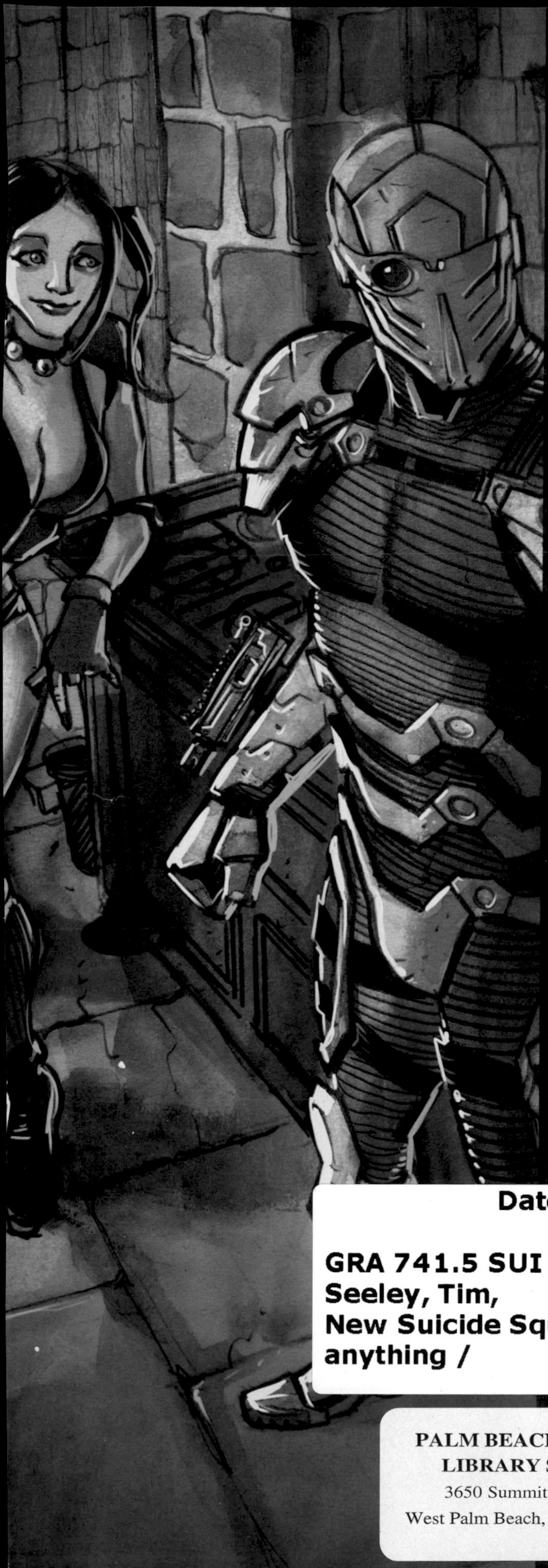

NEW SUICIDE SQUAD

ANYTHING

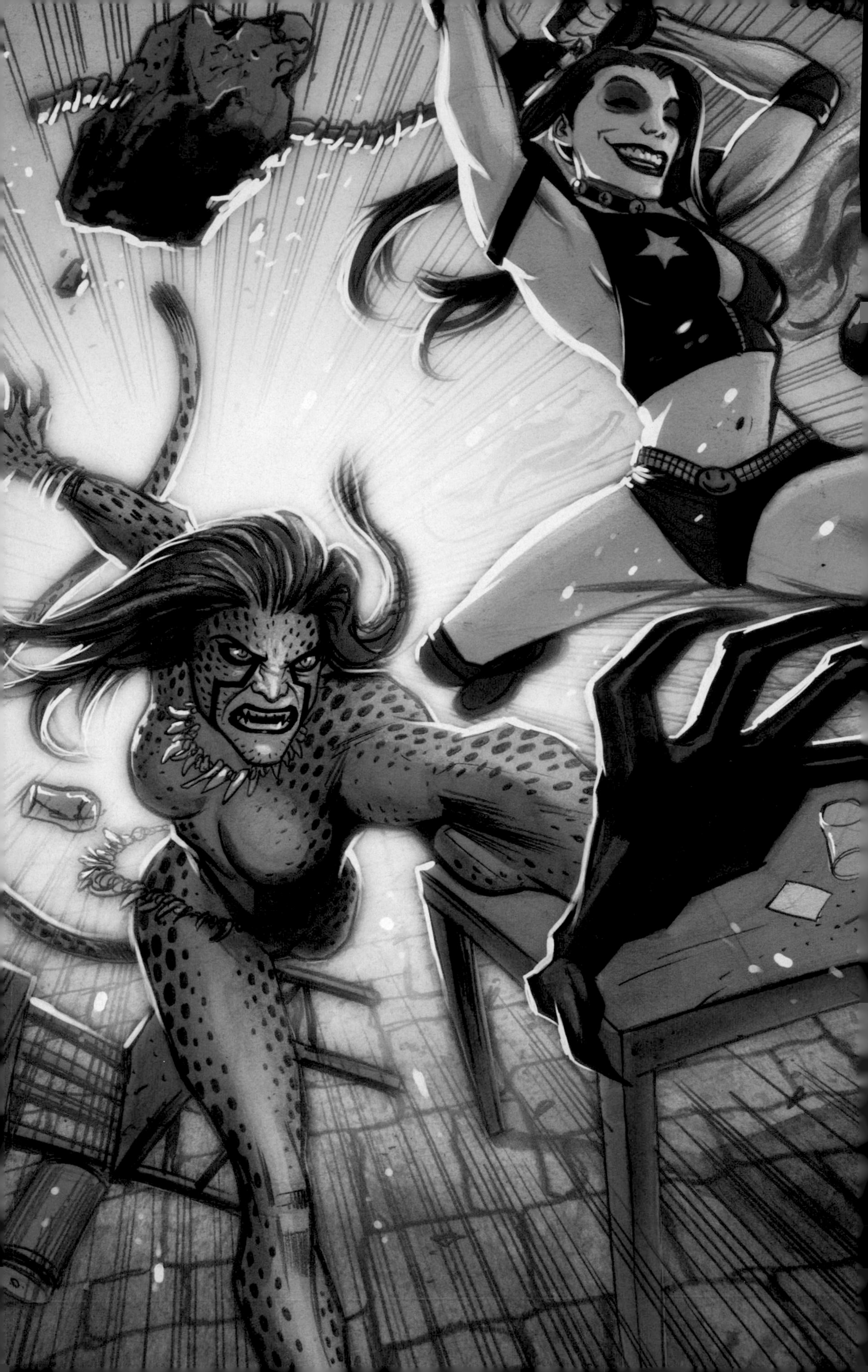

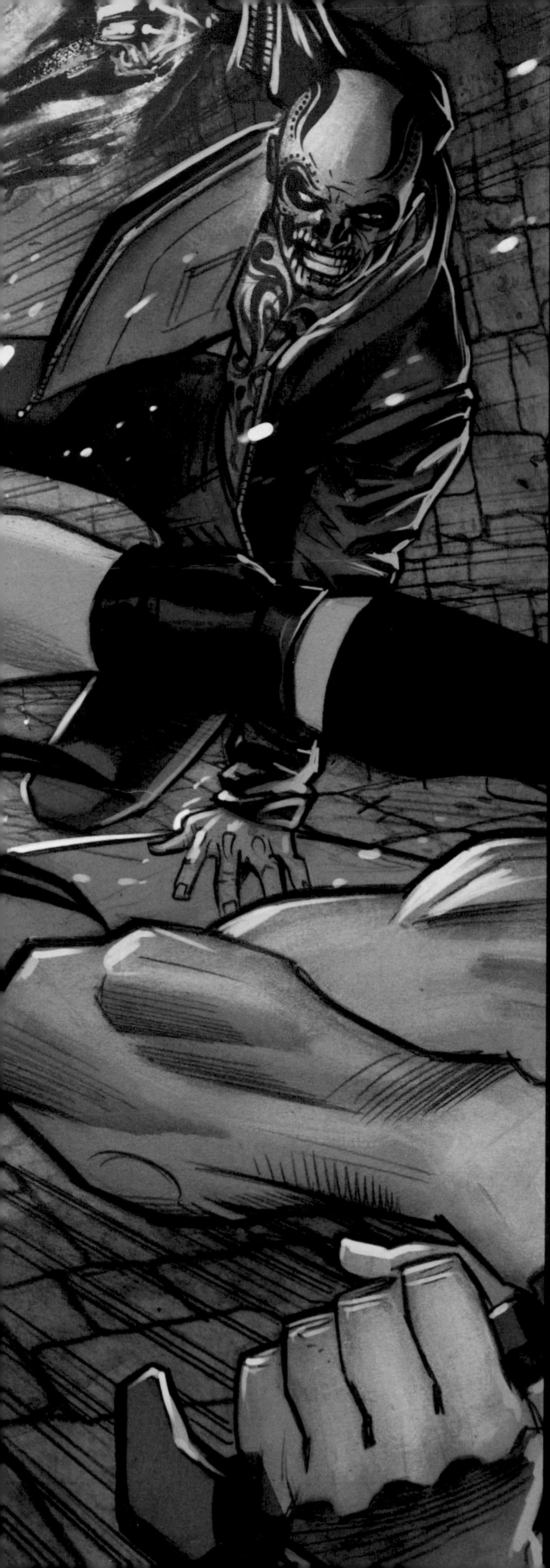

NEW SUICIDE SQUAD

VOLUME 4
KILL ANYTHING

WRITTEN BY
TIM SEELEY
SEAN RYAN

ART BY
JUAN FERREYRA
GUS VAZQUEZ
RONAN CLIQUET

COLOR BY
JUAN FERREYRA
BLOND

LETTERS BY
NATE PIEKOS
DAVE SHARPE

SERIES & COLLECTION
COVER ART BY
JUAN FERREYRA

ANDY KHOURI Editor – Original Series
HARVEY RICHARDS Associate Editor – Original Series
JEB WOODARD Group Editor – Collected Editions
LIZ ERICKSON Editor – Collected Edition
STEVE COOK Design Director – Books
DAMIAN RYLAND Publication Design

BOB HARRAS Senior VP – Editor-in-Chief, DC Comics

DIANE NELSON President
DAN DiDIO Publisher
JIM LEE Publisher
GEOFF JOHNS President & Chief Creative Officer
AMIT DESAI Executive VP – Business & Marketing Strategy, Direct to Consumer & Global Franchise Management
SAM ADES Senior VP – Direct to Consumer
BOBBIE CHASE VP – Talent Development
MARK CHIARELLO Senior VP – Art, Design & Collected Editions
JOHN CUNNINGHAM Senior VP – Sales & Trade Marketing
ANNE DePIES Senior VP – Business Strategy, Finance & Administration
DON FALLETTI VP – Manufacturing Operations
LAWRENCE GANEM VP – Editorial Administration & Talent Relations
ALISON GILL Senior VP – Manufacturing & Operations
HANK KANALZ Senior VP – Editorial Strategy & Administration
JAY KOGAN VP – Legal Affairs
THOMAS LOFTUS VP – Business Affairs
JACK MAHAN VP – Business Affairs
NICK J. NAPOLITANO VP – Manufacturing Administration
EDDIE SCANNELL VP – Consumer Marketing
COURTNEY SIMMONS Senior VP – Publicity & Communications
JIM (SKI) SOKOLOWSKI VP – Comic Book Specialty Sales & Trade Marketing
NANCY SPEARS VP – Mass, Book, Digital Sales & Trade Marketing

NEW SUICIDE SQUAD VOLUME 4: KILL ANYTHING

DC Comics, 2900 West Alameda Avenue, Burbank, CA 91505
Printed by LSC Communications, Salem,VA, USA. 10/14/16. First Printing.
ISBN: 978-1-4012-7000-1

Library of Congress Cataloging-in-Publication Data is available.

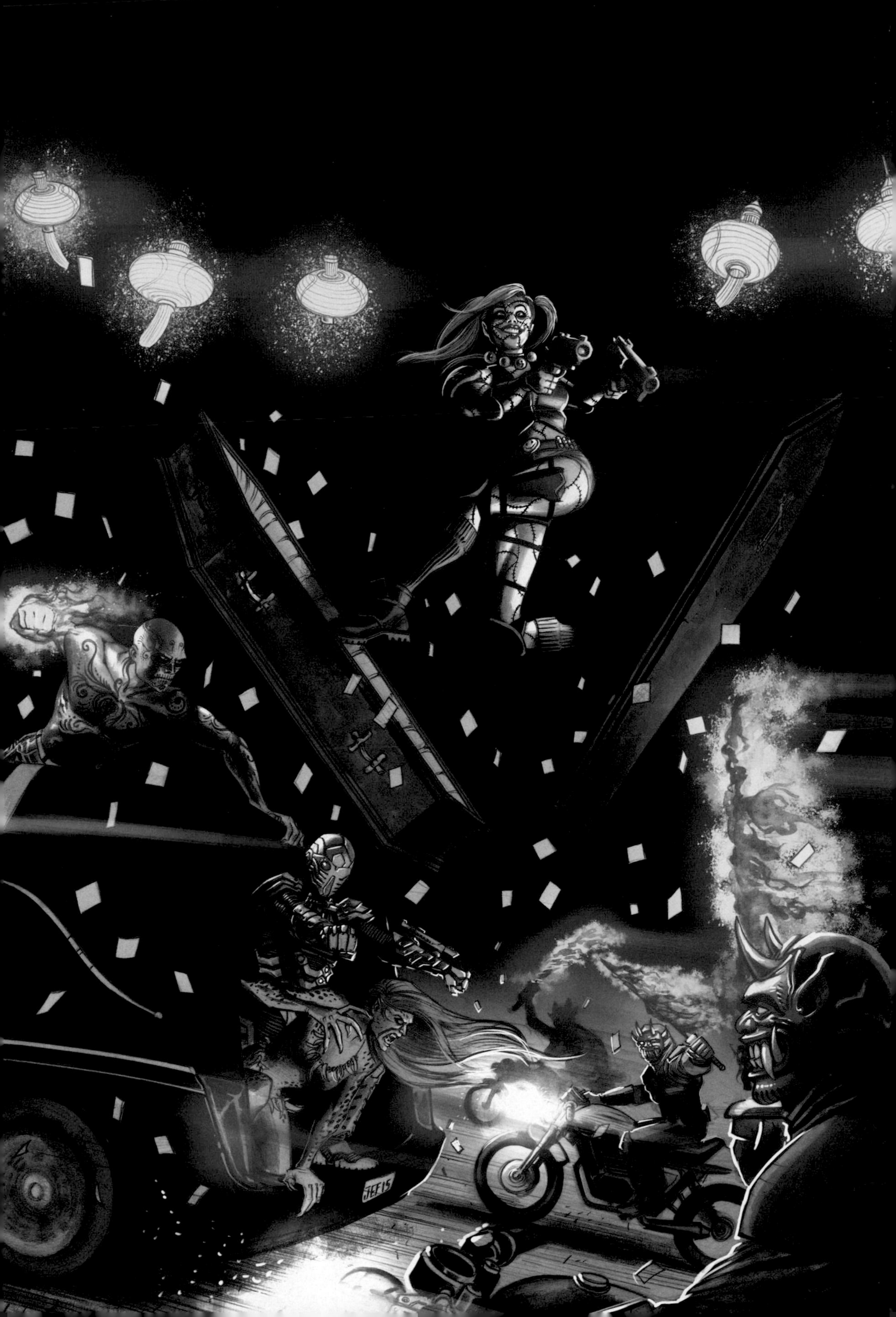

GHOST DAY

TIM SEELEY writer JUAN FERREYRA artist NATE PIEKOS letterer

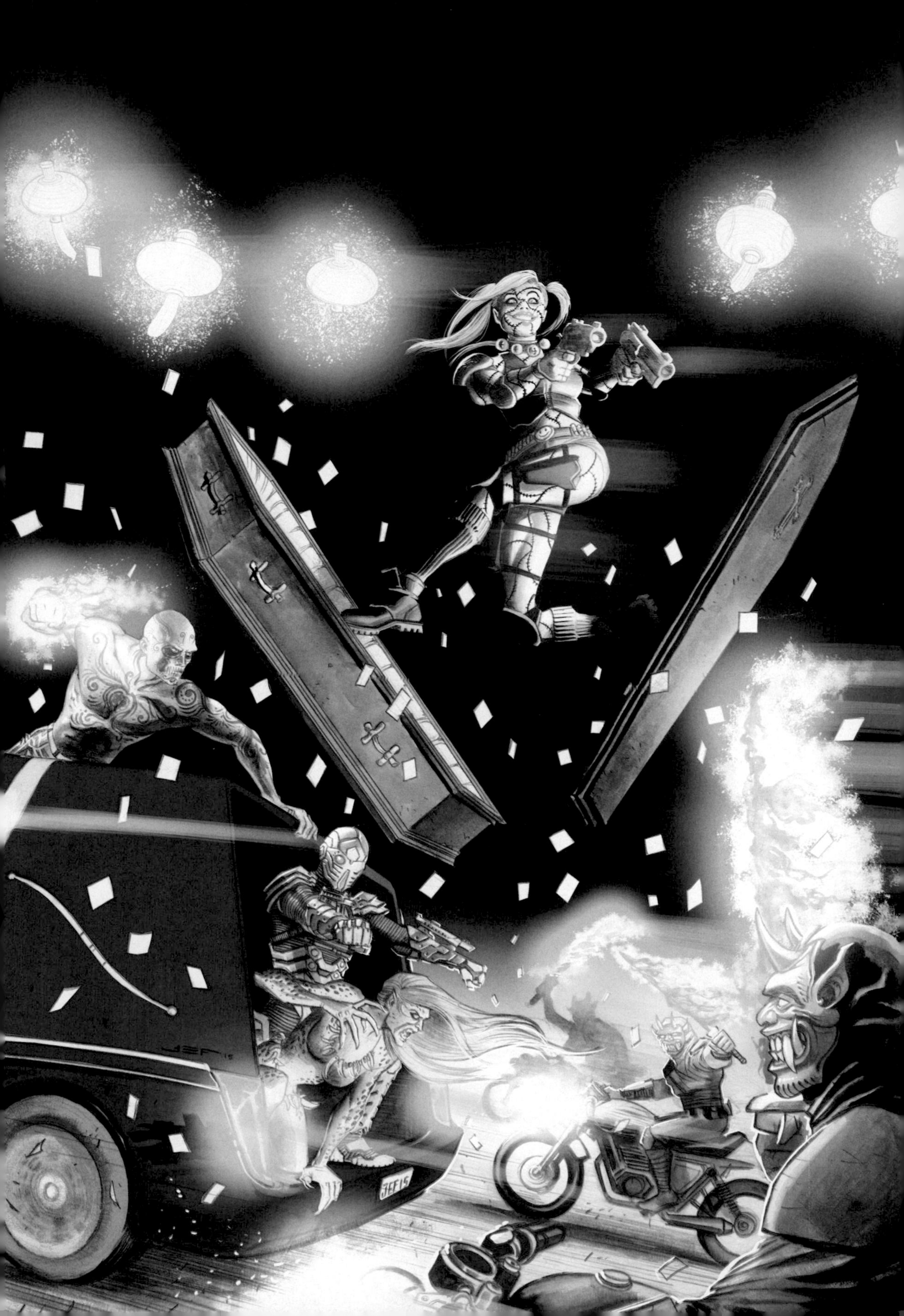

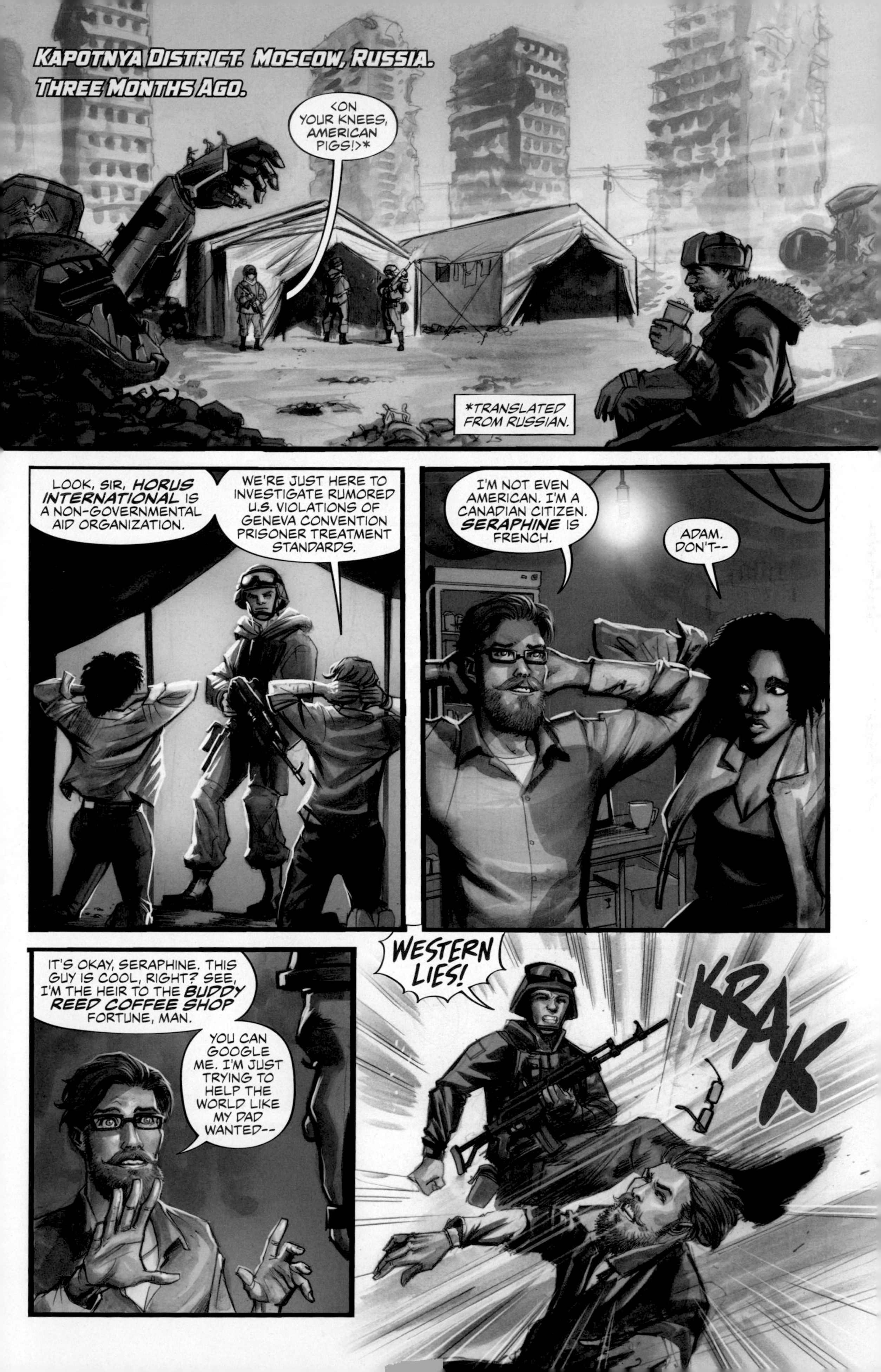
Kapotnya District. Moscow, Russia.
Three Months Ago.
<ON YOUR KNEES, AMERICAN PIGS!>*
*TRANSLATED FROM RUSSIAN.
LOOK, SIR, HORUS INTERNATIONAL IS A NON-GOVERNMENTAL AID ORGANIZATION.
WE'RE JUST HERE TO INVESTIGATE RUMORED U.S. VIOLATIONS OF GENEVA CONVENTION PRISONER TREATMENT STANDARDS.
I'M NOT EVEN AMERICAN. I'M A CANADIAN CITIZEN. SERAPHINE IS FRENCH.
ADAM. DON'T--
IT'S OKAY, SERAPHINE. THIS GUY IS COOL, RIGHT? SEE, I'M THE HEIR TO THE BUDDY REED COFFEE SHOP FORTUNE, MAN.
YOU CAN GOOGLE ME. I'M JUST TRYING TO HELP THE WORLD LIKE MY DAD WANTED--
WESTERN LIES!
KRAK

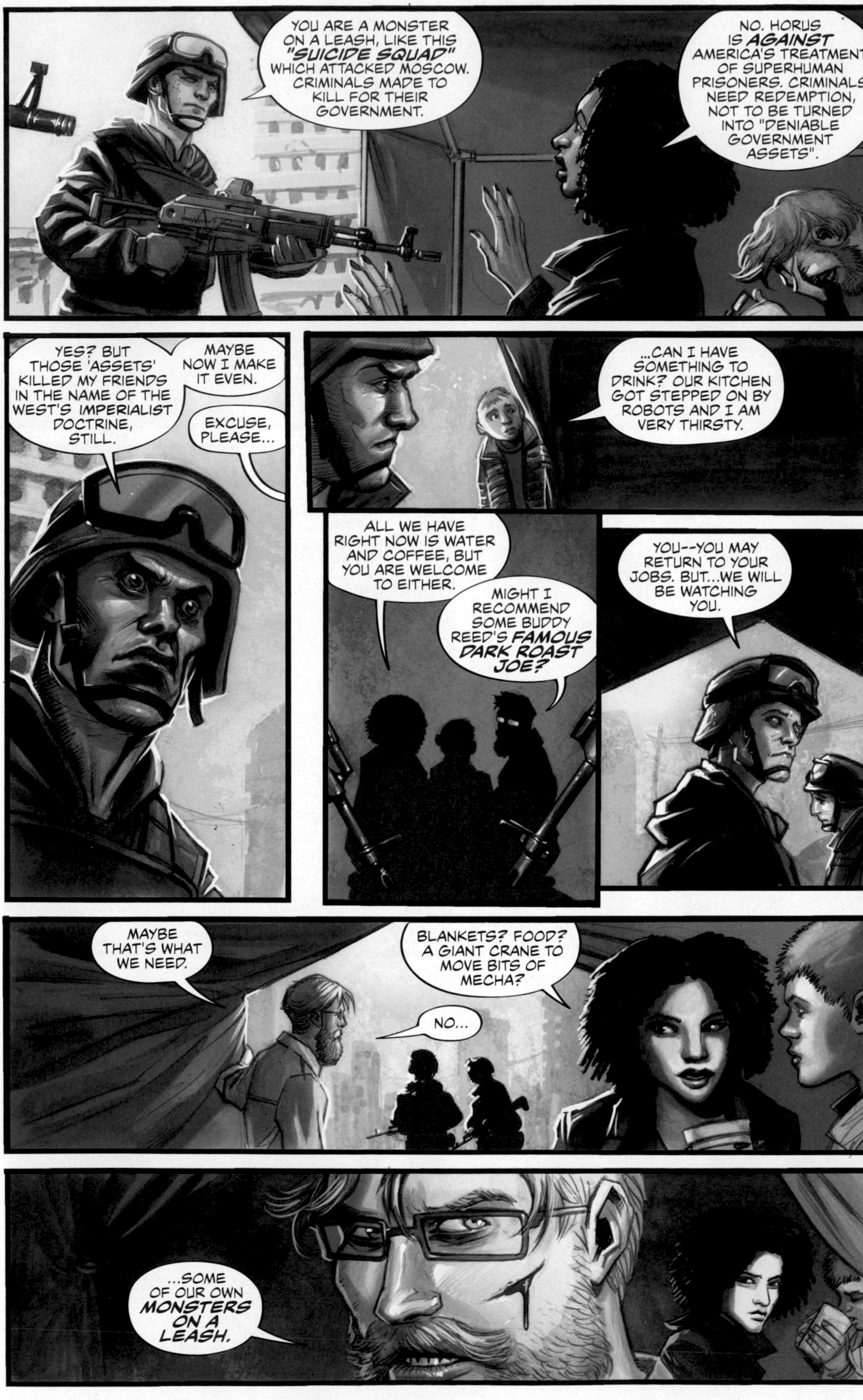
YOU ARE A MONSTER ON A LEASH, LIKE THIS "SUICIDE SQUAD" WHICH ATTACKED MOSCOW. CRIMINALS MADE TO KILL FOR THEIR GOVERNMENT.
NO. HORUS IS AGAINST AMERICA'S TREATMENT OF SUPERHUMAN PRISONERS. CRIMINALS NEED REDEMPTION, NOT TO BE TURNED INTO "DENIABLE GOVERNMENT ASSETS".
YES? BUT THOSE 'ASSETS' KILLED MY FRIENDS IN THE NAME OF THE WEST'S IMPERIALIST DOCTRINE, STILL.
MAYBE NOW I MAKE IT EVEN.
EXCUSE, PLEASE...
...CAN I HAVE SOMETHING TO DRINK? OUR KITCHEN GOT STEPPED ON BY ROBOTS AND I AM VERY THIRSTY.
ALL WE HAVE RIGHT NOW IS WATER AND COFFEE, BUT YOU ARE WELCOME TO EITHER.
MIGHT I RECOMMEND SOME BUDDY REED'S FAMOUS DARK ROAST JOE?
YOU--YOU MAY RETURN TO YOUR JOBS. BUT...WE WILL BE WATCHING YOU.
MAYBE THAT'S WHAT WE NEED.
BLANKETS? FOOD? A GIANT CRANE TO MOVE BITS OF MECHA?
NO...
...SOME OF OUR OWN MONSTERS ON A LEASH.

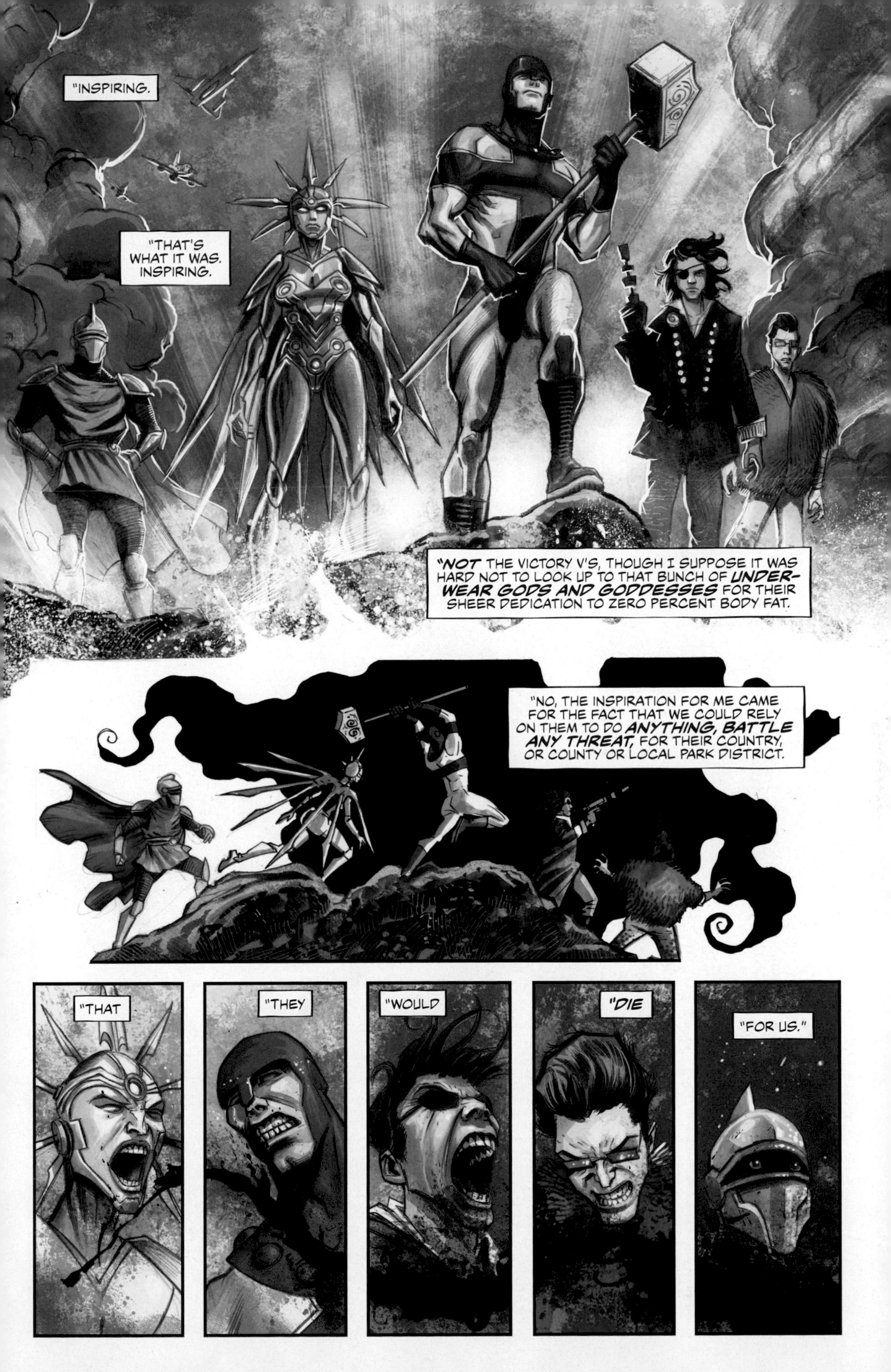
"INSPIRING.
"THAT'S WHAT IT WAS. INSPIRING.
"NOT THE VICTORY V'S, THOUGH I SUPPOSE IT WAS HARD NOT TO LOOK UP TO THAT BUNCH OF UNDERWEAR GODS AND GODDESSES FOR THEIR SHEER DEDICATION TO ZERO PERCENT BODY FAT.
"NO, THE INSPIRATION FOR ME CAME FOR THE FACT THAT WE COULD RELY ON THEM TO DO ANYTHING, BATTLE ANY THREAT, FOR THEIR COUNTRY, OR COUNTY OR LOCAL PARK DISTRICT.
"THAT
"THEY
"WOULD
"DIE
"FOR US."

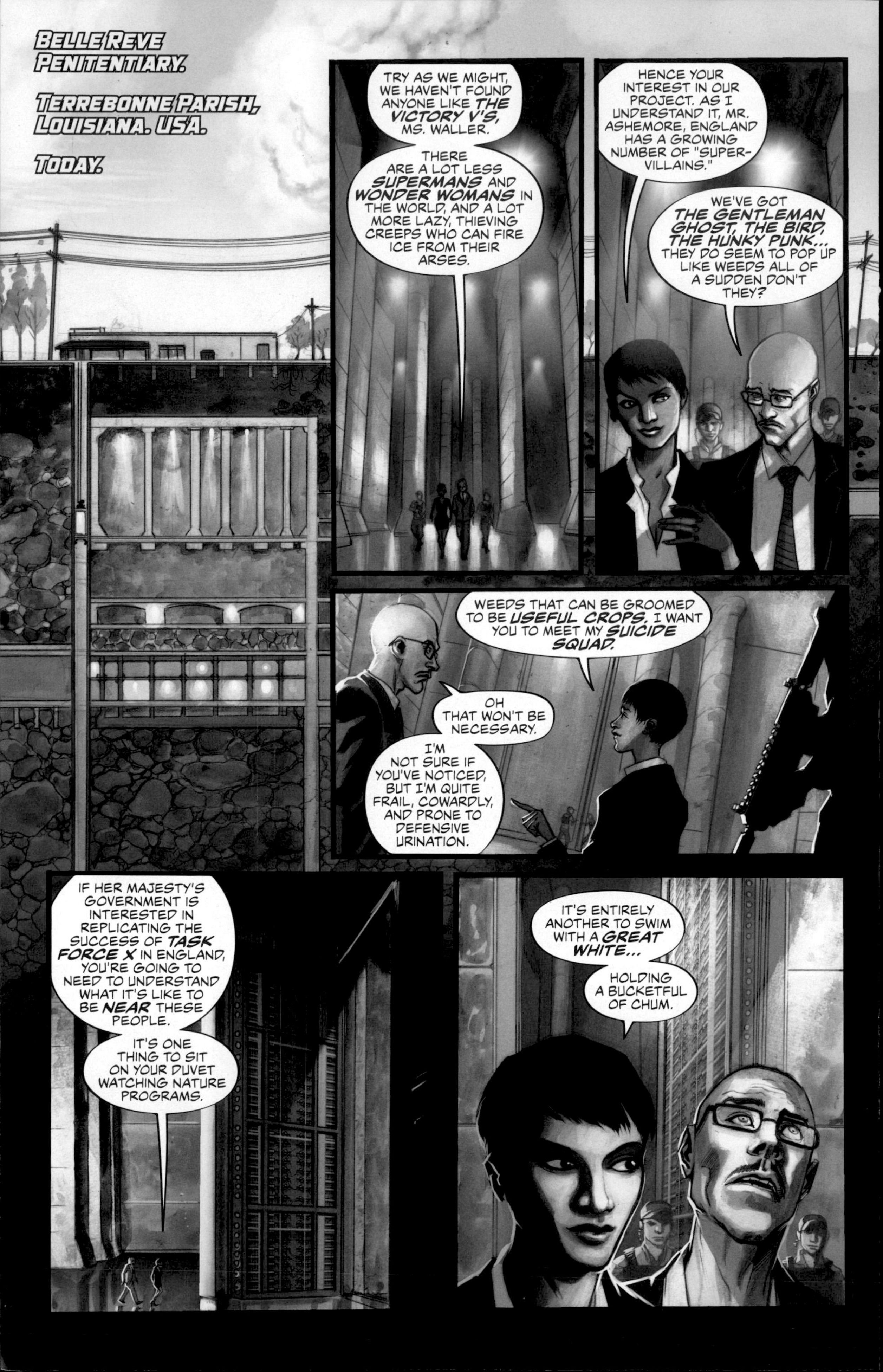
BELLE REVE PENITENTIARY.
TERREBONNE PARISH, LOUISIANA. USA.
TODAY.
TRY AS WE MIGHT, WE HAVEN'T FOUND ANYONE LIKE THE VICTORY V'S, MS. WALLER.
THERE ARE A LOT LESS SUPERMANS AND WONDER WOMANS IN THE WORLD, AND A LOT MORE LAZY, THIEVING CREEPS WHO CAN FIRE ICE FROM THEIR ARSES.
HENCE YOUR INTEREST IN OUR PROJECT. AS I UNDERSTAND IT, MR. ASHEMORE, ENGLAND HAS A GROWING NUMBER OF "SUPER-VILLAINS."
WE'VE GOT THE GENTLEMAN GHOST, THE BIRD, THE HUNKY PUNK... THEY DO SEEM TO POP UP LIKE WEEDS ALL OF A SUDDEN DON'T THEY?
WEEDS THAT CAN BE GROOMED TO BE USEFUL CROPS. I WANT YOU TO MEET MY SUICIDE SQUAD.
OH THAT WON'T BE NECESSARY.
I'M NOT SURE IF YOU'VE NOTICED, BUT I'M QUITE FRAIL, COWARDLY, AND PRONE TO DEFENSIVE URINATION.
IF HER MAJESTY'S GOVERNMENT IS INTERESTED IN REPLICATING THE SUCCESS OF TASK FORCE X IN ENGLAND, YOU'RE GOING TO NEED TO UNDERSTAND WHAT IT'S LIKE TO BE NEAR THESE PEOPLE.
IT'S ONE THING TO SIT ON YOUR DUVET WATCHING NATURE PROGRAMS.
IT'S ENTIRELY ANOTHER TO SWIM WITH A GREAT WHITE...
HOLDING A BUCKETFUL OF CHUM.

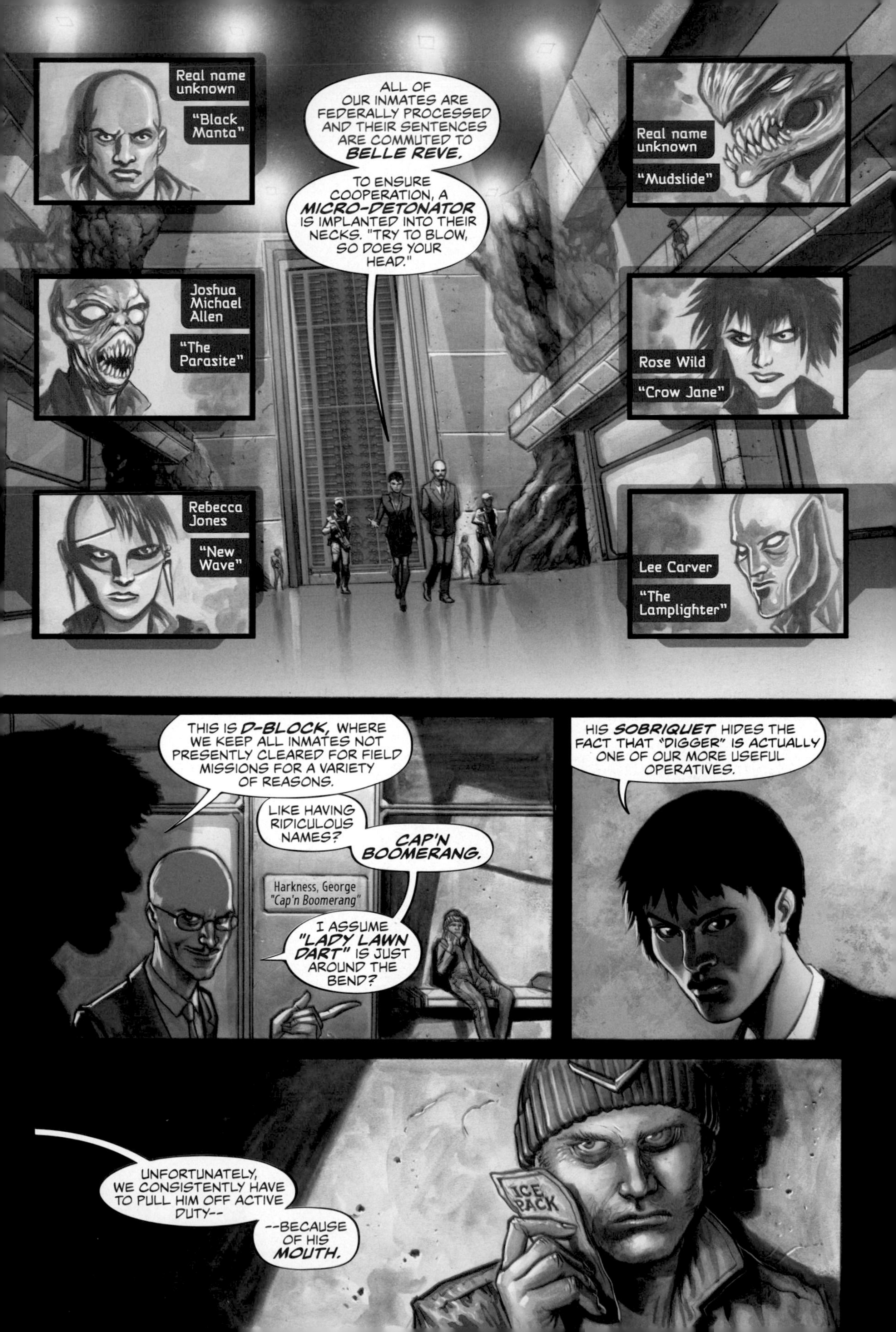
Real name unknown
"Black Manta"
ALL OF OUR INMATES ARE FEDERALLY PROCESSED AND THEIR SENTENCES ARE COMMUTED TO BELLE REVE.
TO ENSURE COOPERATION, A MICRO-DETONATOR IS IMPLANTED INTO THEIR NECKS. "TRY TO BLOW, SO DOES YOUR HEAD."
Real name unknown
"Mudslide"
Joshua Michael Allen
"The Parasite"
Rose Wild
"Crow Jane"
Rebecca Jones
"New Wave"
Lee Carver
"The Lamplighter"
THIS IS D-BLOCK, WHERE WE KEEP ALL INMATES NOT PRESENTLY CLEARED FOR FIELD MISSIONS FOR A VARIETY OF REASONS.
LIKE HAVING RIDICULOUS NAMES?
CAP'N BOOMERANG.
Harkness, George
"Cap'n Boomerang"
I ASSUME "LADY LAWN DART" IS JUST AROUND THE BEND?
HIS SOBRIQUET HIDES THE FACT THAT "DIGGER" IS ACTUALLY ONE OF OUR MORE USEFUL OPERATIVES.
UNFORTUNATELY, WE CONSISTENTLY HAVE TO PULL HIM OFF ACTIVE DUTY--
--BECAUSE OF HIS MOUTH.
ICE PACK

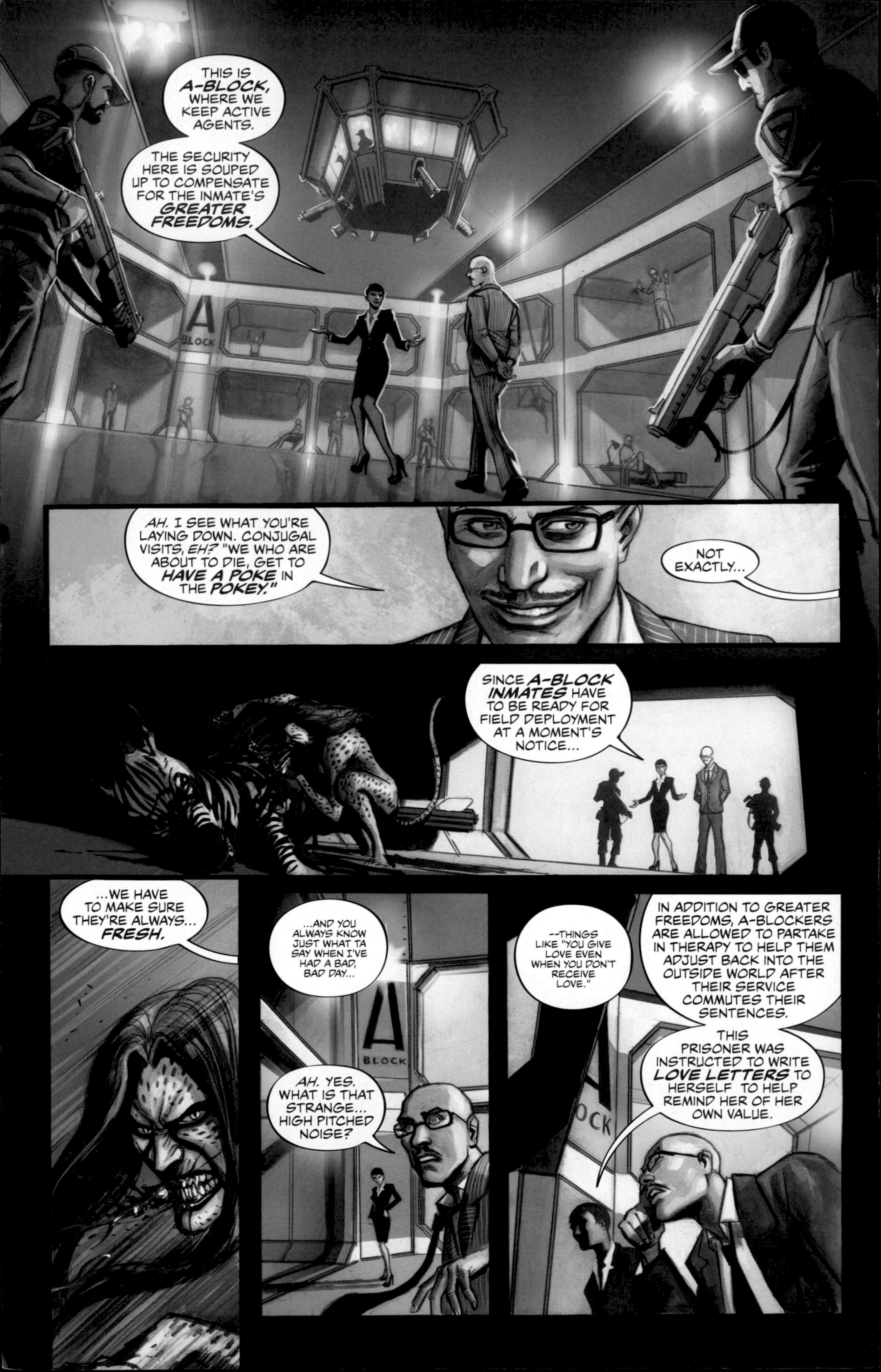

THIS IS A-BLOCK, WHERE WE KEEP ACTIVE AGENTS.
THE SECURITY HERE IS SOUPED UP TO COMPENSATE FOR THE INMATE'S GREATER FREEDOMS.
A BLOCK
AH. I SEE WHAT YOU'RE LAYING DOWN. CONJUGAL VISITS, EH? "WE WHO ARE ABOUT TO DIE, GET TO HAVE A POKE IN THE POKEY."
NOT EXACTLY...
SINCE A-BLOCK INMATES HAVE TO BE READY FOR FIELD DEPLOYMENT AT A MOMENT'S NOTICE...
...WE HAVE TO MAKE SURE THEY'RE ALWAYS... FRESH.
...AND YOU ALWAYS KNOW JUST WHAT TA SAY WHEN I'VE HAD A BAD, BAD DAY...
A BLOCK
AH. YES. WHAT IS THAT STRANGE... HIGH PITCHED NOISE?
--THINGS LIKE "YOU GIVE LOVE EVEN WHEN YOU DON'T RECEIVE LOVE."
IN ADDITION TO GREATER FREEDOMS, A-BLOCKERS ARE ALLOWED TO PARTAKE IN THERAPY TO HELP THEM ADJUST BACK INTO THE OUTSIDE WORLD AFTER THEIR SERVICE COMMUTES THEIR SENTENCES.
THIS PRISONER WAS INSTRUCTED TO WRITE LOVE LETTERS TO HERSELF TO HELP REMIND HER OF HER OWN VALUE.

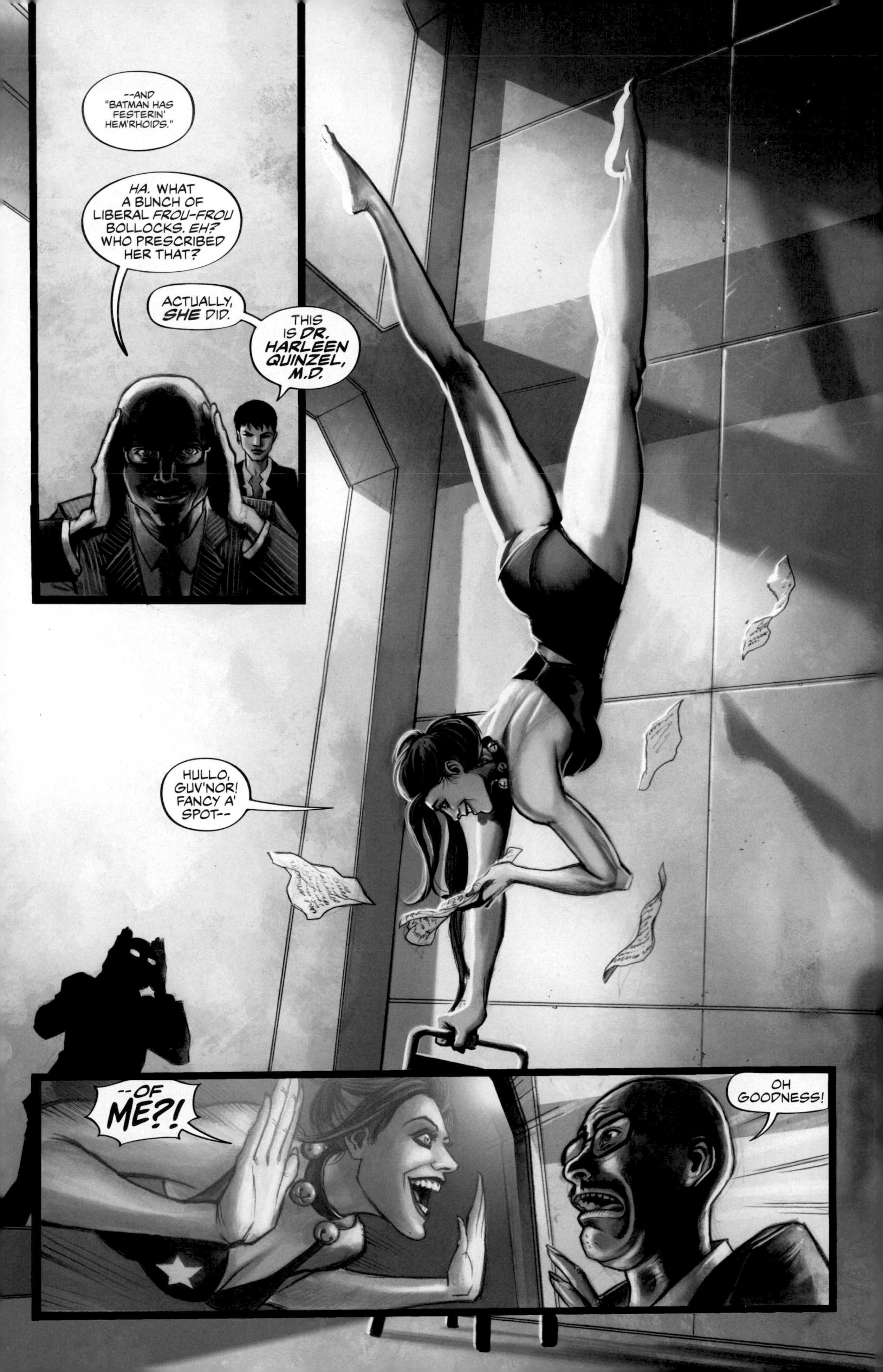
--AND "BATMAN HAS FESTERIN' HEM'RHOIDS."
HA. WHAT A BUNCH OF LIBERAL FROU-FROU BOLLOCKS. EH? WHO PRESCRIBED HER THAT?
ACTUALLY, SHE DID.
THIS IS DR. HARLEEN QUINZEL, M.D.
HULLO, GUV'NOR! FANCY A' SPOT--
--OF ME?!
OH GOODNESS!

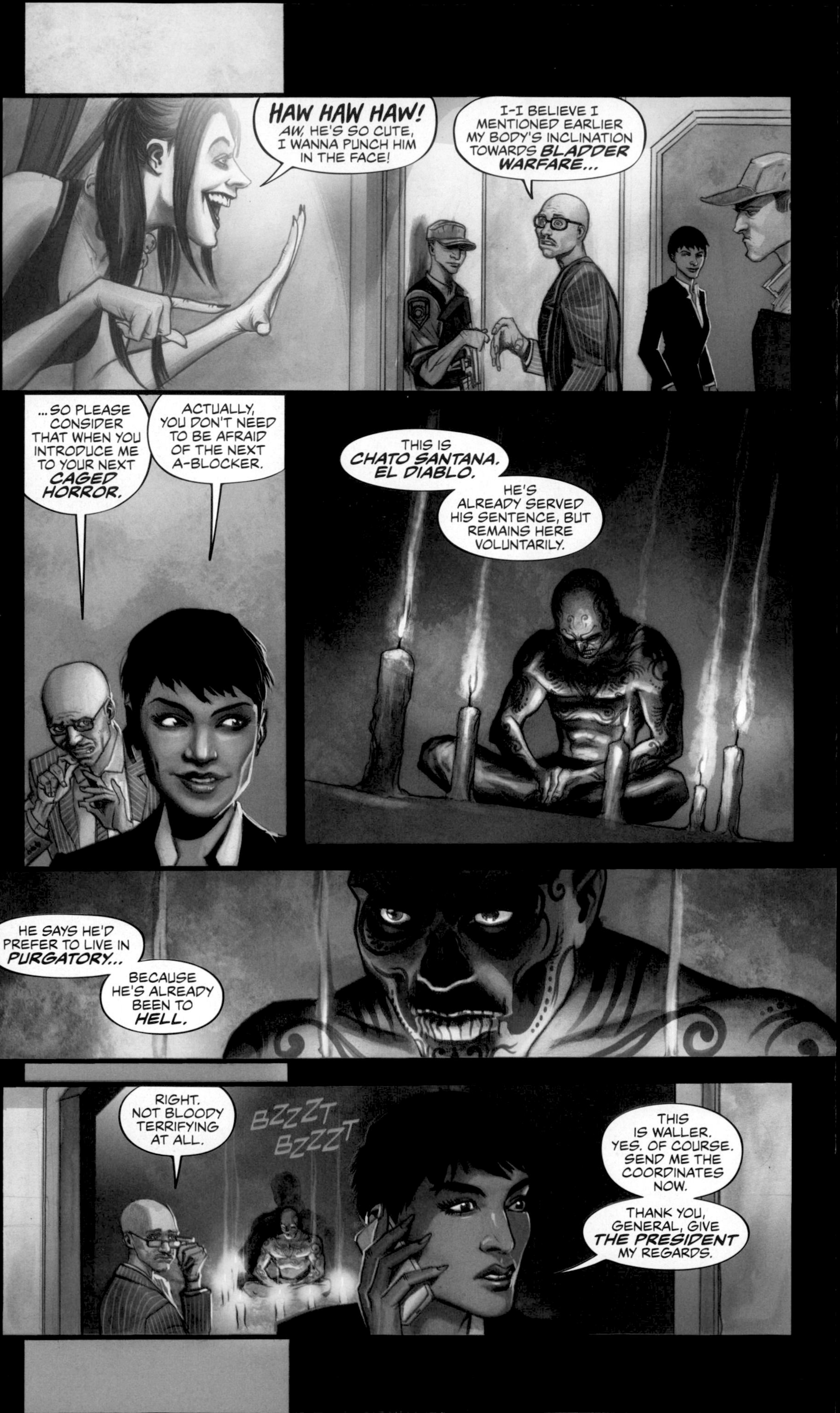
HAW HAW HAW! AW, HE'S SO CUTE, I WANNA PUNCH HIM IN THE FACE!
I-I BELIEVE I MENTIONED EARLIER MY BODY'S INCLINATION TOWARDS BLADDER WARFARE...
...SO PLEASE CONSIDER THAT WHEN YOU INTRODUCE ME TO YOUR NEXT CAGED HORROR.
ACTUALLY, YOU DON'T NEED TO BE AFRAID OF THE NEXT A-BLOCKER.
THIS IS CHATO SANTANA. EL DIABLO.
HE'S ALREADY SERVED HIS SENTENCE, BUT REMAINS HERE VOLUNTARILY.
HE SAYS HE'D PREFER TO LIVE IN PURGATORY...
BECAUSE HE'S ALREADY BEEN TO HELL.
RIGHT. NOT BLOODY TERRIFYING AT ALL.
BZZZT BZZZT
THIS IS WALLER. YES. OF COURSE. SEND ME THE COORDINATES NOW.
THANK YOU, GENERAL, GIVE THE PRESIDENT MY REGARDS.

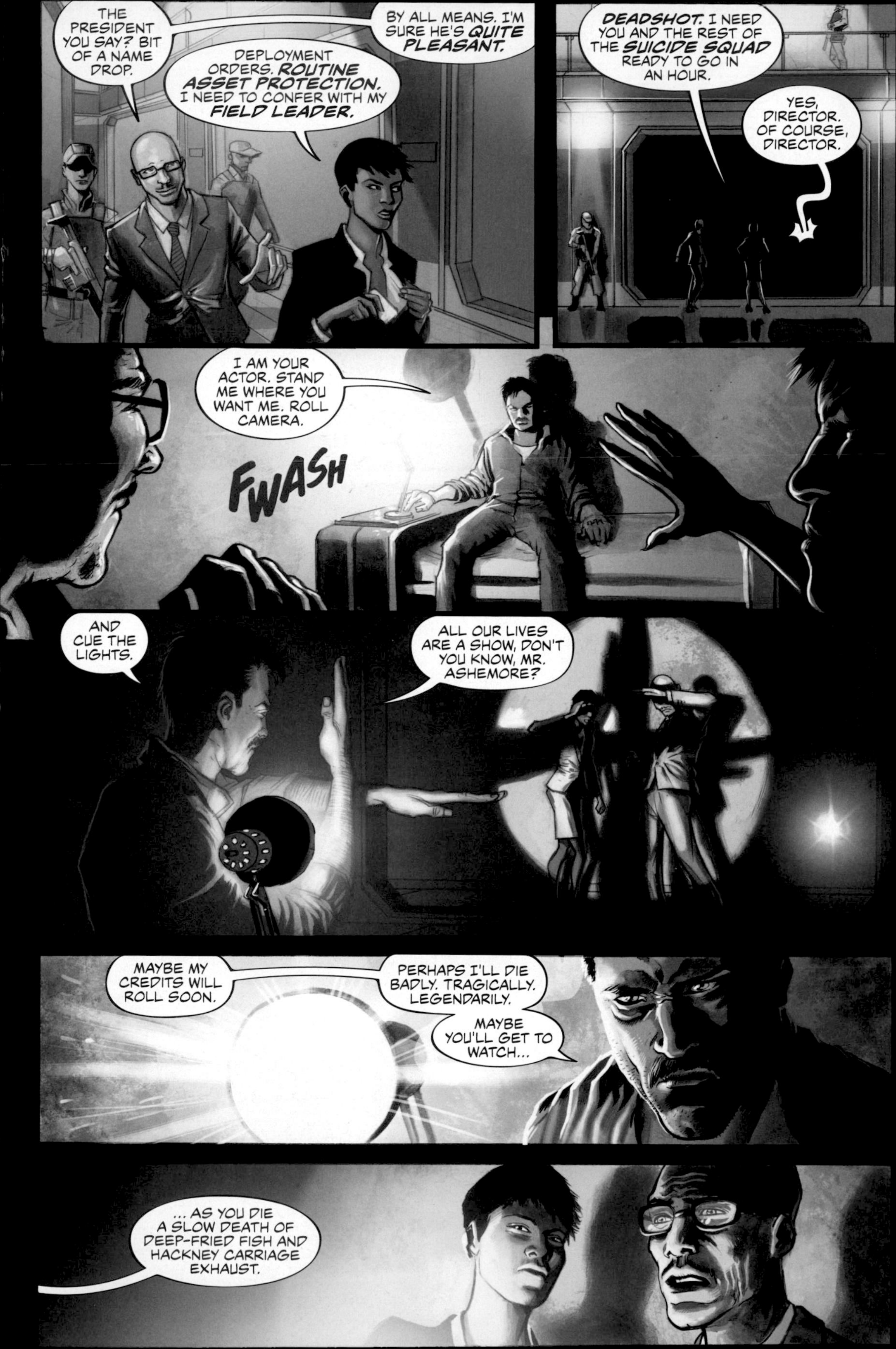
THE PRESIDENT YOU SAY? BIT OF A NAME DROP.
BY ALL MEANS. I'M SURE HE'S QUITE PLEASANT.
DEPLOYMENT ORDERS. ROUTINE ASSET PROTECTION. I NEED TO CONFER WITH MY FIELD LEADER.
DEADSHOT. I NEED YOU AND THE REST OF THE SUICIDE SQUAD READY TO GO IN AN HOUR.
YES, DIRECTOR. OF COURSE, DIRECTOR.
I AM YOUR ACTOR. STAND ME WHERE YOU WANT ME. ROLL CAMERA.
FWASH
AND CUE THE LIGHTS.
ALL OUR LIVES ARE A SHOW, DON'T YOU KNOW, MR. ASHEMORE?
MAYBE MY CREDITS WILL ROLL SOON.
PERHAPS I'LL DIE BADLY. TRAGICALLY. LEGENDARILY.
MAYBE YOU'LL GET TO WATCH...
... AS YOU DIE A SLOW DEATH OF DEEP-FRIED FISH AND HACKNEY CARRIAGE EXHAUST.

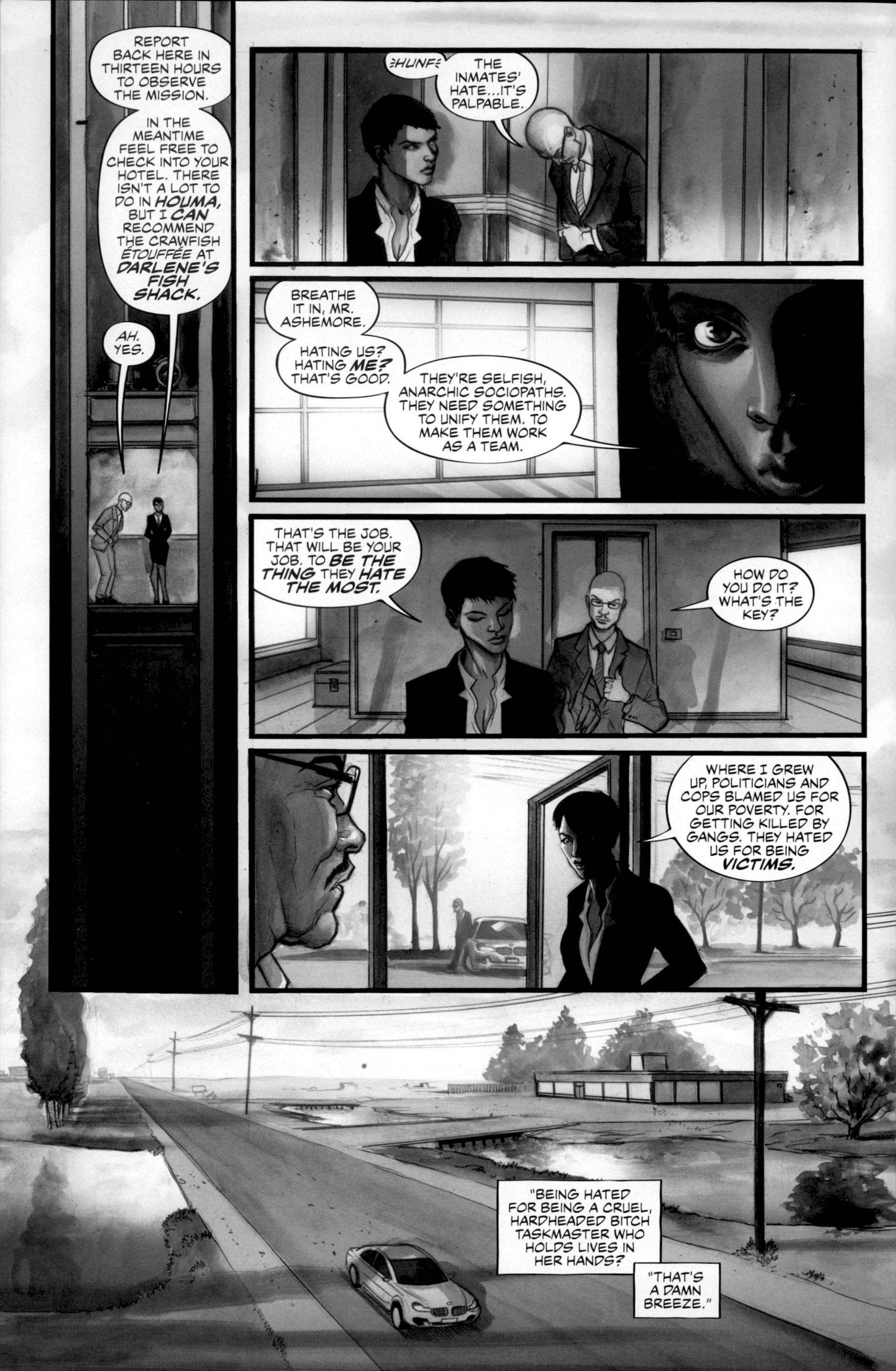
REPORT BACK HERE IN THIRTEEN HOURS TO OBSERVE THE MISSION.
IN THE MEANTIME FEEL FREE TO CHECK INTO YOUR HOTEL. THERE ISN'T A LOT TO DO IN HOUMA, BUT I CAN RECOMMEND THE CRAWFISH ÉTOUFFÉE AT DARLENE'S FISH SHACK.
AH. YES.
HUNF
THE INMATES' HATE...IT'S PALPABLE.
BREATHE IT IN, MR. ASHEMORE.
HATING US? HATING ME? THAT'S GOOD.
THEY'RE SELFISH, ANARCHIC SOCIOPATHS. THEY NEED SOMETHING TO UNIFY THEM. TO MAKE THEM WORK AS A TEAM.
THAT'S THE JOB. THAT WILL BE YOUR JOB. TO BE THE THING THEY HATE THE MOST.
HOW DO YOU DO IT? WHAT'S THE KEY?
WHERE I GREW UP, POLITICIANS AND COPS BLAMED US FOR OUR POVERTY. FOR GETTING KILLED BY GANGS. THEY HATED US FOR BEING VICTIMS.
"BEING HATED FOR BEING A CRUEL, HARDHEADED BITCH TASKMASTER WHO HOLDS LIVES IN HER HANDS?
"THAT'S A DAMN BREEZE."

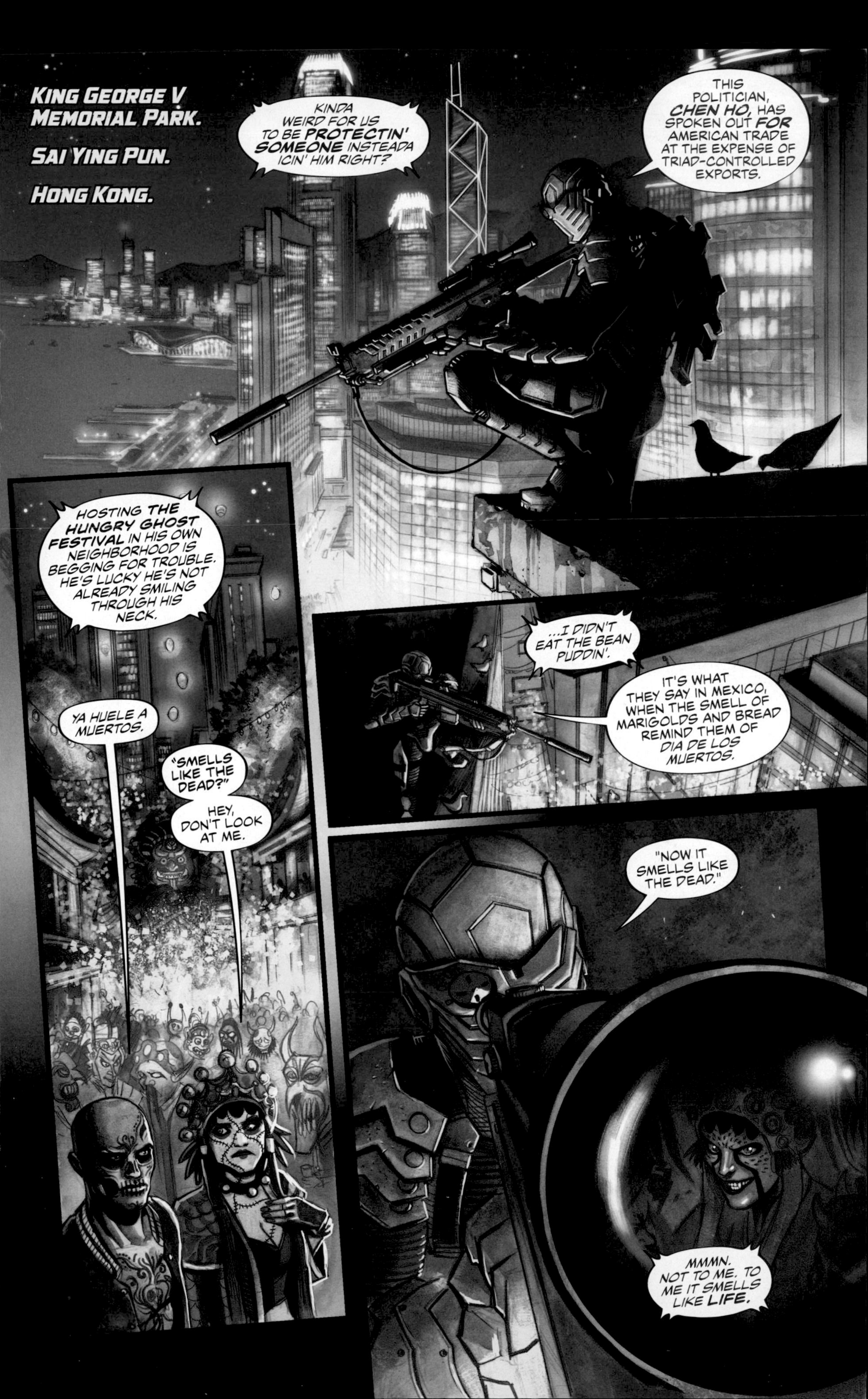
King George V Memorial Park.
Sai Ying Pun.
Hong Kong.
KINDA WEIRD FOR US TO BE PROTECTIN' SOMEONE INSTEADA ICIN' HIM RIGHT?
THIS POLITICIAN, CHEN HO, HAS SPOKEN OUT FOR AMERICAN TRADE AT THE EXPENSE OF TRIAD-CONTROLLED EXPORTS.
HOSTING THE HUNGRY GHOST FESTIVAL IN HIS OWN NEIGHBORHOOD IS BEGGING FOR TROUBLE. HE'S LUCKY HE'S NOT ALREADY SMILING THROUGH HIS NECK.
YA HUELE A MUERTOS.
"SMELLS LIKE THE DEAD?"
HEY, DON'T LOOK AT ME.
...I DIDN'T EAT THE BEAN PUDDIN'.
IT'S WHAT THEY SAY IN MEXICO, WHEN THE SMELL OF MARIGOLDS AND BREAD REMIND THEM OF DIA DE LOS MUERTOS.
"NOW IT SMELLS LIKE THE DEAD."
MMMN. NOT TO ME. TO ME IT SMELLS LIKE LIFE.

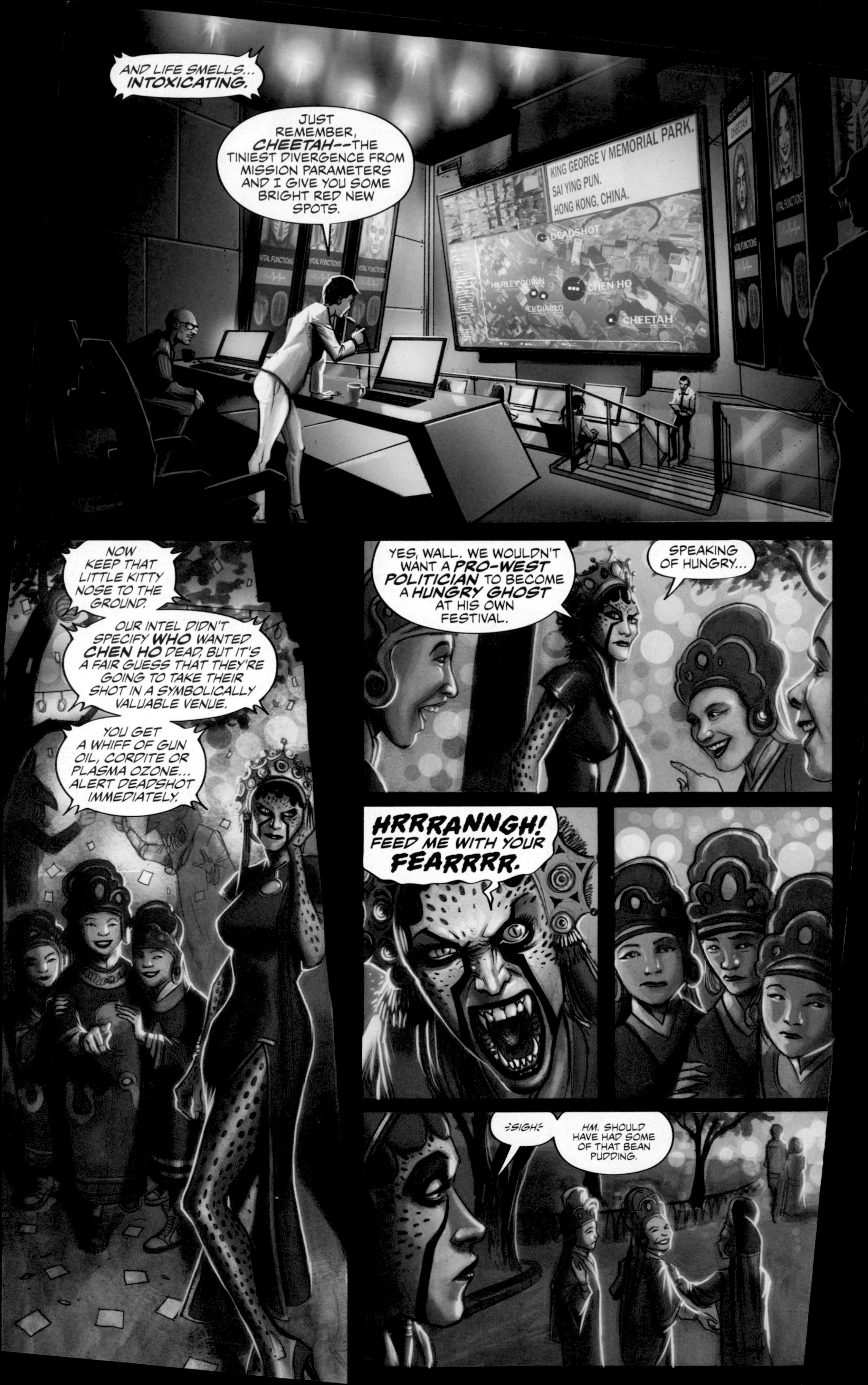

AND LIFE SMELLS... INTOXICATING.
JUST REMEMBER, CHEETAH--THE TINIEST DIVERGENCE FROM MISSION PARAMETERS AND I GIVE YOU SOME BRIGHT RED NEW SPOTS.
KING GEORGE V MEMORIAL PARK.
SAI YING PUN.
HONG KONG, CHINA.
DEADSHOT
HARLEY QUINN
CHEN HO
EL DIABLO
CHEETAH
VITAL FUNCTIONS
CHEETAH
NOW KEEP THAT LITTLE KITTY NOSE TO THE GROUND.
OUR INTEL DIDN'T SPECIFY WHO WANTED CHEN HO DEAD, BUT IT'S A FAIR GUESS THAT THEY'RE GOING TO TAKE THEIR SHOT IN A SYMBOLICALLY VALUABLE VENUE.
YOU GET A WHIFF OF GUN OIL, CORDITE OR PLASMA OZONE... ALERT DEADSHOT IMMEDIATELY.
YES, WALL. WE WOULDN'T WANT A PRO-WEST POLITICIAN TO BECOME A HUNGRY GHOST AT HIS OWN FESTIVAL.
SPEAKING OF HUNGRY...
HRRRANNGH! FEED ME WITH YOUR FEARRRR.
-SIGH-
HM. SHOULD HAVE HAD SOME OF THAT BEAN PUDDING.

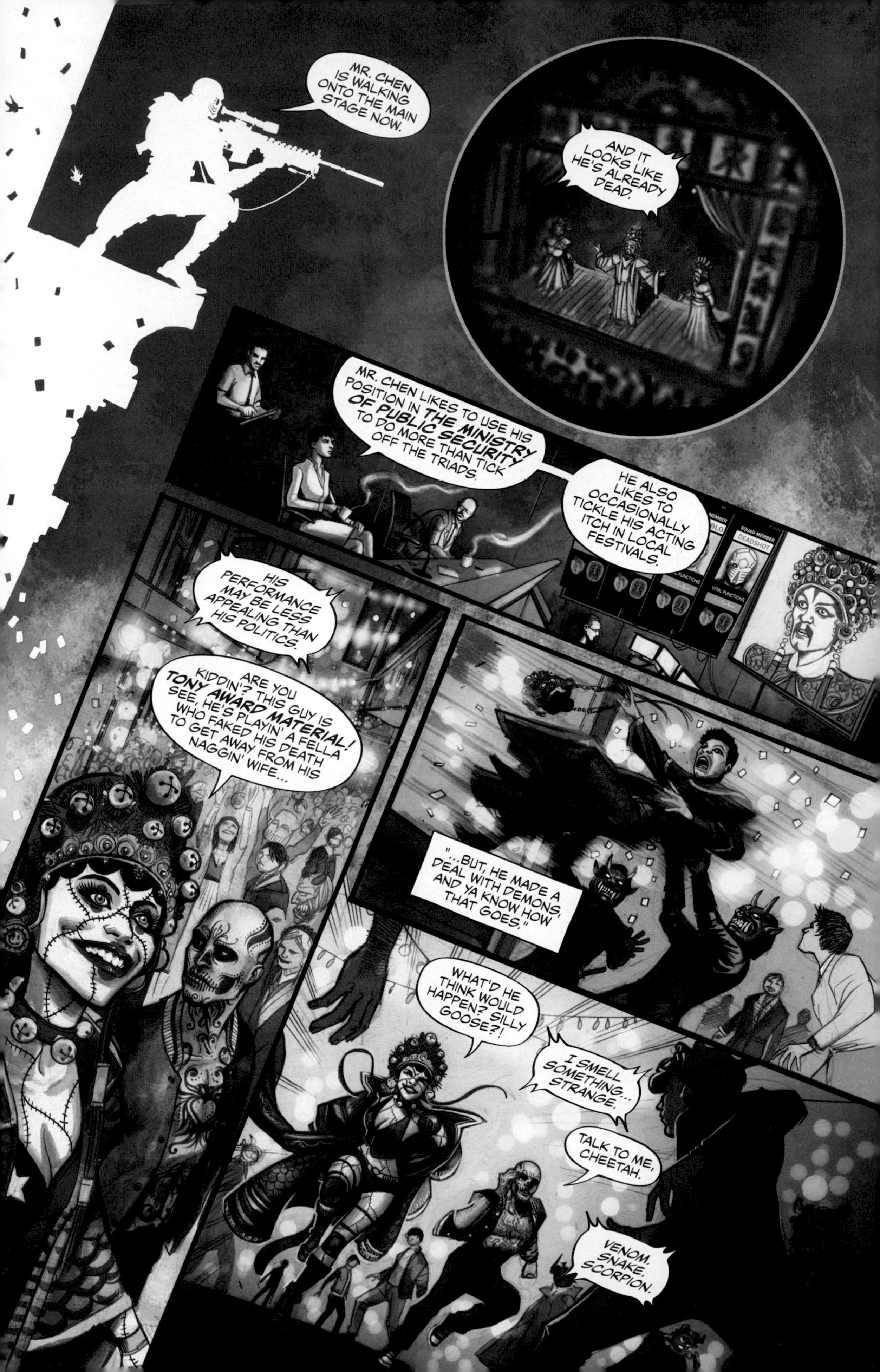
MR. CHEN IS WALKING ONTO THE MAIN STAGE NOW.
AND IT LOOKS LIKE HE'S ALREADY DEAD.
MR. CHEN LIKES TO USE HIS POSITION IN THE MINISTRY OF PUBLIC SECURITY TO DO MORE THAN TICK OFF THE TRIADS.
HE ALSO LIKES TO OCCASIONALLY TICKLE HIS ACTING ITCH IN LOCAL FESTIVALS.
SQUAD MEMBER
DEADSHOT
VITAL FUNCTIONS
HIS PERFORMANCE MAY BE LESS APPEALING THAN HIS POLITICS.
ARE YOU KIDDIN'? THIS GUY IS TONY AWARD MATERIAL! SEE, HE'S PLAYIN' A FELLA WHO FAKED HIS DEATH TO GET AWAY FROM HIS NAGGIN' WIFE...
"...BUT, HE MADE A DEAL WITH DEMONS, AND YA KNOW HOW THAT GOES."
WHAT'D HE THINK WOULD HAPPEN? SILLY GOOSE?!
I SMELL SOMETHING... STRANGE.
TALK TO ME, CHEETAH.
VENOM. SNAKE. SCORPION.

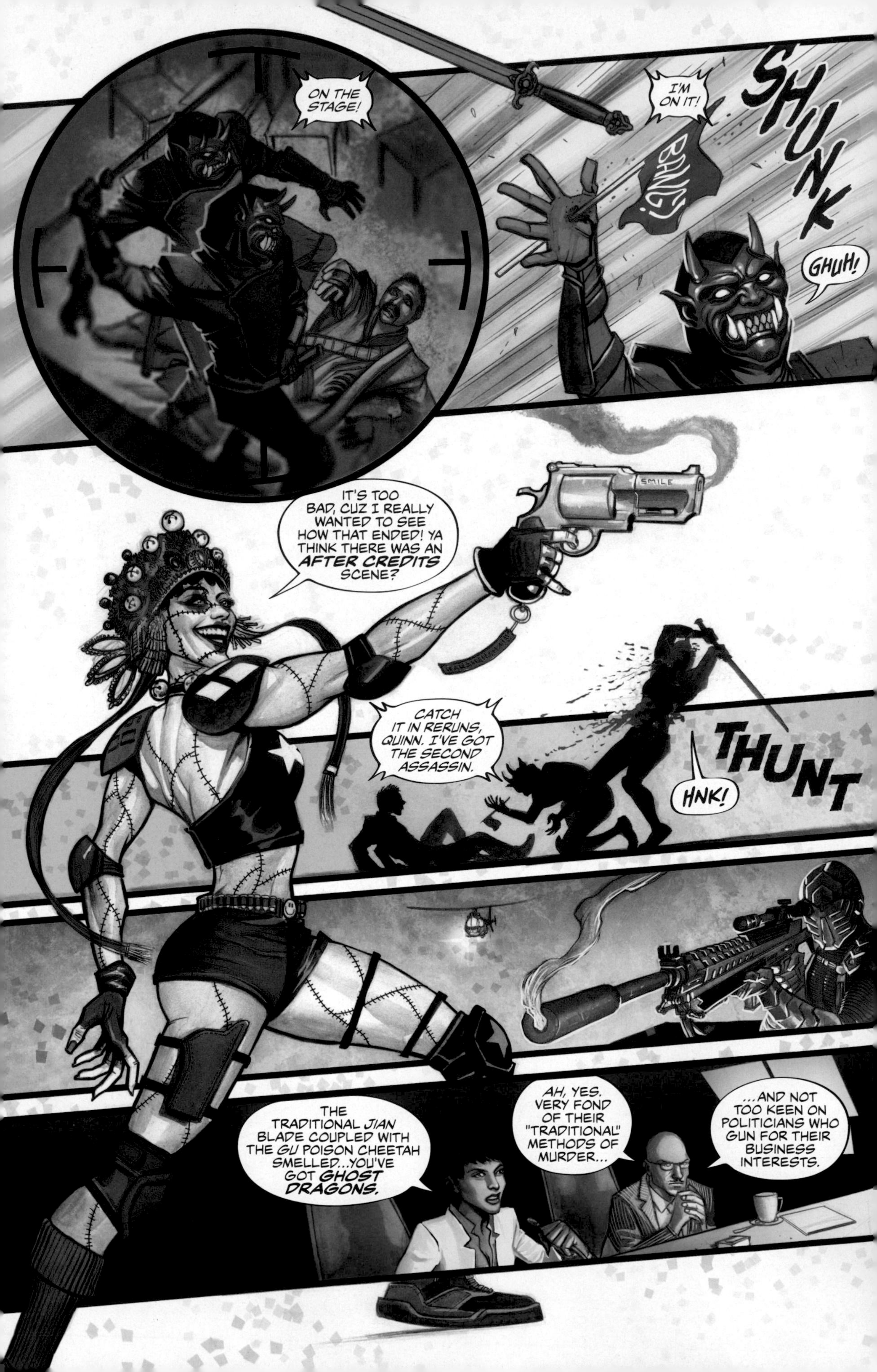
ON THE STAGE!
I'M ON IT!
SHUNK
BANG!
GHUH!
SMILE
IT'S TOO BAD, CUZ I REALLY WANTED TO SEE HOW THAT ENDED! YA THINK THERE WAS AN AFTER CREDITS SCENE?
CATCH IT IN RERUNS, QUINN. I'VE GOT THE SECOND ASSASSIN.
THUNT
HNK!
THE TRADITIONAL JIAN BLADE COUPLED WITH THE GU POISON CHEETAH SMELLED...YOU'VE GOT GHOST DRAGONS.
AH, YES. VERY FOND OF THEIR "TRADITIONAL" METHODS OF MURDER...
...AND NOT TOO KEEN ON POLITICIANS WHO GUN FOR THEIR BUSINESS INTERESTS.

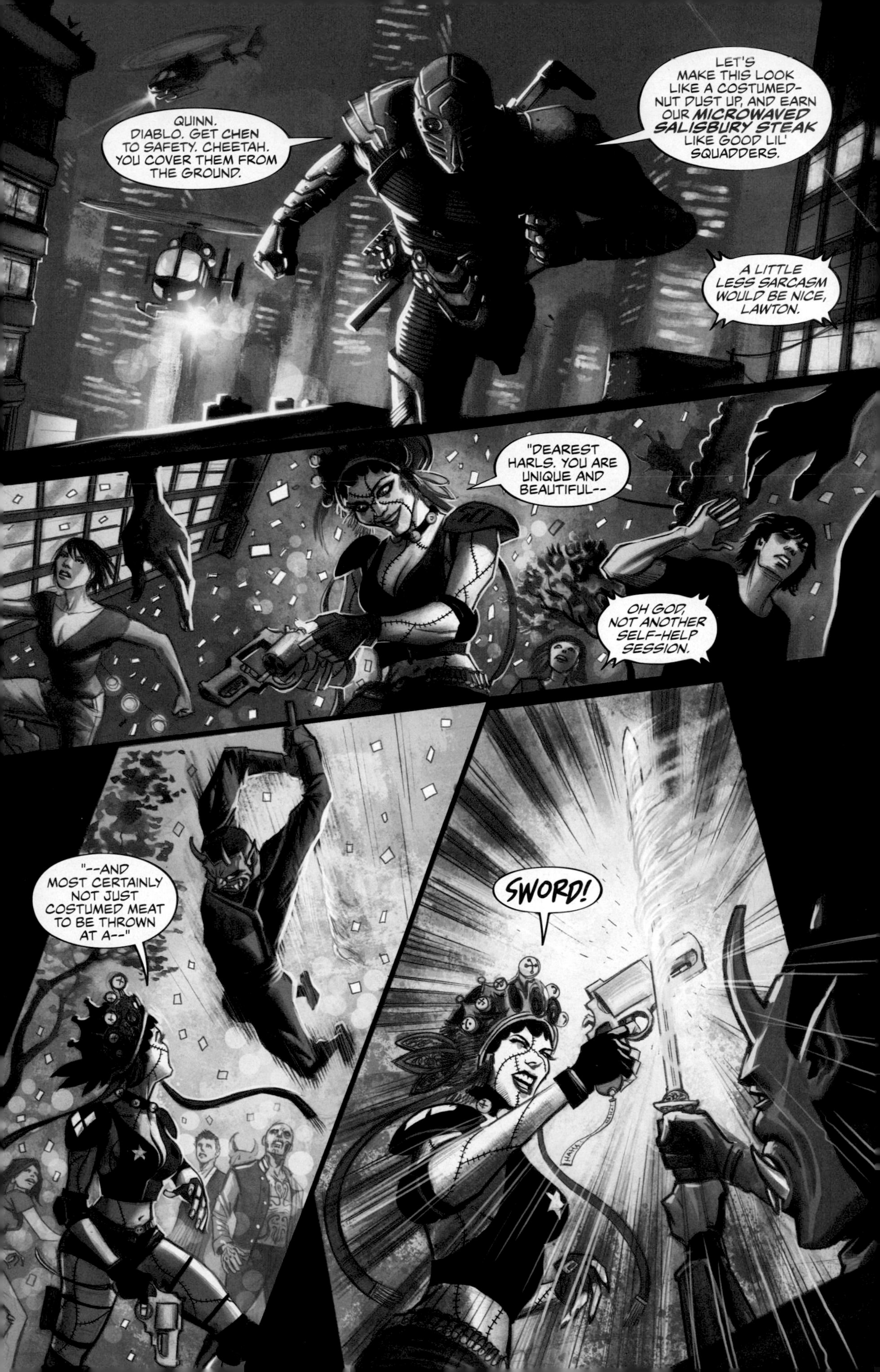
QUINN. DIABLO. GET CHEN TO SAFETY. CHEETAH. YOU COVER THEM FROM THE GROUND.
LET'S MAKE THIS LOOK LIKE A COSTUMED-NUT DUST UP, AND EARN OUR MICROWAVED SALISBURY STEAK LIKE GOOD LIL' SQUADDERS.
A LITTLE LESS SARCASM WOULD BE NICE, LAWTON.
"DEAREST HARLS. YOU ARE UNIQUE AND BEAUTIFUL--
OH GOD, NOT ANOTHER SELF-HELP SESSION.
"--AND MOST CERTAINLY NOT JUST COSTUMED MEAT TO BE THROWN AT A--"
SWORD!

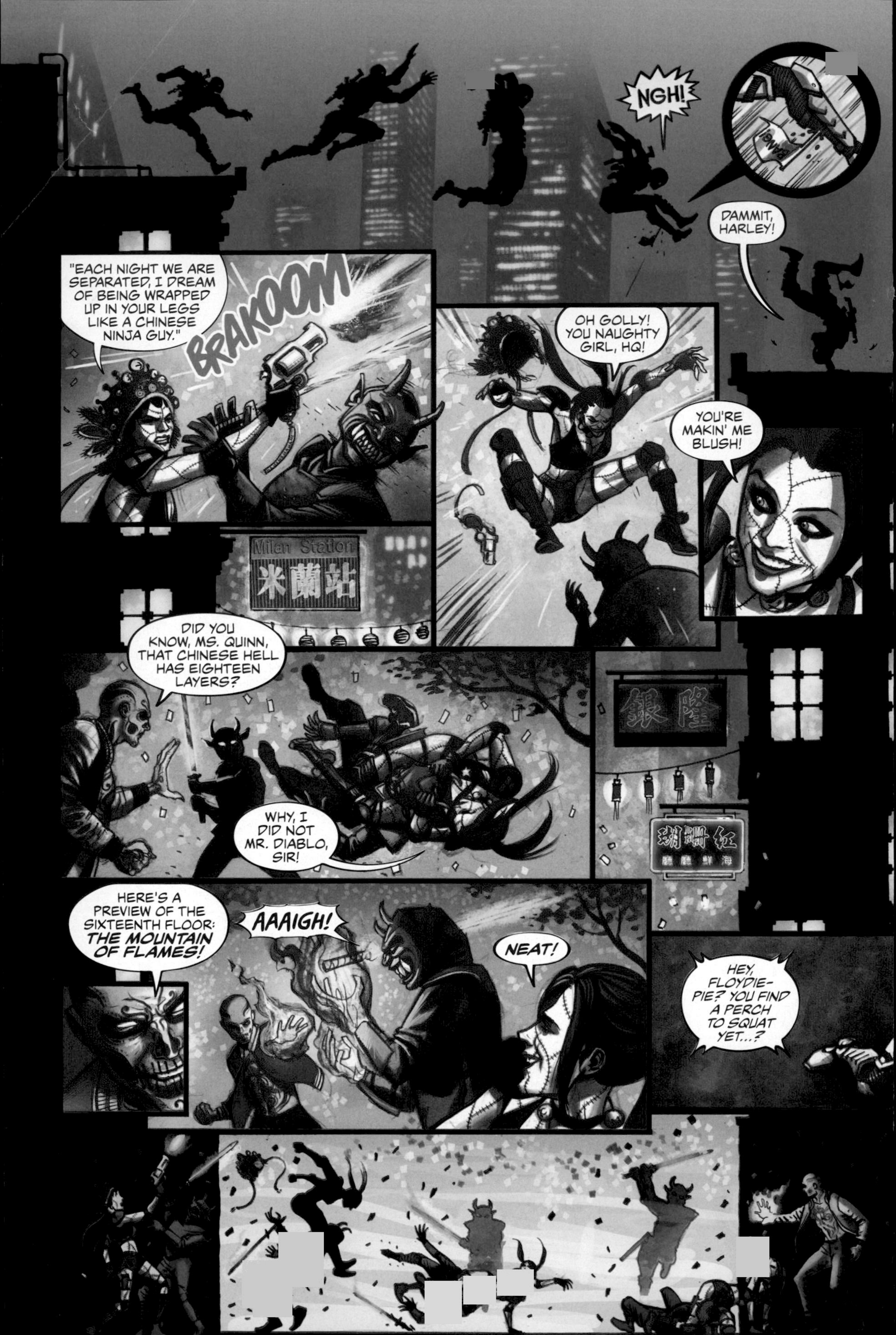
NGH!
DAMMIT, HARLEY!
"EACH NIGHT WE ARE SEPARATED, I DREAM OF BEING WRAPPED UP IN YOUR LEGS LIKE A CHINESE NINJA GUY."
BRAKOOM
OH GOLLY! YOU NAUGHTY GIRL, HQ!
YOU'RE MAKIN' ME BLUSH!
Milan Station
米蘭站
DID YOU KNOW, MS. QUINN, THAT CHINESE HELL HAS EIGHTEEN LAYERS?
WHY, I DID NOT MR. DIABLO, SIR!
HERE'S A PREVIEW OF THE SIXTEENTH FLOOR: *THE MOUNTAIN OF FLAMES!*
AAAIGH!
NEAT!
HEY, FLOYDIE-PIE? YOU FIND A PERCH TO SQUAT YET...?

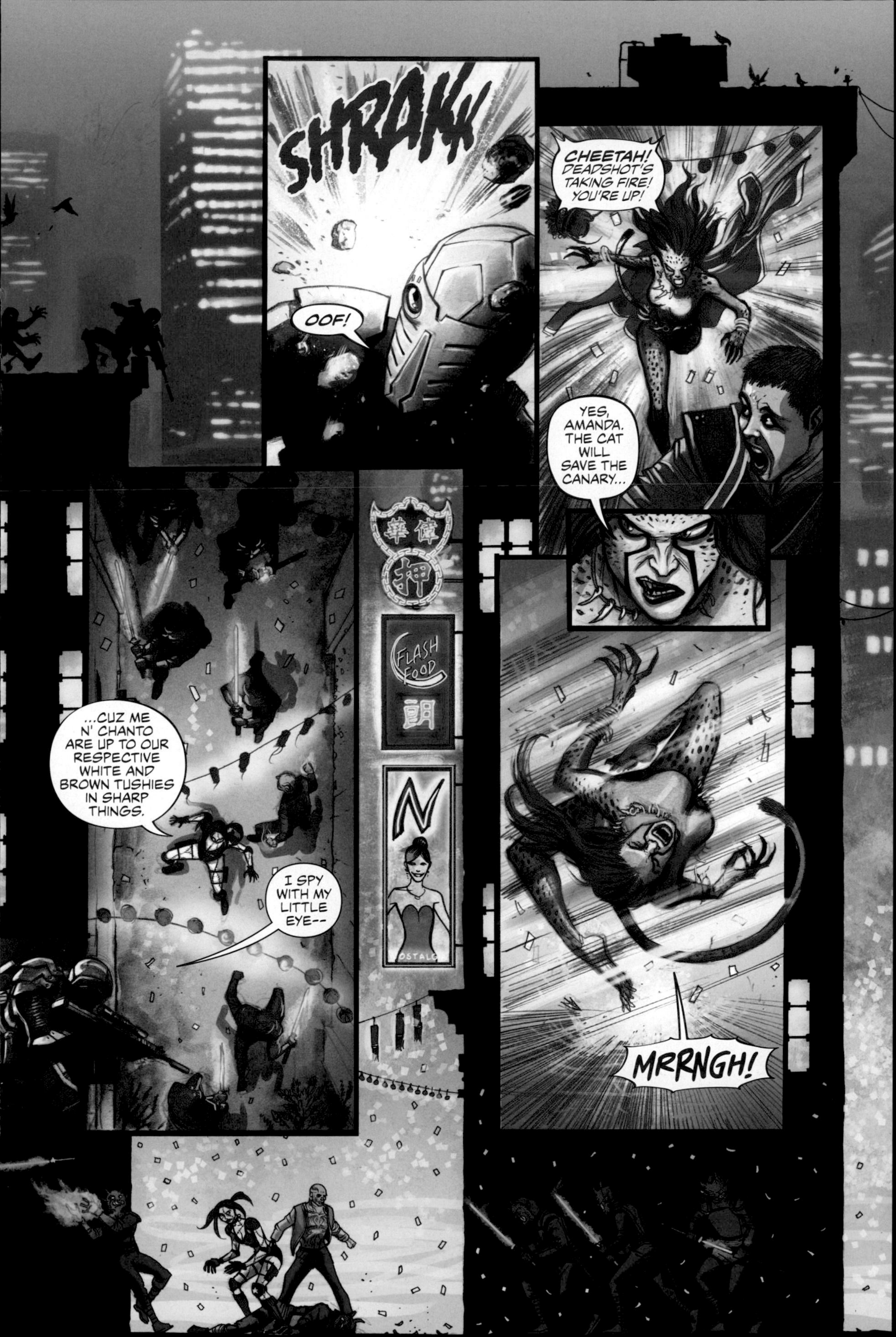
SHRAKK
OOF!
CHEETAH! DEADSHOT'S TAKING FIRE! YOU'RE UP!
YES, AMANDA. THE CAT WILL SAVE THE CANARY...
...CUZ ME N' CHANTO ARE UP TO OUR RESPECTIVE WHITE AND BROWN TUSHIES IN SHARP THINGS.
I SPY WITH MY LITTLE EYE--
華偉
押
FLASH FOOD
朗
N
MRRNGH!

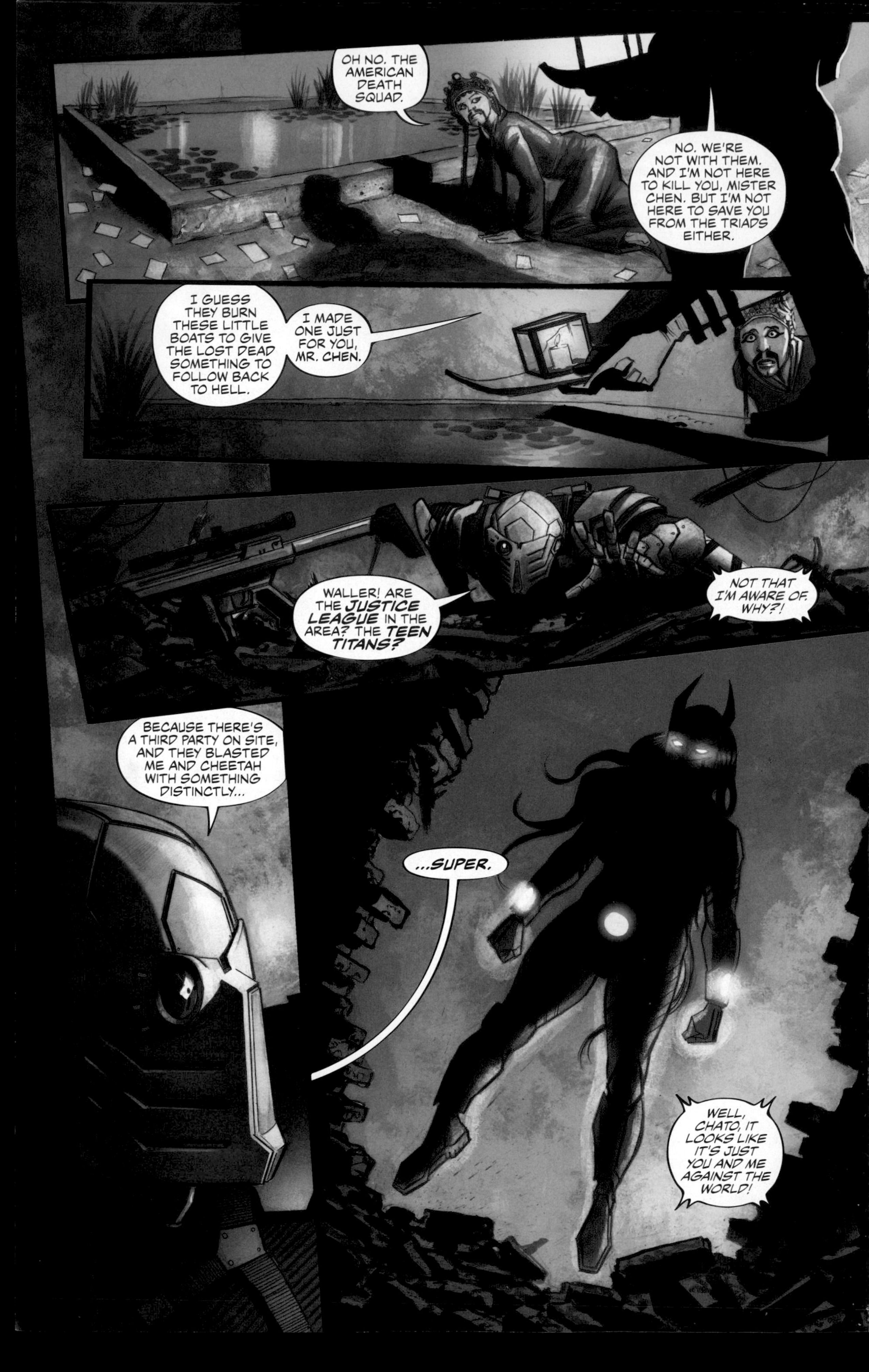
OH NO. THE AMERICAN DEATH SQUAD.
NO. WE'RE NOT WITH THEM. AND I'M NOT HERE TO KILL YOU, MISTER CHEN. BUT I'M NOT HERE TO SAVE YOU FROM THE TRIADS EITHER.
I GUESS THEY BURN THESE LITTLE BOATS TO GIVE THE LOST DEAD SOMETHING TO FOLLOW BACK TO HELL.
I MADE ONE JUST FOR YOU, MR. CHEN.
WALLER! ARE THE JUSTICE LEAGUE IN THE AREA? THE TEEN TITANS?
NOT THAT I'M AWARE OF. WHY?!
BECAUSE THERE'S A THIRD PARTY ON SITE, AND THEY BLASTED ME AND CHEETAH WITH SOMETHING DISTINCTLY...
...SUPER.
WELL, CHATO, IT LOOKS LIKE IT'S JUST YOU AND ME AGAINST THE WORLD!

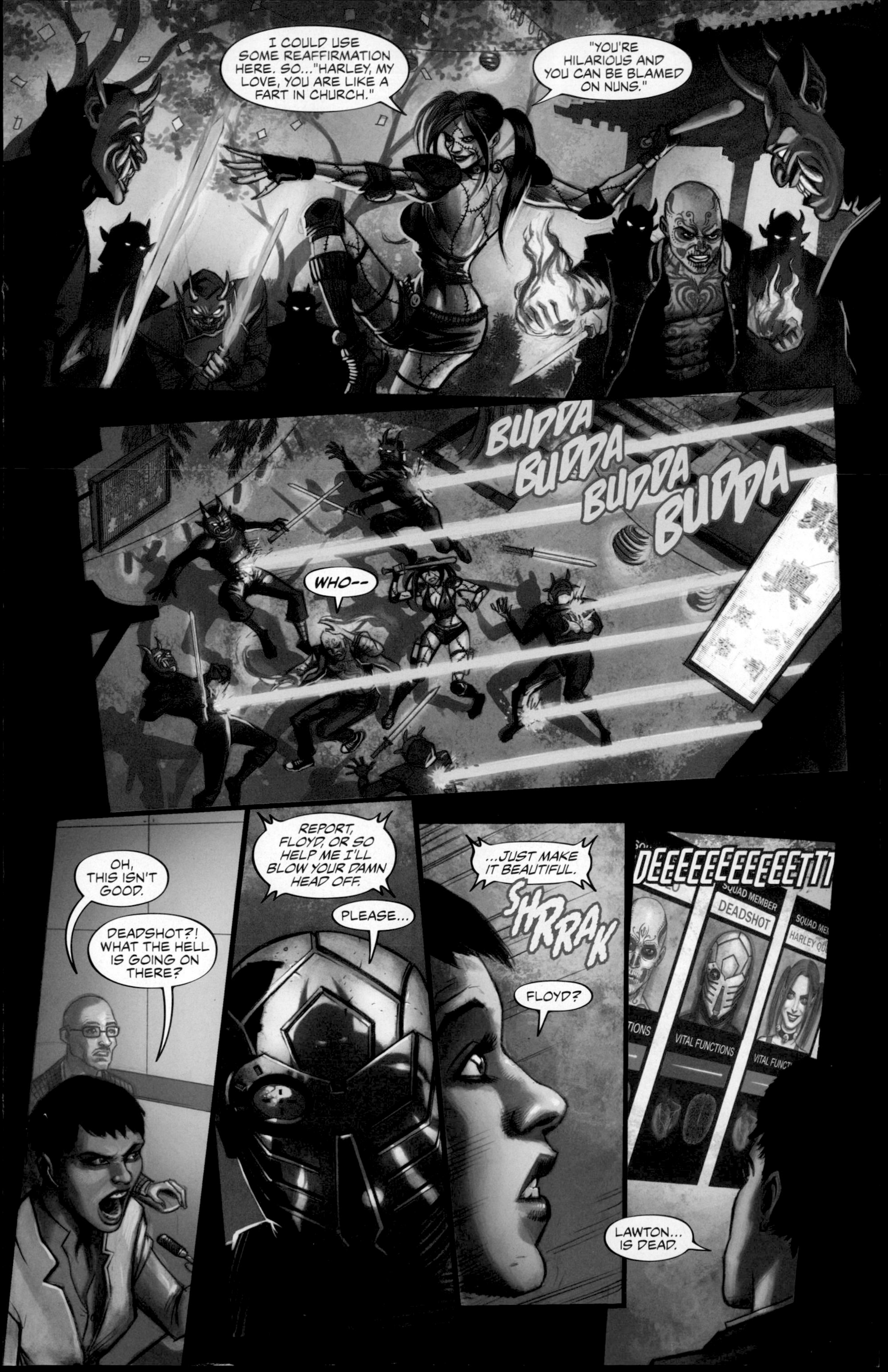
I COULD USE SOME REAFFIRMATION HERE. SO... "HARLEY, MY LOVE, YOU ARE LIKE A FART IN CHURCH."
"YOU'RE HILARIOUS AND YOU CAN BE BLAMED ON NUNS."
BUDDA BUDDA BUDDA BUDDA
WHO--
OH, THIS ISN'T GOOD.
DEADSHOT?! WHAT THE HELL IS GOING ON THERE?
REPORT, FLOYD, OR SO HELP ME I'LL BLOW YOUR DAMN HEAD OFF.
PLEASE...
...JUST MAKE IT BEAUTIFUL.
SHRRAK
FLOYD?
DEEEEEEEEEEEETTT
SQUAD MEMBER
DEADSHOT
VITAL FUNCTIONS
LAWTON... IS DEAD.

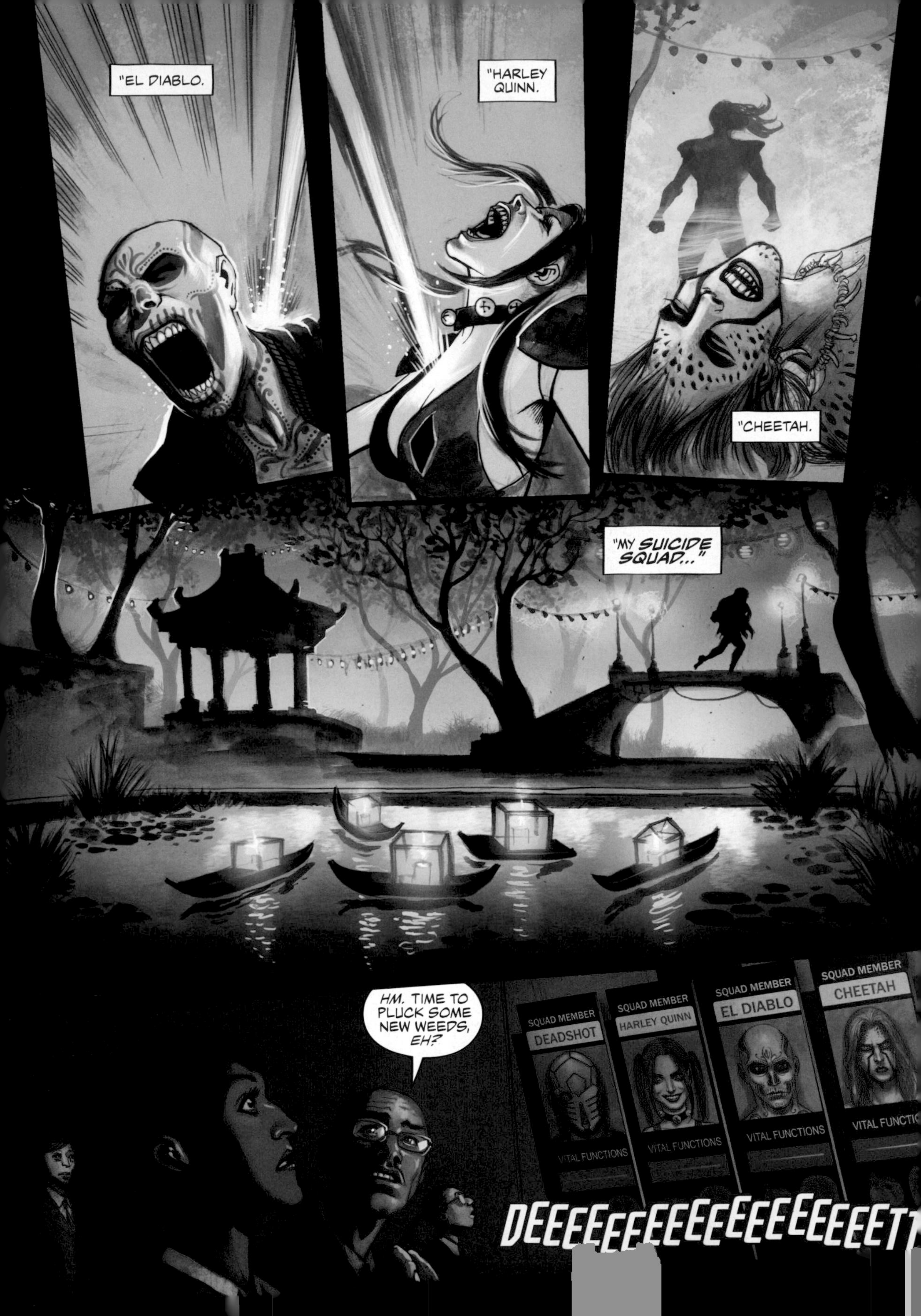

"EL DIABLO.
"HARLEY QUINN.
"CHEETAH.
"MY SUICIDE SQUAD..."
HM. TIME TO PLUCK SOME NEW WEEDS, EH?
SQUAD MEMBER
DEADSHOT
VITAL FUNCTIONS
SQUAD MEMBER
HARLEY QUINN
VITAL FUNCTIONS
SQUAD MEMBER
EL DIABLO
VITAL FUNCTIONS
SQUAD MEMBER
CHEETAH
DEEEEEEEEEEEEEEEEEETT

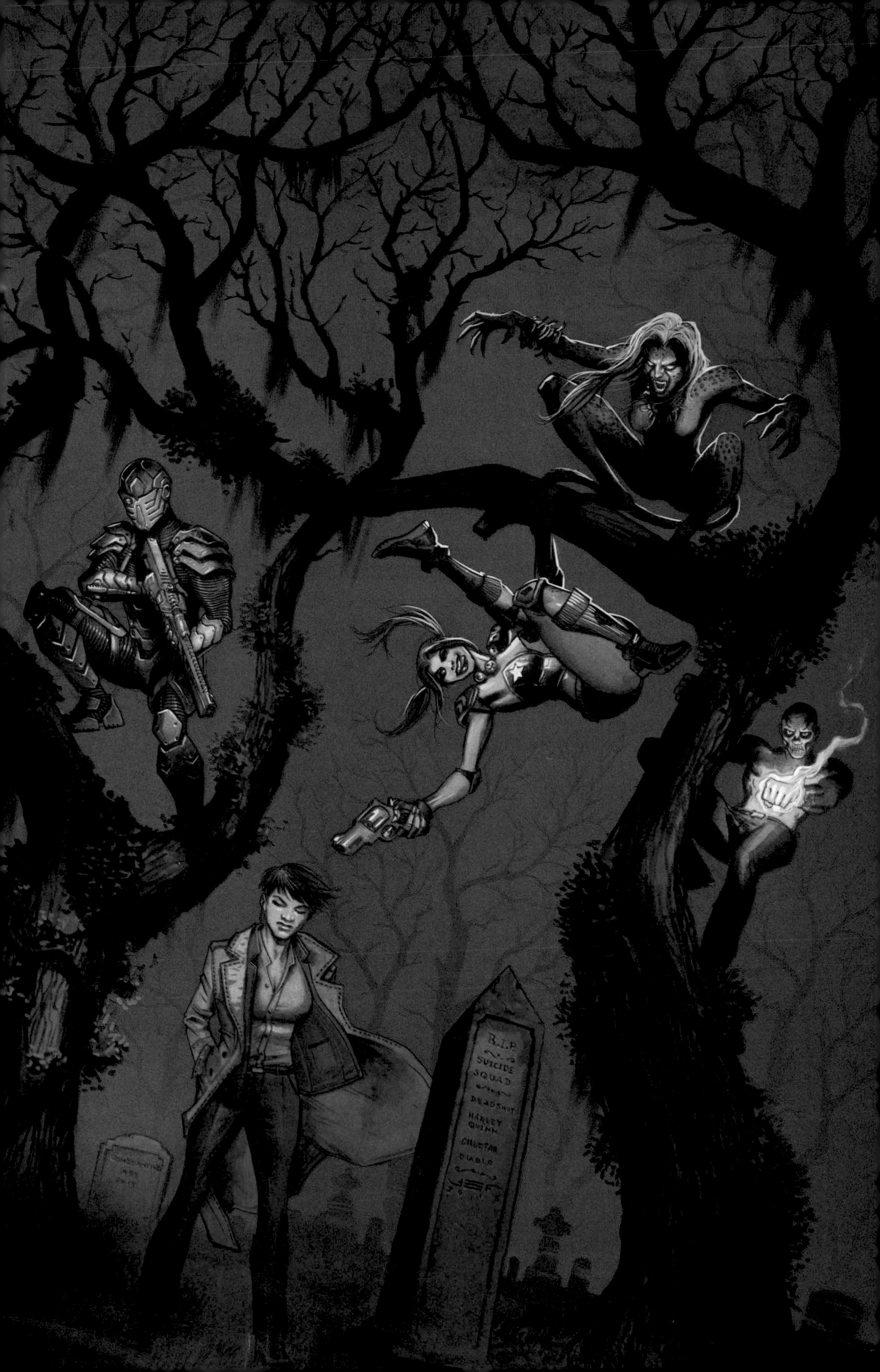
R.I.P.
SUICIDE SQUAD
DEADSHOT
HARLEY QUINN
DIABLO

A LUNCH LADY NAMED MARLENE?

TIM SEELEY writer JUAN FERREYRA artist NATE PIEKOS letterer

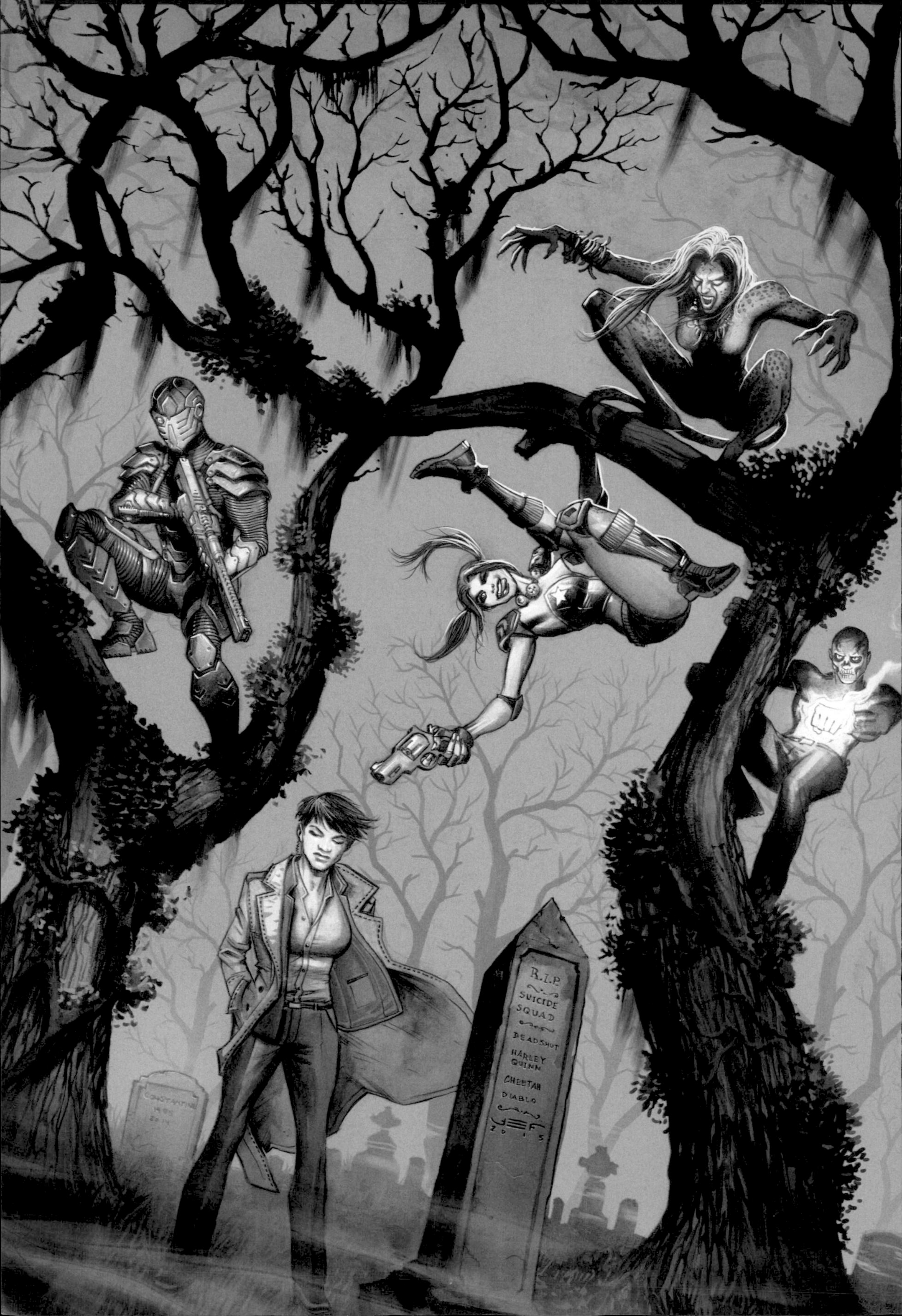
R.I.P.
SUICIDE SQUAD
DEADSHOT
HARLEY QUINN
CHEETAH
DIABLO

"IT ALL BEGINS WITH A LUNCH LADY NAMED **MARLENE.**"

"'**MAULING?**' THAT'S NOT A NAME, DEAR, THAT'S A PLEASURABLE ACTIVITY."

"HEY, IT'S NOT MY FAULT YER MOMMA DIDN'T LEARN YA PROPER **BROOKLYN ENGLISH.** MARLENE! **MAR**-LENE!"

"ANYWAYS, MARLENE WORKS AT **BELLE REVE PENITENTIARY** IN TERREBONNE PARISH, LOUISIANA, SEE. MAYBE YOU HEARD OF IT?"

"SO, MARLENE'S FAVORITE MAN-MEAT SASHAYS IN ONE DAY--"

"I DON'T SASHAY."

"YOU GUYS GONNA LET ME TELL THIS STORY OR NOT?!"

"--AHEM-- SO FLOYD SAYS--"

I'LL HAVE A SLICE OF PIZZA, PLEASE. SAUSAGE.

THANK YOU, **MARLENE,** YOU LOOK LOVELY TODAY.

OH, WELL THANK **YOU,** MISTER LAWTON.

DID YOU DO SOMETHING DIFFERENT WITH YOUR HAIR? OH, NO, WAIT, I'VE GOT IT...

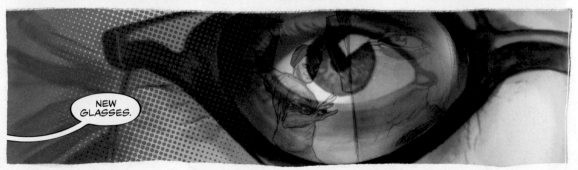

NEW GLASSES.

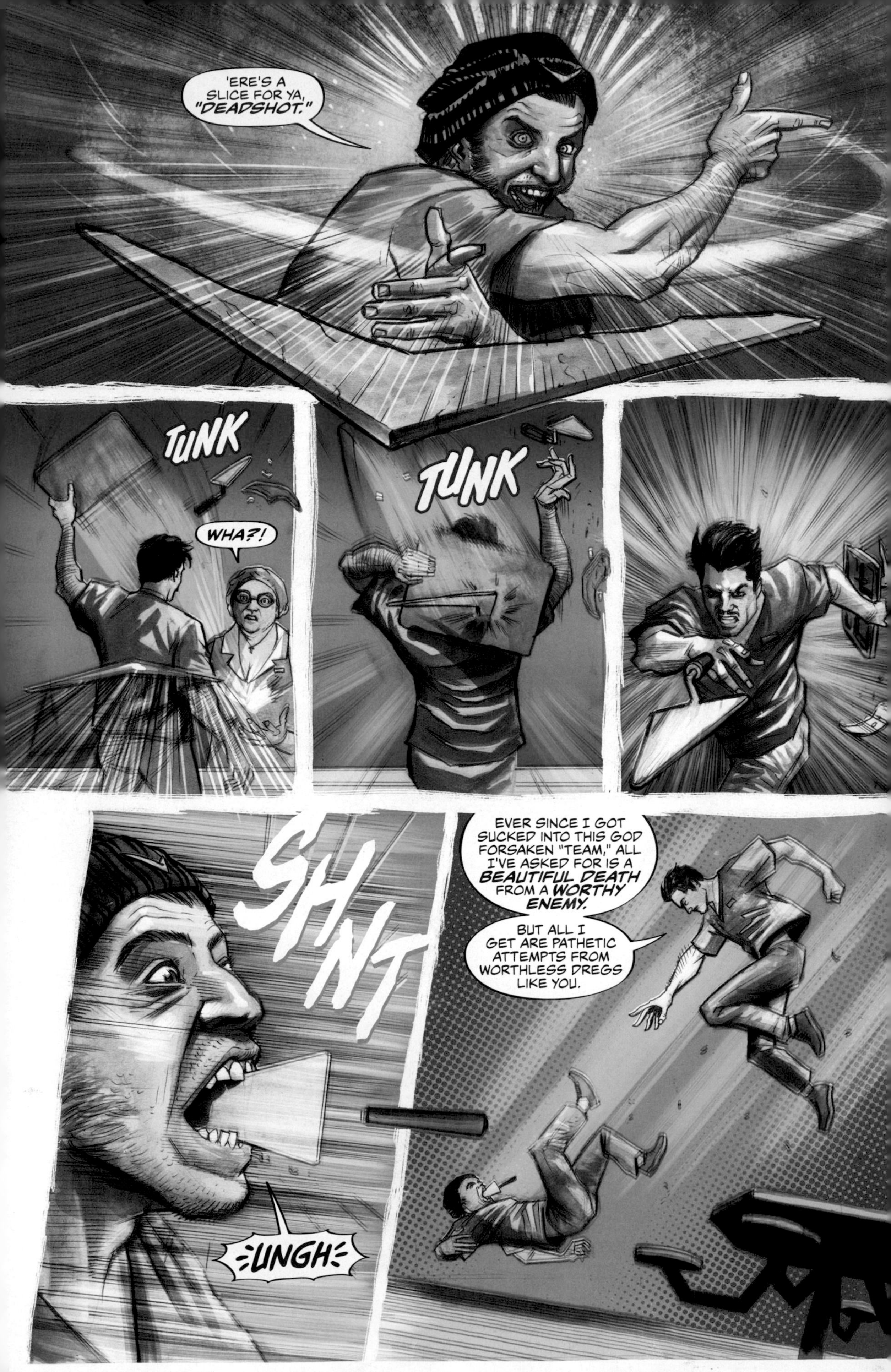
'ERE'S A SLICE FOR YA, "DEADSHOT."
TUNK
WHA?!
TUNK
SHNT
UNGH
EVER SINCE I GOT SUCKED INTO THIS GOD FORSAKEN "TEAM," ALL I'VE ASKED FOR IS A BEAUTIFUL DEATH FROM A WORTHY ENEMY.
BUT ALL I GET ARE PATHETIC ATTEMPTS FROM WORTHLESS DREGS LIKE YOU.

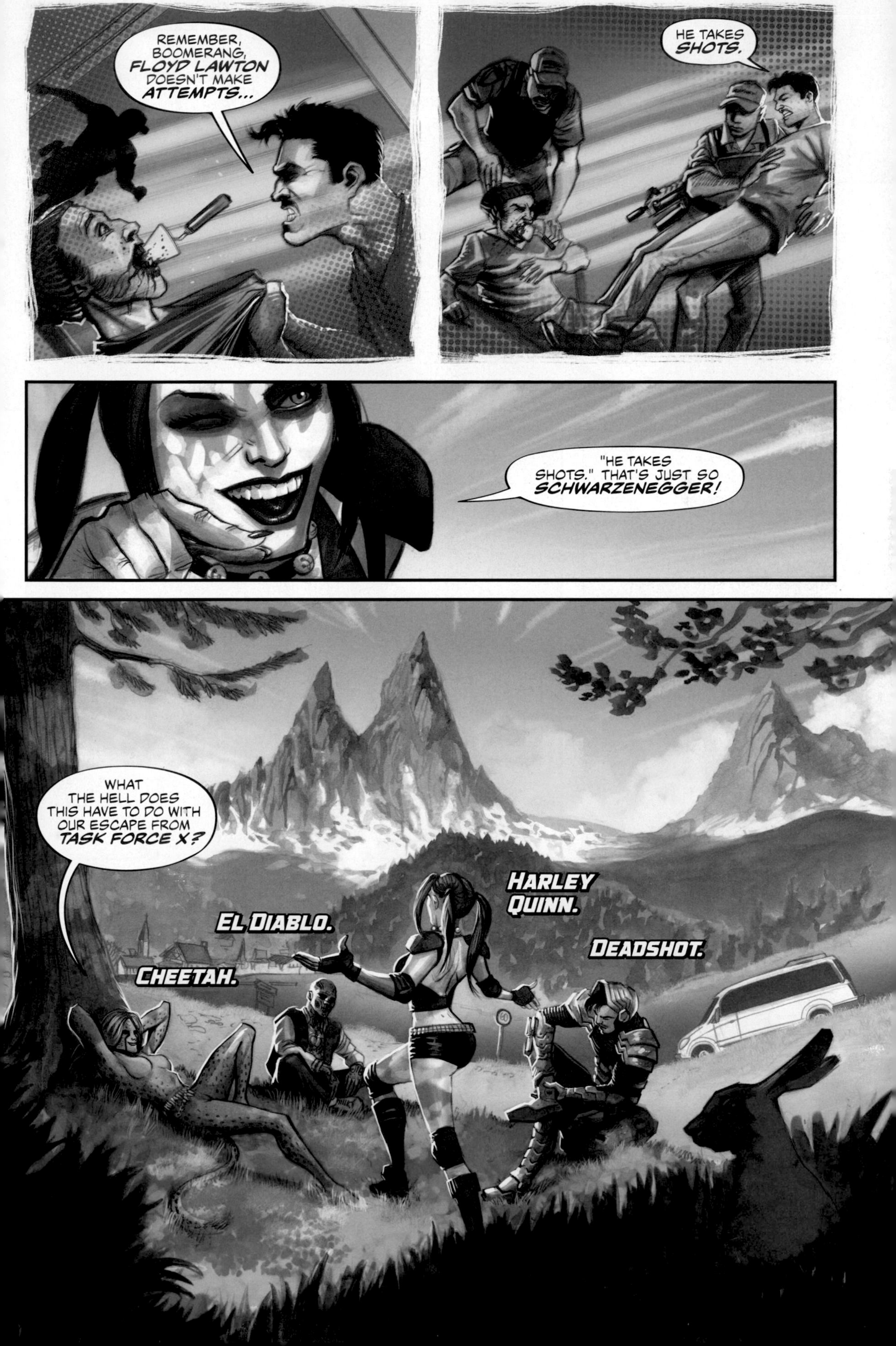
REMEMBER, BOOMERANG, FLOYD LAWTON DOESN'T MAKE ATTEMPTS...
HE TAKES SHOTS.
"HE TAKES SHOTS." THAT'S JUST SO SCHWARZENEGGER!
WHAT THE HELL DOES THIS HAVE TO DO WITH OUR ESCAPE FROM TASK FORCE X?
HARLEY QUINN.
EL DIABLO.
DEADSHOT.
CHEETAH.

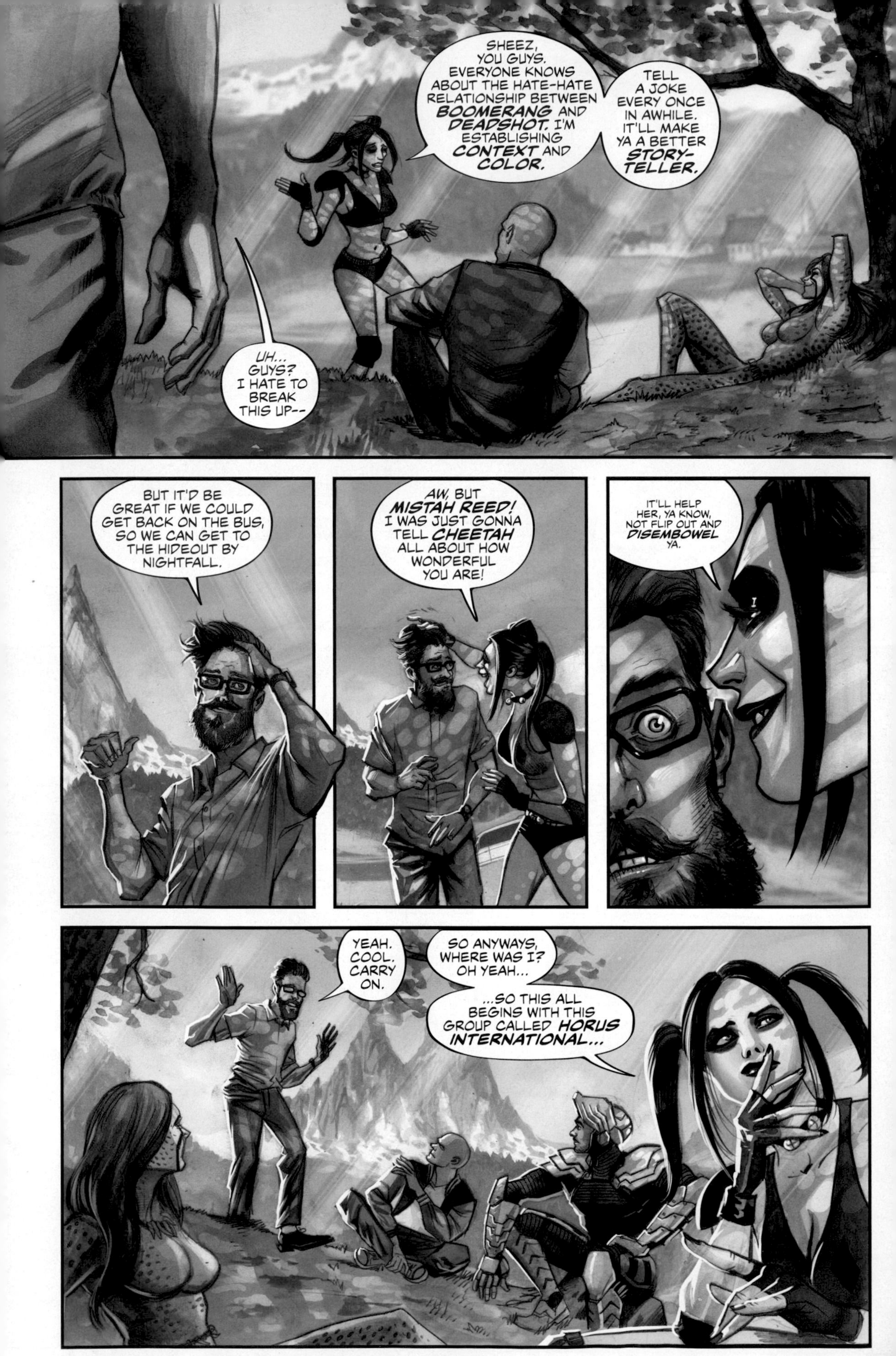
SHEEZ, YOU GUYS. EVERYONE KNOWS ABOUT THE HATE-HATE RELATIONSHIP BETWEEN BOOMERANG AND DEADSHOT. I'M ESTABLISHING CONTEXT AND COLOR.
TELL A JOKE EVERY ONCE IN AWHILE. IT'LL MAKE YA A BETTER STORY-TELLER.
UH... GUYS? I HATE TO BREAK THIS UP--
BUT IT'D BE GREAT IF WE COULD GET BACK ON THE BUS, SO WE CAN GET TO THE HIDEOUT BY NIGHTFALL.
AW, BUT MISTAH REED! I WAS JUST GONNA TELL CHEETAH ALL ABOUT HOW WONDERFUL YOU ARE!
IT'LL HELP HER, YA KNOW, NOT FLIP OUT AND DISEMBOWEL YA.
YEAH. COOL. CARRY ON.
SO ANYWAYS, WHERE WAS I? OH YEAH...
...SO THIS ALL BEGINS WITH THIS GROUP CALLED HORUS INTERNATIONAL...

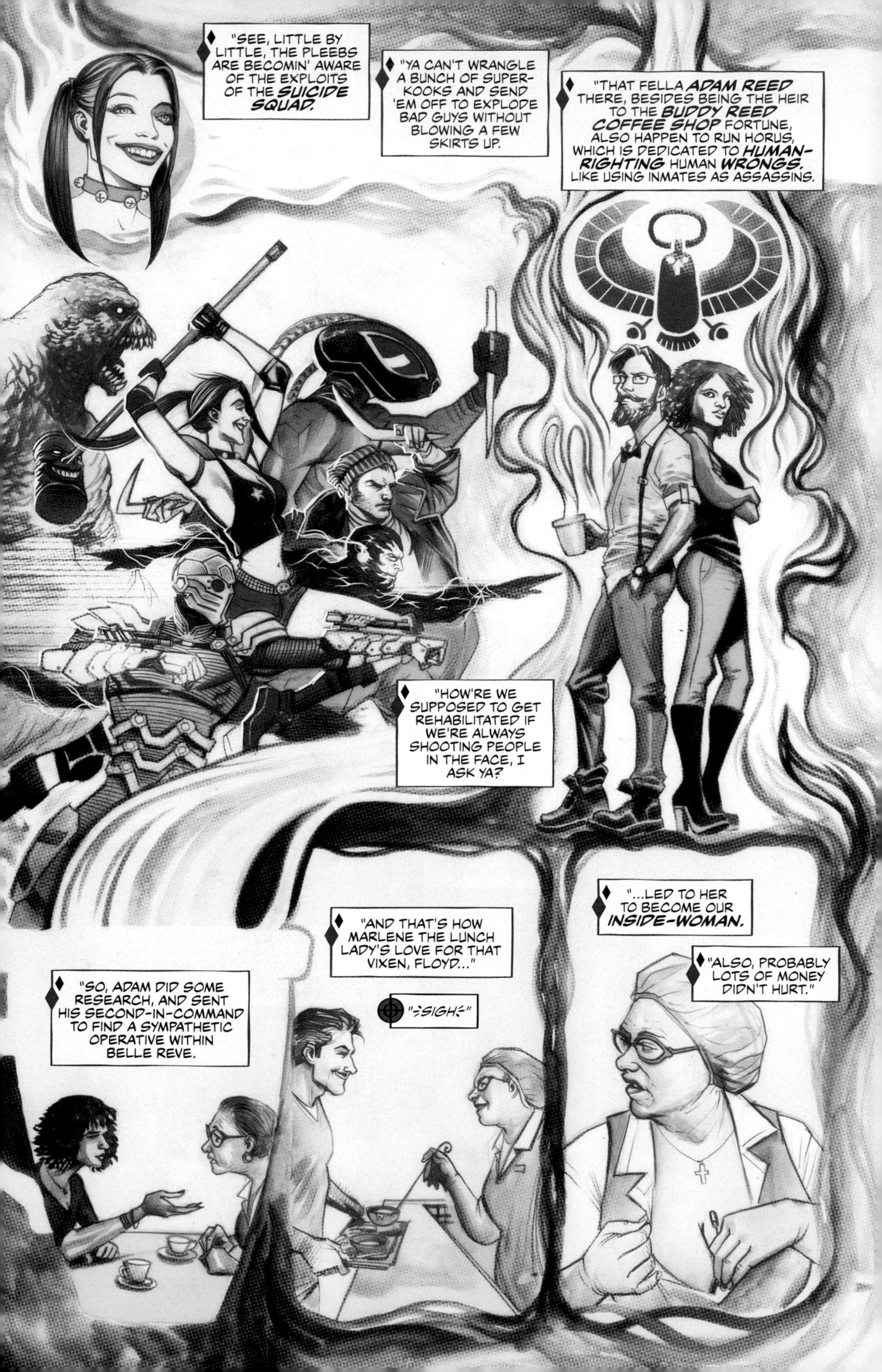
"SEE, LITTLE BY LITTLE, THE PLEEBS ARE BECOMIN' AWARE OF THE EXPLOITS OF THE SUICIDE SQUAD.
"YA CAN'T WRANGLE A BUNCH OF SUPER-KOOKS AND SEND 'EM OFF TO EXPLODE BAD GUYS WITHOUT BLOWING A FEW SKIRTS UP.
"THAT FELLA ADAM REED THERE, BESIDES BEING THE HEIR TO THE BUDDY REED COFFEE SHOP FORTUNE, ALSO HAPPEN TO RUN HORUS, WHICH IS DEDICATED TO HUMAN-RIGHTING HUMAN WRONGS. LIKE USING INMATES AS ASSASSINS.
"HOW'RE WE SUPPOSED TO GET REHABILITATED IF WE'RE ALWAYS SHOOTING PEOPLE IN THE FACE, I ASK YA?
"SO, ADAM DID SOME RESEARCH, AND SENT HIS SECOND-IN-COMMAND TO FIND A SYMPATHETIC OPERATIVE WITHIN BELLE REVE.
"AND THAT'S HOW MARLENE THE LUNCH LADY'S LOVE FOR THAT VIXEN, FLOYD..."
"SIGH"
"...LED TO HER TO BECOME OUR INSIDE-WOMAN.
"ALSO, PROBABLY LOTS OF MONEY DIDN'T HURT."

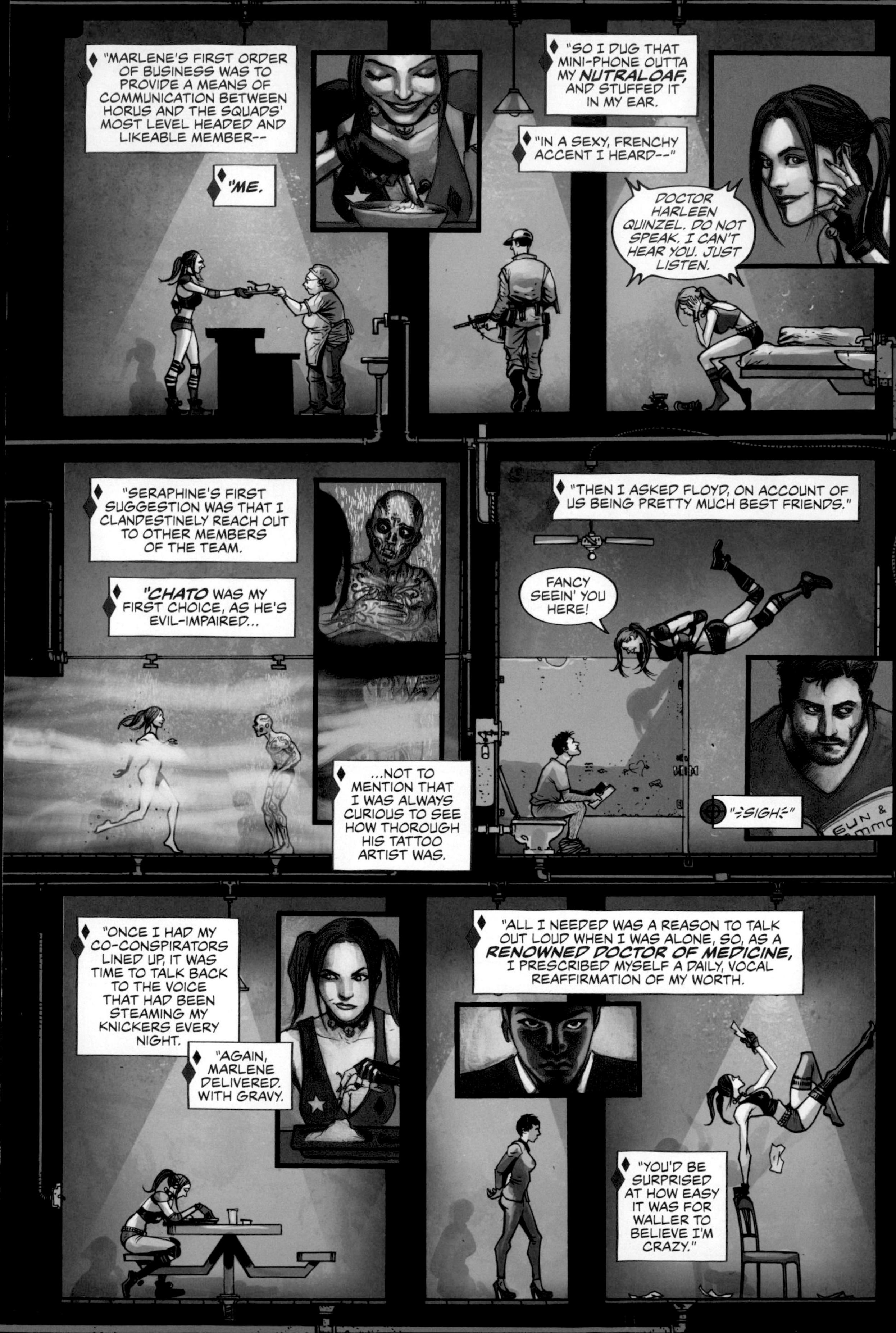
"MARLENE'S FIRST ORDER OF BUSINESS WAS TO PROVIDE A MEANS OF COMMUNICATION BETWEEN HORUS AND THE SQUADS' MOST LEVEL HEADED AND LIKEABLE MEMBER--
"ME.
"SO I DUG THAT MINI-PHONE OUTTA MY NUTRALOAF, AND STUFFED IT IN MY EAR.
"IN A SEXY, FRENCHY ACCENT I HEARD--"
DOCTOR HARLEEN QUINZEL. DO NOT SPEAK. I CAN'T HEAR YOU. JUST LISTEN.
"SERAPHINE'S FIRST SUGGESTION WAS THAT I CLANDESTINELY REACH OUT TO OTHER MEMBERS OF THE TEAM.
"CHATO WAS MY FIRST CHOICE, AS HE'S EVIL-IMPAIRED...
...NOT TO MENTION THAT I WAS ALWAYS CURIOUS TO SEE HOW THOROUGH HIS TATTOO ARTIST WAS.
"THEN I ASKED FLOYD, ON ACCOUNT OF US BEING PRETTY MUCH BEST FRIENDS."
FANCY SEEIN' YOU HERE!
"*SIGH*"
"ONCE I HAD MY CO-CONSPIRATORS LINED UP, IT WAS TIME TO TALK BACK TO THE VOICE THAT HAD BEEN STEAMING MY KNICKERS EVERY NIGHT.
"AGAIN, MARLENE DELIVERED. WITH GRAVY.
"ALL I NEEDED WAS A REASON TO TALK OUT LOUD WHEN I WAS ALONE, SO, AS A RENOWNED DOCTOR OF MEDICINE, I PRESCRIBED MYSELF A DAILY, VOCAL REAFFIRMATION OF MY WORTH.
"YOU'D BE SURPRISED AT HOW EASY IT WAS FOR WALLER TO BELIEVE I'M CRAZY."

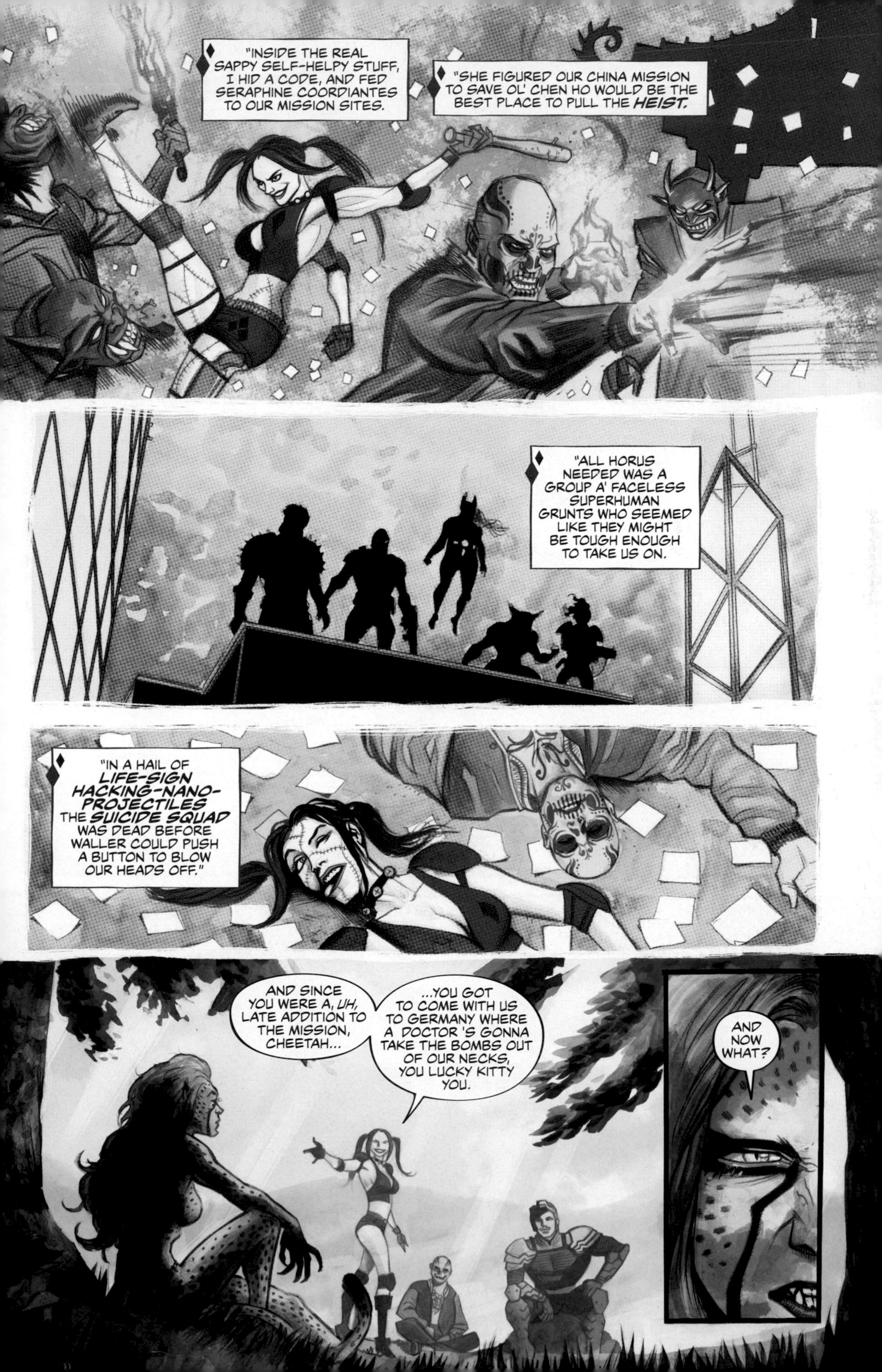
"INSIDE THE REAL SAPPY SELF-HELPY STUFF, I HID A CODE, AND FED SERAPHINE COORDIANTES TO OUR MISSION SITES.
"SHE FIGURED OUR CHINA MISSION TO SAVE OL' CHEN HO WOULD BE THE BEST PLACE TO PULL THE *HEIST.*
"ALL HORUS NEEDED WAS A GROUP A' FACELESS SUPERHUMAN GRUNTS WHO SEEMED LIKE THEY MIGHT BE TOUGH ENOUGH TO TAKE US ON.
"IN A HAIL OF *LIFE-SIGN HACKING-NANO-PROJECTILES* THE *SUICIDE SQUAD* WAS DEAD BEFORE WALLER COULD PUSH A BUTTON TO BLOW OUR HEADS OFF."
AND SINCE YOU WERE A, *UH,* LATE ADDITION TO THE MISSION, CHEETAH...
...YOU GOT TO COME WITH US TO GERMANY WHERE A DOCTOR 'S GONNA TAKE THE BOMBS OUT OF OUR NECKS, YOU LUCKY KITTY YOU.
AND NOW WHAT?

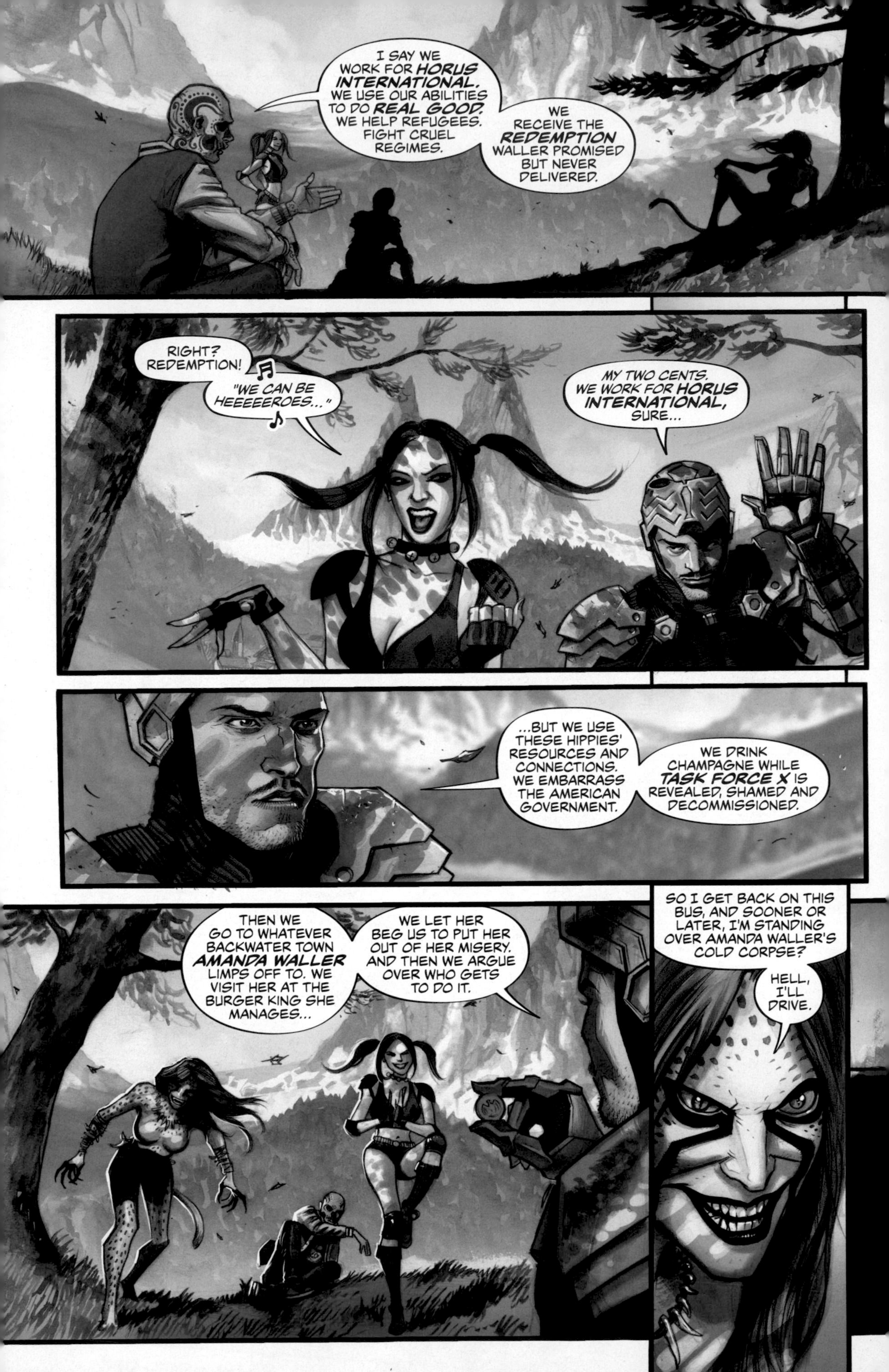
I SAY WE WORK FOR HORUS INTERNATIONAL. WE USE OUR ABILITIES TO DO REAL GOOD. WE HELP REFUGEES. FIGHT CRUEL REGIMES.
WE RECEIVE THE REDEMPTION WALLER PROMISED BUT NEVER DELIVERED.
RIGHT? REDEMPTION!
"WE CAN BE HEEEEEROES..."
MY TWO CENTS. WE WORK FOR HORUS INTERNATIONAL, SURE...
...BUT WE USE THESE HIPPIES' RESOURCES AND CONNECTIONS. WE EMBARRASS THE AMERICAN GOVERNMENT.
WE DRINK CHAMPAGNE WHILE TASK FORCE X IS REVEALED, SHAMED AND DECOMMISSIONED.
THEN WE GO TO WHATEVER BACKWATER TOWN AMANDA WALLER LIMPS OFF TO. WE VISIT HER AT THE BURGER KING SHE MANAGES...
WE LET HER BEG US TO PUT HER OUT OF HER MISERY. AND THEN WE ARGUE OVER WHO GETS TO DO IT.
SO I GET BACK ON THIS BUS, AND SOONER OR LATER, I'M STANDING OVER AMANDA WALLER'S COLD CORPSE?
HELL, I'LL DRIVE.

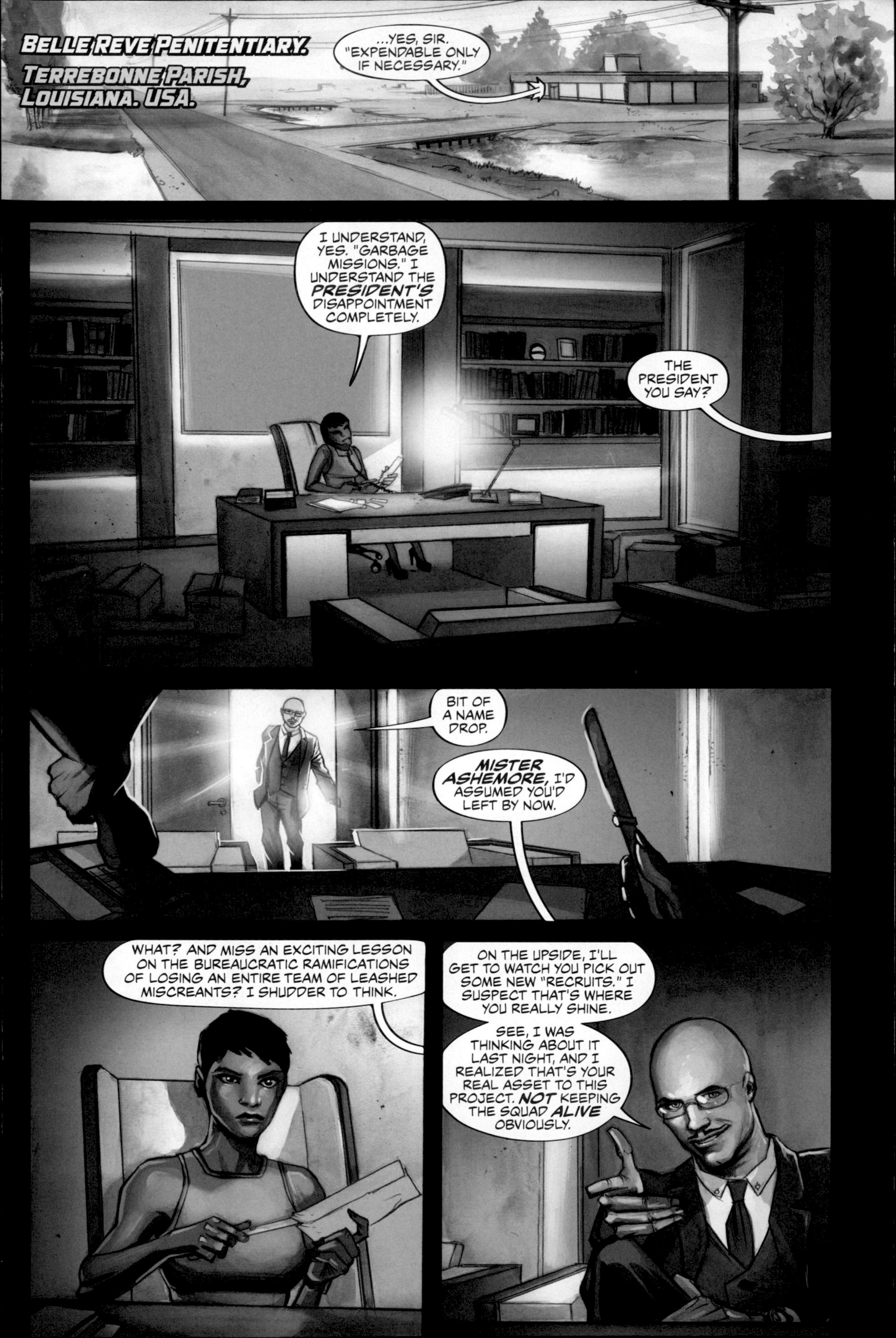
BELLE REVE PENITENTIARY.
TERREBONNE PARISH, LOUISIANA. USA.
...YES, SIR. "EXPENDABLE ONLY IF NECESSARY."
I UNDERSTAND, YES. "GARBAGE MISSIONS." I UNDERSTAND THE PRESIDENT'S DISAPPOINTMENT COMPLETELY.
THE PRESIDENT YOU SAY?
BIT OF A NAME DROP.
MISTER ASHEMORE, I'D ASSUMED YOU'D LEFT BY NOW.
WHAT? AND MISS AN EXCITING LESSON ON THE BUREAUCRATIC RAMIFICATIONS OF LOSING AN ENTIRE TEAM OF LEASHED MISCREANTS? I SHUDDER TO THINK.
ON THE UPSIDE, I'LL GET TO WATCH YOU PICK OUT SOME NEW "RECRUITS." I SUSPECT THAT'S WHERE YOU REALLY SHINE.
SEE, I WAS THINKING ABOUT IT LAST NIGHT, AND I REALIZED THAT'S YOUR REAL ASSET TO THIS PROJECT. NOT KEEPING THE SQUAD ALIVE OBVIOUSLY.

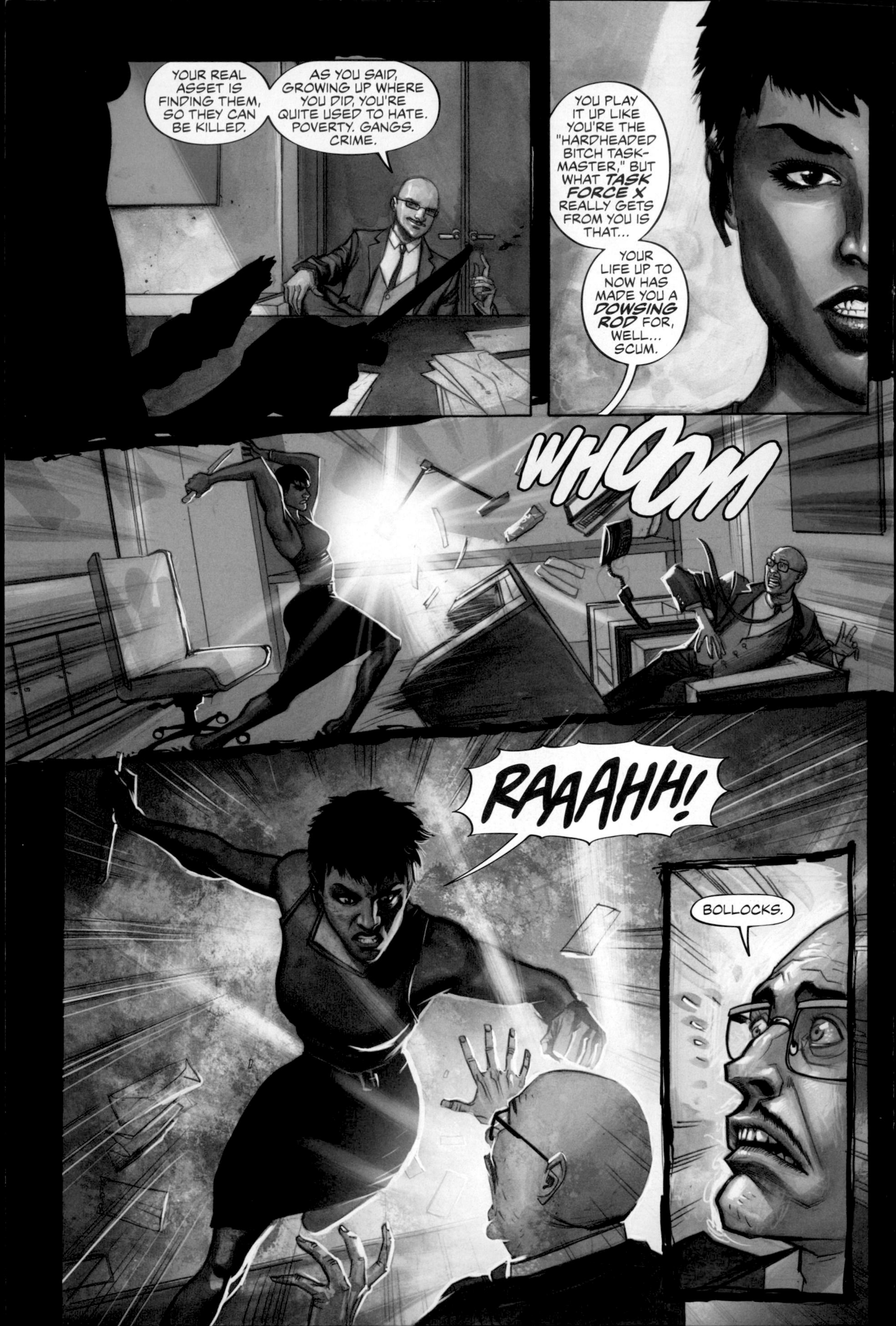
YOUR REAL ASSET IS FINDING THEM, SO THEY CAN BE KILLED.
AS YOU SAID, GROWING UP WHERE YOU DID, YOU'RE QUITE USED TO HATE. POVERTY. GANGS. CRIME.
YOU PLAY IT UP LIKE YOU'RE THE "HARDHEADED BITCH TASK-MASTER," BUT WHAT TASK FORCE X REALLY GETS FROM YOU IS THAT...
YOUR LIFE UP TO NOW HAS MADE YOU A DOWSING ROD FOR, WELL... SCUM.
WHOOM
RAAAHH!
BOLLOCKS.

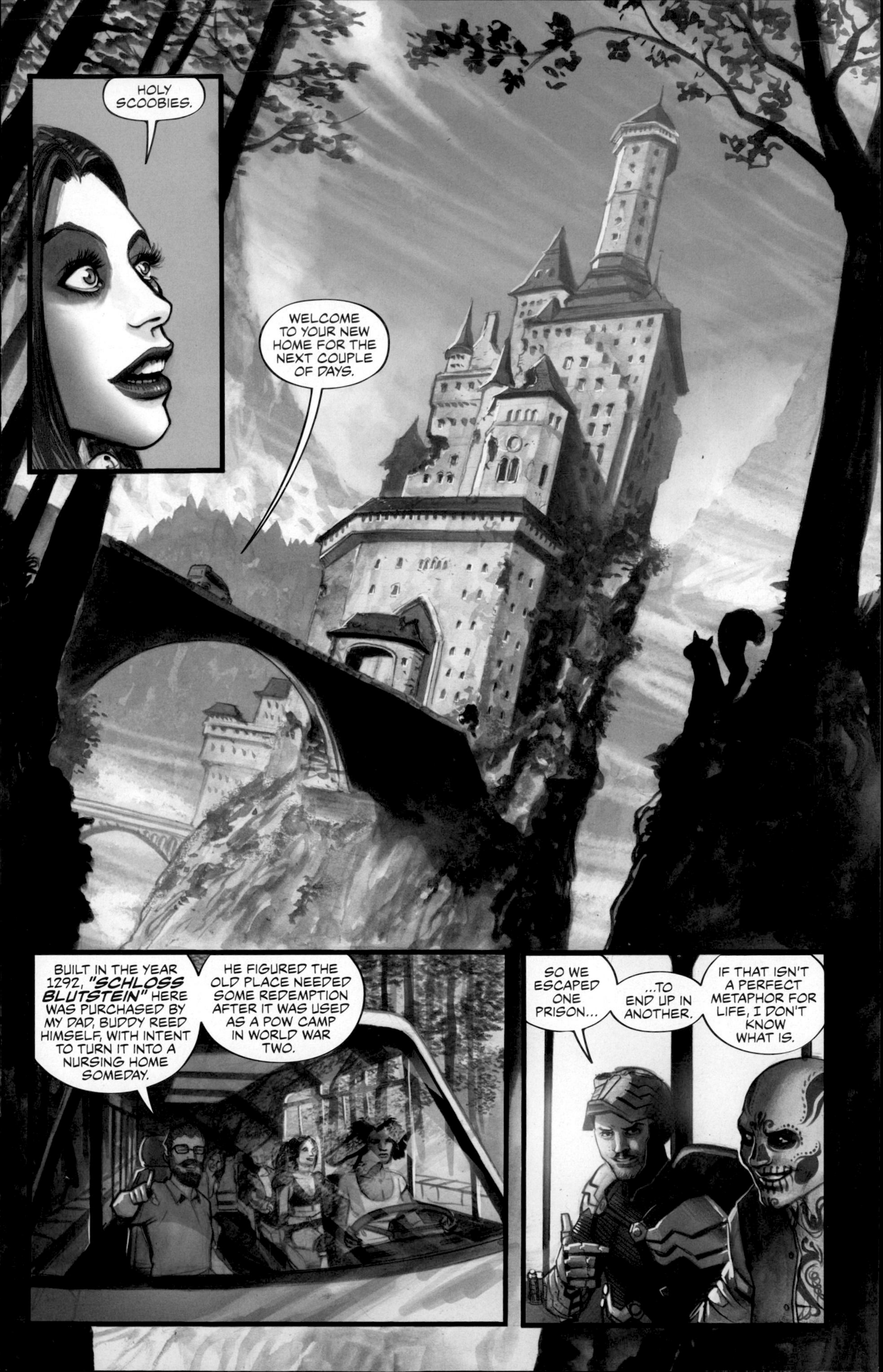
HOLY SCOOBIES.
WELCOME TO YOUR NEW HOME FOR THE NEXT COUPLE OF DAYS.
BUILT IN THE YEAR 1292, "SCHLOSS BLUTSTEIN" HERE WAS PURCHASED BY MY DAD, BUDDY REED HIMSELF, WITH INTENT TO TURN IT INTO A NURSING HOME SOMEDAY.
HE FIGURED THE OLD PLACE NEEDED SOME REDEMPTION AFTER IT WAS USED AS A POW CAMP IN WORLD WAR TWO.
SO WE ESCAPED ONE PRISON...
...TO END UP IN ANOTHER.
IF THAT ISN'T A PERFECT METAPHOR FOR LIFE, I DON'T KNOW WHAT IS.

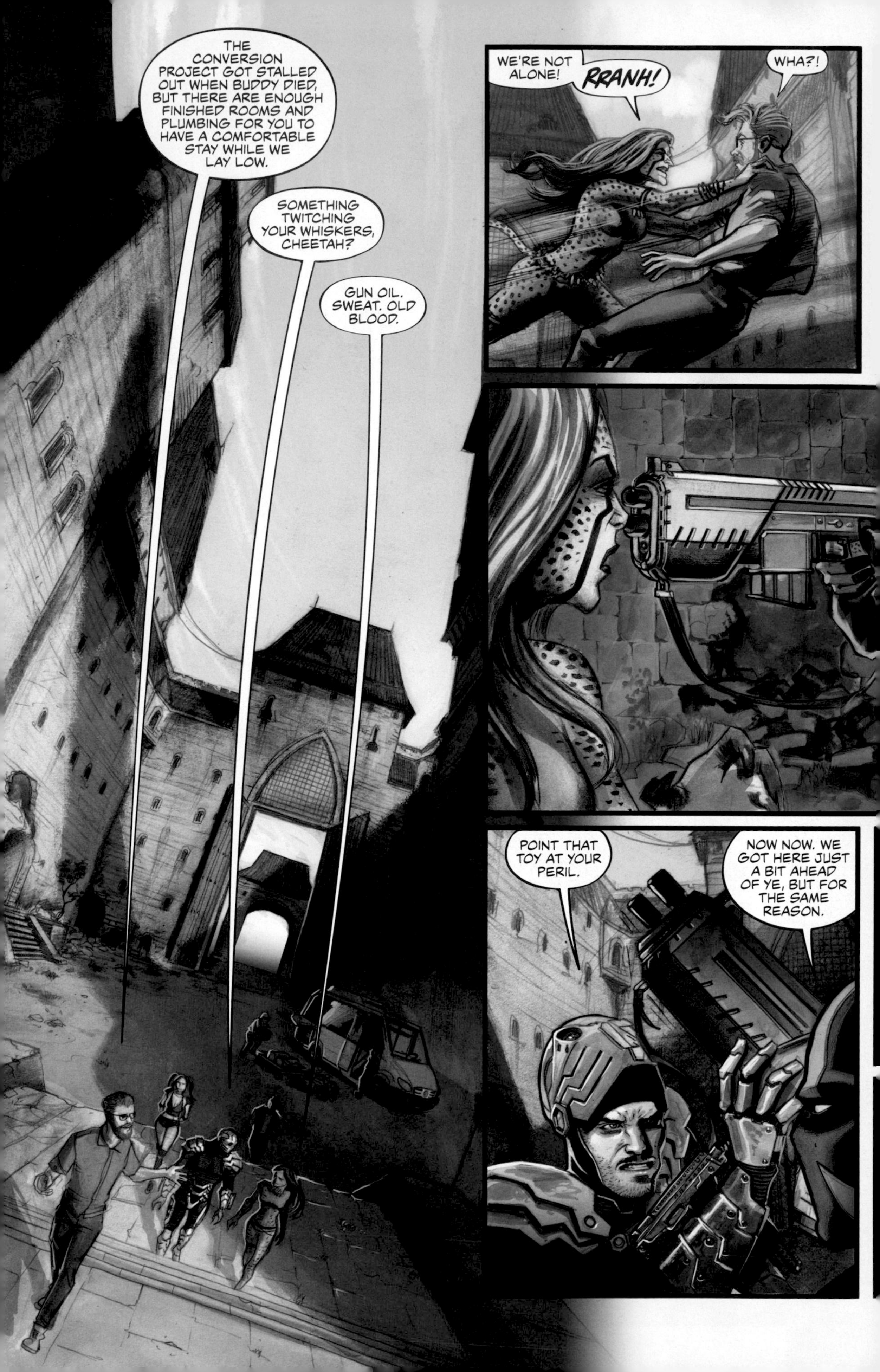
THE CONVERSION PROJECT GOT STALLED OUT WHEN BUDDY DIED, BUT THERE ARE ENOUGH FINISHED ROOMS AND PLUMBING FOR YOU TO HAVE A COMFORTABLE STAY WHILE WE LAY LOW.
SOMETHING TWITCHING YOUR WHISKERS, CHEETAH?
GUN OIL. SWEAT. OLD BLOOD.
WE'RE NOT ALONE!
RRANH!
WHA?!
POINT THAT TOY AT YOUR PERIL.
NOW NOW. WE GOT HERE JUST A BIT AHEAD OF YE, BUT FOR THE SAME REASON.

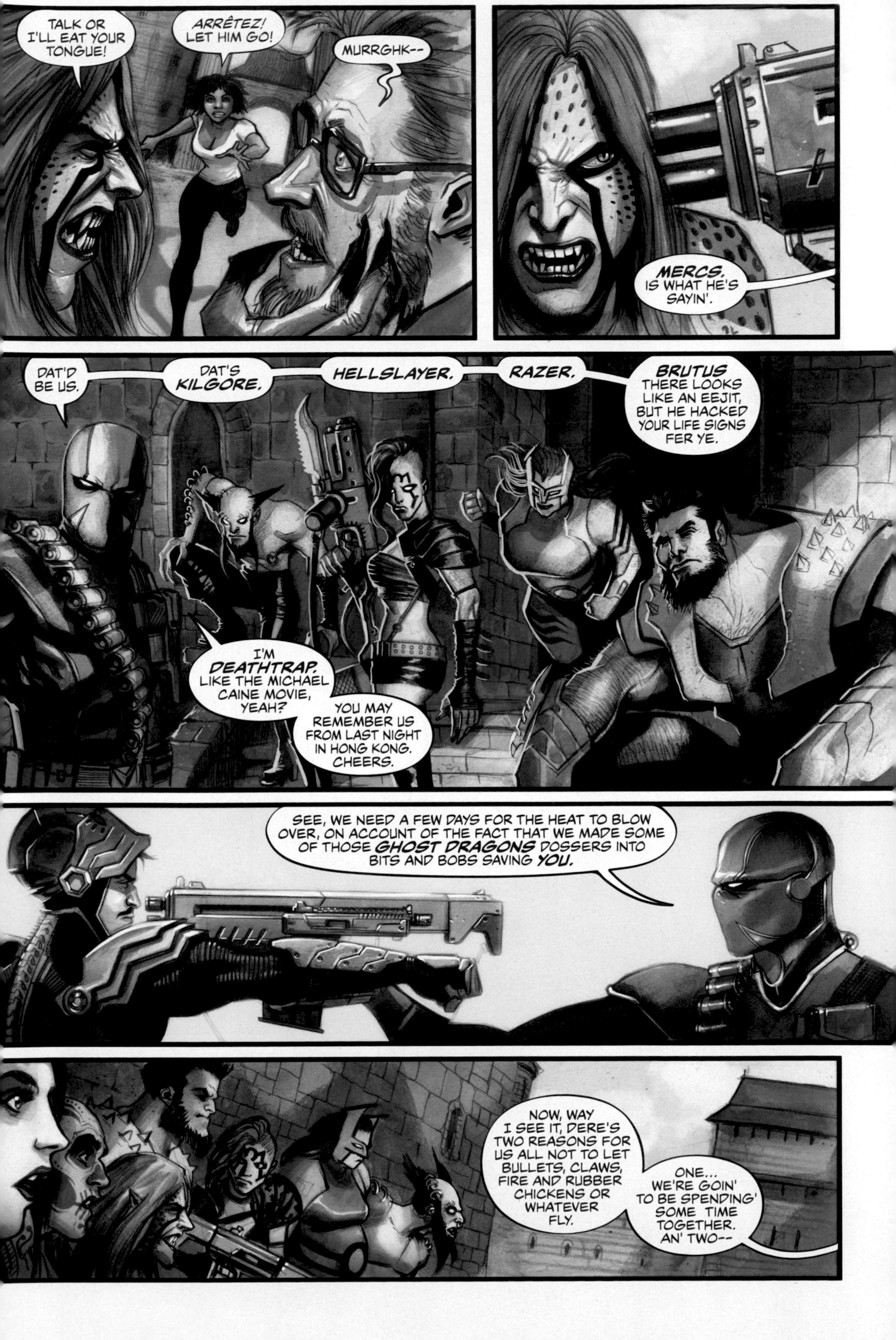
TALK OR I'LL EAT YOUR TONGUE!
ARRÊTEZ! LET HIM GO!
MURRGHK--
MERCS. IS WHAT HE'S SAYIN'.
DAT'D BE US.
DAT'S KILGORE.
HELLSLAYER.
RAZER.
BRUTUS THERE LOOKS LIKE AN EEJIT, BUT HE HACKED YOUR LIFE SIGNS FER YE.
I'M DEATHTRAP. LIKE THE MICHAEL CAINE MOVIE, YEAH?
YOU MAY REMEMBER US FROM LAST NIGHT IN HONG KONG. CHEERS.
SEE, WE NEED A FEW DAYS FOR THE HEAT TO BLOW OVER, ON ACCOUNT OF THE FACT THAT WE MADE SOME OF THOSE GHOST DRAGONS DOSSERS INTO BITS AND BOBS SAVING YOU.
NOW, WAY I SEE IT, DERE'S TWO REASONS FOR US ALL NOT TO LET BULLETS, CLAWS, FIRE AND RUBBER CHICKENS OR WHATEVER FLY.
ONE... WE'RE GOIN' TO BE SPENDING' SOME TIME TOGETHER. AN' TWO--

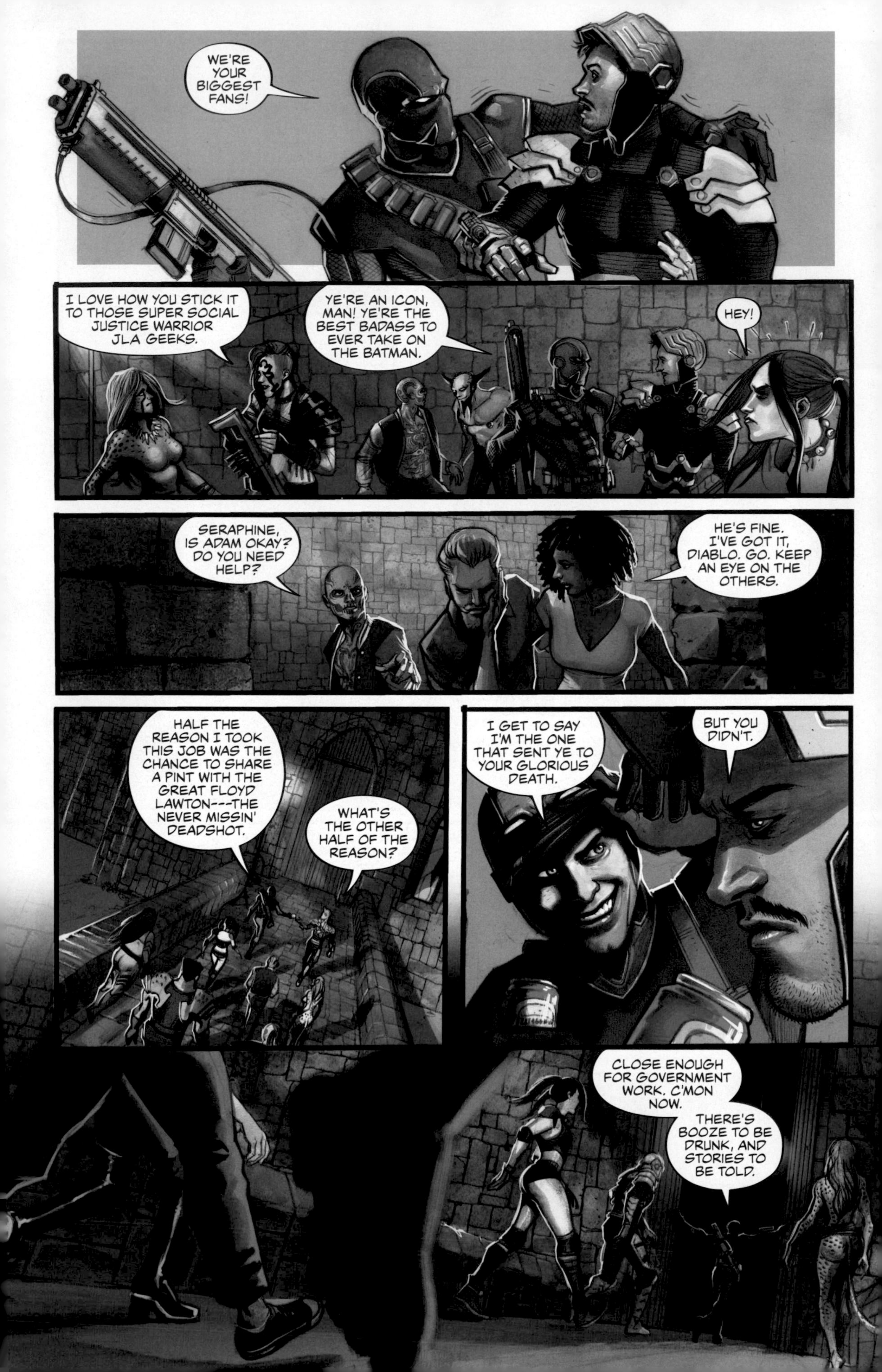
WE'RE YOUR BIGGEST FANS!
I LOVE HOW YOU STICK IT TO THOSE SUPER SOCIAL JUSTICE WARRIOR JLA GEEKS.
YE'RE AN ICON, MAN! YE'RE THE BEST BADASS TO EVER TAKE ON THE BATMAN.
HEY!
SERAPHINE, IS ADAM OKAY? DO YOU NEED HELP?
HE'S FINE. I'VE GOT IT, DIABLO. GO. KEEP AN EYE ON THE OTHERS.
HALF THE REASON I TOOK THIS JOB WAS THE CHANCE TO SHARE A PINT WITH THE GREAT FLOYD LAWTON---THE NEVER MISSIN' DEADSHOT.
WHAT'S THE OTHER HALF OF THE REASON?
I GET TO SAY I'M THE ONE THAT SENT YE TO YOUR GLORIOUS DEATH.
BUT YOU DIDN'T.
CLOSE ENOUGH FOR GOVERNMENT WORK. C'MON NOW.
THERE'S BOOZE TO BE DRUNK, AND STORIES TO BE TOLD.

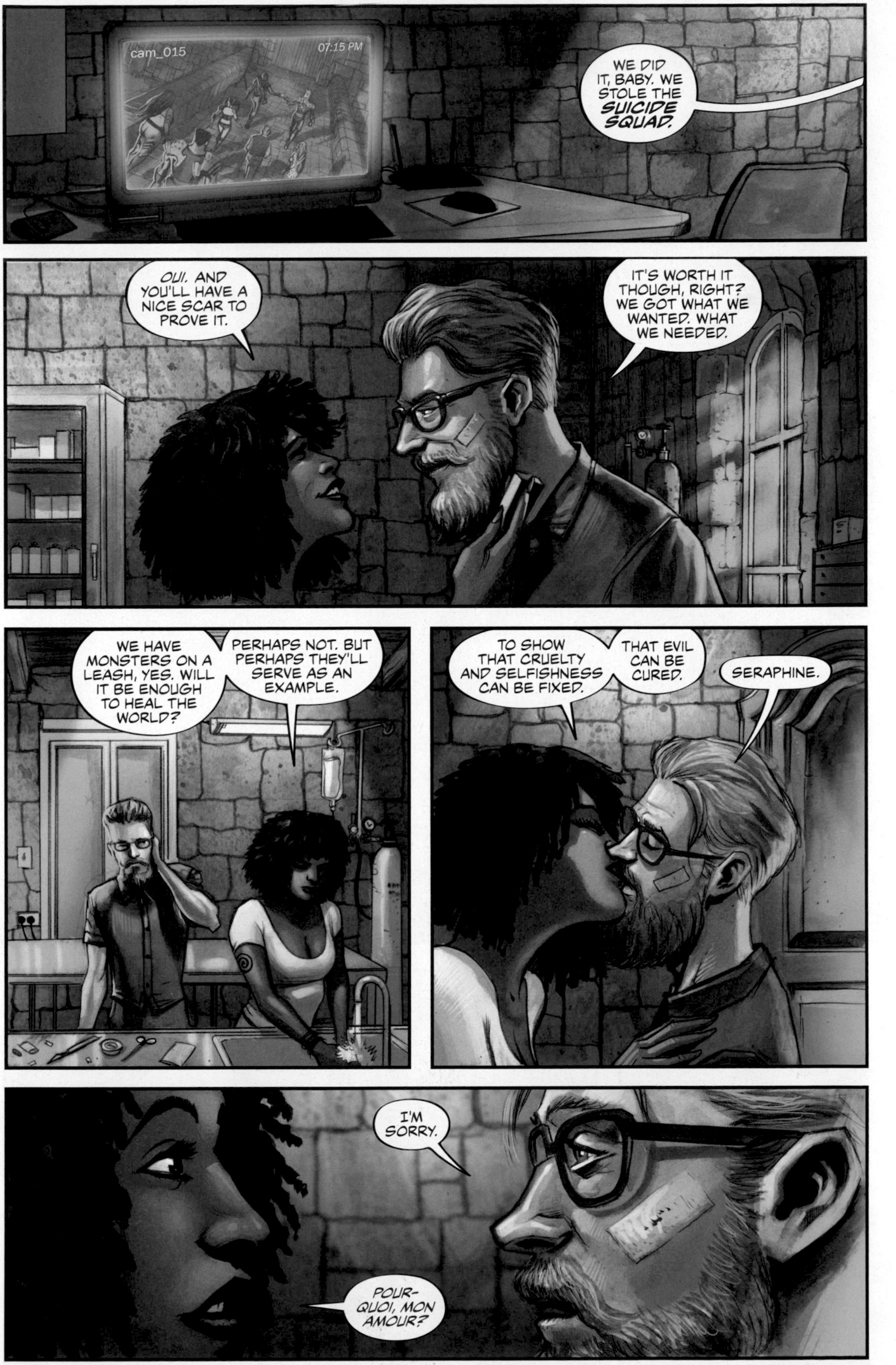
cam_015
07:15 PM
WE DID IT, BABY. WE STOLE THE SUICIDE SQUAD.
OUI. AND YOU'LL HAVE A NICE SCAR TO PROVE IT.
IT'S WORTH IT THOUGH, RIGHT? WE GOT WHAT WE WANTED. WHAT WE NEEDED.
WE HAVE MONSTERS ON A LEASH, YES. WILL IT BE ENOUGH TO HEAL THE WORLD?
PERHAPS NOT. BUT PERHAPS THEY'LL SERVE AS AN EXAMPLE.
TO SHOW THAT CRUELTY AND SELFISHNESS CAN BE FIXED.
THAT EVIL CAN BE CURED.
SERAPHINE.
I'M SORRY.
POURQUOI, MON AMOUR?

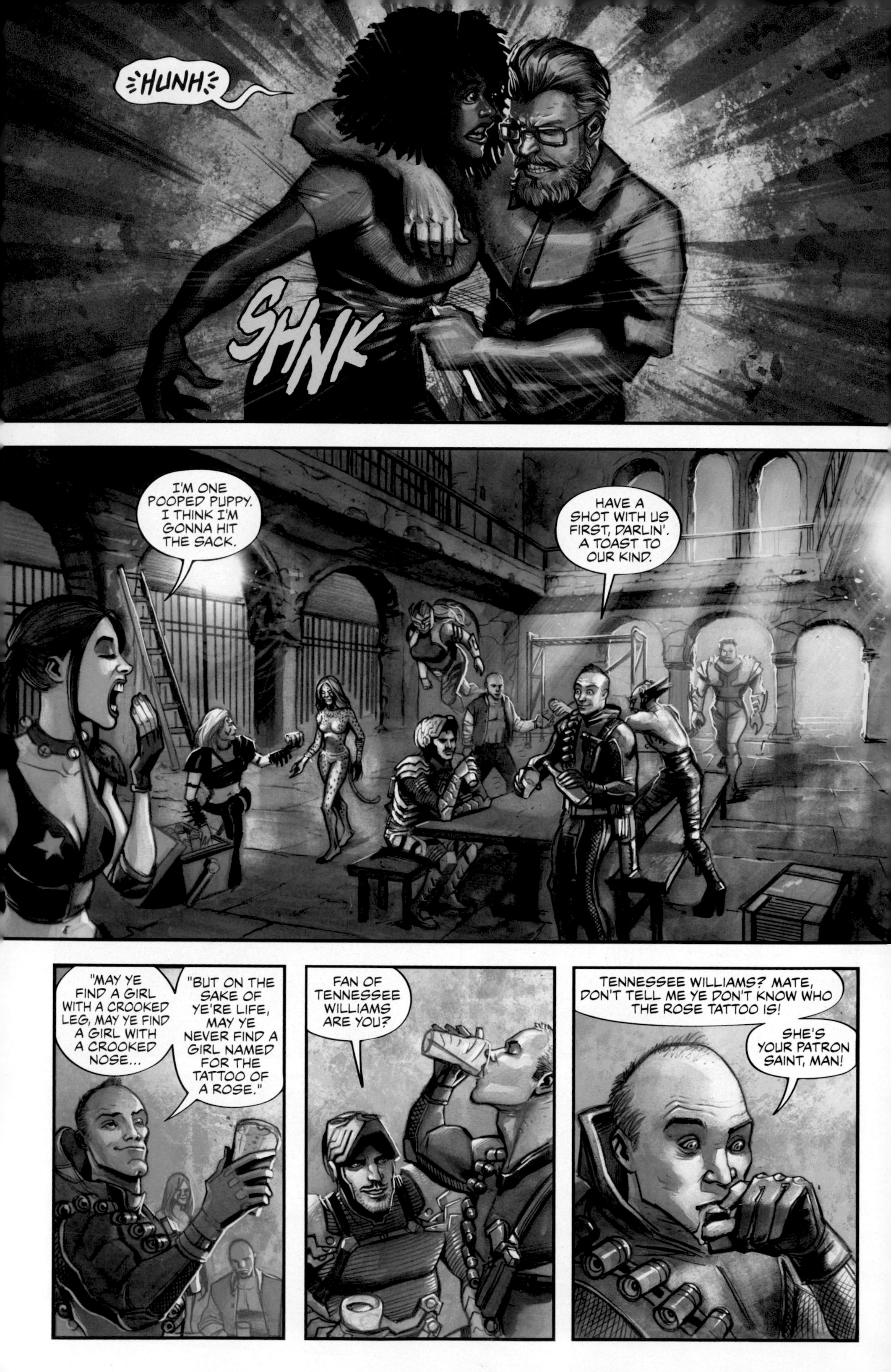
HUNH
SHNK
I'M ONE POOPED PUPPY. I THINK I'M GONNA HIT THE SACK.
HAVE A SHOT WITH US FIRST, DARLIN'. A TOAST TO OUR KIND.
"MAY YE FIND A GIRL WITH A CROOKED LEG, MAY YE FIND A GIRL WITH A CROOKED NOSE...
"BUT ON THE SAKE OF YE'RE LIFE, MAY YE NEVER FIND A GIRL NAMED FOR THE TATTOO OF A ROSE."
FAN OF TENNESSEE WILLIAMS ARE YOU?
TENNESSEE WILLIAMS? MATE, DON'T TELL ME YE DON'T KNOW WHO THE ROSE TATTOO IS!
SHE'S YOUR PATRON SAINT, MAN!

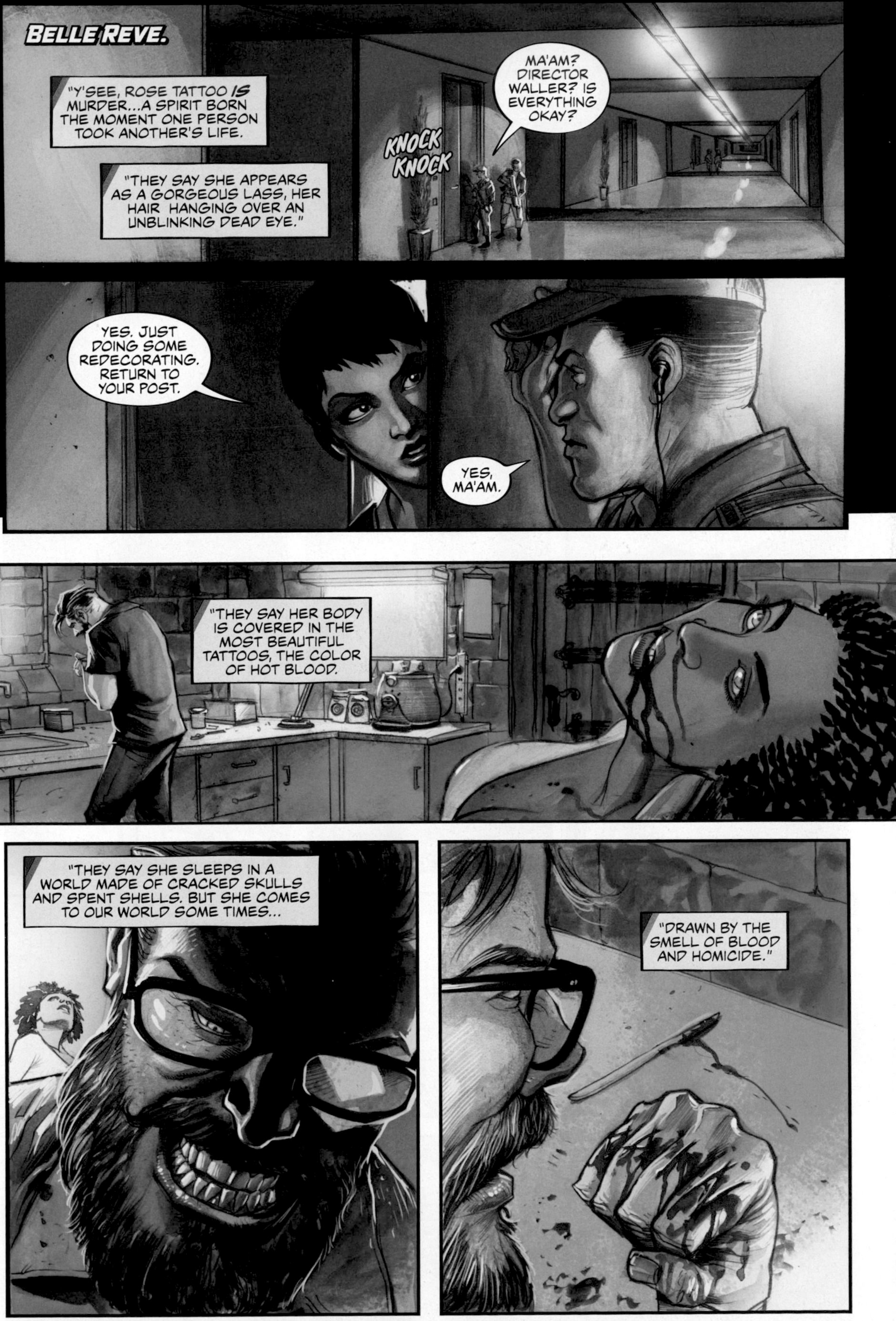
BELLE REVE.
"Y'SEE, ROSE TATTOO IS MURDER...A SPIRIT BORN THE MOMENT ONE PERSON TOOK ANOTHER'S LIFE.
"THEY SAY SHE APPEARS AS A GORGEOUS LASS, HER HAIR HANGING OVER AN UNBLINKING DEAD EYE."
KNOCK KNOCK
MA'AM? DIRECTOR WALLER? IS EVERYTHING OKAY?
YES. JUST DOING SOME REDECORATING. RETURN TO YOUR POST.
YES, MA'AM.
"THEY SAY HER BODY IS COVERED IN THE MOST BEAUTIFUL TATTOOS, THE COLOR OF HOT BLOOD.
"THEY SAY SHE SLEEPS IN A WORLD MADE OF CRACKED SKULLS AND SPENT SHELLS. BUT SHE COMES TO OUR WORLD SOME TIMES...
"DRAWN BY THE SMELL OF BLOOD AND HOMICIDE."

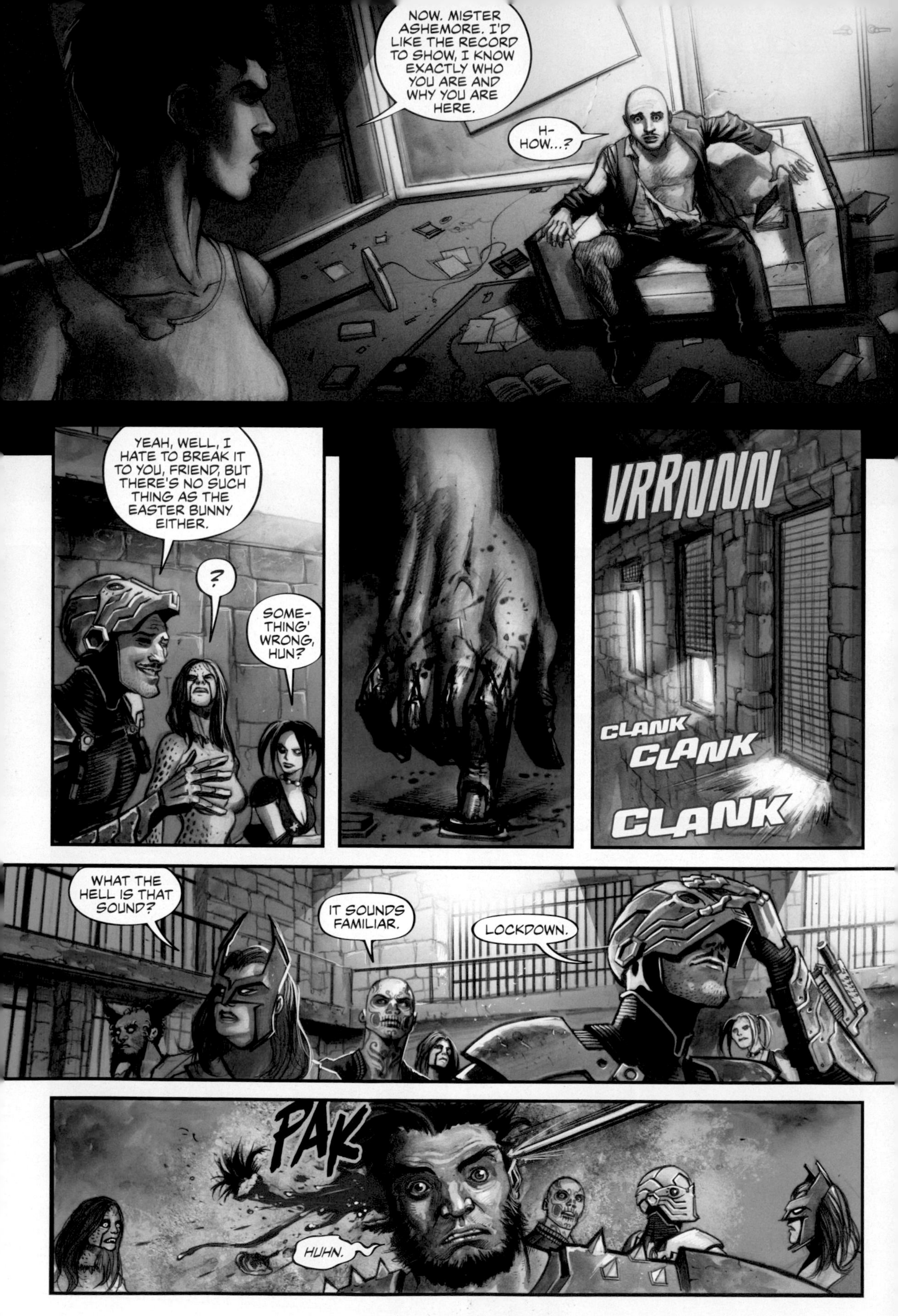
NOW. MISTER ASHEMORE. I'D LIKE THE RECORD TO SHOW, I KNOW EXACTLY WHO YOU ARE AND WHY YOU ARE HERE.
H- HOW...?
YEAH, WELL, I HATE TO BREAK IT TO YOU, FRIEND, BUT THERE'S NO SUCH THING AS THE EASTER BUNNY EITHER.
?
SOME-THING' WRONG, HUN?
VRRNNN
CLANK
CLANK
CLANK
WHAT THE HELL IS THAT SOUND?
IT SOUNDS FAMILIAR.
LOCKDOWN.
PAK
HUHN.

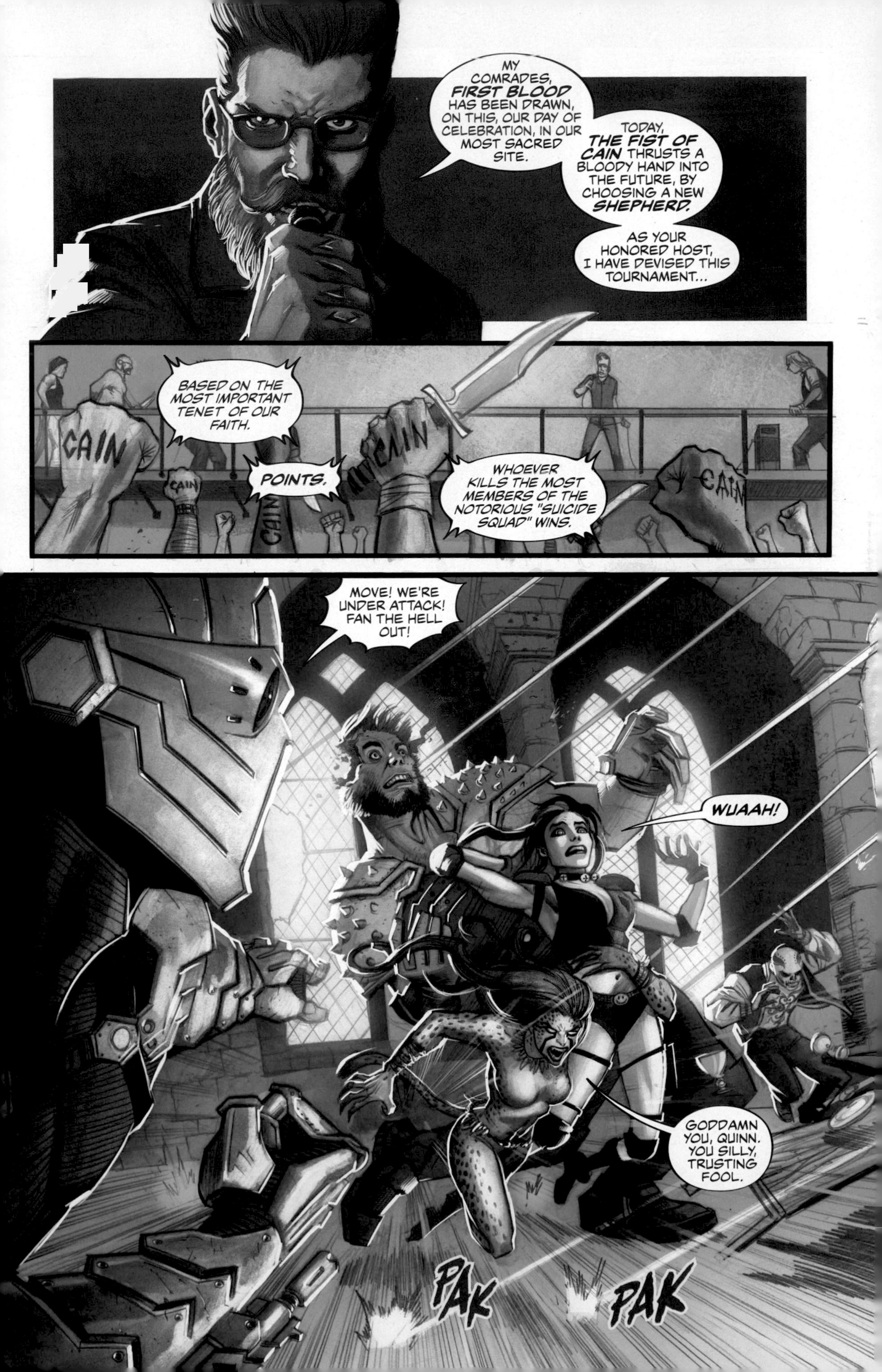
MY COMRADES, FIRST BLOOD HAS BEEN DRAWN, ON THIS, OUR DAY OF CELEBRATION, IN OUR MOST SACRED SITE.
TODAY, THE FIST OF CAIN THRUSTS A BLOODY HAND INTO THE FUTURE, BY CHOOSING A NEW SHEPHERD.
AS YOUR HONORED HOST, I HAVE DEVISED THIS TOURNAMENT...
BASED ON THE MOST IMPORTANT TENET OF OUR FAITH.
POINTS.
WHOEVER KILLS THE MOST MEMBERS OF THE NOTORIOUS "SUICIDE SQUAD" WINS.
CAIN
CAIN
CAIN
CAIN
CAIN
CAIN
MOVE! WE'RE UNDER ATTACK! FAN THE HELL OUT!
WUAAH!
GODDAMN YOU, QUINN. YOU SILLY, TRUSTING FOOL.
PAK
PAK

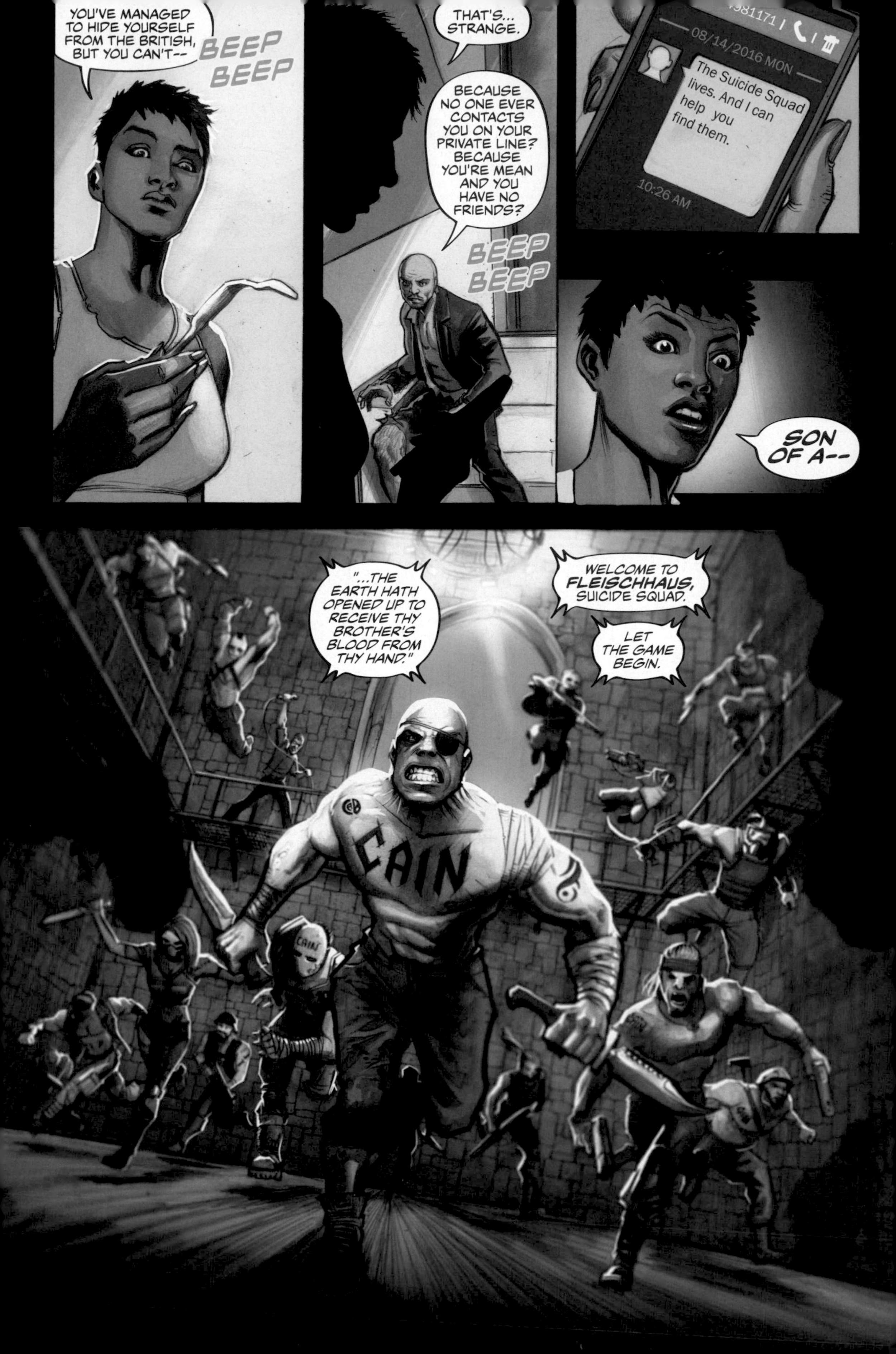
YOU'VE MANAGED TO HIDE YOURSELF FROM THE BRITISH, BUT YOU CAN'T--
BEEP BEEP
THAT'S... STRANGE.
BECAUSE NO ONE EVER CONTACTS YOU ON YOUR PRIVATE LINE? BECAUSE YOU'RE MEAN AND YOU HAVE NO FRIENDS?
BEEP BEEP
08/14/2016 MON
The Suicide Squad lives. And I can help you find them.
10:26 AM
SON OF A--
"...THE EARTH HATH OPENED UP TO RECEIVE THY BROTHER'S BLOOD FROM THY HAND."
WELCOME TO FLEISCHHAUS, SUICIDE SQUAD.
LET THE GAME BEGIN.
CAIN

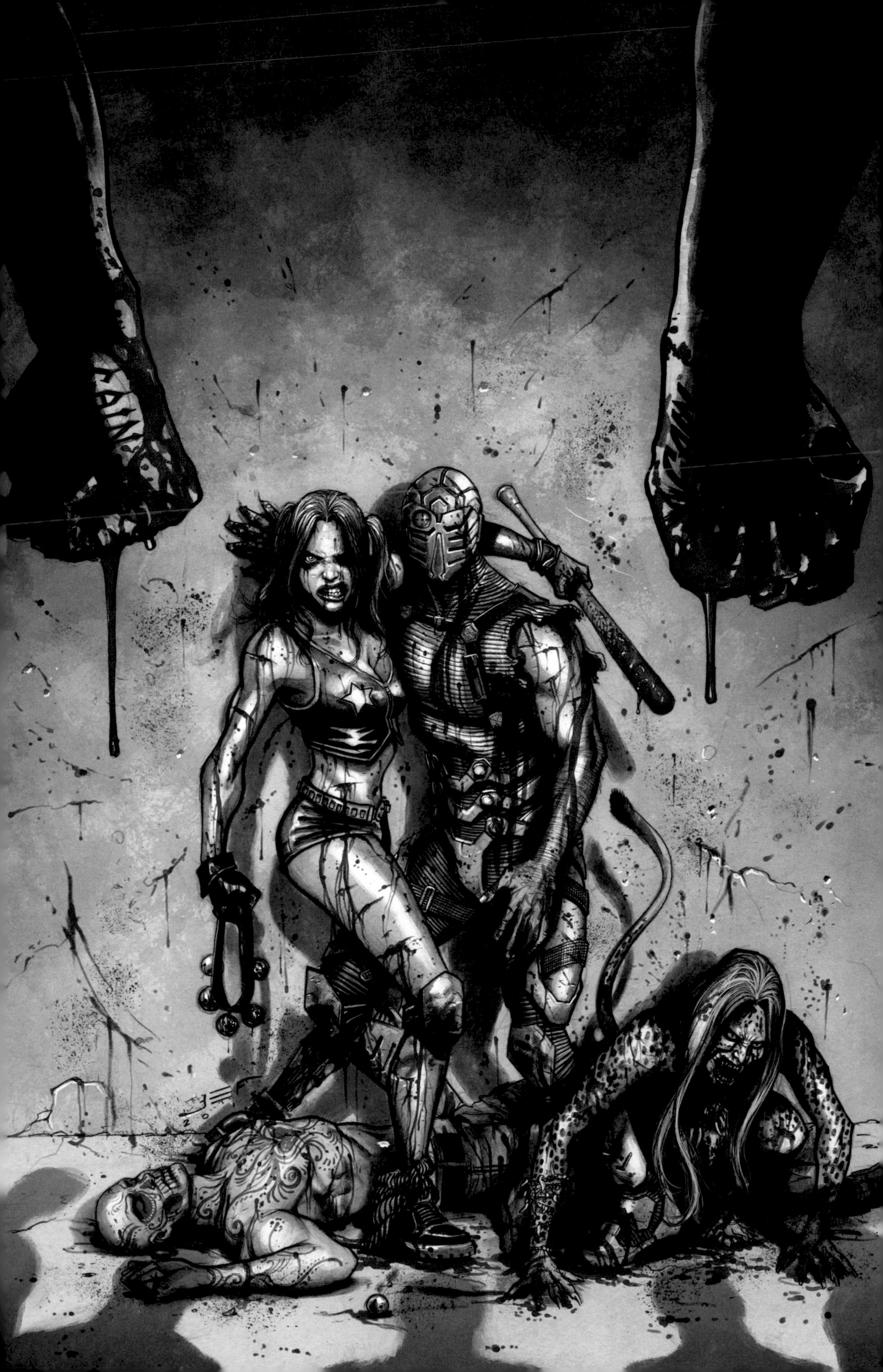
CAIN
CAIN

THE HOUSE OF MEAT

TIM SEELEY writer JUAN FERREYRA artist NATE PIEKOS letterer

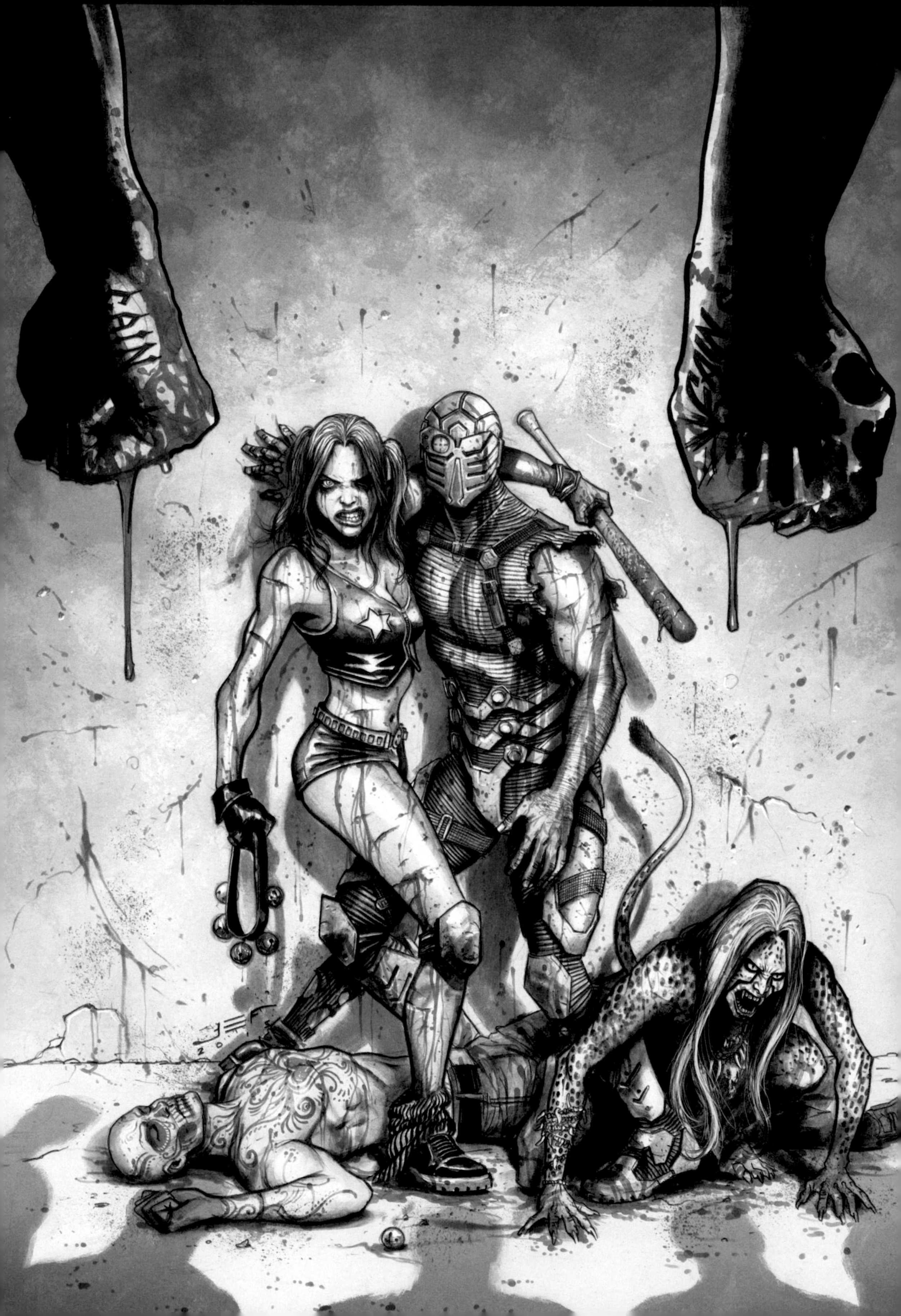
CAIN
CAIN

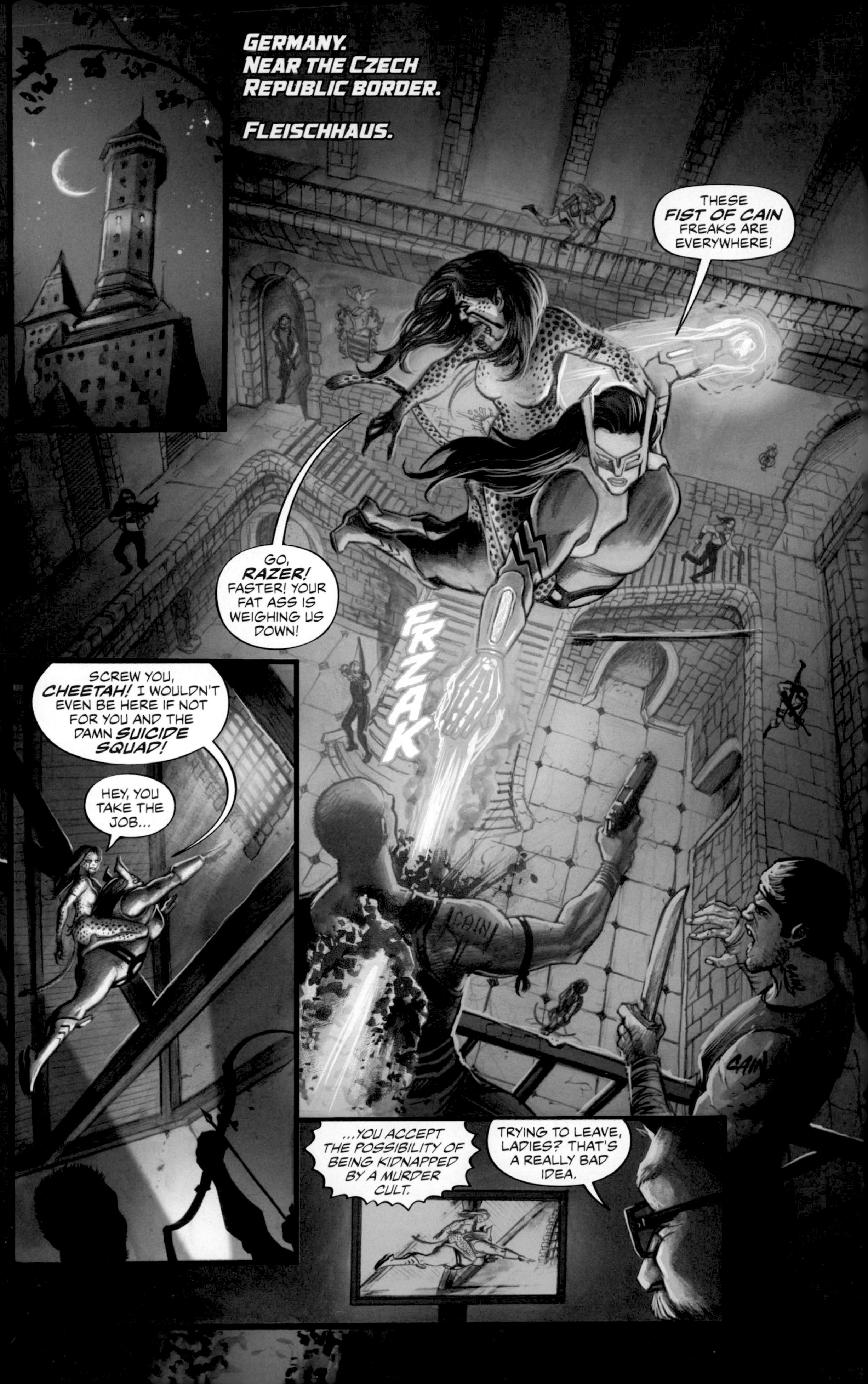
GERMANY. NEAR THE CZECH REPUBLIC BORDER.
FLEISCHHAUS.
THESE FIST OF CAIN FREAKS ARE EVERYWHERE!
GO, RAZER! FASTER! YOUR FAT ASS IS WEIGHING US DOWN!
FRZAK
SCREW YOU, CHEETAH! I WOULDN'T EVEN BE HERE IF NOT FOR YOU AND THE DAMN SUICIDE SQUAD!
HEY, YOU TAKE THE JOB...
...YOU ACCEPT THE POSSIBILITY OF BEING KIDNAPPED BY A MURDER CULT.
TRYING TO LEAVE, LADIES? THAT'S A REALLY BAD IDEA.

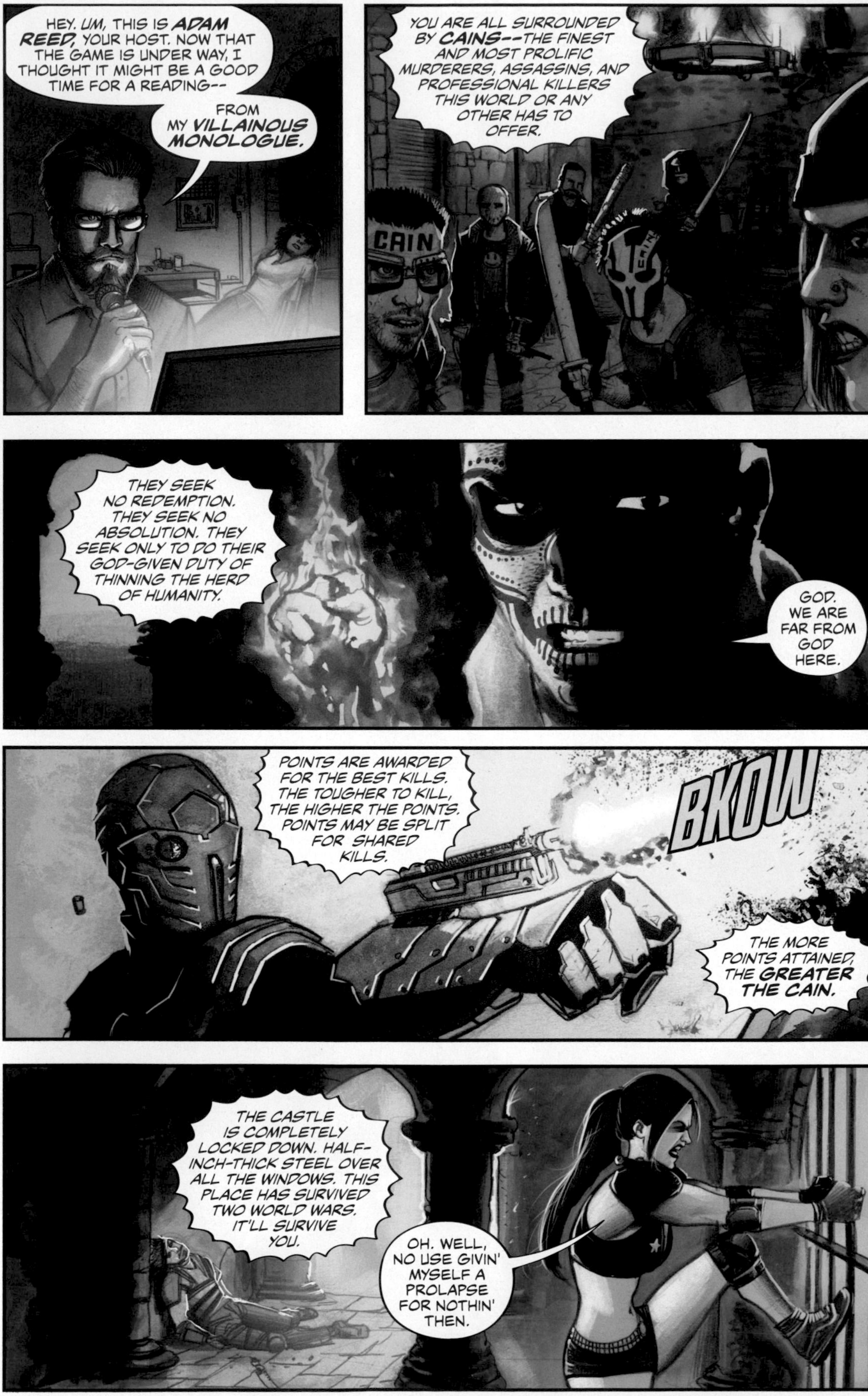
HEY. UM, THIS IS ADAM REED, YOUR HOST. NOW THAT THE GAME IS UNDER WAY, I THOUGHT IT MIGHT BE A GOOD TIME FOR A READING--
FROM MY VILLAINOUS MONOLOGUE.
YOU ARE ALL SURROUNDED BY CAINS--THE FINEST AND MOST PROLIFIC MURDERERS, ASSASSINS, AND PROFESSIONAL KILLERS THIS WORLD OR ANY OTHER HAS TO OFFER.
CAIN
THEY SEEK NO REDEMPTION. THEY SEEK NO ABSOLUTION. THEY SEEK ONLY TO DO THEIR GOD-GIVEN DUTY OF THINNING THE HERD OF HUMANITY.
GOD. WE ARE FAR FROM GOD HERE.
POINTS ARE AWARDED FOR THE BEST KILLS. THE TOUGHER TO KILL, THE HIGHER THE POINTS. POINTS MAY BE SPLIT FOR SHARED KILLS.
BKOW
THE MORE POINTS ATTAINED, THE GREATER THE CAIN.
THE CASTLE IS COMPLETELY LOCKED DOWN. HALF-INCH-THICK STEEL OVER ALL THE WINDOWS. THIS PLACE HAS SURVIVED TWO WORLD WARS. IT'LL SURVIVE YOU.
OH. WELL, NO USE GIVIN' MYSELF A PROLAPSE FOR NOTHIN' THEN.

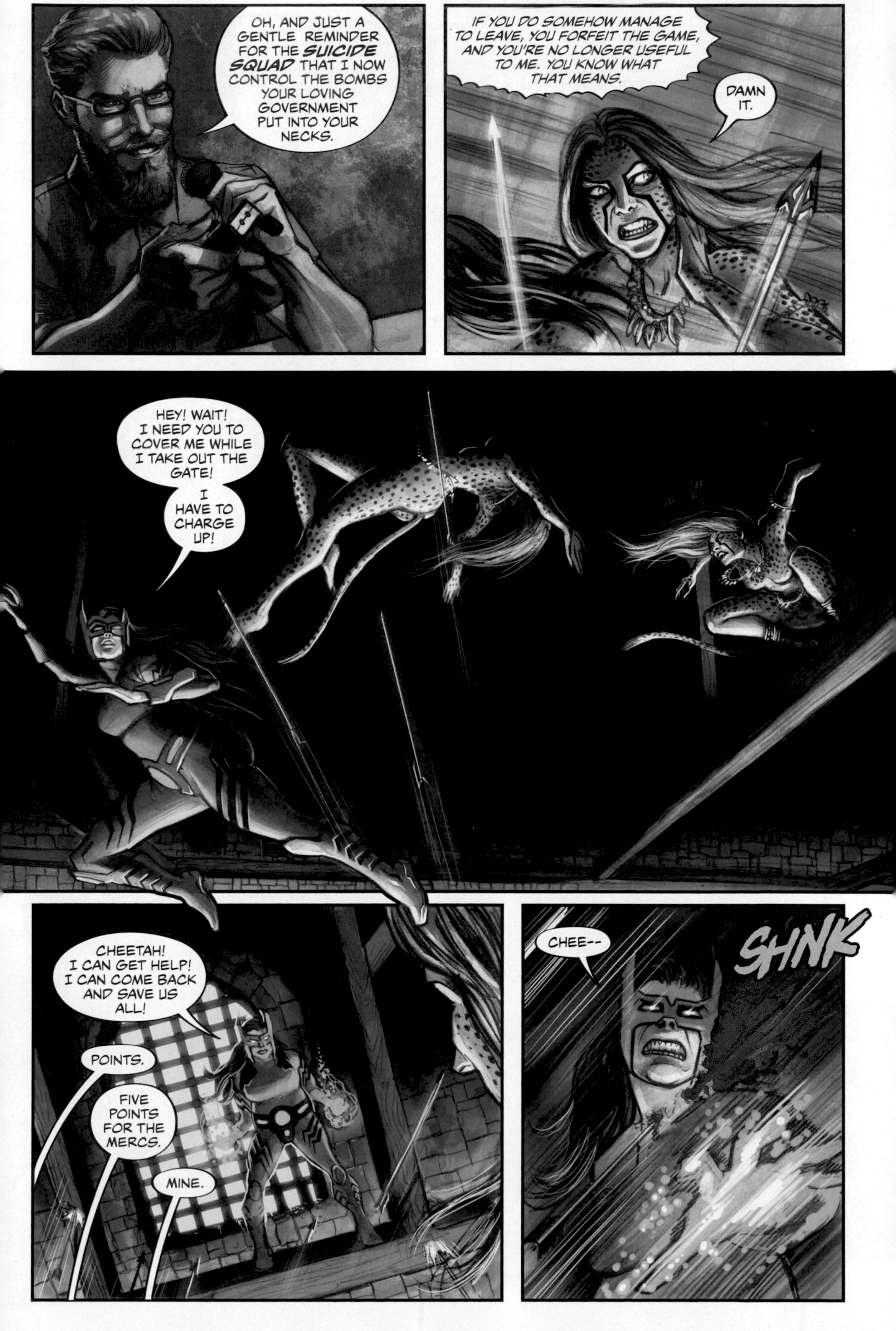
OH, AND JUST A GENTLE REMINDER FOR THE SUICIDE SQUAD THAT I NOW CONTROL THE BOMBS YOUR LOVING GOVERNMENT PUT INTO YOUR NECKS.
IF YOU DO SOMEHOW MANAGE TO LEAVE, YOU FORFEIT THE GAME, AND YOU'RE NO LONGER USEFUL TO ME. YOU KNOW WHAT THAT MEANS.
DAMN IT.
HEY! WAIT! I NEED YOU TO COVER ME WHILE I TAKE OUT THE GATE!
I HAVE TO CHARGE UP!
CHEETAH! I CAN GET HELP! I CAN COME BACK AND SAVE US ALL!
POINTS.
FIVE POINTS FOR THE MERCS.
MINE.
CHEE--
SHNK

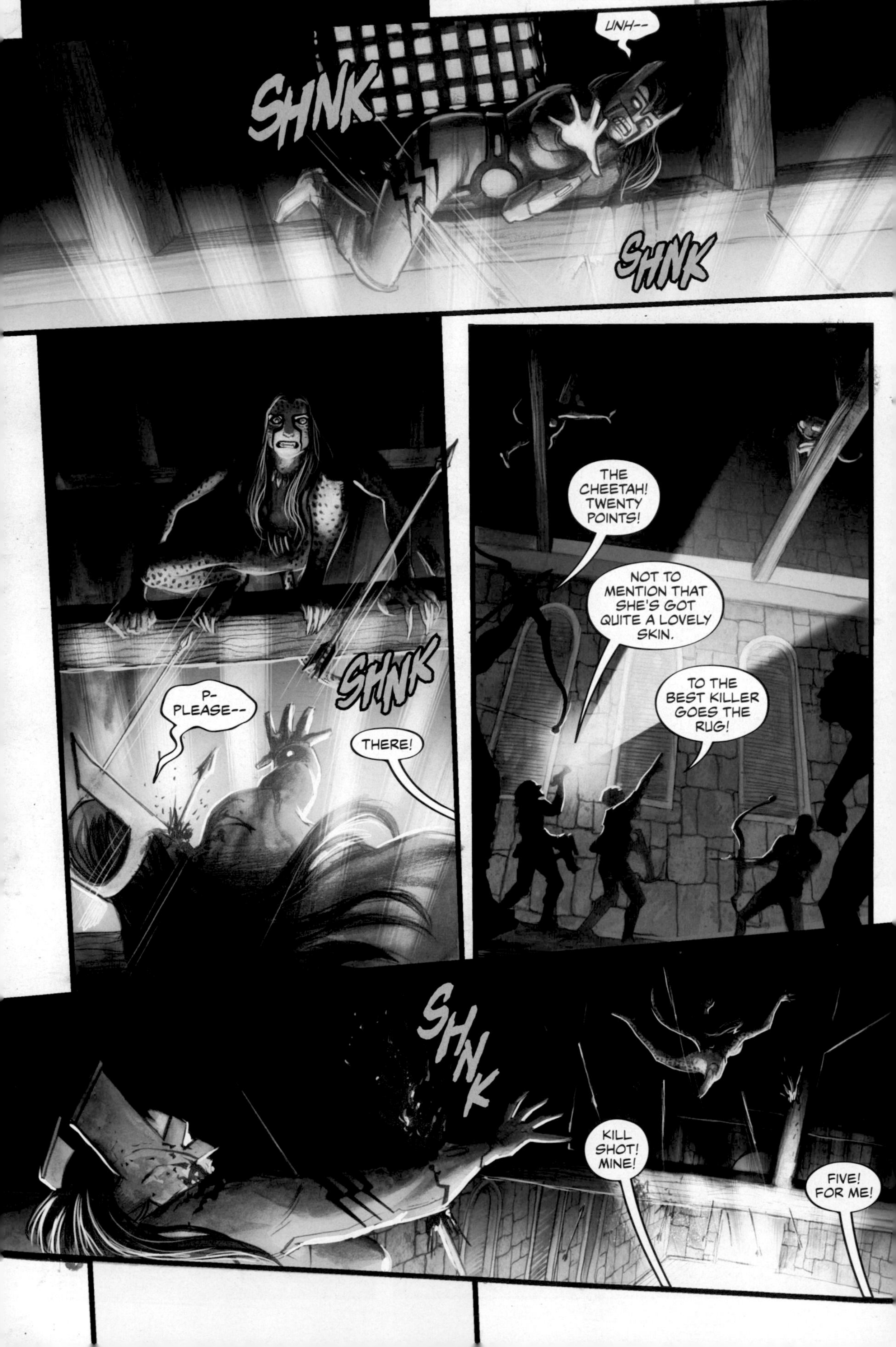
UNH--
SHNK
SHNK
SHNK
P-PLEASE--
THERE!
THE CHEETAH! TWENTY POINTS!
NOT TO MENTION THAT SHE'S GOT QUITE A LOVELY SKIN.
TO THE BEST KILLER GOES THE RUG!
SHNK
KILL SHOT! MINE!
FIVE! FOR ME!

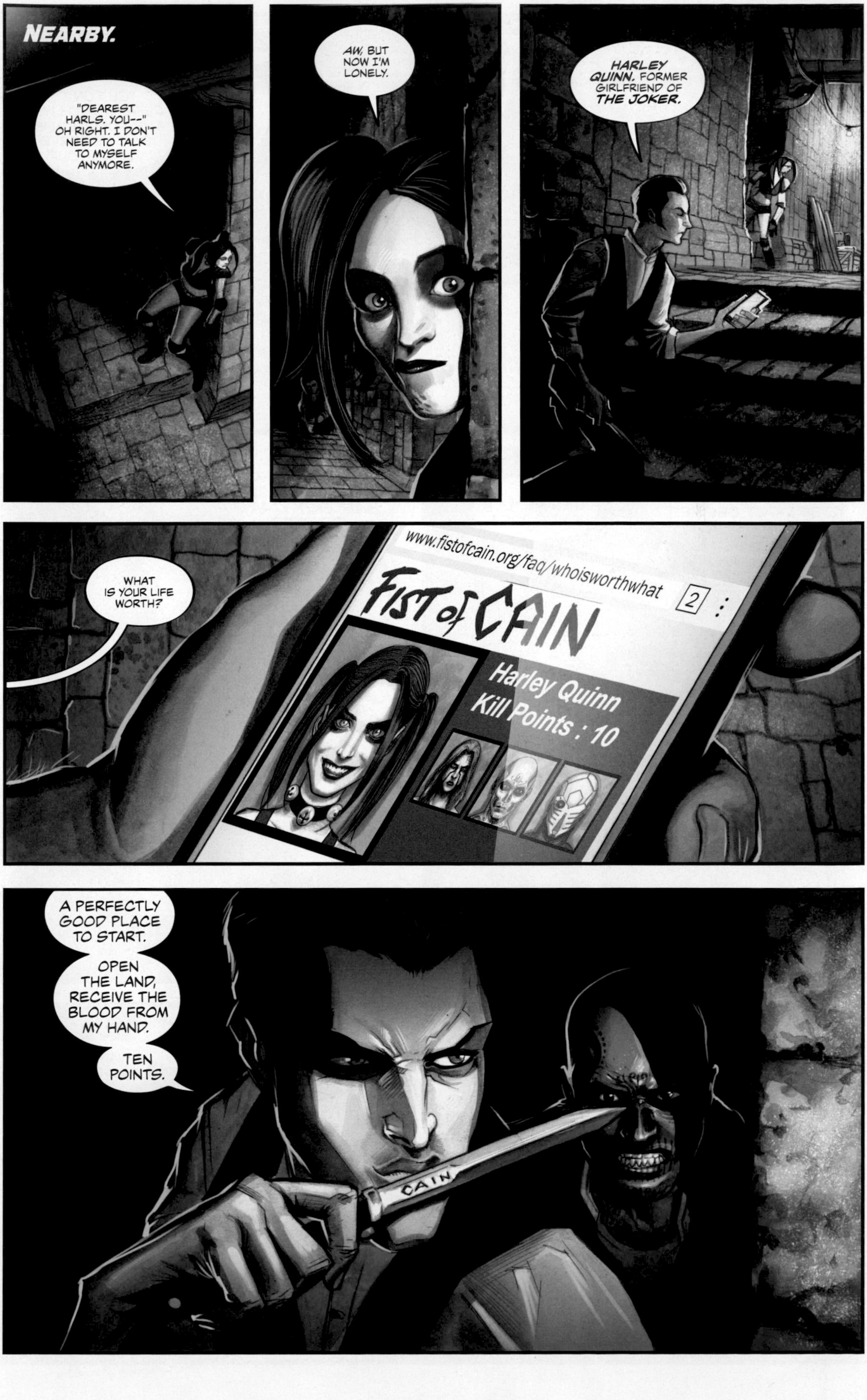
NEARBY.
"DEAREST HARLS. YOU--" OH RIGHT. I DON'T NEED TO TALK TO MYSELF ANYMORE.
AW, BUT NOW I'M LONELY.
HARLEY QUINN. FORMER GIRLFRIEND OF THE JOKER.
WHAT IS YOUR LIFE WORTH?
www.fistofcain.org/faq/whoisworthwhat
2
FIST of CAIN
Harley Quinn
Kill Points : 10
A PERFECTLY GOOD PLACE TO START.
OPEN THE LAND, RECEIVE THE BLOOD FROM MY HAND.
TEN POINTS.
CAIN

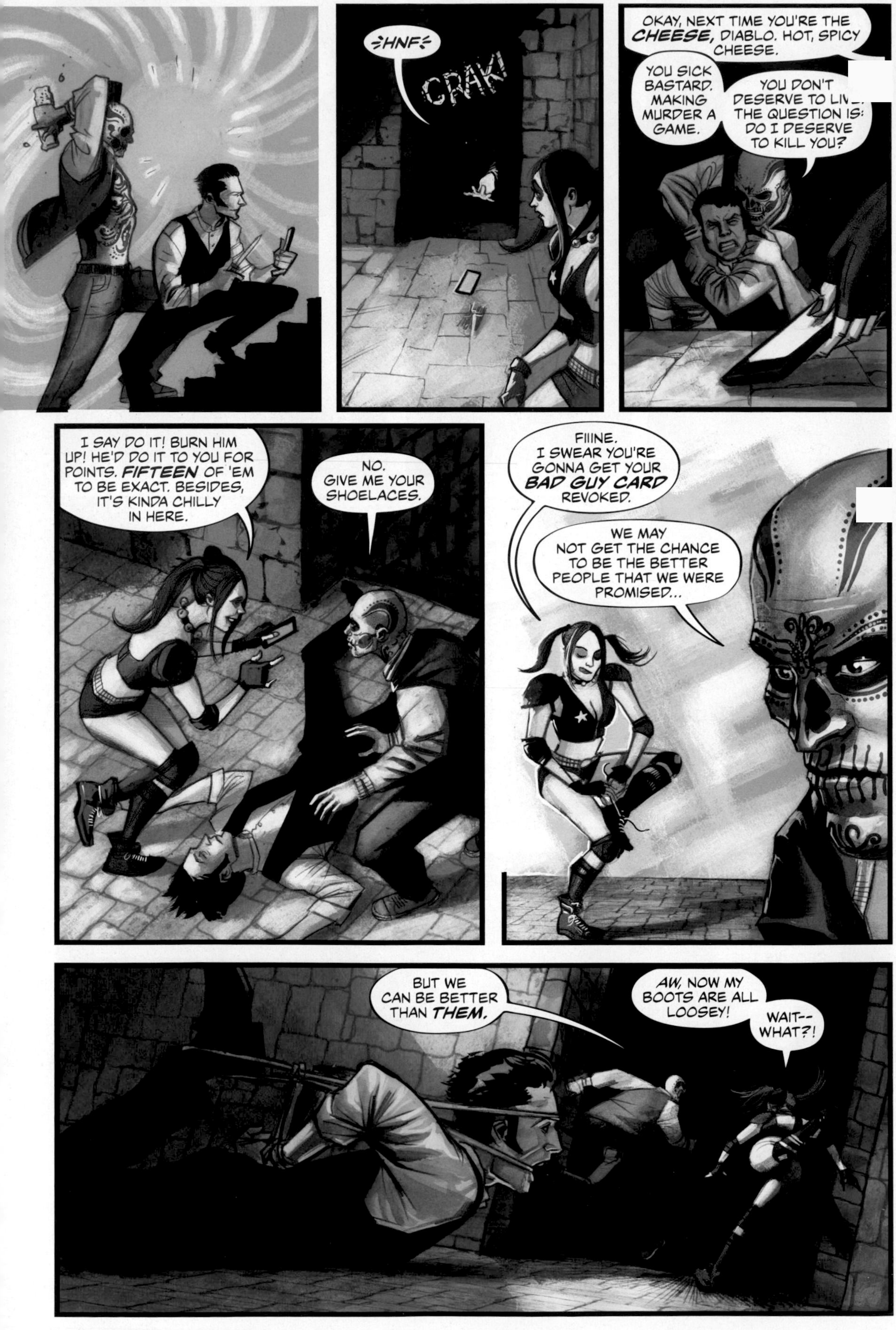

HNF
CRAK!
OKAY, NEXT TIME YOU'RE THE CHEESE, DIABLO. HOT, SPICY CHEESE.
YOU SICK BASTARD. MAKING MURDER A GAME.
YOU DON'T DESERVE TO LIVE. THE QUESTION IS: DO I DESERVE TO KILL YOU?
I SAY DO IT! BURN HIM UP! HE'D DO IT TO YOU FOR POINTS. FIFTEEN OF 'EM TO BE EXACT. BESIDES, IT'S KINDA CHILLY IN HERE.
NO. GIVE ME YOUR SHOELACES.
FIIINE. I SWEAR YOU'RE GONNA GET YOUR BAD GUY CARD REVOKED.
WE MAY NOT GET THE CHANCE TO BE THE BETTER PEOPLE THAT WE WERE PROMISED...
BUT WE CAN BE BETTER THAN THEM.
AW, NOW MY BOOTS ARE ALL LOOSEY!
WAIT-- WHAT?!

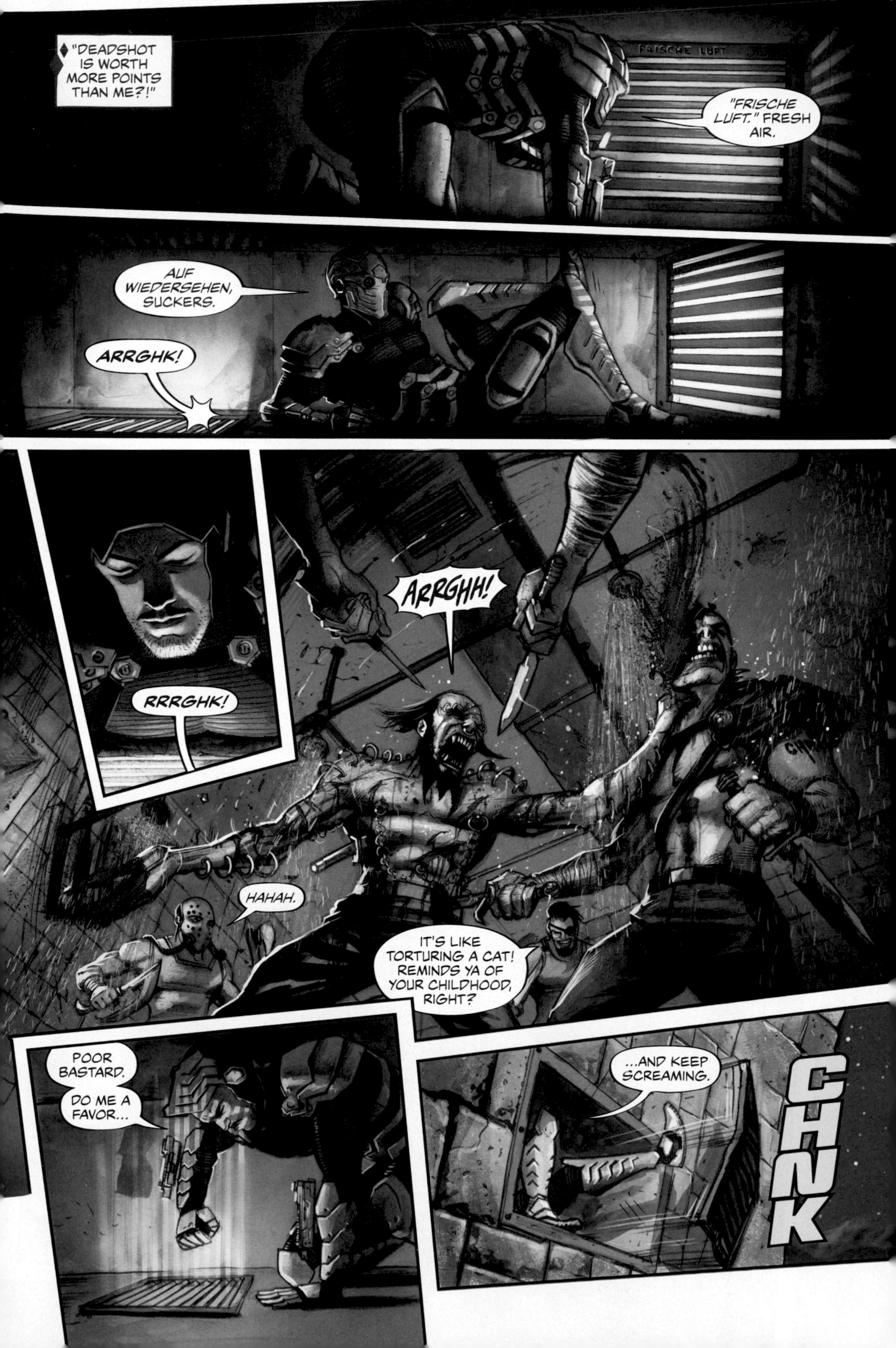
"DEADSHOT IS WORTH MORE POINTS THAN ME?!"
FRISCHE LUFT
"FRISCHE LUFT." FRESH AIR.
AUF WIEDERSEHEN, SUCKERS.
ARRGHK!
RRRGHK!
ARRGHH!
HAHAH.
IT'S LIKE TORTURING A CAT! REMINDS YA OF YOUR CHILDHOOD, RIGHT?
POOR BASTARD.
DO ME A FAVOR...
...AND KEEP SCREAMING.
CHNK

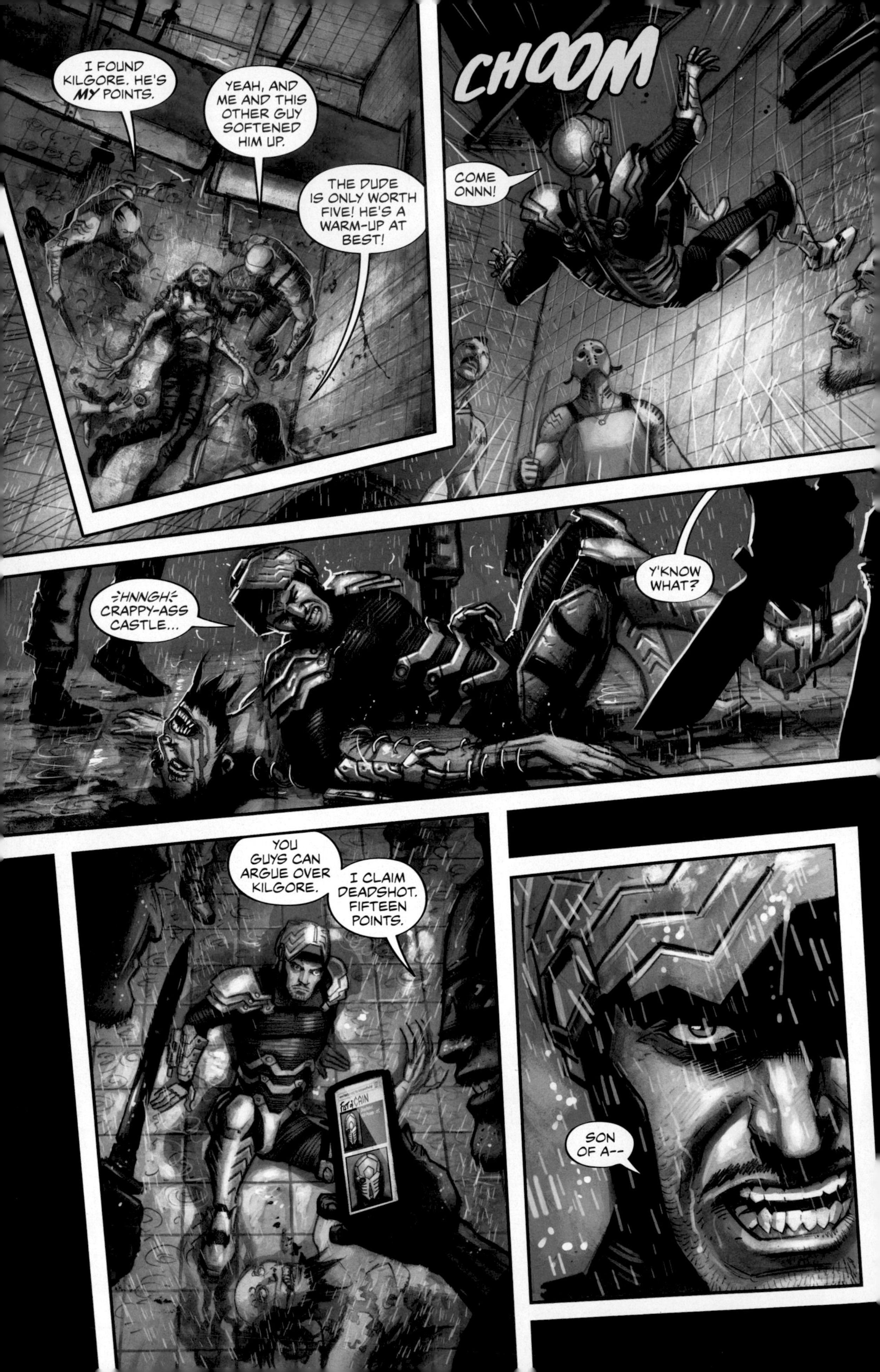
I FOUND KILGORE. HE'S MY POINTS.
YEAH, AND ME AND THIS OTHER GUY SOFTENED HIM UP.
THE DUDE IS ONLY WORTH FIVE! HE'S A WARM-UP AT BEST!
CHOOM
COME ONNN!
HNNGH CRAPPY-ASS CASTLE...
Y'KNOW WHAT?
YOU GUYS CAN ARGUE OVER KILGORE.
I CLAIM DEADSHOT. FIFTEEN POINTS.
SON OF A--

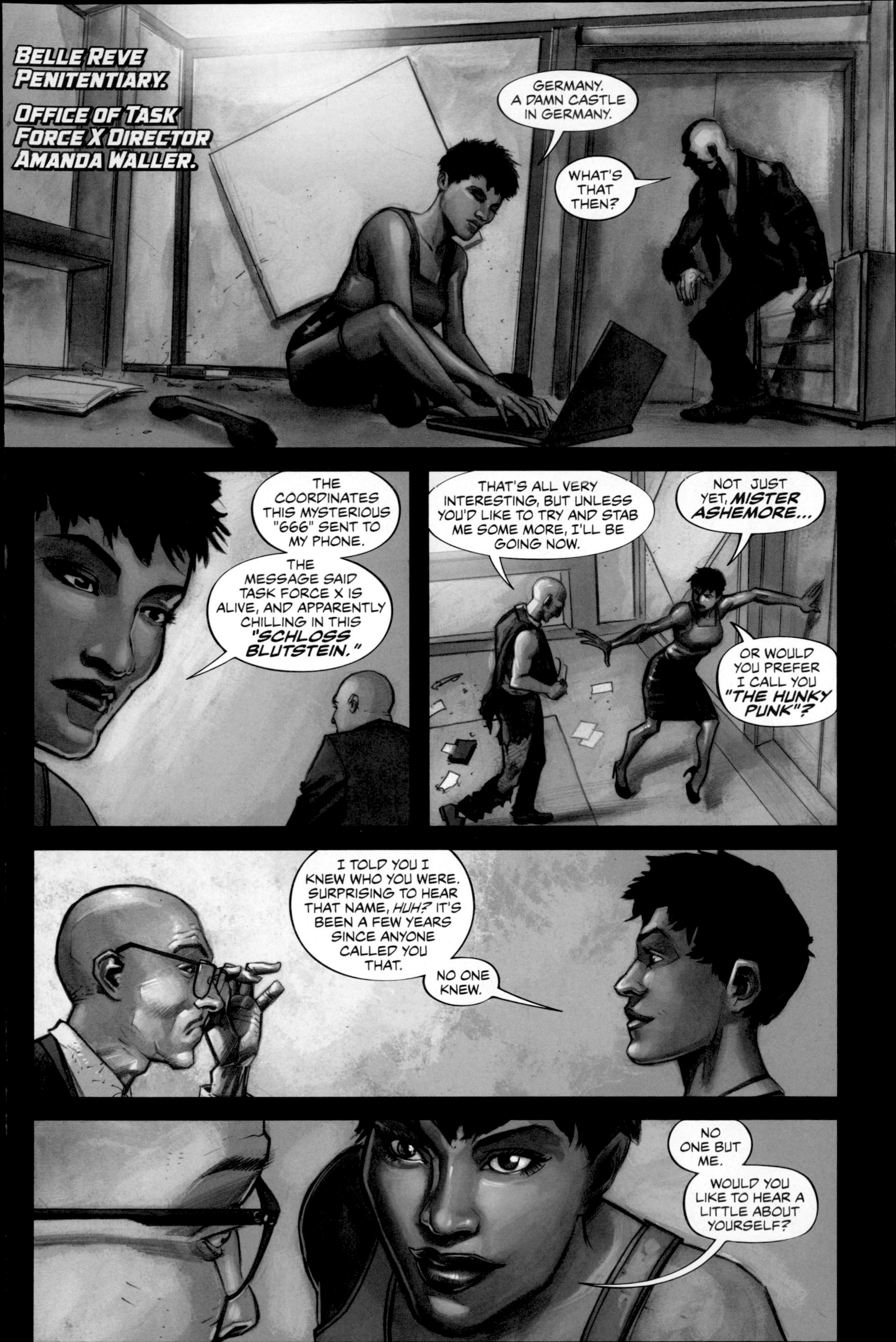
BELLE REVE PENITENTIARY.
OFFICE OF TASK FORCE X DIRECTOR AMANDA WALLER.
GERMANY. A DAMN CASTLE IN GERMANY.
WHAT'S THAT THEN?
THE COORDINATES THIS MYSTERIOUS "666" SENT TO MY PHONE.
THE MESSAGE SAID TASK FORCE X IS ALIVE, AND APPARENTLY CHILLING IN THIS "SCHLOSS BLUTSTEIN."
THAT'S ALL VERY INTERESTING, BUT UNLESS YOU'D LIKE TO TRY AND STAB ME SOME MORE, I'LL BE GOING NOW.
NOT JUST YET, MISTER ASHEMORE...
OR WOULD YOU PREFER I CALL YOU "THE HUNKY PUNK"?
I TOLD YOU I KNEW WHO YOU WERE. SURPRISING TO HEAR THAT NAME, HUH? IT'S BEEN A FEW YEARS SINCE ANYONE CALLED YOU THAT.
NO ONE KNEW.
NO ONE BUT ME.
WOULD YOU LIKE TO HEAR A LITTLE ABOUT YOURSELF?

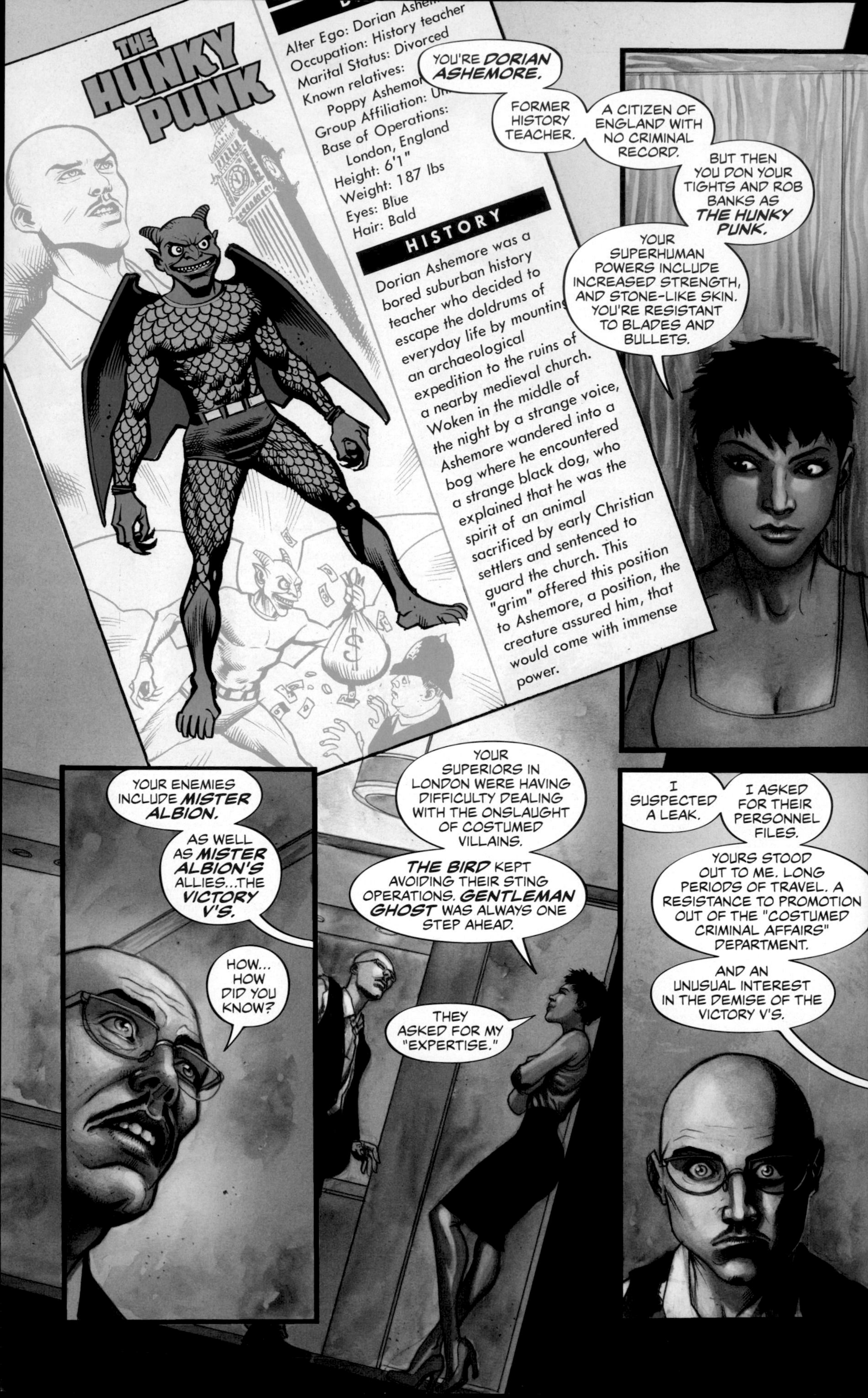

THE HUNKY PUNK
Alter Ego: Dorian Ashe
Occupation: History teacher
Marital Status: Divorced
Known relatives:
Poppy Ashemo
Group Affiliation: Un
Base of Operations:
London, England
Height: 6'1"
Weight: 187 lbs
Eyes: Blue
Hair: Bald
HISTORY
Dorian Ashemore was a bored suburban history teacher who decided to escape the doldrums of everyday life by mountin an archaeological expedition to the ruins of a nearby medieval church. Woken in the middle of the night by a strange voice, Ashemore wandered into a bog where he encountered a strange black dog, who explained that he was the spirit of an animal sacrificed by early Christian settlers and sentenced to guard the church. This "grim" offered this position to Ashemore, a position, the creature assured him, that would come with immense power.
YOU'RE DORIAN ASHEMORE.
FORMER HISTORY TEACHER.
A CITIZEN OF ENGLAND WITH NO CRIMINAL RECORD.
BUT THEN YOU DON YOUR TIGHTS AND ROB BANKS AS THE HUNKY PUNK.
YOUR SUPERHUMAN POWERS INCLUDE INCREASED STRENGTH, AND STONE-LIKE SKIN. YOU'RE RESISTANT TO BLADES AND BULLETS.
YOUR ENEMIES INCLUDE MISTER ALBION.
AS WELL AS MISTER ALBION'S ALLIES...THE VICTORY V'S.
HOW... HOW DID YOU KNOW?
YOUR SUPERIORS IN LONDON WERE HAVING DIFFICULTY DEALING WITH THE ONSLAUGHT OF COSTUMED VILLAINS.
THE BIRD KEPT AVOIDING THEIR STING OPERATIONS. GENTLEMAN GHOST WAS ALWAYS ONE STEP AHEAD.
THEY ASKED FOR MY "EXPERTISE."
I SUSPECTED A LEAK.
I ASKED FOR THEIR PERSONNEL FILES.
YOURS STOOD OUT TO ME. LONG PERIODS OF TRAVEL. A RESISTANCE TO PROMOTION OUT OF THE "COSTUMED CRIMINAL AFFAIRS" DEPARTMENT.
AND AN UNUSUAL INTEREST IN THE DEMISE OF THE VICTORY V'S.

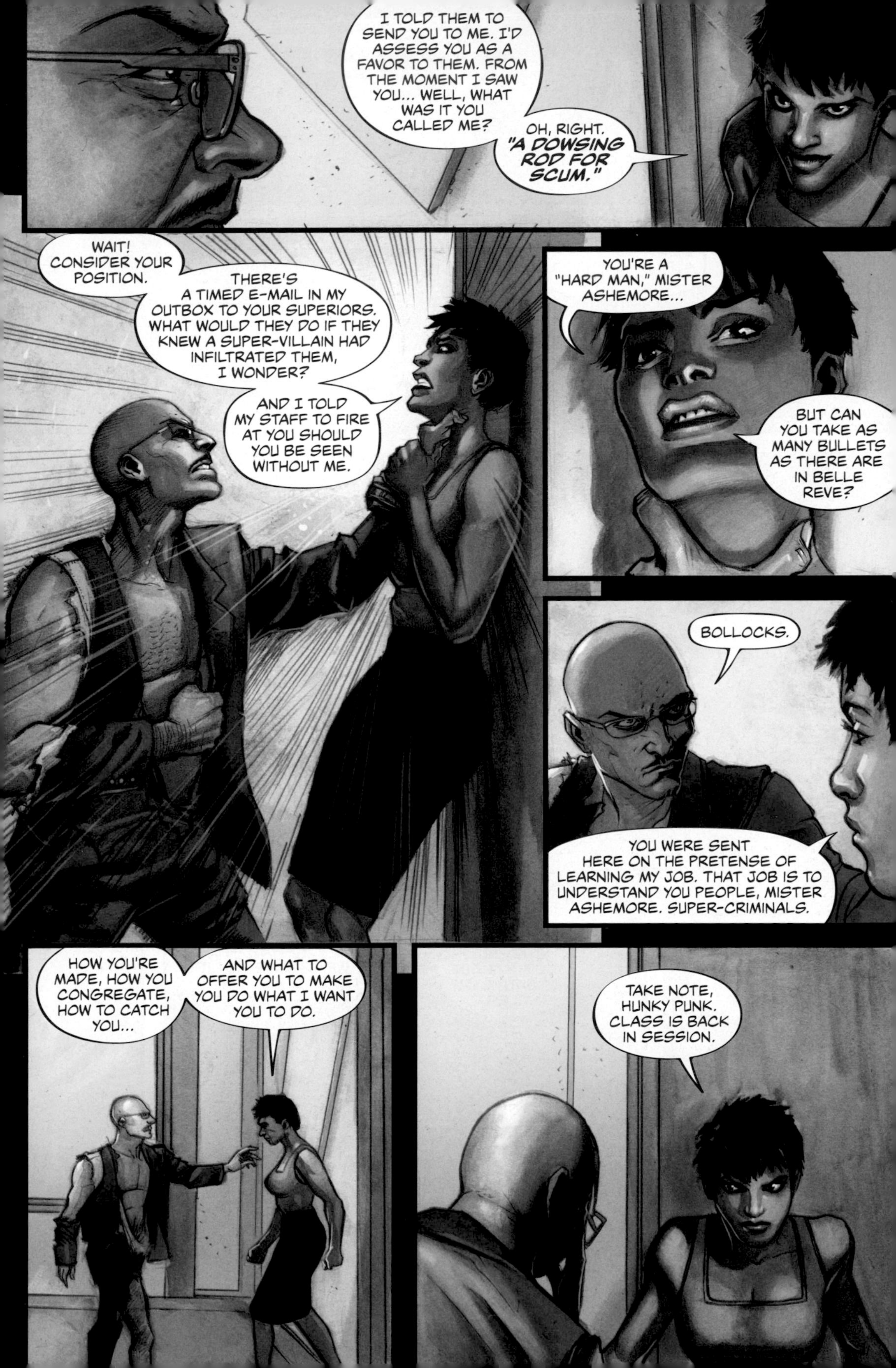
I TOLD THEM TO SEND YOU TO ME. I'D ASSESS YOU AS A FAVOR TO THEM. FROM THE MOMENT I SAW YOU... WELL, WHAT WAS IT YOU CALLED ME?
OH, RIGHT. "A DOWSING ROD FOR SCUM."
WAIT! CONSIDER YOUR POSITION.
THERE'S A TIMED E-MAIL IN MY OUTBOX TO YOUR SUPERIORS. WHAT WOULD THEY DO IF THEY KNEW A SUPER-VILLAIN HAD INFILTRATED THEM, I WONDER?
AND I TOLD MY STAFF TO FIRE AT YOU SHOULD YOU BE SEEN WITHOUT ME.
YOU'RE A "HARD MAN," MISTER ASHEMORE...
BUT CAN YOU TAKE AS MANY BULLETS AS THERE ARE IN BELLE REVE?
BOLLOCKS.
YOU WERE SENT HERE ON THE PRETENSE OF LEARNING MY JOB. THAT JOB IS TO UNDERSTAND YOU PEOPLE, MISTER ASHEMORE. SUPER-CRIMINALS.
HOW YOU'RE MADE, HOW YOU CONGREGATE, HOW TO CATCH YOU...
AND WHAT TO OFFER YOU TO MAKE YOU DO WHAT I WANT YOU TO DO.
TAKE NOTE, HUNKY PUNK. CLASS IS BACK IN SESSION.

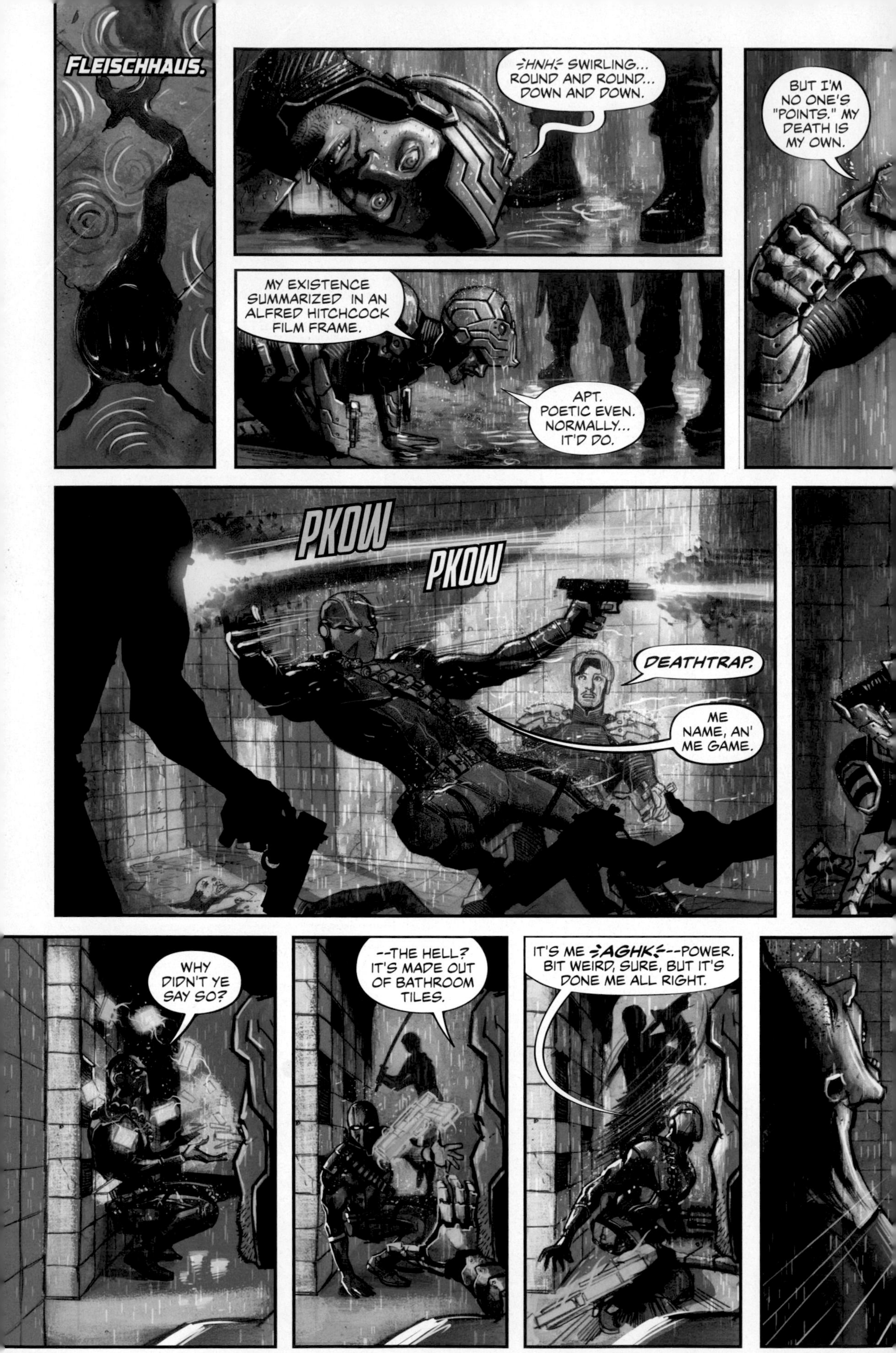
FLEISCHHAUS.
=HNH= SWIRLING... ROUND AND ROUND... DOWN AND DOWN.
BUT I'M NO ONE'S "POINTS." MY DEATH IS MY OWN.
MY EXISTENCE SUMMARIZED IN AN ALFRED HITCHCOCK FILM FRAME.
APT. POETIC EVEN. NORMALLY... IT'D DO.
PKOW
PKOW
DEATHTRAP.
ME NAME, AN' ME GAME.
WHY DIDN'T YE SAY SO?
--THE HELL? IT'S MADE OUT OF BATHROOM TILES.
IT'S ME =AGHK=--POWER. BIT WEIRD, SURE, BUT IT'S DONE ME ALL RIGHT.

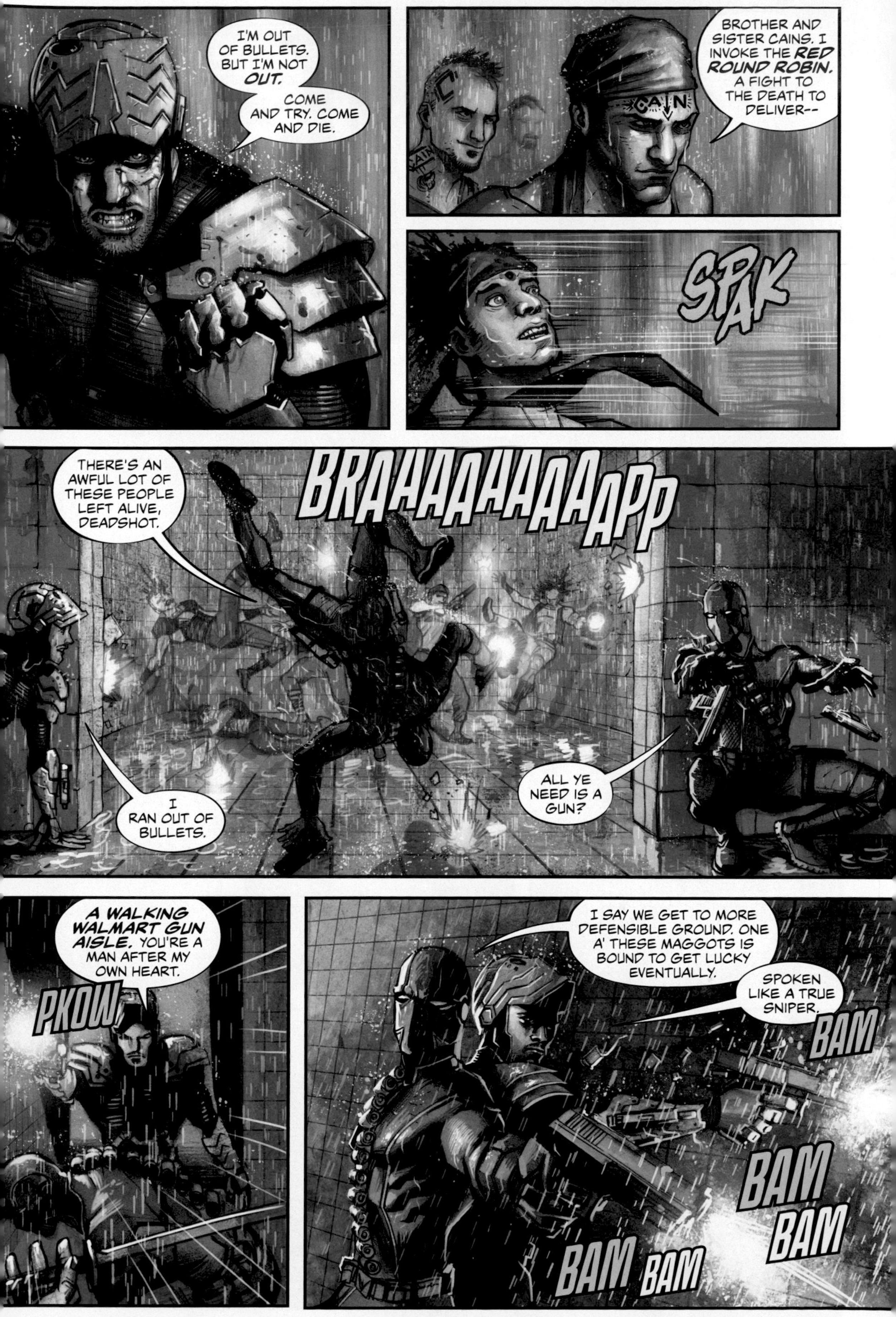
I'M OUT OF BULLETS. BUT I'M NOT OUT.
COME AND TRY. COME AND DIE.
BROTHER AND SISTER CAINS. I INVOKE THE RED ROUND ROBIN. A FIGHT TO THE DEATH TO DELIVER--
CAIN
SPAK
BRAAAAAAAAAAPP
THERE'S AN AWFUL LOT OF THESE PEOPLE LEFT ALIVE, DEADSHOT.
I RAN OUT OF BULLETS.
ALL YE NEED IS A GUN?
A WALKING WALMART GUN AISLE. YOU'RE A MAN AFTER MY OWN HEART.
PKOW
I SAY WE GET TO MORE DEFENSIBLE GROUND. ONE A' THESE MAGGOTS IS BOUND TO GET LUCKY EVENTUALLY.
SPOKEN LIKE A TRUE SNIPER.
BAM
BAM
BAM
BAM BAM

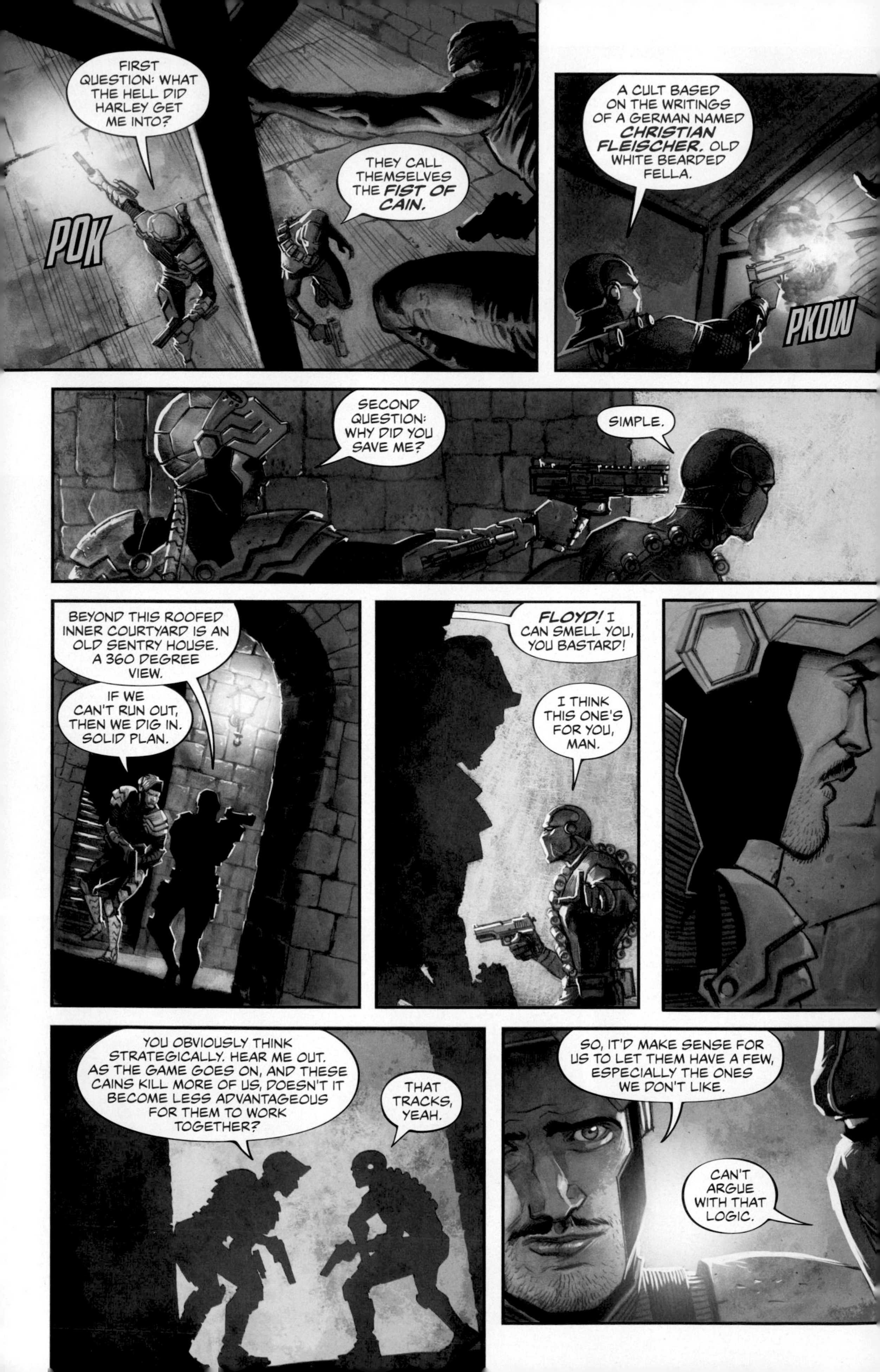

FIRST QUESTION: WHAT THE HELL DID HARLEY GET ME INTO?
POK
THEY CALL THEMSELVES THE FIST OF CAIN.
A CULT BASED ON THE WRITINGS OF A GERMAN NAMED CHRISTIAN FLEISCHER. OLD WHITE BEARDED FELLA.
PKOW
SECOND QUESTION: WHY DID YOU SAVE ME?
SIMPLE.
BEYOND THIS ROOFED INNER COURTYARD IS AN OLD SENTRY HOUSE. A 360 DEGREE VIEW.
IF WE CAN'T RUN OUT, THEN WE DIG IN. SOLID PLAN.
FLOYD! I CAN SMELL YOU, YOU BASTARD!
I THINK THIS ONE'S FOR YOU, MAN.
YOU OBVIOUSLY THINK STRATEGICALLY. HEAR ME OUT. AS THE GAME GOES ON, AND THESE CAINS KILL MORE OF US, DOESN'T IT BECOME LESS ADVANTAGEOUS FOR THEM TO WORK TOGETHER?
THAT TRACKS, YEAH.
SO, IT'D MAKE SENSE FOR US TO LET THEM HAVE A FEW, ESPECIALLY THE ONES WE DON'T LIKE.
CAN'T ARGUE WITH THAT LOGIC.

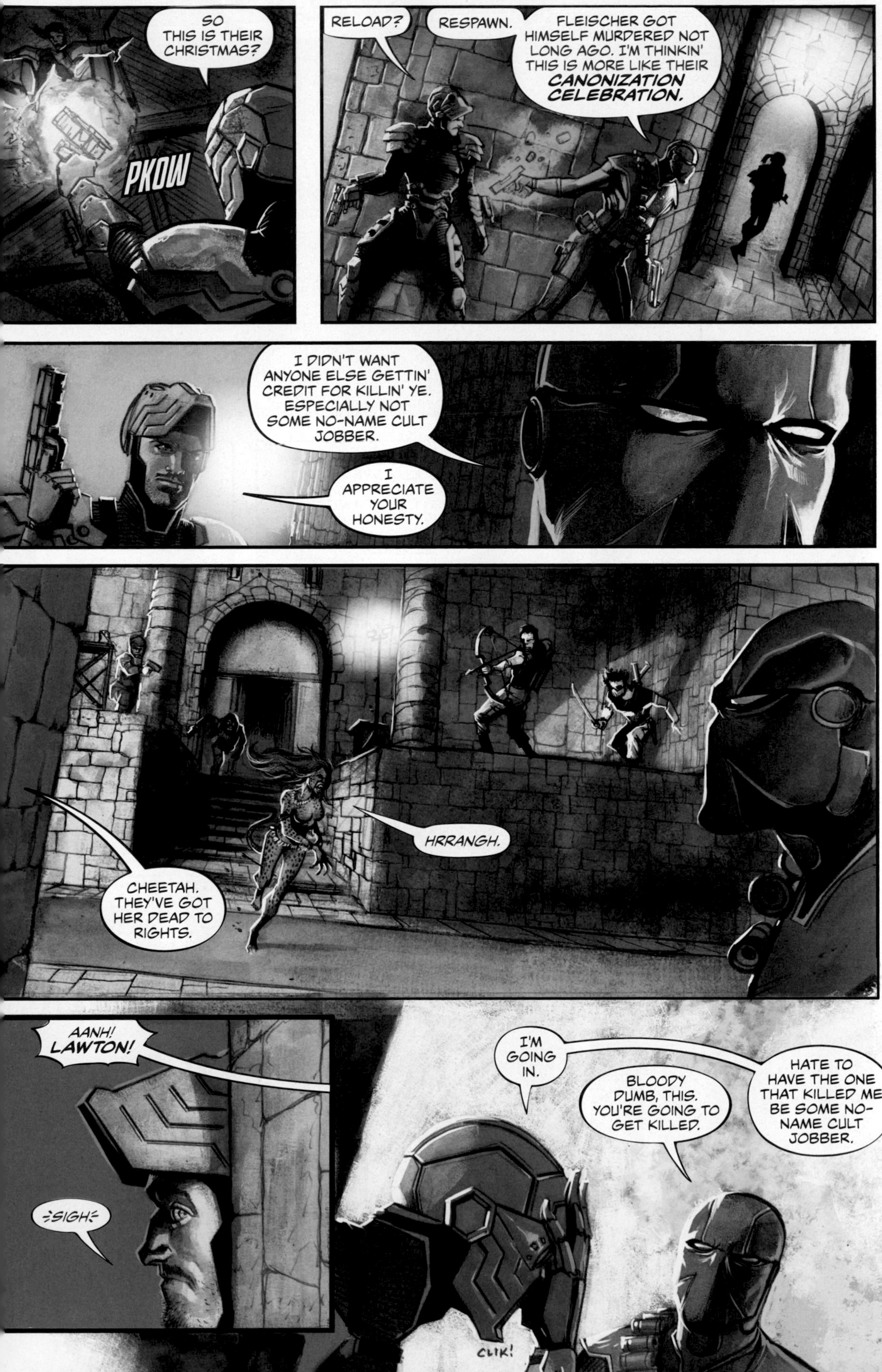
SO THIS IS THEIR CHRISTMAS?
PKOW
RELOAD?
RESPAWN.
FLEISCHER GOT HIMSELF MURDERED NOT LONG AGO. I'M THINKIN' THIS IS MORE LIKE THEIR CANONIZATION CELEBRATION.
I DIDN'T WANT ANYONE ELSE GETTIN' CREDIT FOR KILLIN' YE. ESPECIALLY NOT SOME NO-NAME CULT JOBBER.
I APPRECIATE YOUR HONESTY.
HRRANGH.
CHEETAH. THEY'VE GOT HER DEAD TO RIGHTS.
AANH! LAWTON!
SIGH
I'M GOING IN.
BLOODY DUMB, THIS. YOU'RE GOING TO GET KILLED.
HATE TO HAVE THE ONE THAT KILLED ME BE SOME NO-NAME CULT JOBBER.
CLIK!

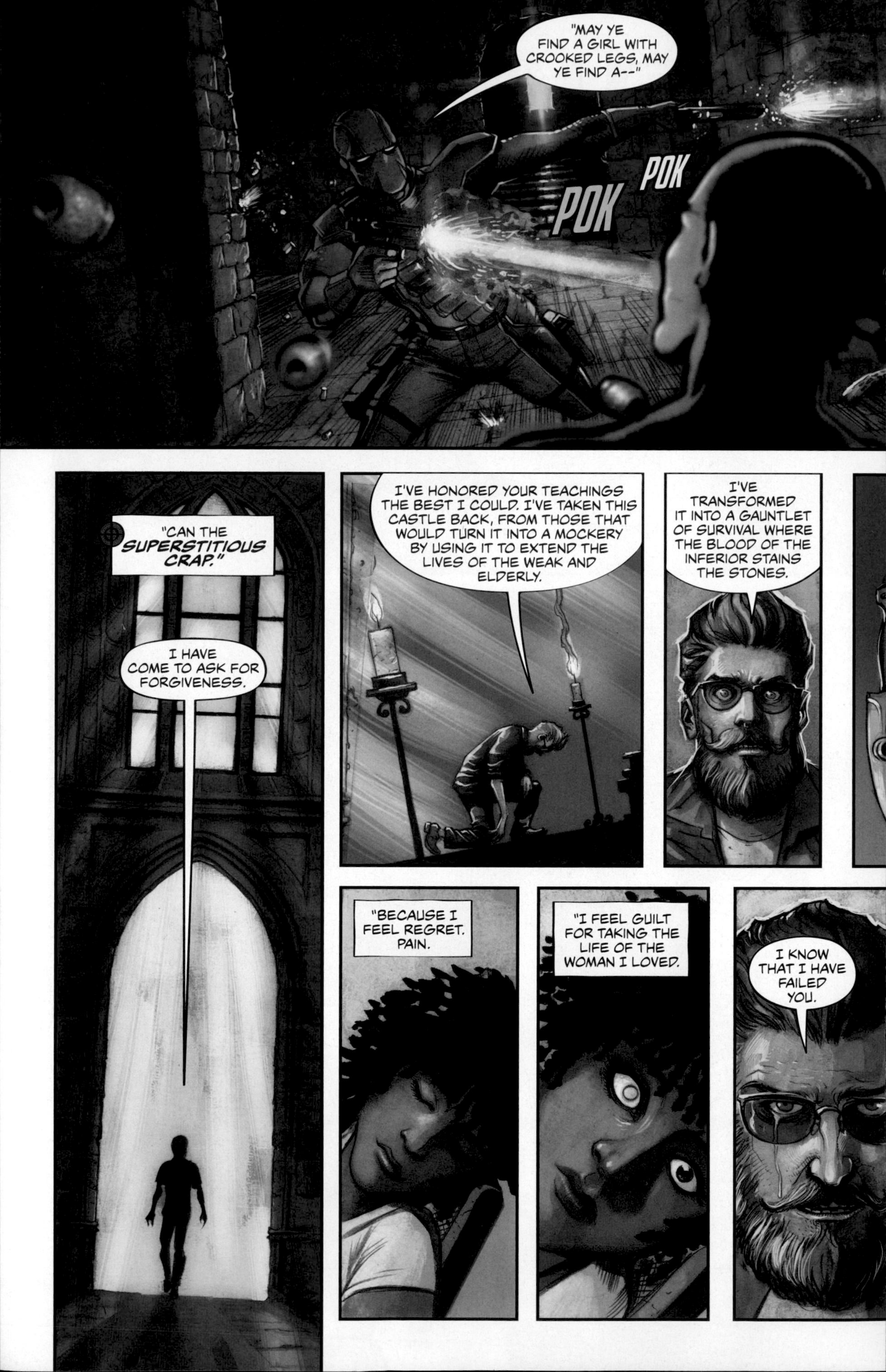
"MAY YE FIND A GIRL WITH CROOKED LEGS, MAY YE FIND A--"
POK
POK
"CAN THE SUPERSTITIOUS CRAP."
I HAVE COME TO ASK FOR FORGIVENESS.
I'VE HONORED YOUR TEACHINGS THE BEST I COULD. I'VE TAKEN THIS CASTLE BACK, FROM THOSE THAT WOULD TURN IT INTO A MOCKERY BY USING IT TO EXTEND THE LIVES OF THE WEAK AND ELDERLY.
I'VE TRANSFORMED IT INTO A GAUNTLET OF SURVIVAL WHERE THE BLOOD OF THE INFERIOR STAINS THE STONES.
"BECAUSE I FEEL REGRET. PAIN.
"I FEEL GUILT FOR TAKING THE LIFE OF THE WOMAN I LOVED.
I KNOW THAT I HAVE FAILED YOU.

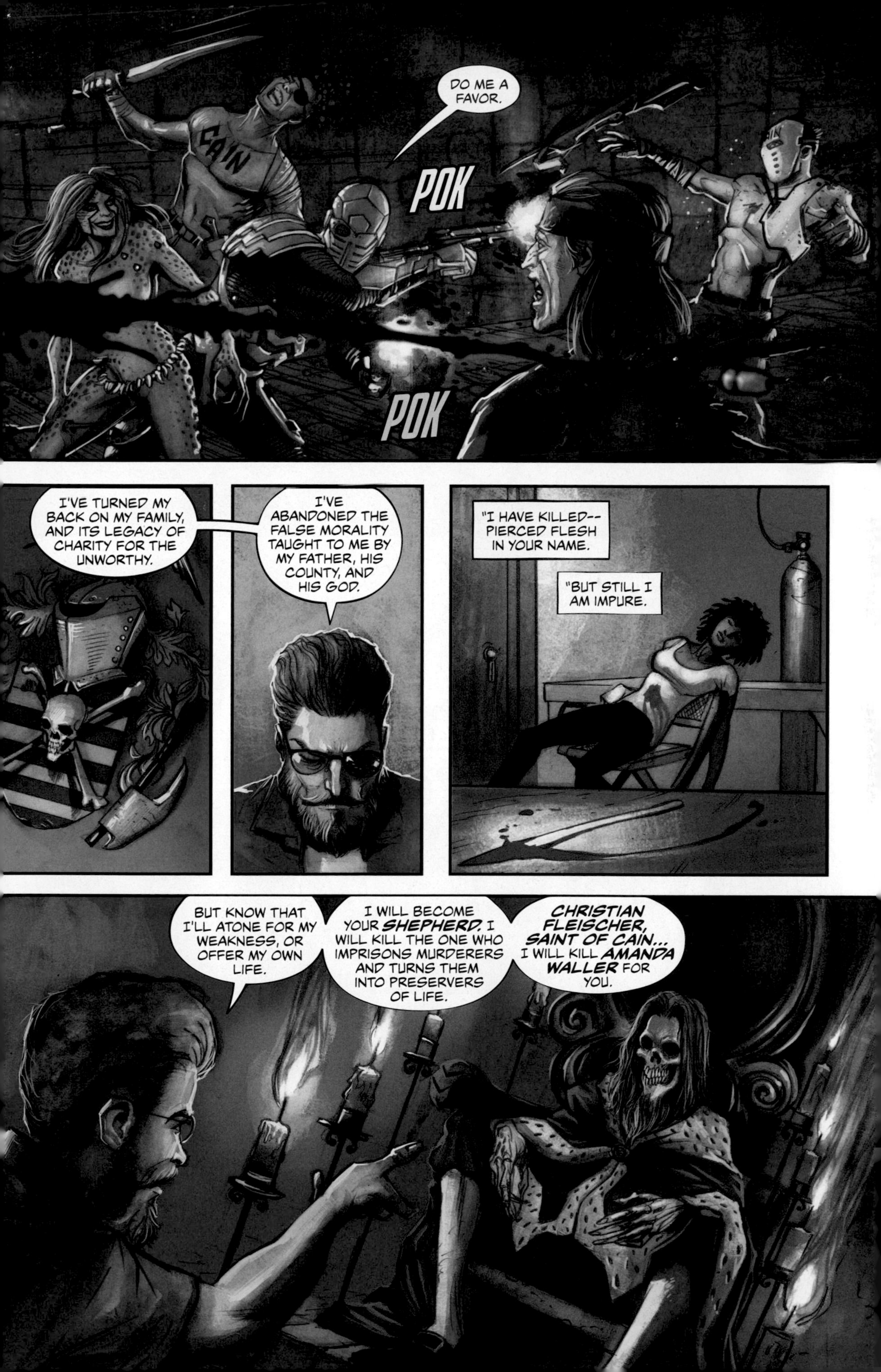

DO ME A FAVOR.
CAIN
POK
POK
I'VE TURNED MY BACK ON MY FAMILY, AND ITS LEGACY OF CHARITY FOR THE UNWORTHY.
I'VE ABANDONED THE FALSE MORALITY TAUGHT TO ME BY MY FATHER, HIS COUNTY, AND HIS GOD.
"I HAVE KILLED-- PIERCED FLESH IN YOUR NAME.
"BUT STILL I AM IMPURE.
BUT KNOW THAT I'LL ATONE FOR MY WEAKNESS, OR OFFER MY OWN LIFE.
I WILL BECOME YOUR SHEPHERD. I WILL KILL THE ONE WHO IMPRISONS MURDERERS AND TURNS THEM INTO PRESERVERS OF LIFE.
CHRISTIAN FLEISCHER, SAINT OF CAIN... I WILL KILL AMANDA WALLER FOR YOU.

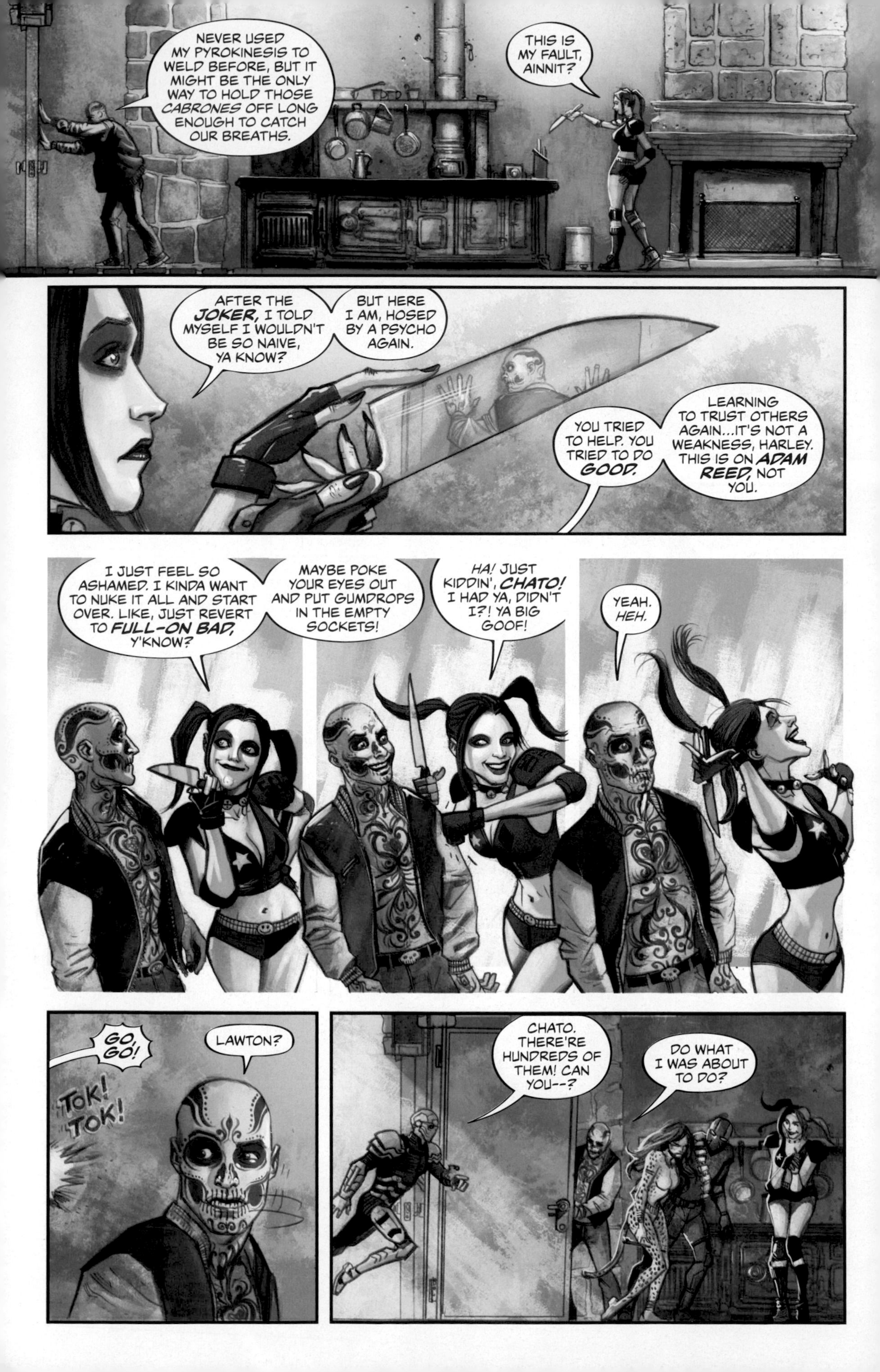

NEVER USED MY PYROKINESIS TO WELD BEFORE, BUT IT MIGHT BE THE ONLY WAY TO HOLD THOSE CABRONES OFF LONG ENOUGH TO CATCH OUR BREATHS.
THIS IS MY FAULT, AINNIT?
AFTER THE JOKER, I TOLD MYSELF I WOULDN'T BE SO NAIVE, YA KNOW?
BUT HERE I AM, HOSED BY A PSYCHO AGAIN.
YOU TRIED TO HELP. YOU TRIED TO DO GOOD.
LEARNING TO TRUST OTHERS AGAIN...IT'S NOT A WEAKNESS, HARLEY. THIS IS ON ADAM REED, NOT YOU.
I JUST FEEL SO ASHAMED. I KINDA WANT TO NUKE IT ALL AND START OVER. LIKE, JUST REVERT TO FULL-ON BAD, Y'KNOW?
MAYBE POKE YOUR EYES OUT AND PUT GUMDROPS IN THE EMPTY SOCKETS!
HA! JUST KIDDIN', CHATO! I HAD YA, DIDN'T I?! YA BIG GOOF!
YEAH. HEH.
GO, GO!
LAWTON?
TOK! TOK!
CHATO. THERE'RE HUNDREDS OF THEM! CAN YOU--?
DO WHAT I WAS ABOUT TO DO?

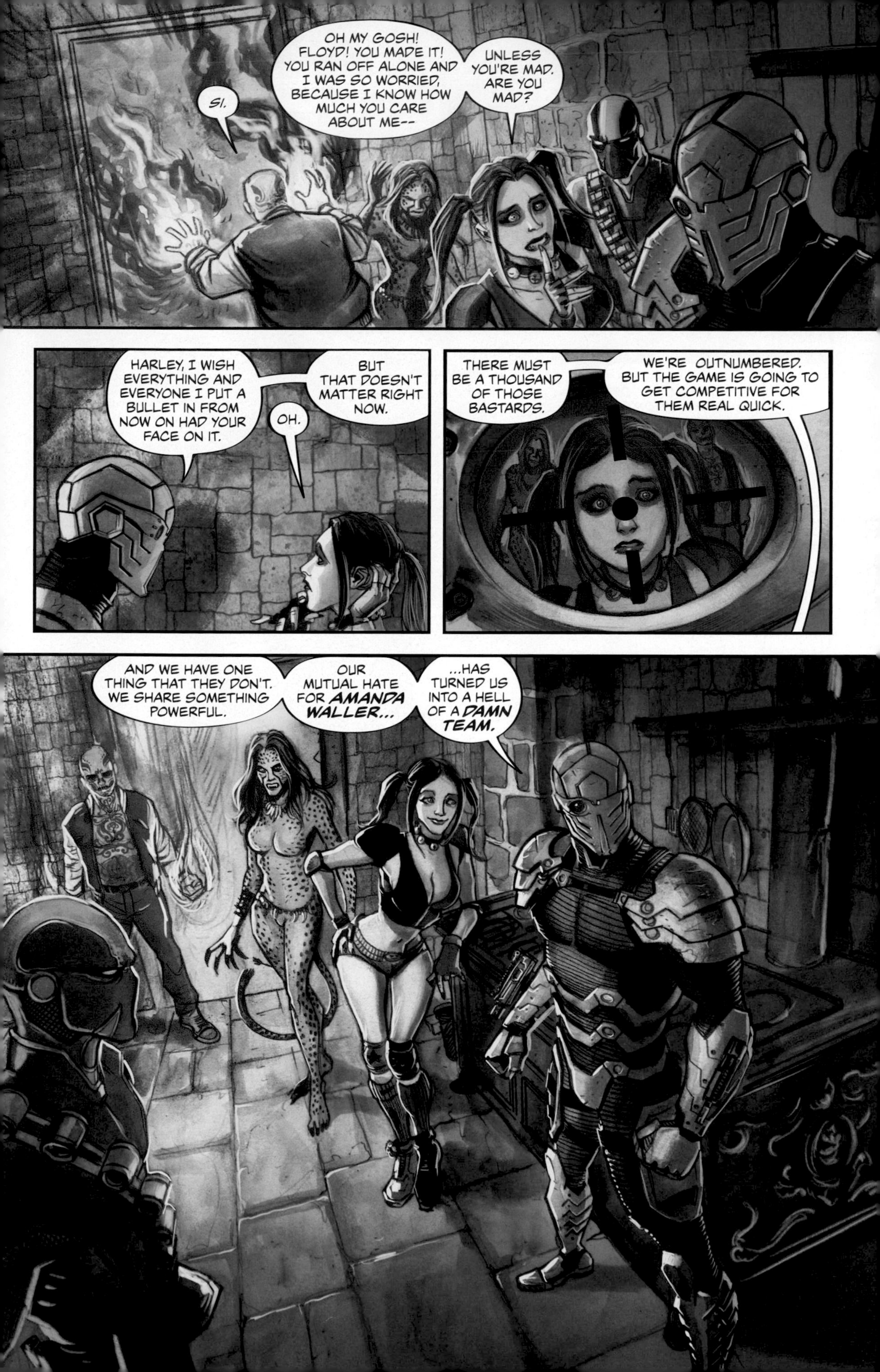
SI.
OH MY GOSH! FLOYD! YOU MADE IT! YOU RAN OFF ALONE AND I WAS SO WORRIED, BECAUSE I KNOW HOW MUCH YOU CARE ABOUT ME--
UNLESS YOU'RE MAD. ARE YOU MAD?
HARLEY, I WISH EVERYTHING AND EVERYONE I PUT A BULLET IN FROM NOW ON HAD YOUR FACE ON IT.
BUT THAT DOESN'T MATTER RIGHT NOW.
OH.
THERE MUST BE A THOUSAND OF THOSE BASTARDS.
WE'RE OUTNUMBERED. BUT THE GAME IS GOING TO GET COMPETITIVE FOR THEM REAL QUICK.
AND WE HAVE ONE THING THAT THEY DON'T. WE SHARE SOMETHING POWERFUL.
OUR MUTUAL HATE FOR AMANDA WALLER...
...HAS TURNED US INTO A HELL OF A DAMN TEAM.

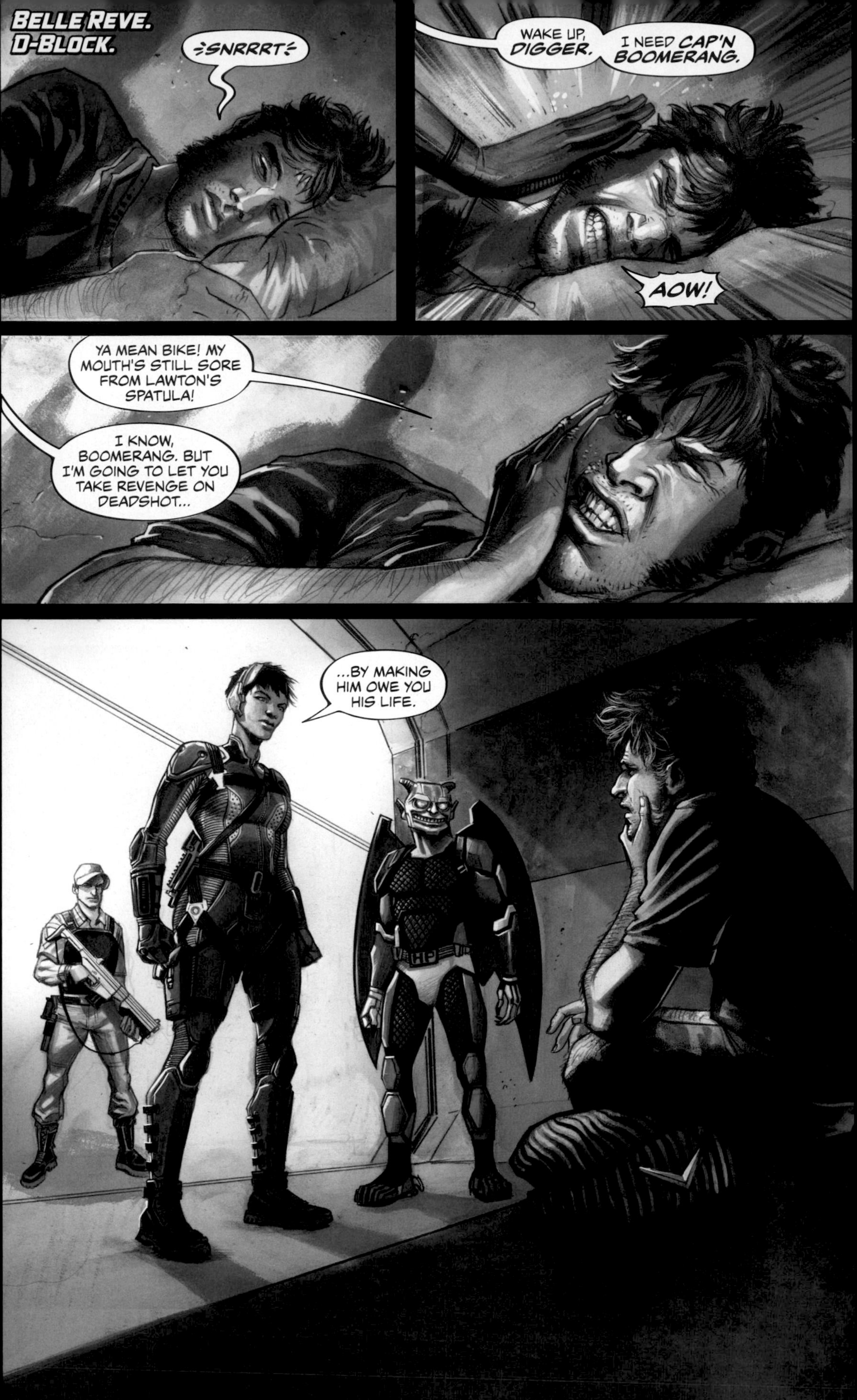
BELLE REVE. D-BLOCK.
SNRRRT
WAKE UP, DIGGER.
I NEED CAP'N BOOMERANG.
AOW!
YA MEAN BIKE! MY MOUTH'S STILL SORE FROM LAWTON'S SPATULA!
I KNOW, BOOMERANG. BUT I'M GOING TO LET YOU TAKE REVENGE ON DEADSHOT...
...BY MAKING HIM OWE YOU HIS LIFE.

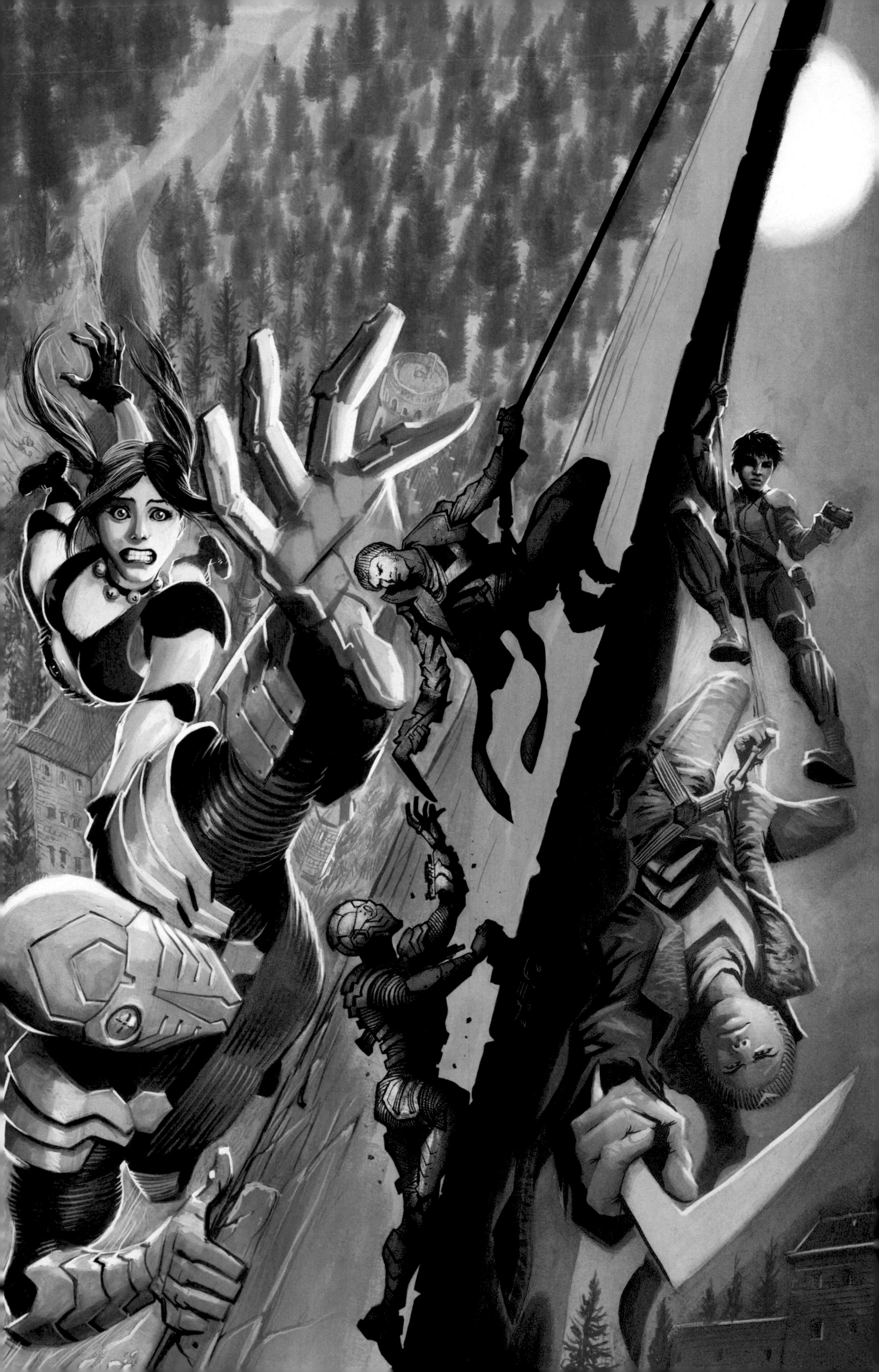

DOUBLE TEAMED

TIM SEELEY writer JUAN FERREYRA artist NATE PIEKOS letterer

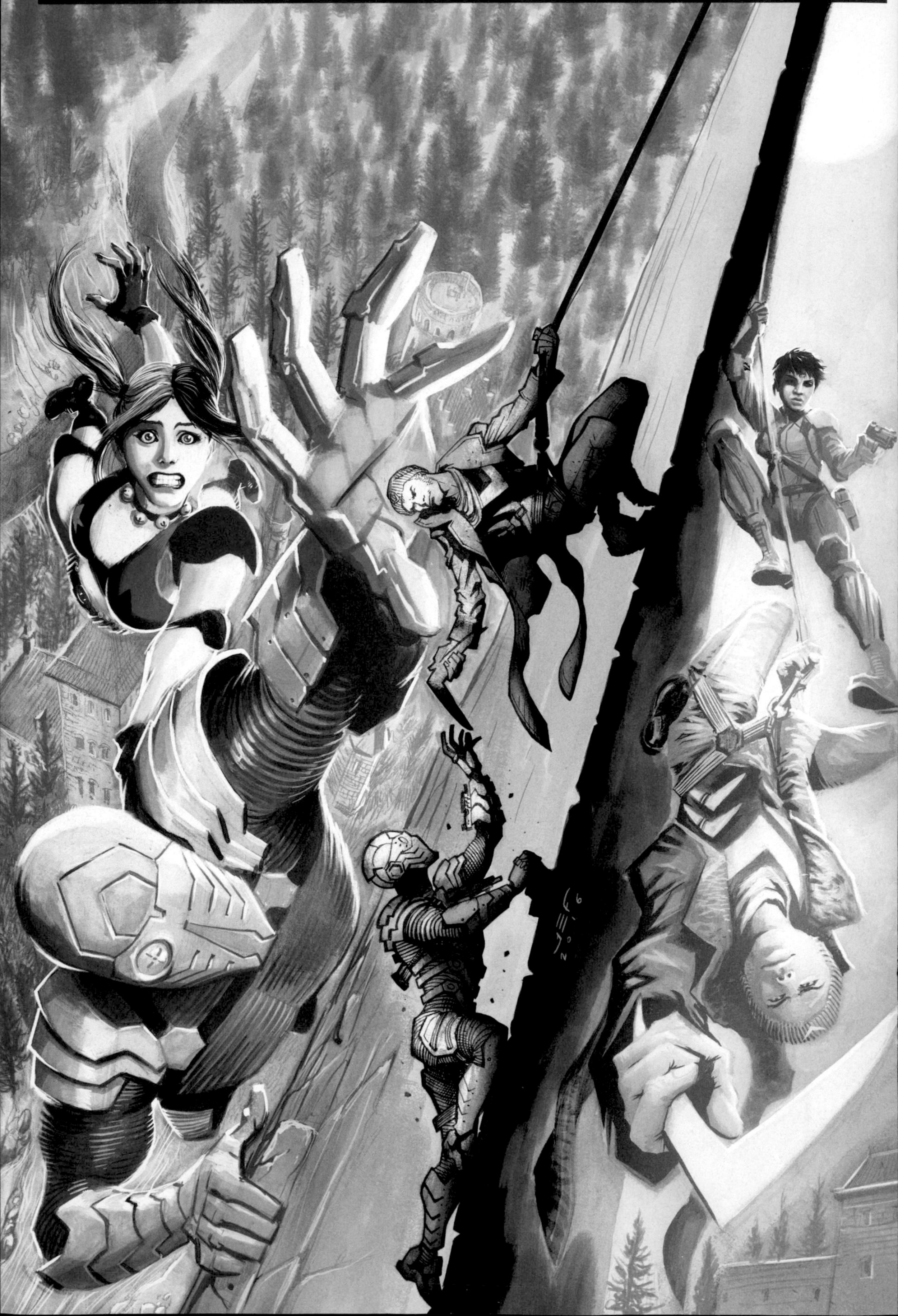

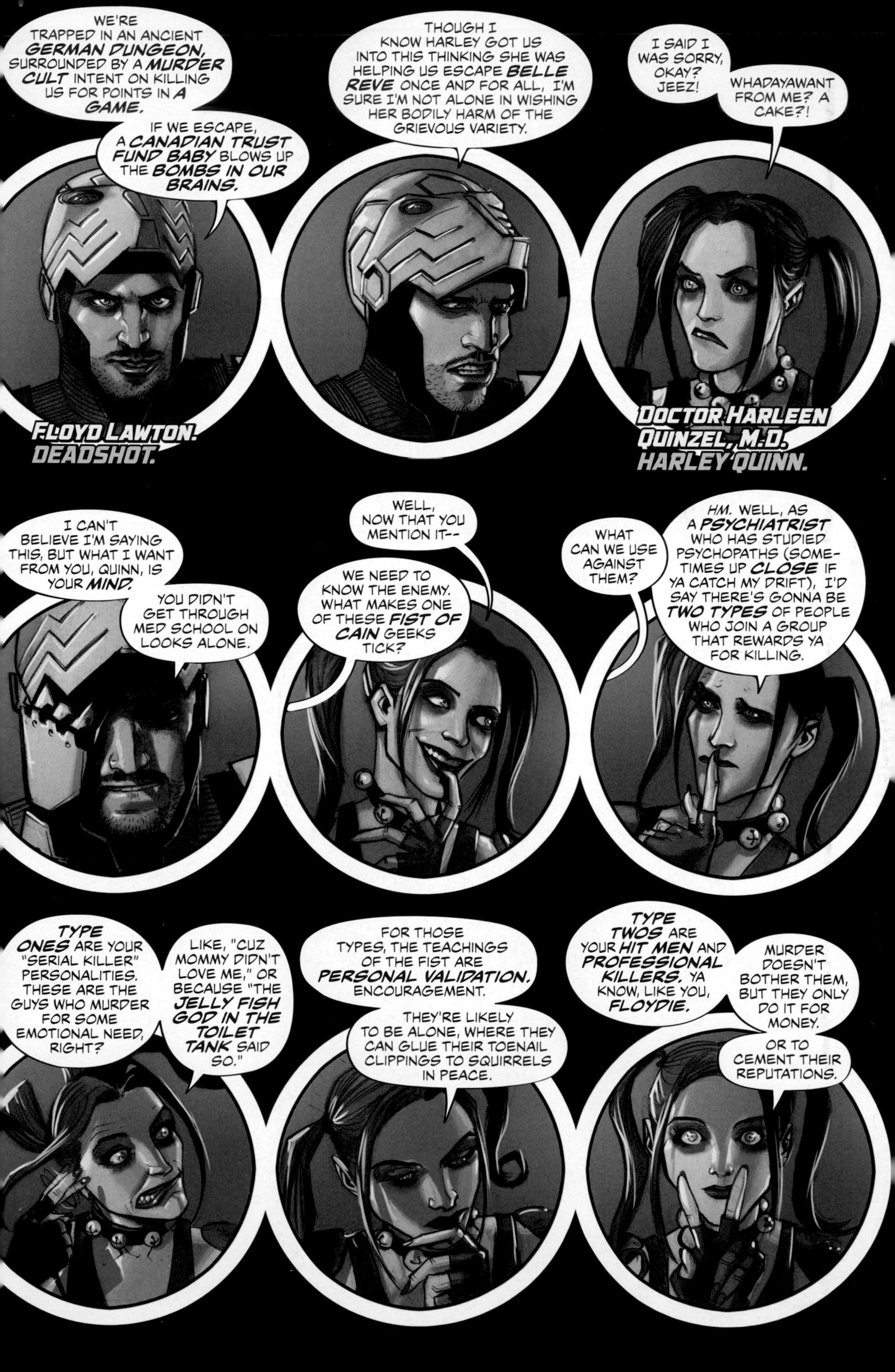
WE'RE TRAPPED IN AN ANCIENT GERMAN DUNGEON, SURROUNDED BY A MURDER CULT INTENT ON KILLING US FOR POINTS IN A GAME.
IF WE ESCAPE, A CANADIAN TRUST FUND BABY BLOWS UP THE BOMBS IN OUR BRAINS.
FLOYD LAWTON. DEADSHOT.
THOUGH I KNOW HARLEY GOT US INTO THIS THINKING SHE WAS HELPING US ESCAPE BELLE REVE ONCE AND FOR ALL, I'M SURE I'M NOT ALONE IN WISHING HER BODILY HARM OF THE GRIEVOUS VARIETY.
I SAID I WAS SORRY, OKAY? JEEZ!
WHADAYAWANT FROM ME? A CAKE?!
DOCTOR HARLEEN QUINZEL, M.D. HARLEY QUINN.
I CAN'T BELIEVE I'M SAYING THIS, BUT WHAT I WANT FROM YOU, QUINN, IS YOUR MIND.
YOU DIDN'T GET THROUGH MED SCHOOL ON LOOKS ALONE.
WELL, NOW THAT YOU MENTION IT--
WE NEED TO KNOW THE ENEMY. WHAT MAKES ONE OF THESE FIST OF CAIN GEEKS TICK?
WHAT CAN WE USE AGAINST THEM?
HM. WELL, AS A PSYCHIATRIST WHO HAS STUDIED PSYCHOPATHS (SOMETIMES UP CLOSE IF YA CATCH MY DRIFT), I'D SAY THERE'S GONNA BE TWO TYPES OF PEOPLE WHO JOIN A GROUP THAT REWARDS YA FOR KILLING.
TYPE ONES ARE YOUR "SERIAL KILLER" PERSONALITIES. THESE ARE THE GUYS WHO MURDER FOR SOME EMOTIONAL NEED, RIGHT?
LIKE, "CUZ MOMMY DIDN'T LOVE ME," OR BECAUSE "THE JELLY FISH GOD IN THE TOILET TANK SAID SO."
FOR THOSE TYPES, THE TEACHINGS OF THE FIST ARE PERSONAL VALIDATION. ENCOURAGEMENT.
THEY'RE LIKELY TO BE ALONE, WHERE THEY CAN GLUE THEIR TOENAIL CLIPPINGS TO SQUIRRELS IN PEACE.
TYPE TWOS ARE YOUR HIT MEN AND PROFESSIONAL KILLERS. YA KNOW, LIKE YOU, FLOYDIE.
MURDER DOESN'T BOTHER THEM, BUT THEY ONLY DO IT FOR MONEY.
OR TO CEMENT THEIR REPUTATIONS.

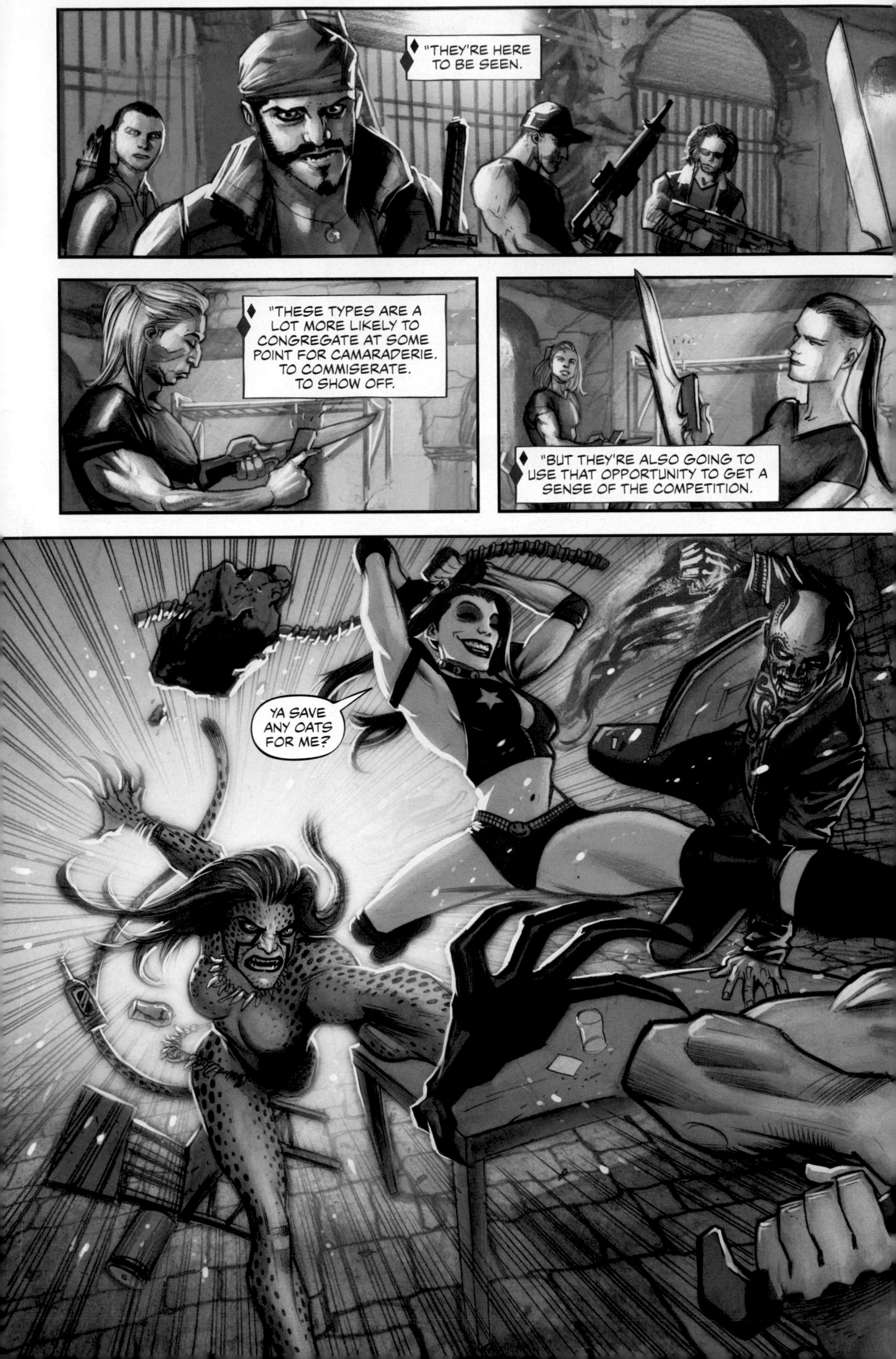
"THEY'RE HERE TO BE SEEN.
"THESE TYPES ARE A LOT MORE LIKELY TO CONGREGATE AT SOME POINT FOR CAMARADERIE. TO COMMISERATE. TO SHOW OFF.
"BUT THEY'RE ALSO GOING TO USE THAT OPPORTUNITY TO GET A SENSE OF THE COMPETITION.
YA SAVE ANY OATS FOR ME?

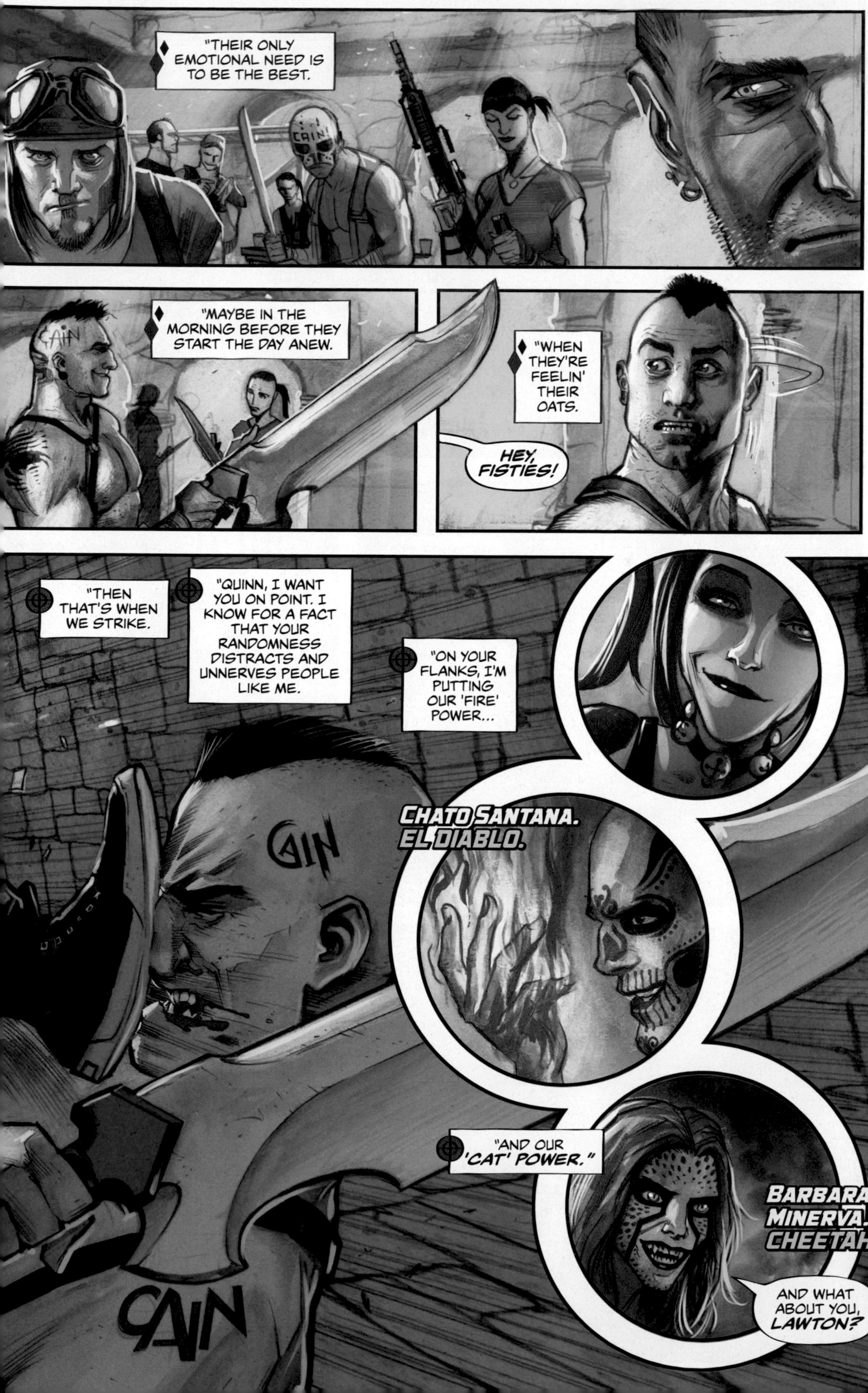
"THEIR ONLY EMOTIONAL NEED IS TO BE THE BEST.
CAIN
CAIN
"MAYBE IN THE MORNING BEFORE THEY START THE DAY ANEW.
"WHEN THEY'RE FEELIN' THEIR OATS.
HEY, FISTIES!
"THEN THAT'S WHEN WE STRIKE.
"QUINN, I WANT YOU ON POINT. I KNOW FOR A FACT THAT YOUR RANDOMNESS DISTRACTS AND UNNERVES PEOPLE LIKE ME.
"ON YOUR FLANKS, I'M PUTTING OUR 'FIRE' POWER...
CAIN
CHATO SANTANA. EL DIABLO.
"AND OUR 'CAT' POWER."
BARBARA MINERVA. CHEETAH.
AND WHAT ABOUT YOU, LAWTON?
CAIN

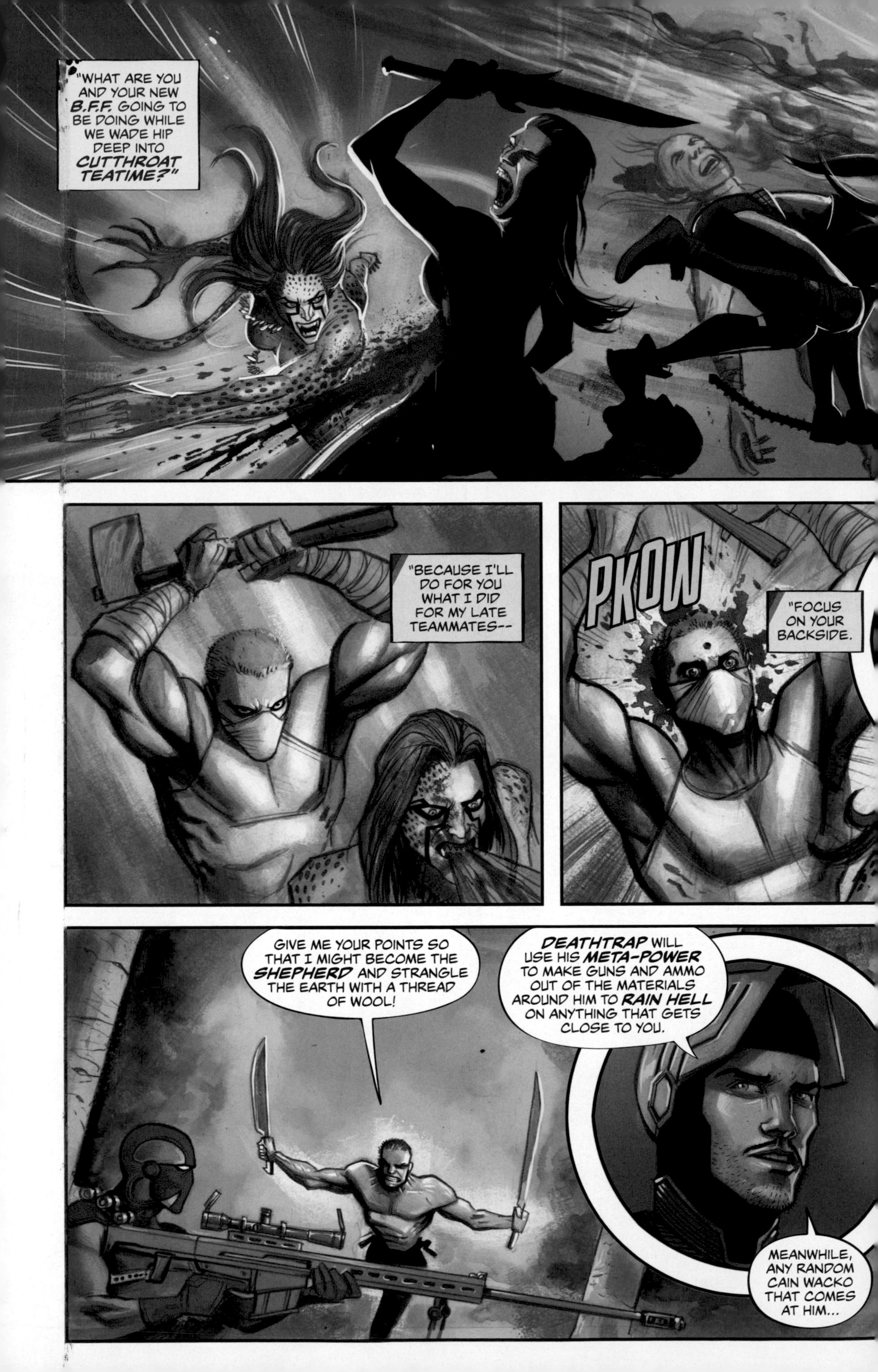
"WHAT ARE YOU AND YOUR NEW B.F.F. GOING TO BE DOING WHILE WE WADE HIP DEEP INTO CUTTHROAT TEATIME?"
"BECAUSE I'LL DO FOR YOU WHAT I DID FOR MY LATE TEAMMATES--
PKOW
"FOCUS ON YOUR BACKSIDE.
GIVE ME YOUR POINTS SO THAT I MIGHT BECOME THE SHEPHERD AND STRANGLE THE EARTH WITH A THREAD OF WOOL!
DEATHTRAP WILL USE HIS META-POWER TO MAKE GUNS AND AMMO OUT OF THE MATERIALS AROUND HIM TO RAIN HELL ON ANYTHING THAT GETS CLOSE TO YOU.
MEANWHILE, ANY RANDOM CAIN WACKO THAT COMES AT HIM...

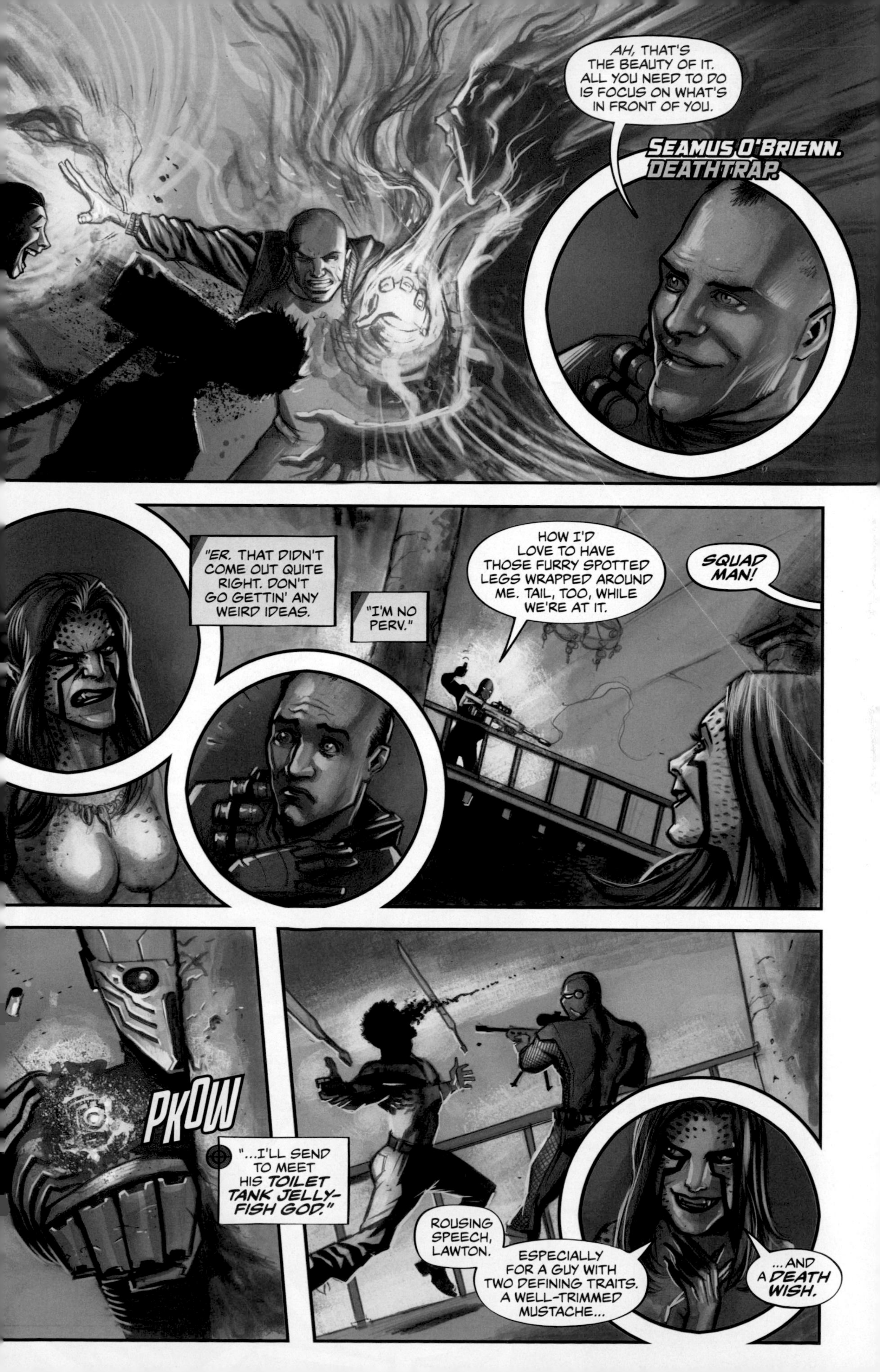
AH, THAT'S THE BEAUTY OF IT. ALL YOU NEED TO DO IS FOCUS ON WHAT'S IN FRONT OF YOU.
SEAMUS O'BRIENN. DEATHTRAP.
"ER. THAT DIDN'T COME OUT QUITE RIGHT. DON'T GO GETTIN' ANY WEIRD IDEAS.
"I'M NO PERV."
HOW I'D LOVE TO HAVE THOSE FURRY SPOTTED LEGS WRAPPED AROUND ME. TAIL, TOO, WHILE WE'RE AT IT.
SQUAD MAN!
PKOW
"...I'LL SEND TO MEET HIS TOILET TANK JELLY-FISH GOD."
ROUSING SPEECH, LAWTON.
ESPECIALLY FOR A GUY WITH TWO DEFINING TRAITS. A WELL-TRIMMED MUSTACHE...
...AND A DEATH WISH.

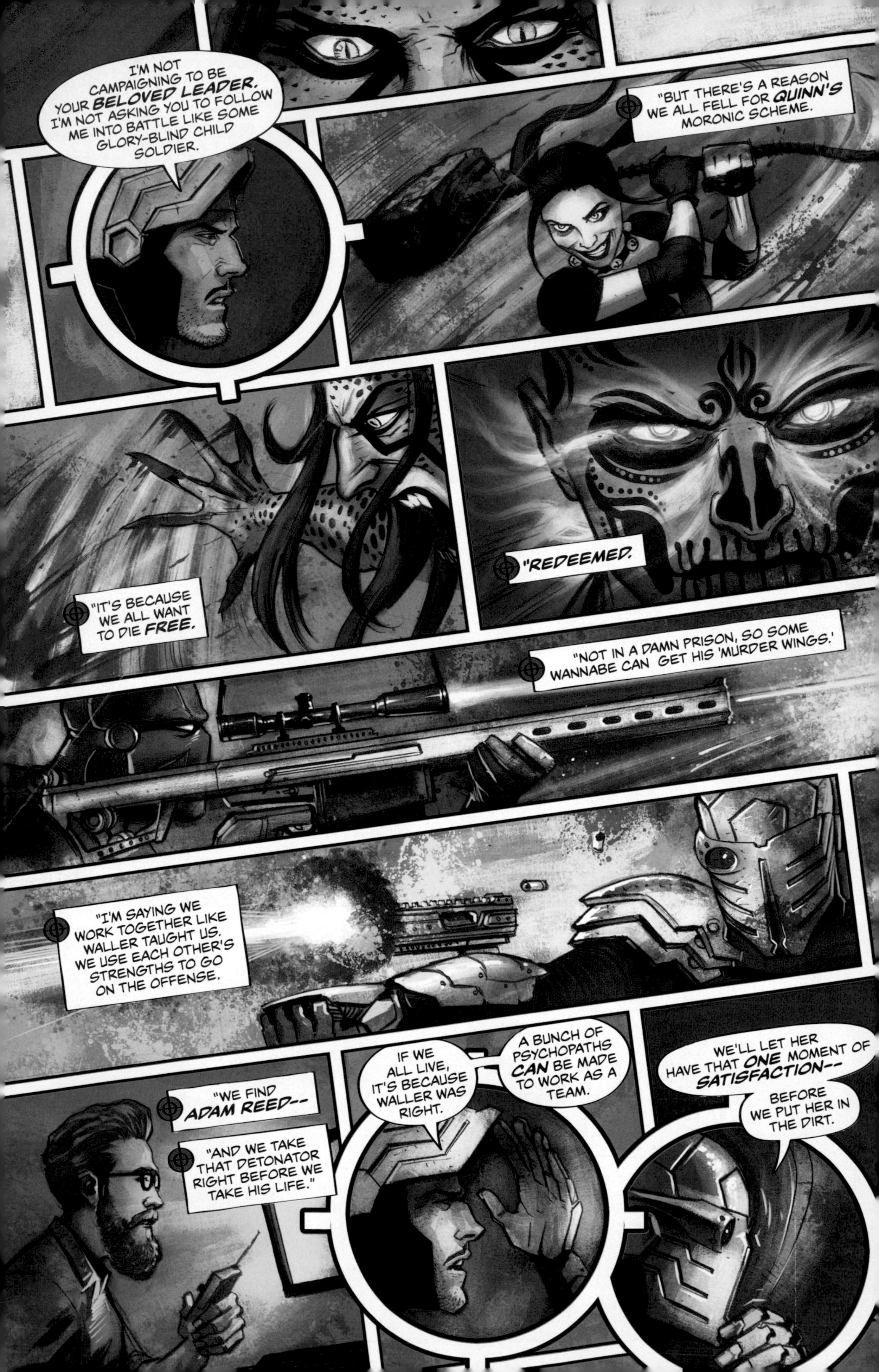
I'M NOT CAMPAIGNING TO BE YOUR BELOVED LEADER. I'M NOT ASKING YOU TO FOLLOW ME INTO BATTLE LIKE SOME GLORY-BLIND CHILD SOLDIER.
"BUT THERE'S A REASON WE ALL FELL FOR QUINN'S MORONIC SCHEME.
"IT'S BECAUSE WE ALL WANT TO DIE FREE.
"REDEEMED.
"NOT IN A DAMN PRISON, SO SOME WANNABE CAN GET HIS 'MURDER WINGS.'
"I'M SAYING WE WORK TOGETHER LIKE WALLER TAUGHT US. WE USE EACH OTHER'S STRENGTHS TO GO ON THE OFFENSE.
"WE FIND ADAM REED--
"AND WE TAKE THAT DETONATOR RIGHT BEFORE WE TAKE HIS LIFE."
IF WE ALL LIVE, IT'S BECAUSE WALLER WAS RIGHT.
A BUNCH OF PSYCHOPATHS CAN BE MADE TO WORK AS A TEAM.
WE'LL LET HER HAVE THAT ONE MOMENT OF SATISFACTION--
BEFORE WE PUT HER IN THE DIRT.

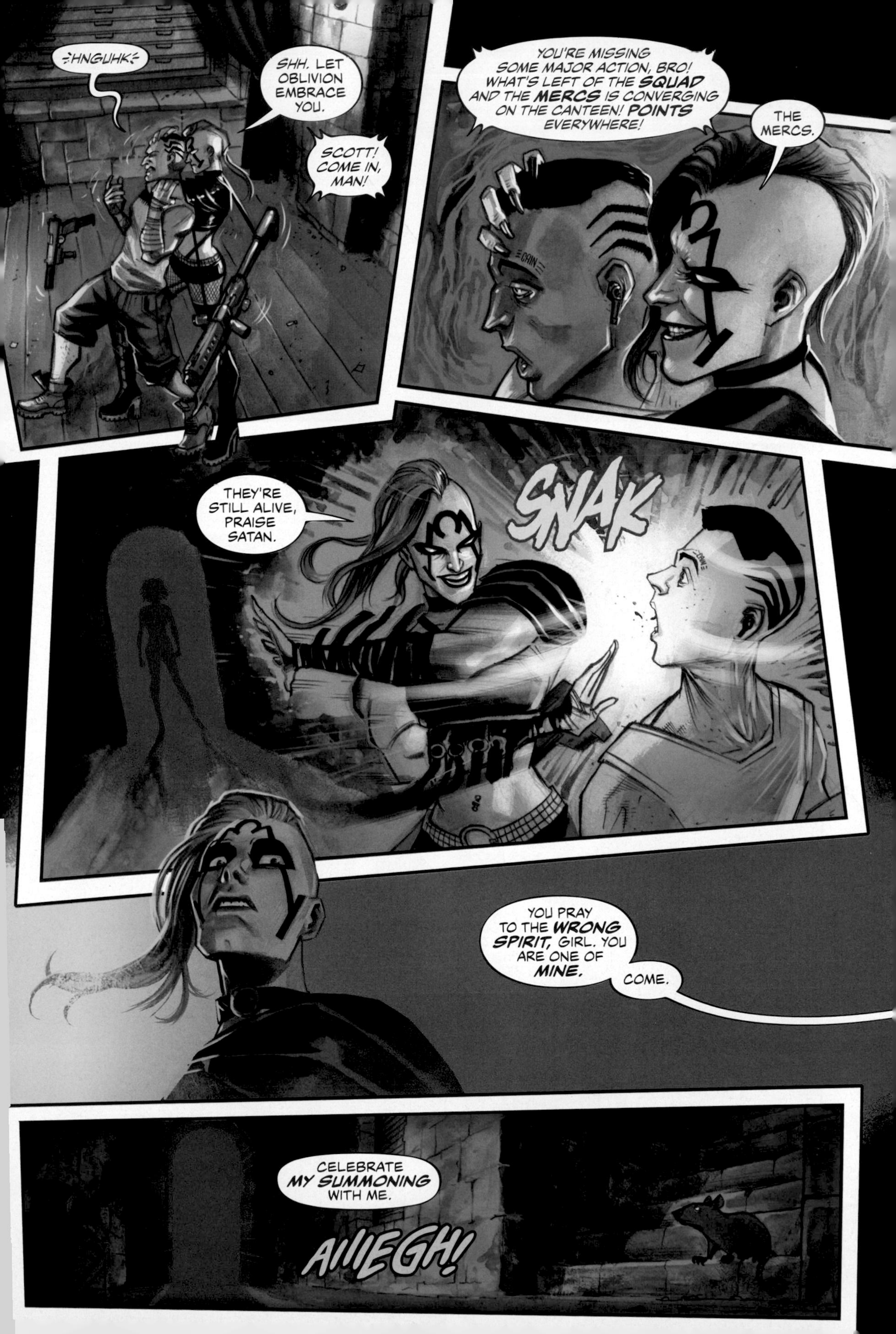
HNGUHK
SHH. LET OBLIVION EMBRACE YOU.
SCOTT! COME IN, MAN!
YOU'RE MISSING SOME MAJOR ACTION, BRO! WHAT'S LEFT OF THE SQUAD AND THE MERCS IS CONVERGING ON THE CANTEEN! POINTS EVERYWHERE!
THE MERCS.
THEY'RE STILL ALIVE, PRAISE SATAN.
SNAK
YOU PRAY TO THE WRONG SPIRIT, GIRL. YOU ARE ONE OF MINE.
COME.
CELEBRATE MY SUMMONING WITH ME.
AIIIEGH!

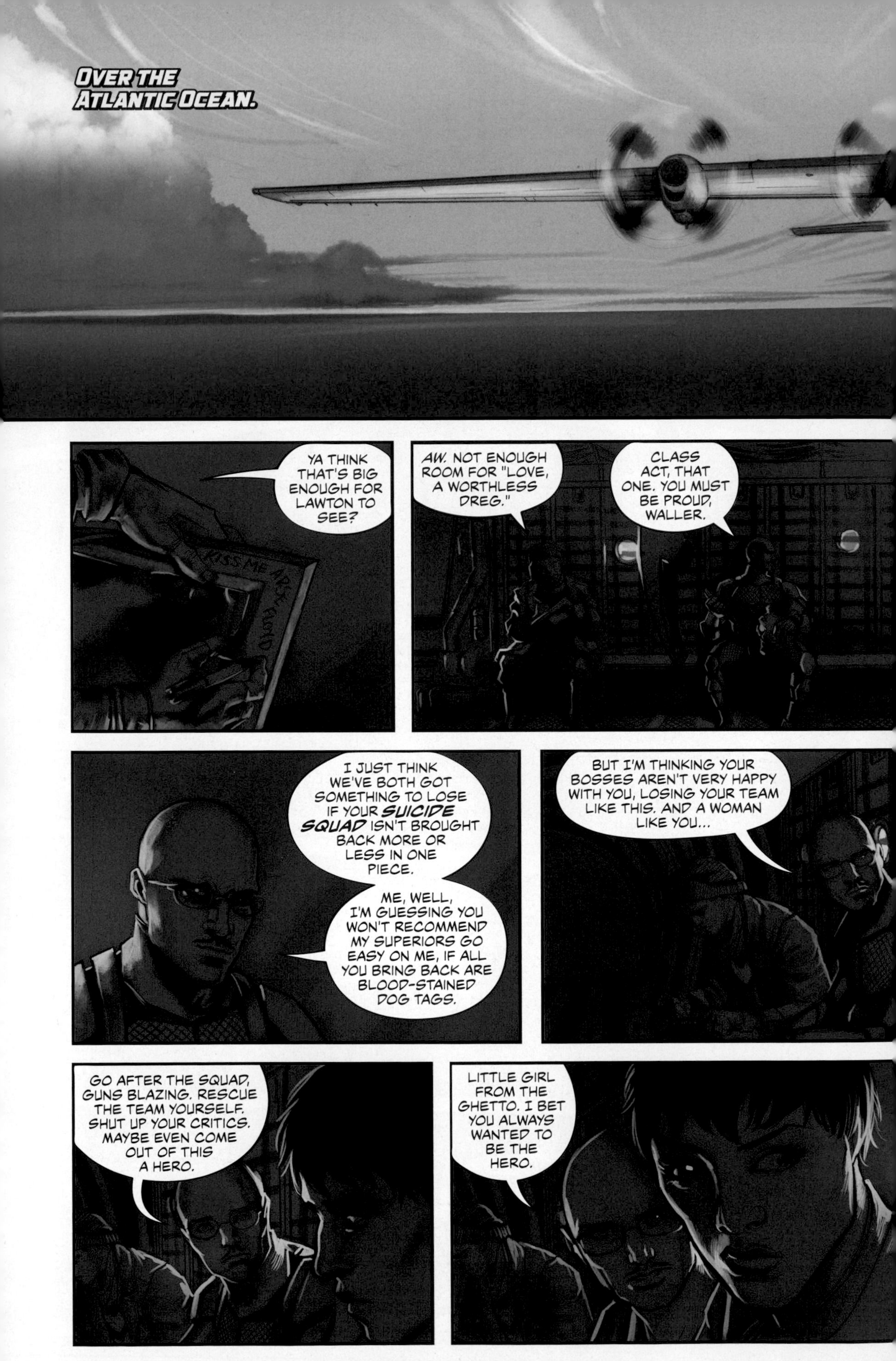
OVER THE ATLANTIC OCEAN.
YA THINK THAT'S BIG ENOUGH FOR LAWTON TO SEE?
AW. NOT ENOUGH ROOM FOR "LOVE, A WORTHLESS DREG."
CLASS ACT, THAT ONE. YOU MUST BE PROUD, WALLER.
I JUST THINK WE'VE BOTH GOT SOMETHING TO LOSE IF YOUR SUICIDE SQUAD ISN'T BROUGHT BACK MORE OR LESS IN ONE PIECE.
ME, WELL, I'M GUESSING YOU WON'T RECOMMEND MY SUPERIORS GO EASY ON ME, IF ALL YOU BRING BACK ARE BLOOD-STAINED DOG TAGS.
BUT I'M THINKING YOUR BOSSES AREN'T VERY HAPPY WITH YOU, LOSING YOUR TEAM LIKE THIS. AND A WOMAN LIKE YOU...
GO AFTER THE SQUAD, GUNS BLAZING. RESCUE THE TEAM YOURSELF. SHUT UP YOUR CRITICS. MAYBE EVEN COME OUT OF THIS A HERO.
LITTLE GIRL FROM THE GHETTO. I BET YOU ALWAYS WANTED TO BE THE HERO.

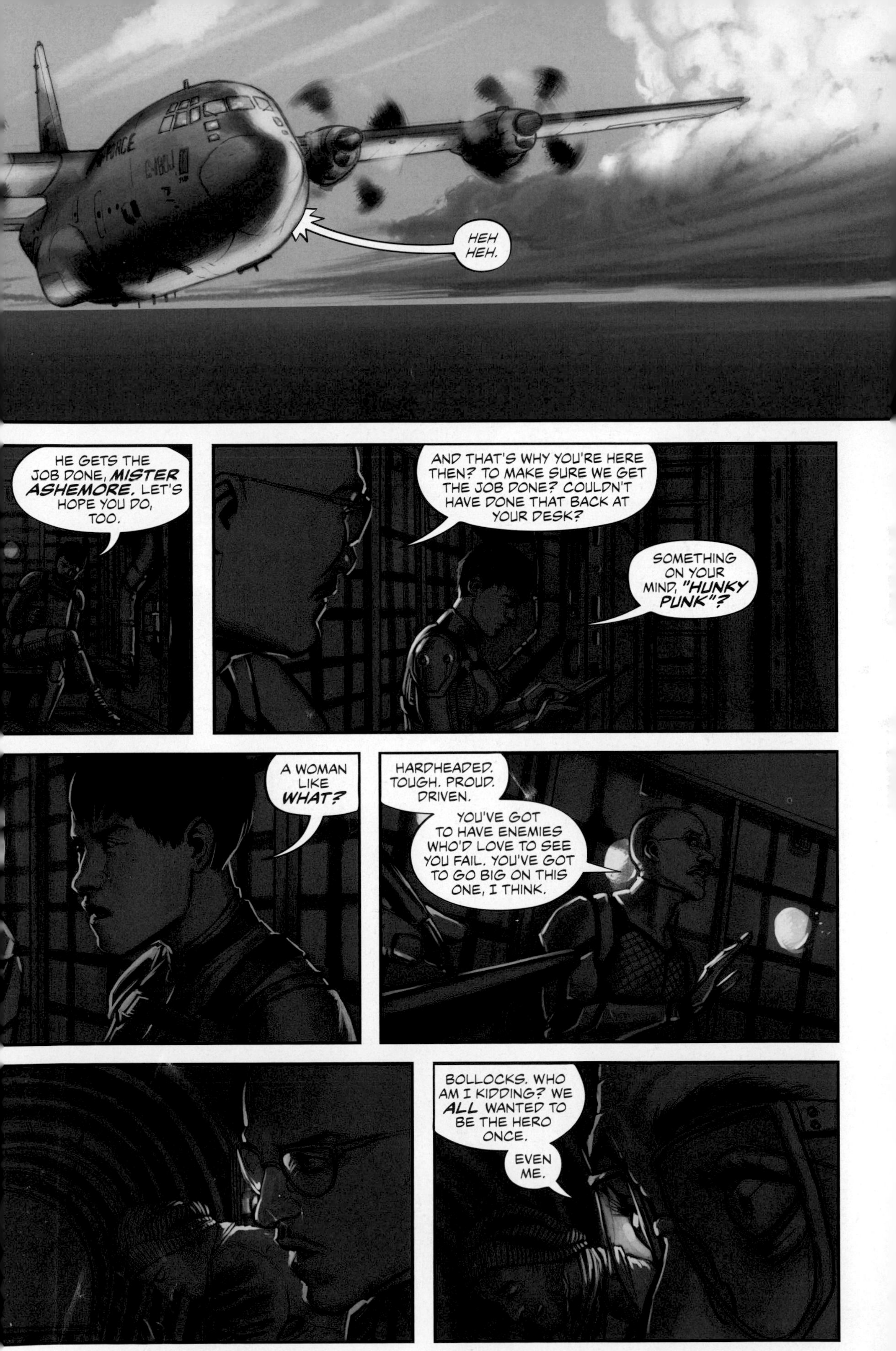
HEH HEH.
HE GETS THE JOB DONE, MISTER ASHEMORE. LET'S HOPE YOU DO, TOO.
AND THAT'S WHY YOU'RE HERE THEN? TO MAKE SURE WE GET THE JOB DONE? COULDN'T HAVE DONE THAT BACK AT YOUR DESK?
SOMETHING ON YOUR MIND, "HUNKY PUNK"?
A WOMAN LIKE WHAT?
HARDHEADED. TOUGH. PROUD. DRIVEN.
YOU'VE GOT TO HAVE ENEMIES WHO'D LOVE TO SEE YOU FAIL. YOU'VE GOT TO GO BIG ON THIS ONE, I THINK.
BOLLOCKS. WHO AM I KIDDING? WE ALL WANTED TO BE THE HERO ONCE.
EVEN ME.

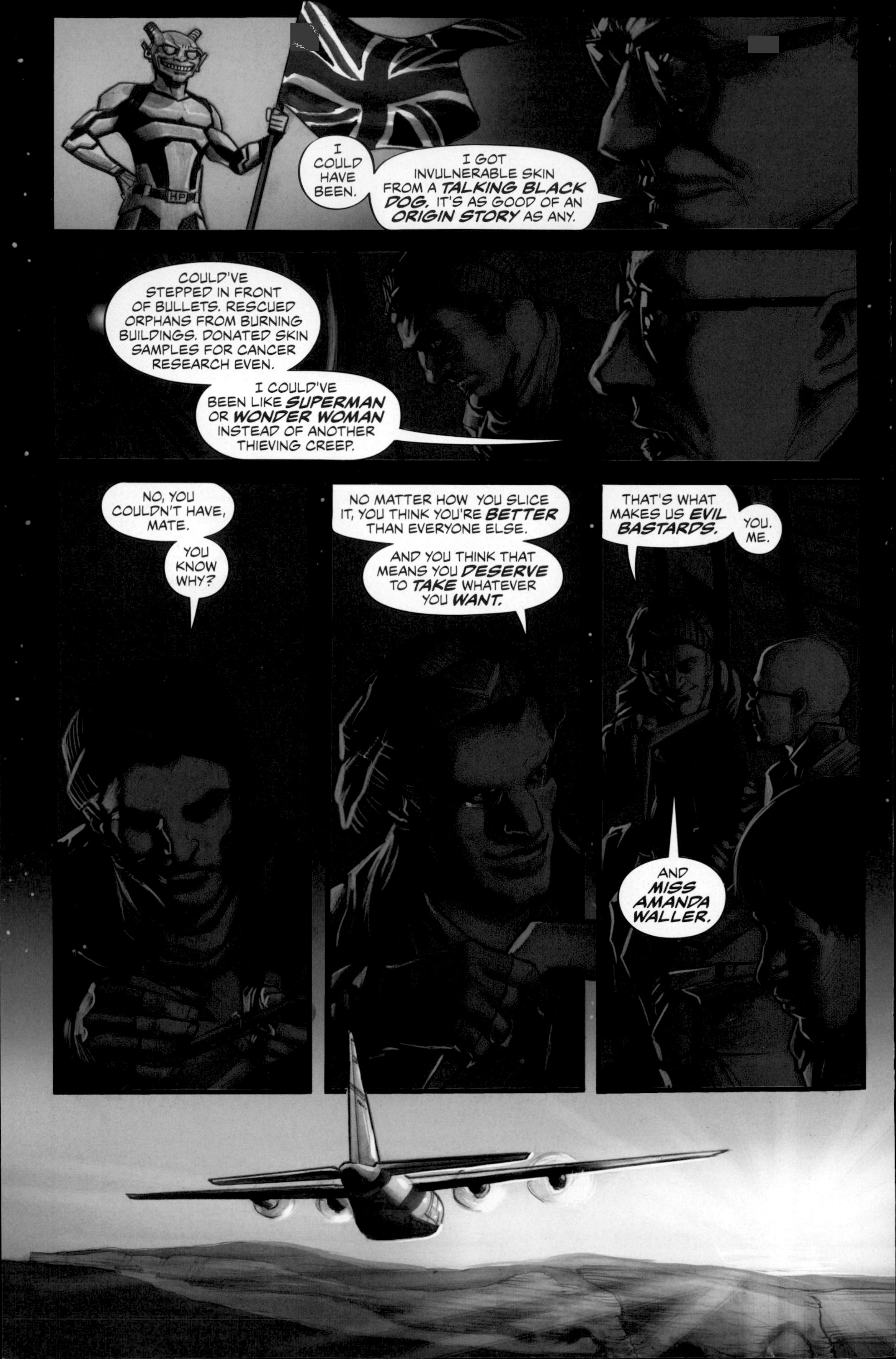
I COULD HAVE BEEN.
I GOT INVULNERABLE SKIN FROM A TALKING BLACK DOG. IT'S AS GOOD OF AN ORIGIN STORY AS ANY.
COULD'VE STEPPED IN FRONT OF BULLETS. RESCUED ORPHANS FROM BURNING BUILDINGS. DONATED SKIN SAMPLES FOR CANCER RESEARCH EVEN.
I COULD'VE BEEN LIKE SUPERMAN OR WONDER WOMAN INSTEAD OF ANOTHER THIEVING CREEP.
NO, YOU COULDN'T HAVE, MATE.
YOU KNOW WHY?
NO MATTER HOW YOU SLICE IT, YOU THINK YOU'RE BETTER THAN EVERYONE ELSE.
AND YOU THINK THAT MEANS YOU DESERVE TO TAKE WHATEVER YOU WANT.
THAT'S WHAT MAKES US EVIL BASTARDS.
YOU. ME.
AND MISS AMANDA WALLER.

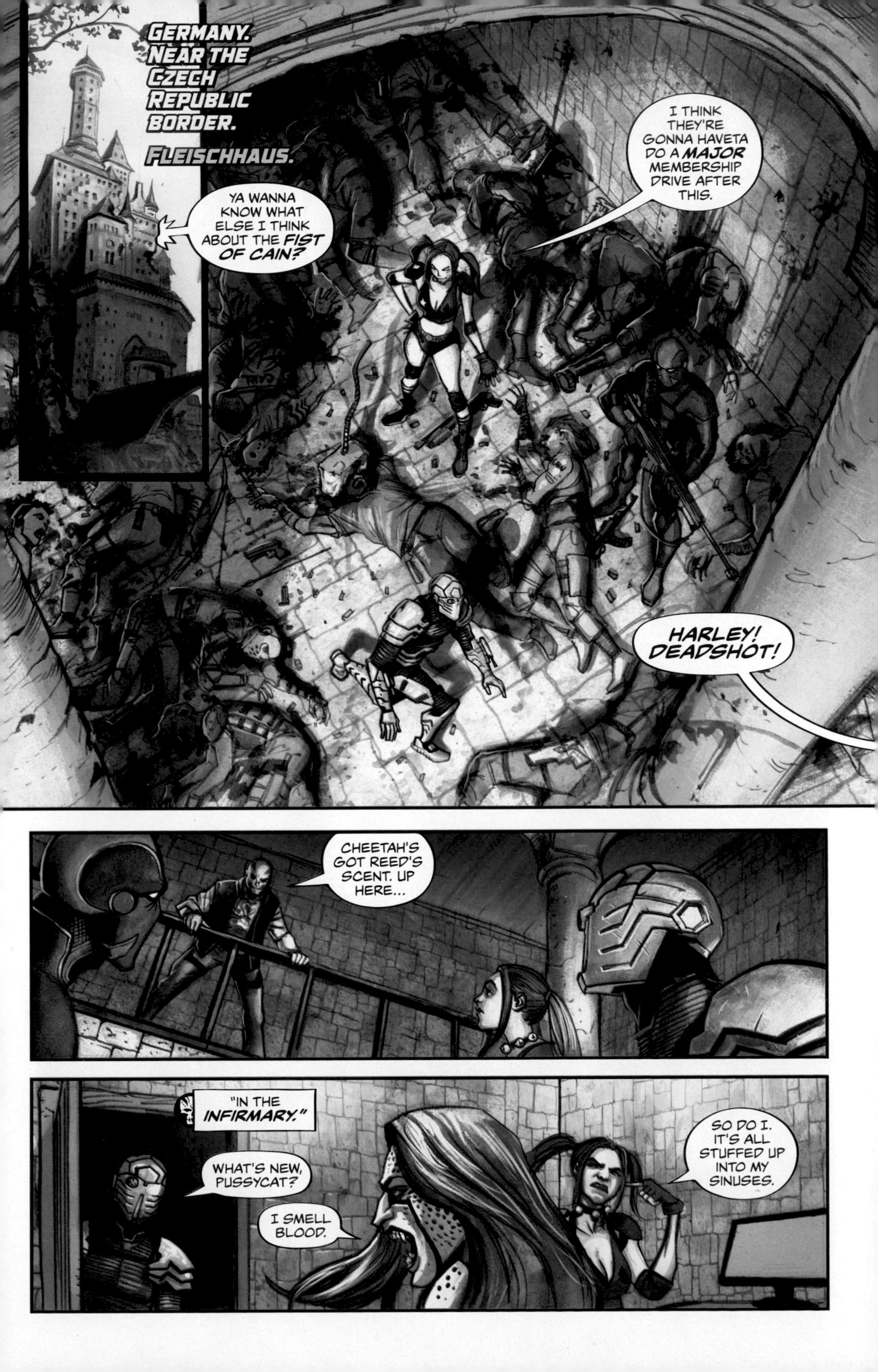
GERMANY. NEAR THE CZECH REPUBLIC BORDER.
FLEISCHHAUS.
YA WANNA KNOW WHAT ELSE I THINK ABOUT THE FIST OF CAIN?
I THINK THEY'RE GONNA HAVETA DO A MAJOR MEMBERSHIP DRIVE AFTER THIS.
HARLEY! DEADSHOT!
CHEETAH'S GOT REED'S SCENT. UP HERE...
"IN THE INFIRMARY."
WHAT'S NEW, PUSSYCAT?
I SMELL BLOOD.
SO DO I. IT'S ALL STUFFED UP INTO MY SINUSES.

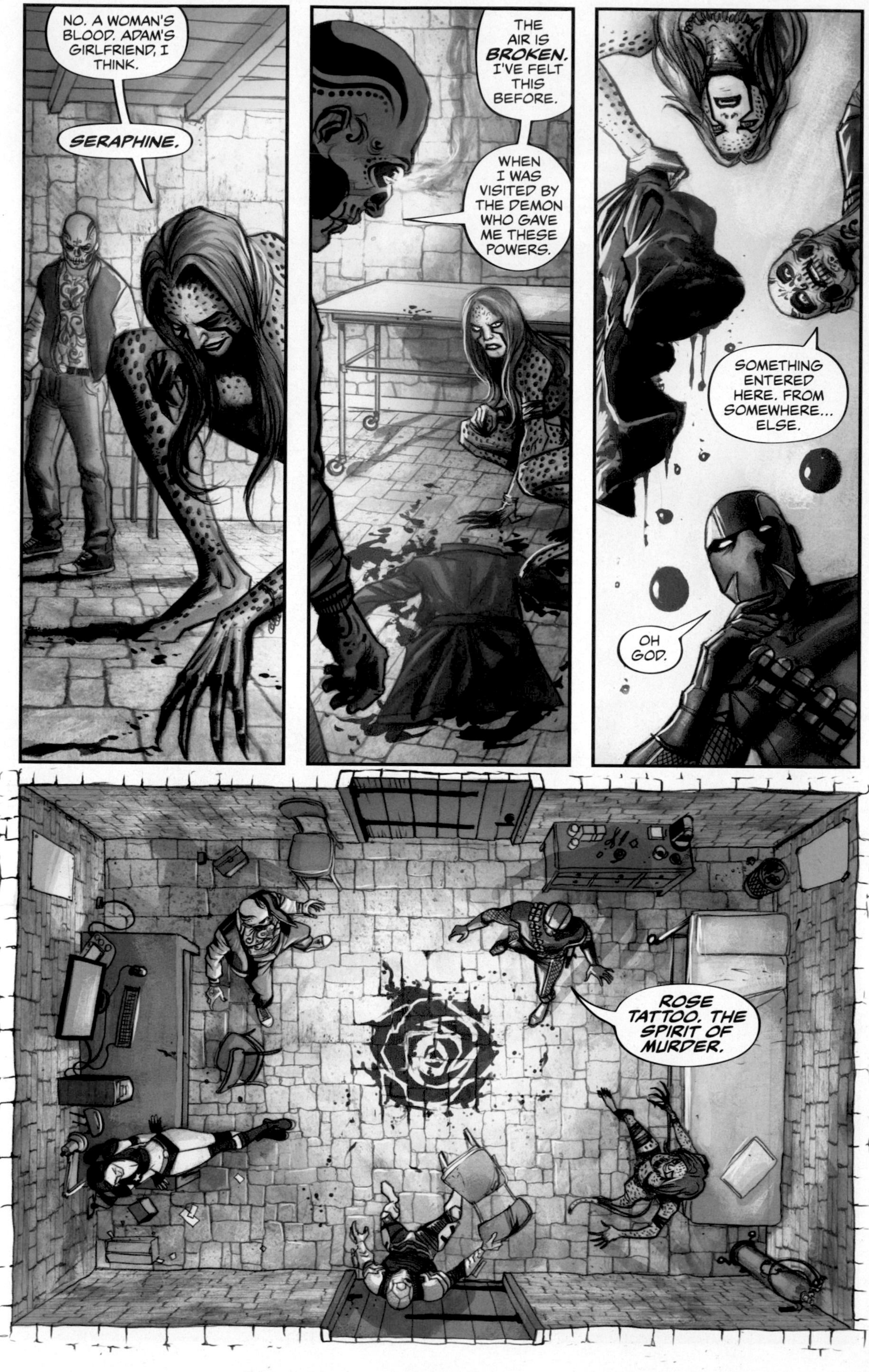
NO. A WOMAN'S BLOOD. ADAM'S GIRLFRIEND, I THINK.
SERAPHINE.
THE AIR IS BROKEN. I'VE FELT THIS BEFORE.
WHEN I WAS VISITED BY THE DEMON WHO GAVE ME THESE POWERS.
SOMETHING ENTERED HERE. FROM SOMEWHERE... ELSE.
OH GOD.
ROSE TATTOO. THE SPIRIT OF MURDER.

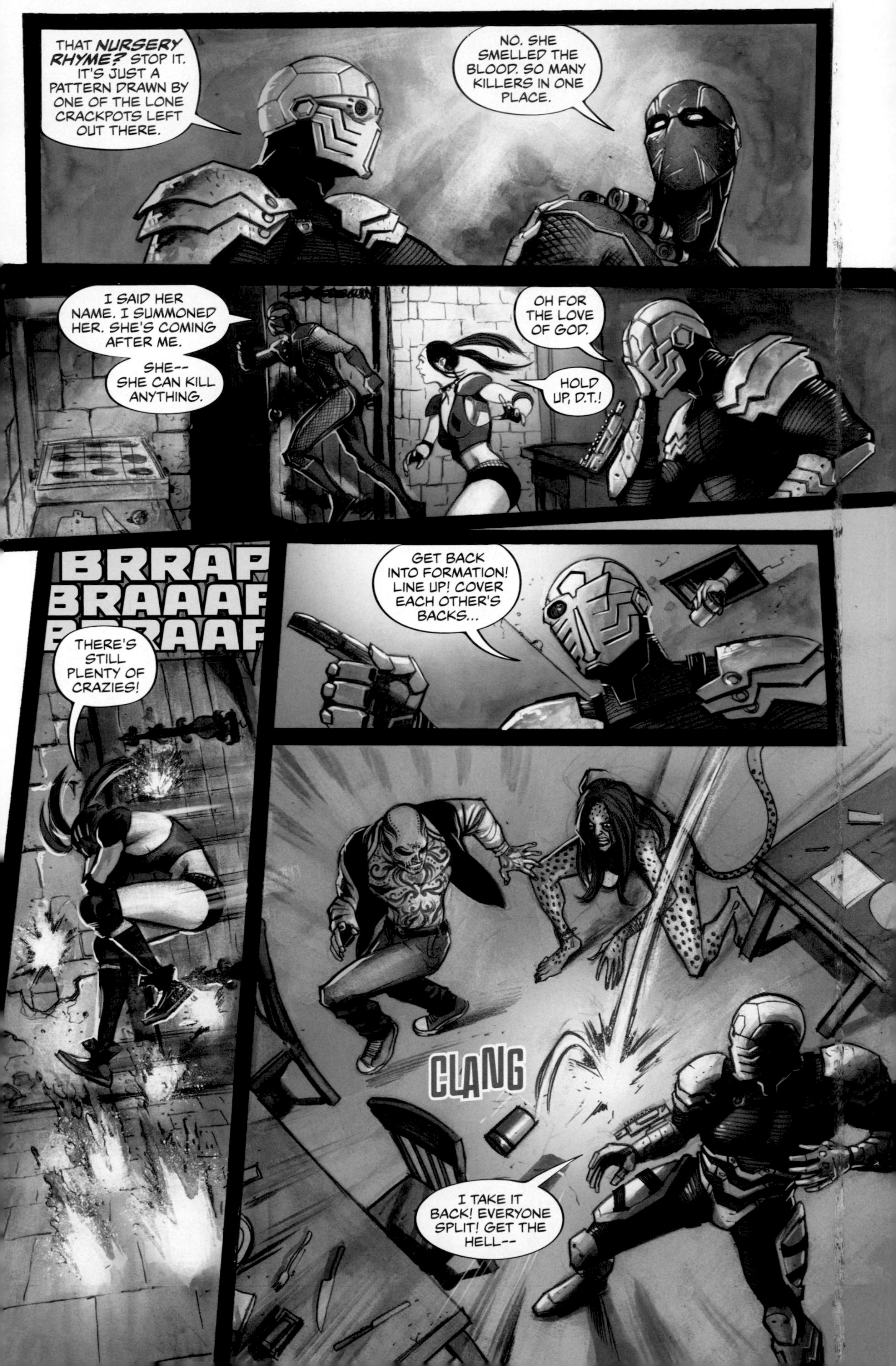
THAT NURSERY RHYME? STOP IT. IT'S JUST A PATTERN DRAWN BY ONE OF THE LONE CRACKPOTS LEFT OUT THERE.
NO. SHE SMELLED THE BLOOD. SO MANY KILLERS IN ONE PLACE.
I SAID HER NAME. I SUMMONED HER. SHE'S COMING AFTER ME.
SHE-- SHE CAN KILL ANYTHING.
OH FOR THE LOVE OF GOD.
HOLD UP, D.T.!
THERE'S STILL PLENTY OF CRAZIES!
GET BACK INTO FORMATION! LINE UP! COVER EACH OTHER'S BACKS...
CLANG
I TAKE IT BACK! EVERYONE SPLIT! GET THE HELL--

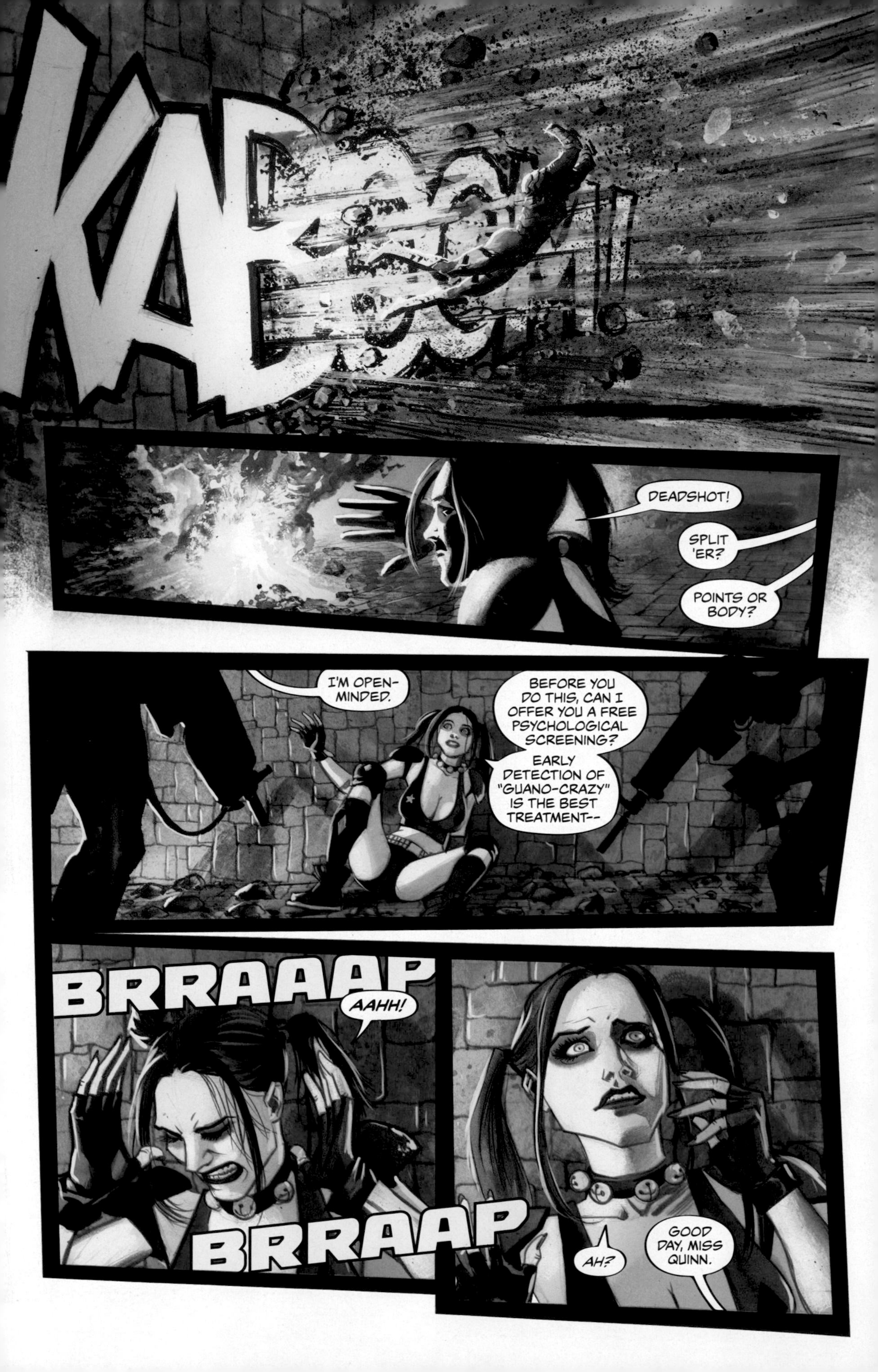
KA-BOOM!
DEADSHOT!
SPLIT 'ER?
POINTS OR BODY?
I'M OPEN-MINDED.
BEFORE YOU DO THIS, CAN I OFFER YOU A FREE PSYCHOLOGICAL SCREENING?
EARLY DETECTION OF "GUANO-CRAZY" IS THE BEST TREATMENT--
BRRAAAP
AAHH!
BRRAAAP
AH?
GOOD DAY, MISS QUINN.

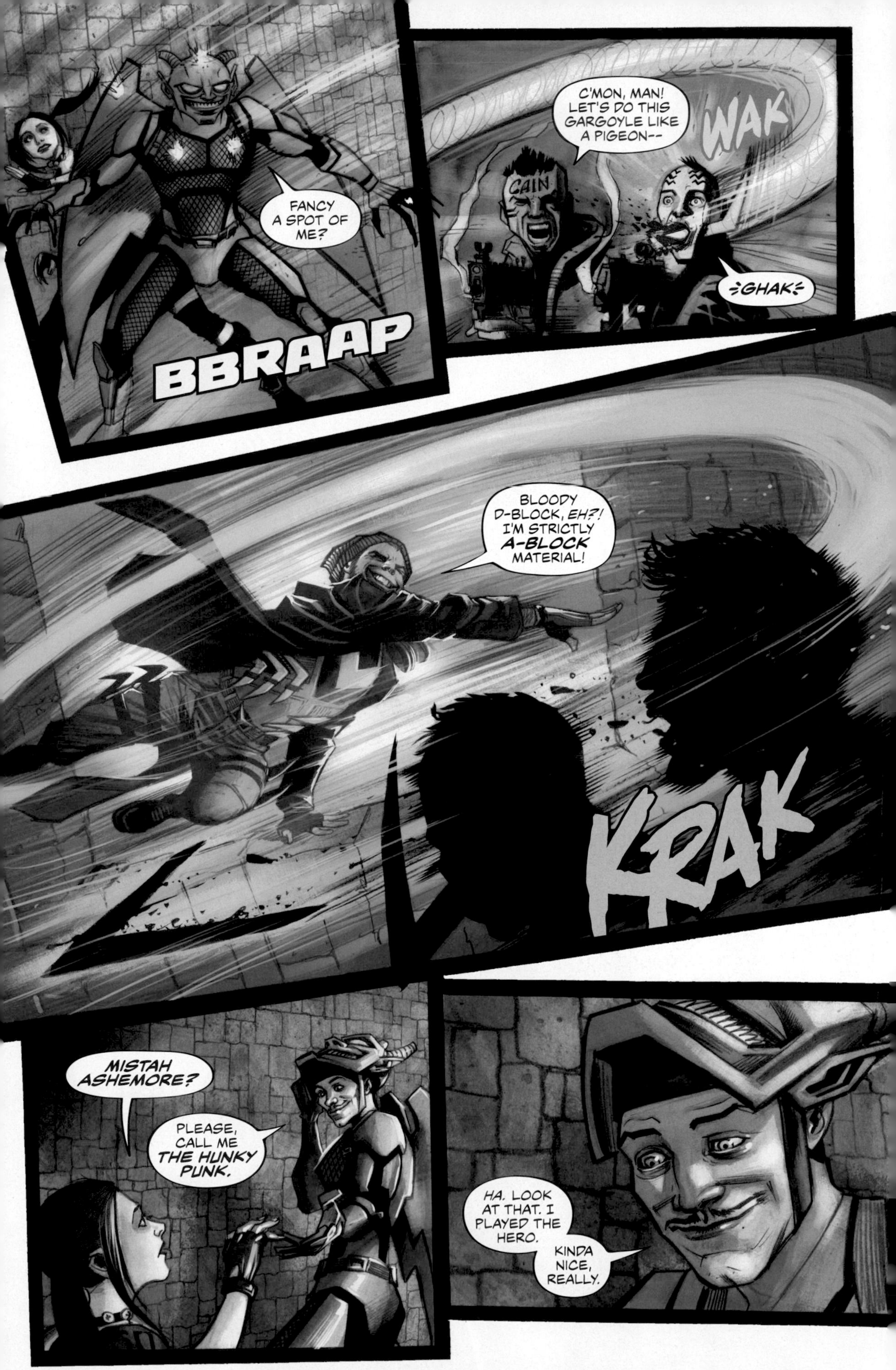
FANCY A SPOT OF ME?
BBRAAP
C'MON, MAN! LET'S DO THIS GARGOYLE LIKE A PIGEON--
WAK
CAIN
GHAK
BLOODY D-BLOCK, *EH?!* I'M STRICTLY ***A-BLOCK*** MATERIAL!
KRAK
MISTAH ASHEMORE?
PLEASE, CALL ME ***THE HUNKY PUNK.***
HA. LOOK AT THAT. I PLAYED THE HERO.
KINDA NICE, REALLY.

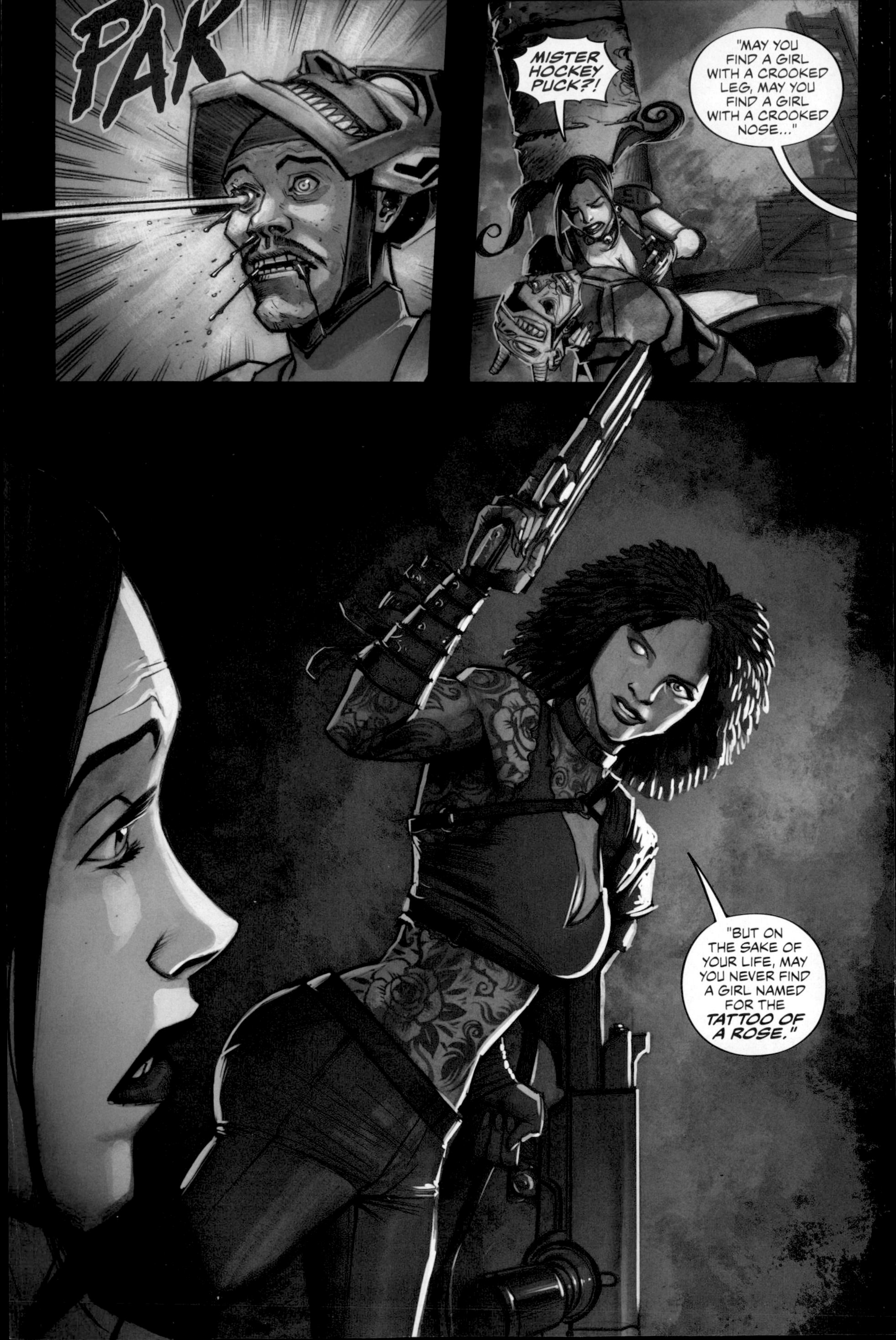
PAK
MISTER HOCKEY PUCK?!
"MAY YOU FIND A GIRL WITH A CROOKED LEG, MAY YOU FIND A GIRL WITH A CROOKED NOSE..."
"BUT ON THE SAKE OF YOUR LIFE, MAY YOU NEVER FIND A GIRL NAMED FOR THE TATTOO OF A ROSE."

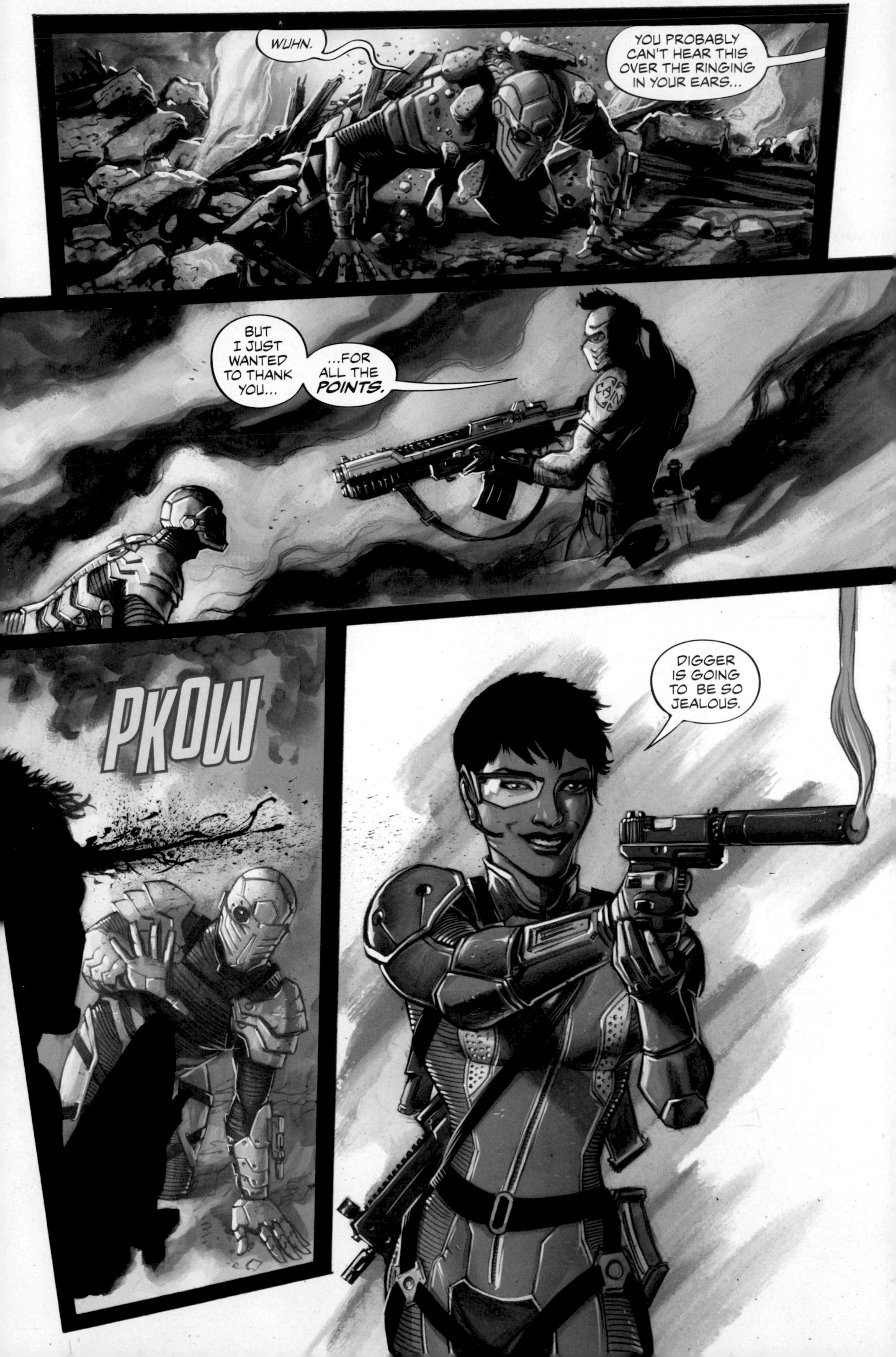
WUHN.
YOU PROBABLY CAN'T HEAR THIS OVER THE RINGING IN YOUR EARS...
BUT I JUST WANTED TO THANK YOU...
...FOR ALL THE POINTS.
PKOW
DIGGER IS GOING TO BE SO JEALOUS.

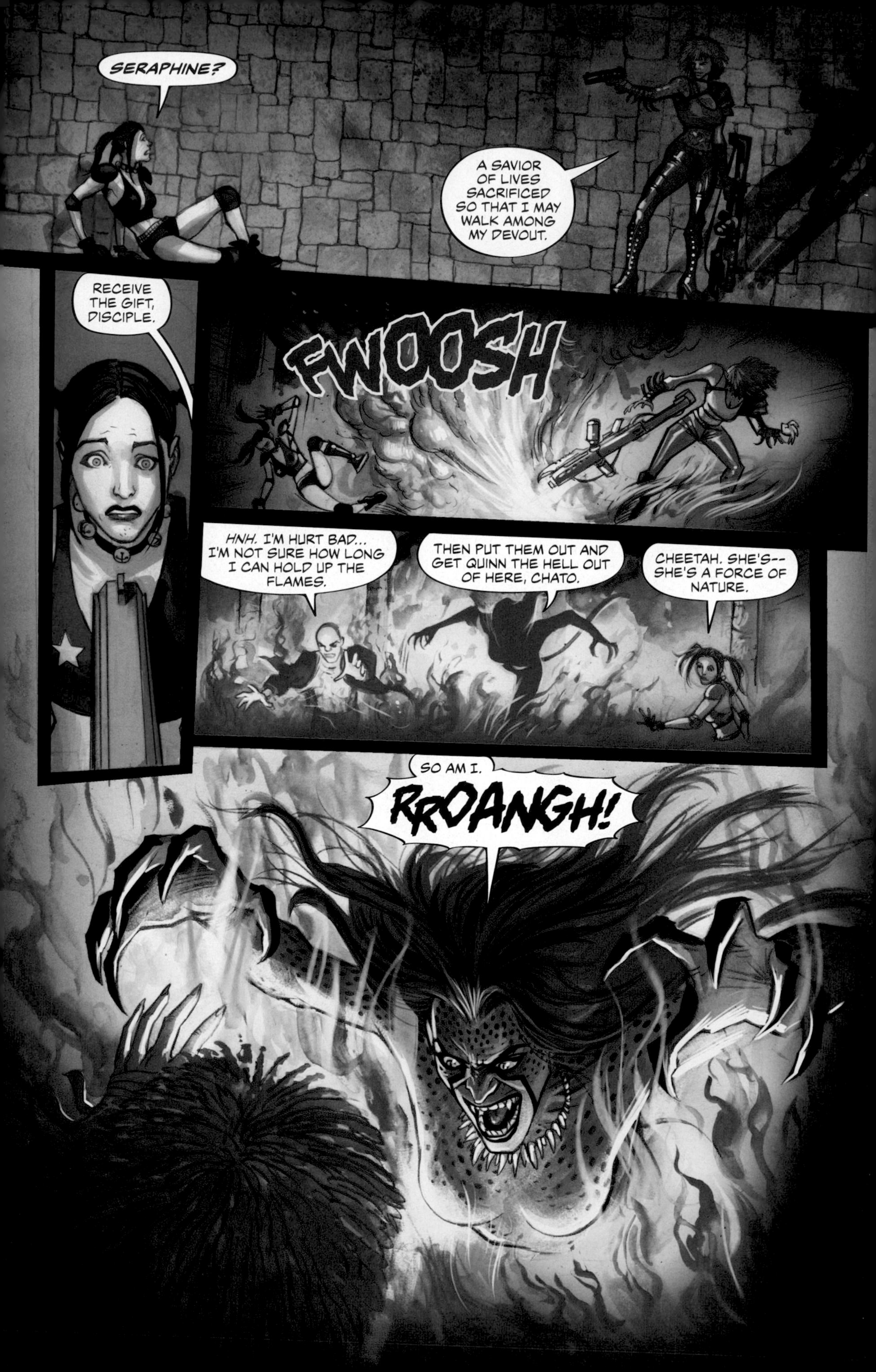
SERAPHINE?
A SAVIOR OF LIVES SACRIFICED SO THAT I MAY WALK AMONG MY DEVOUT.
RECEIVE THE GIFT, DISCIPLE.
FWOOSH
HNH. I'M HURT BAD... I'M NOT SURE HOW LONG I CAN HOLD UP THE FLAMES.
THEN PUT THEM OUT AND GET QUINN THE HELL OUT OF HERE, CHATO.
CHEETAH. SHE'S-- SHE'S A FORCE OF NATURE.
SO AM I.
RROANGH!

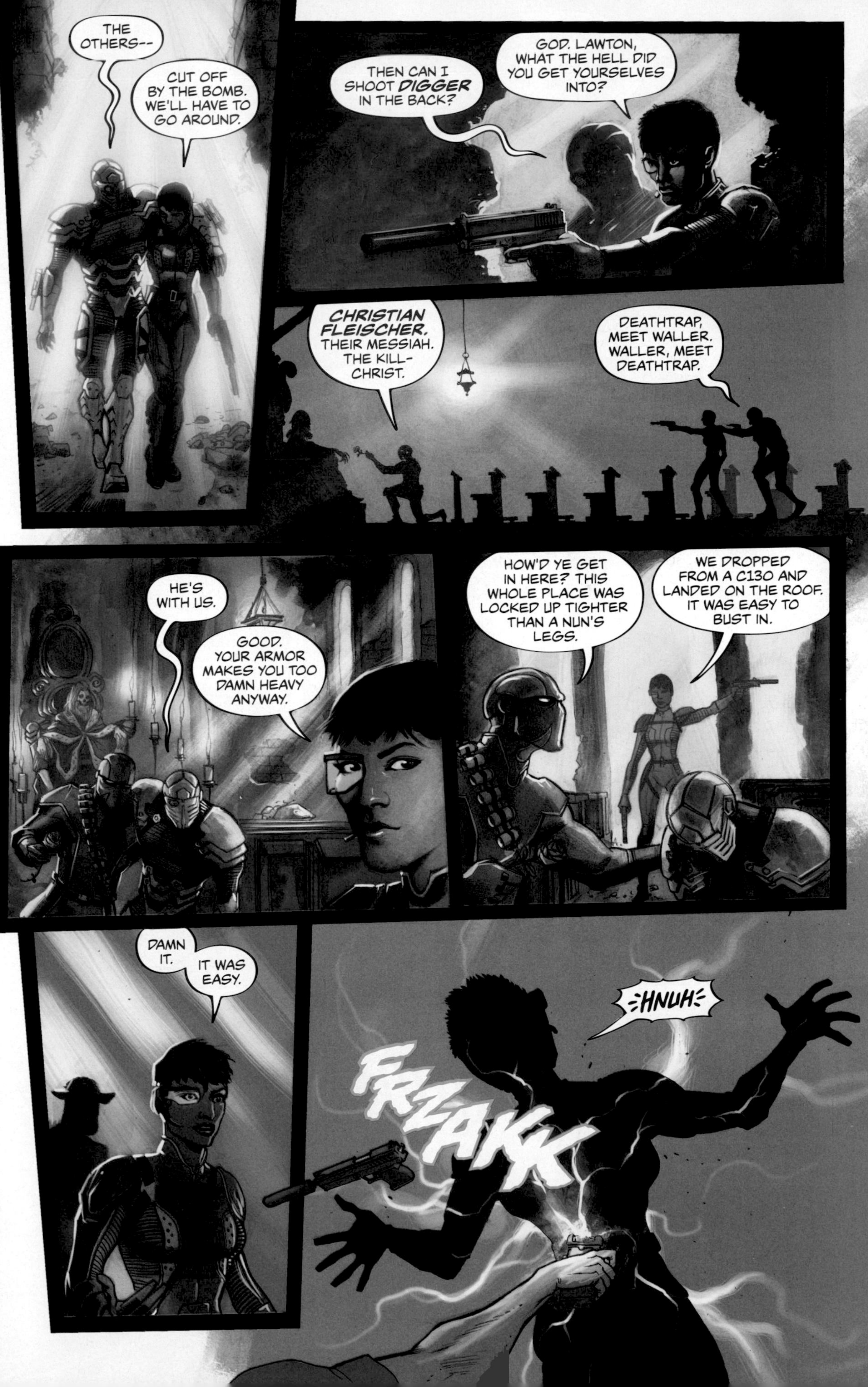
THE OTHERS--
CUT OFF BY THE BOMB. WE'LL HAVE TO GO AROUND.
THEN CAN I SHOOT DIGGER IN THE BACK?
GOD. LAWTON, WHAT THE HELL DID YOU GET YOURSELVES INTO?
CHRISTIAN FLEISCHER. THEIR MESSIAH. THE KILL-CHRIST.
DEATHTRAP, MEET WALLER. WALLER, MEET DEATHTRAP.
HE'S WITH US.
GOOD. YOUR ARMOR MAKES YOU TOO DAMN HEAVY ANYWAY.
HOW'D YE GET IN HERE? THIS WHOLE PLACE WAS LOCKED UP TIGHTER THAN A NUN'S LEGS.
WE DROPPED FROM A C130 AND LANDED ON THE ROOF. IT WAS EASY TO BUST IN.
DAMN IT.
IT WAS EASY.
HNUH
FRZAKK

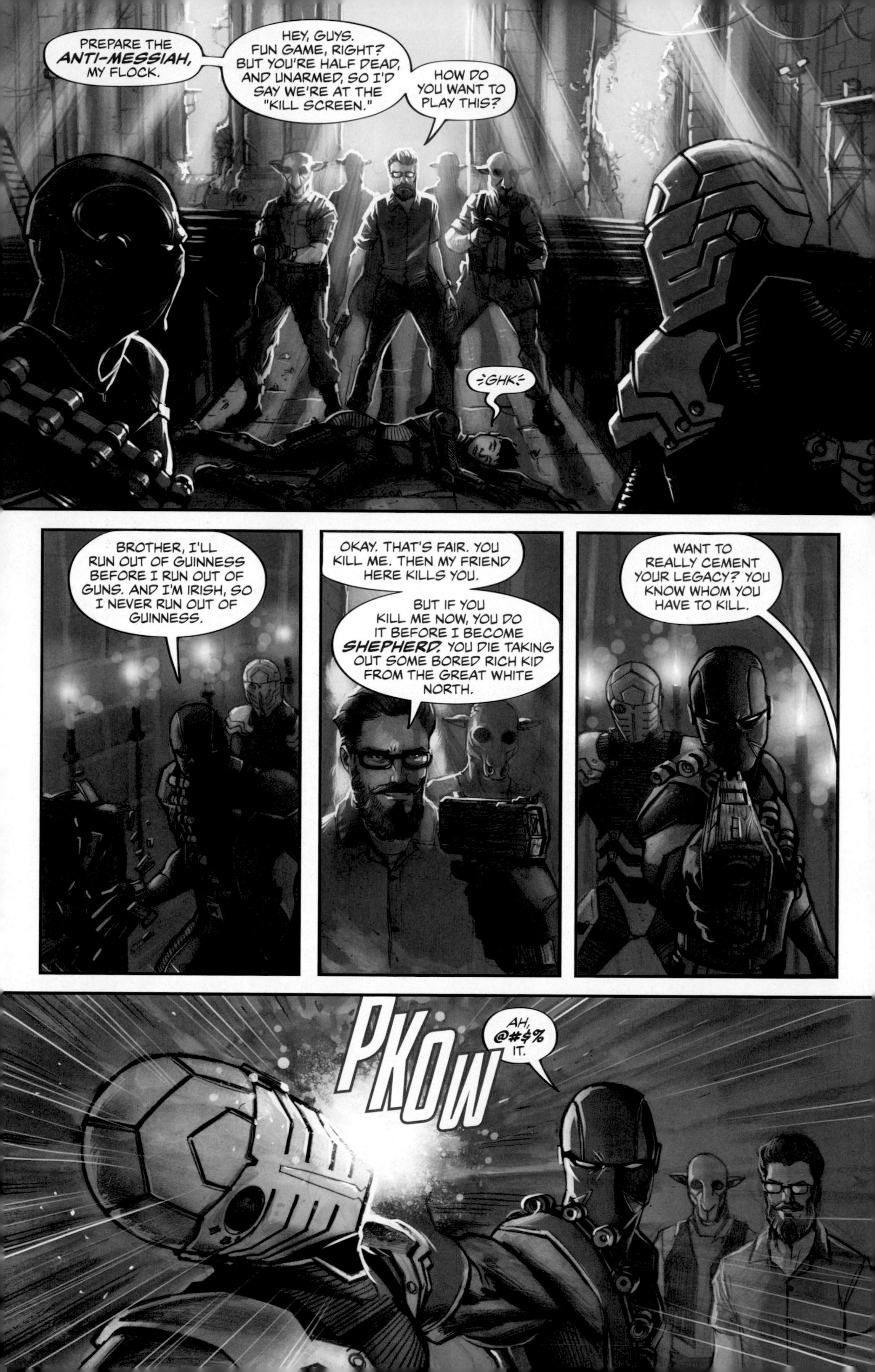
PREPARE THE **ANTI-MESSIAH,** MY FLOCK.
HEY, GUYS. FUN GAME, RIGHT? BUT YOU'RE HALF DEAD, AND UNARMED, SO I'D SAY WE'RE AT THE "KILL SCREEN."
HOW DO YOU WANT TO PLAY THIS?
GHK
BROTHER, I'LL RUN OUT OF GUINNESS BEFORE I RUN OUT OF GUNS. AND I'M IRISH, SO I NEVER RUN OUT OF GUINNESS.
OKAY. THAT'S FAIR. YOU KILL ME. THEN MY FRIEND HERE KILLS YOU.
BUT IF YOU KILL ME NOW, YOU DO IT BEFORE I BECOME **SHEPHERD.** YOU DIE TAKING OUT SOME BORED RICH KID FROM THE GREAT WHITE NORTH.
WANT TO REALLY CEMENT YOUR LEGACY? YOU KNOW WHOM YOU HAVE TO KILL.
PKOW
AH, @#$% IT.

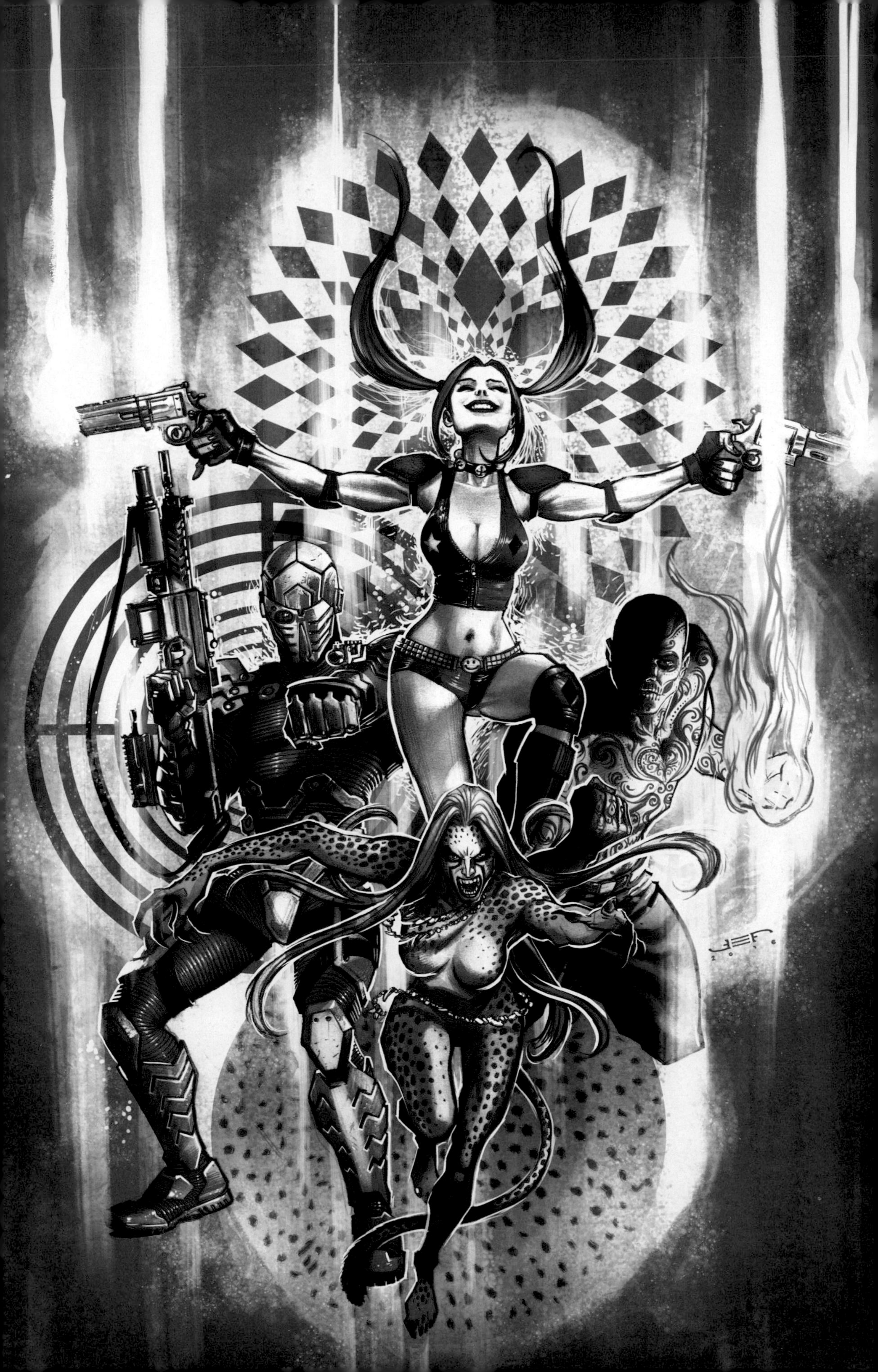

KILL ANYTHING

TIM SEELEY writer GUS VAZQUEZ artist JUAN FERREYRA breakdowns, colorist NATE PIEKOS letterer

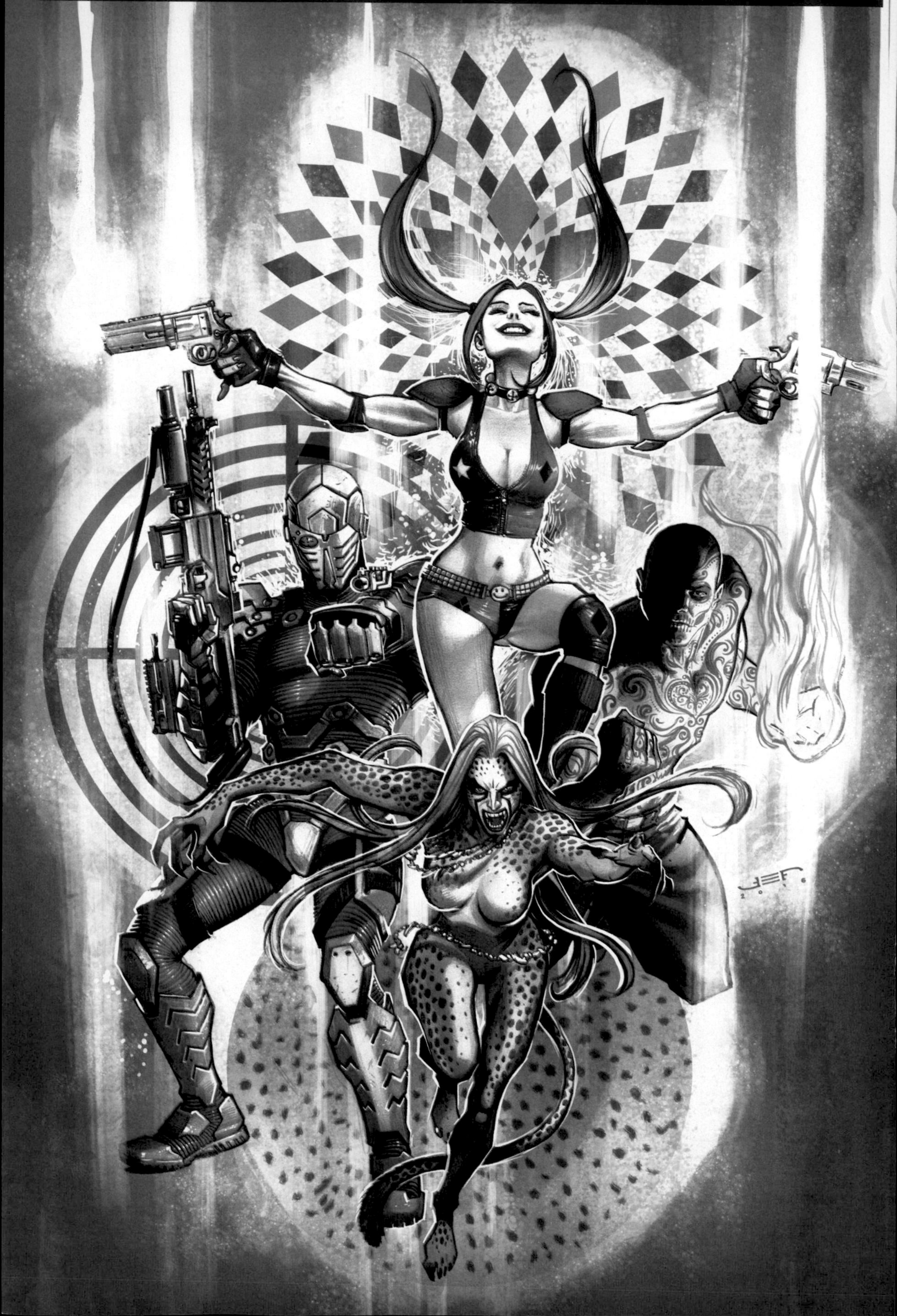

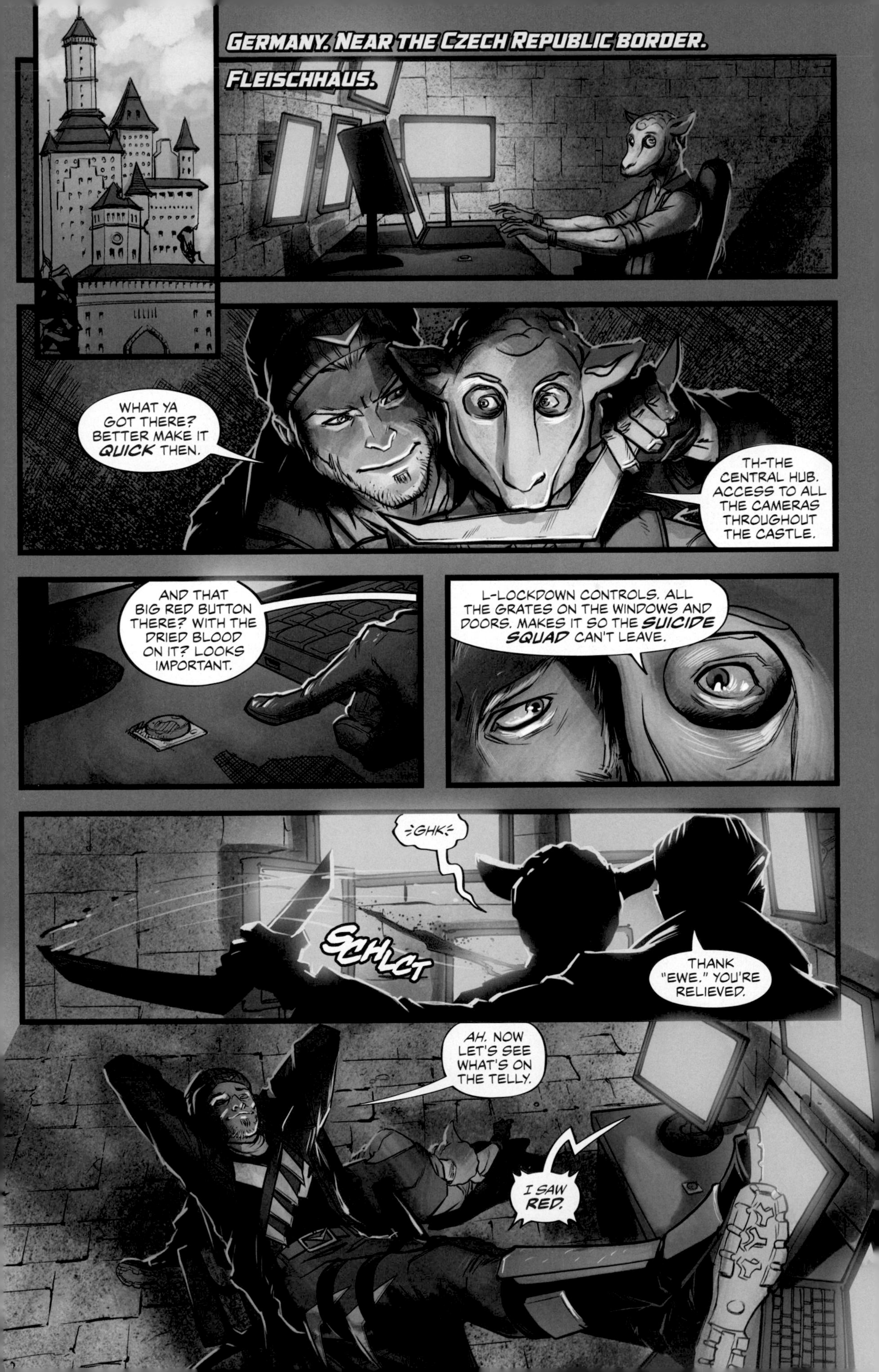
GERMANY. NEAR THE CZECH REPUBLIC BORDER.
FLEISCHHAUS.
WHAT YA GOT THERE? BETTER MAKE IT QUICK THEN.
TH-THE CENTRAL HUB. ACCESS TO ALL THE CAMERAS THROUGHOUT THE CASTLE.
AND THAT BIG RED BUTTON THERE? WITH THE DRIED BLOOD ON IT? LOOKS IMPORTANT.
L-LOCKDOWN CONTROLS. ALL THE GRATES ON THE WINDOWS AND DOORS. MAKES IT SO THE SUICIDE SQUAD CAN'T LEAVE.
GHK
SCHLCT
THANK "EWE." YOU'RE RELIEVED.
AH. NOW LET'S SEE WHAT'S ON THE TELLY.
I SAW RED.

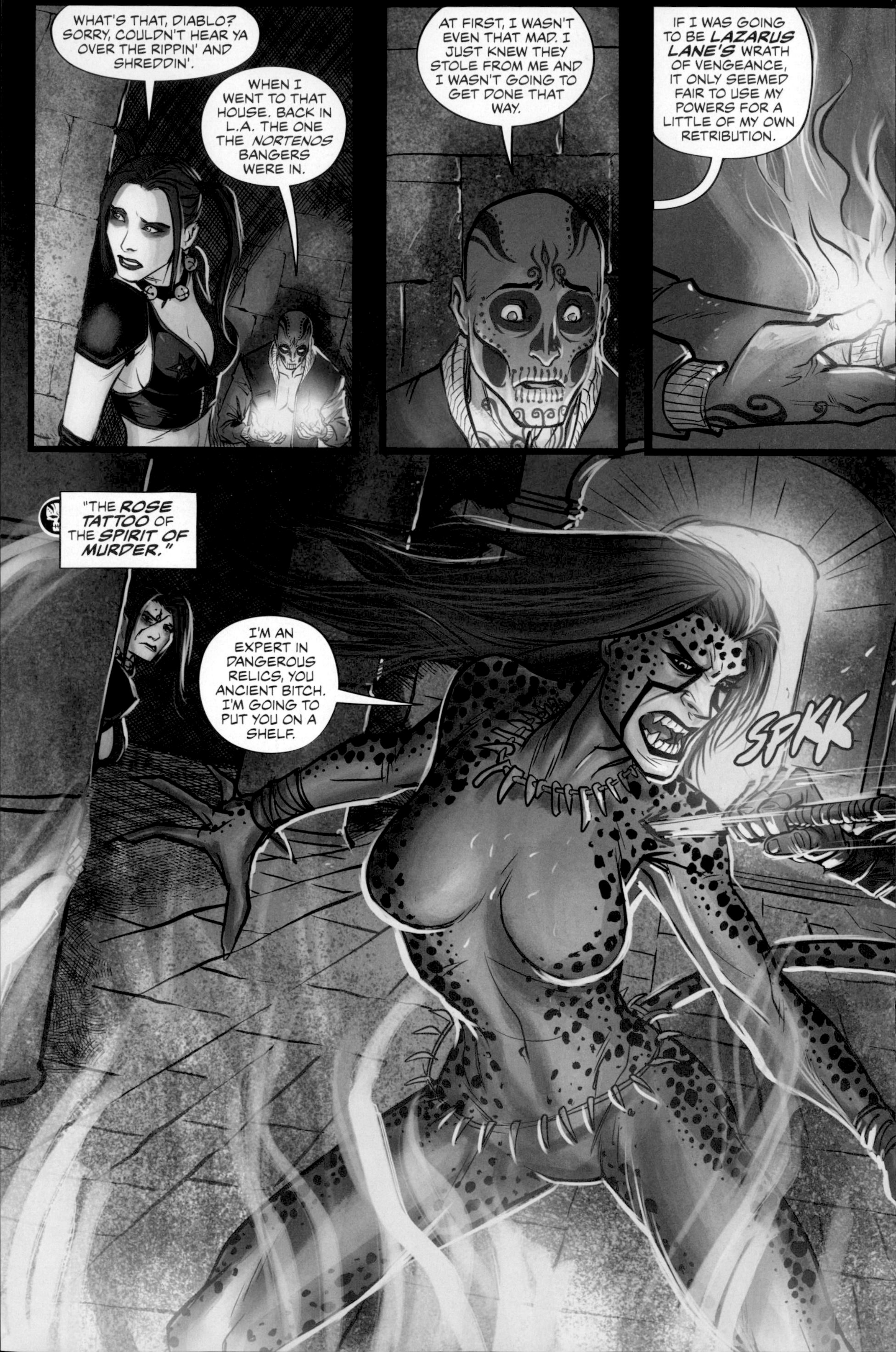
WHAT'S THAT, DIABLO? SORRY, COULDN'T HEAR YA OVER THE RIPPIN' AND SHREDDIN'.
WHEN I WENT TO THAT HOUSE. BACK IN L.A. THE ONE THE NORTENOS BANGERS WERE IN.
AT FIRST, I WASN'T EVEN THAT MAD. I JUST KNEW THEY STOLE FROM ME AND I WASN'T GOING TO GET DONE THAT WAY.
IF I WAS GOING TO BE LAZARUS LANE'S WRATH OF VENGEANCE, IT ONLY SEEMED FAIR TO USE MY POWERS FOR A LITTLE OF MY OWN RETRIBUTION.
"THE ROSE TATTOO OF THE SPIRIT OF MURDER."
I'M AN EXPERT IN DANGEROUS RELICS, YOU ANCIENT BITCH. I'M GOING TO PUT YOU ON A SHELF.
SPKK

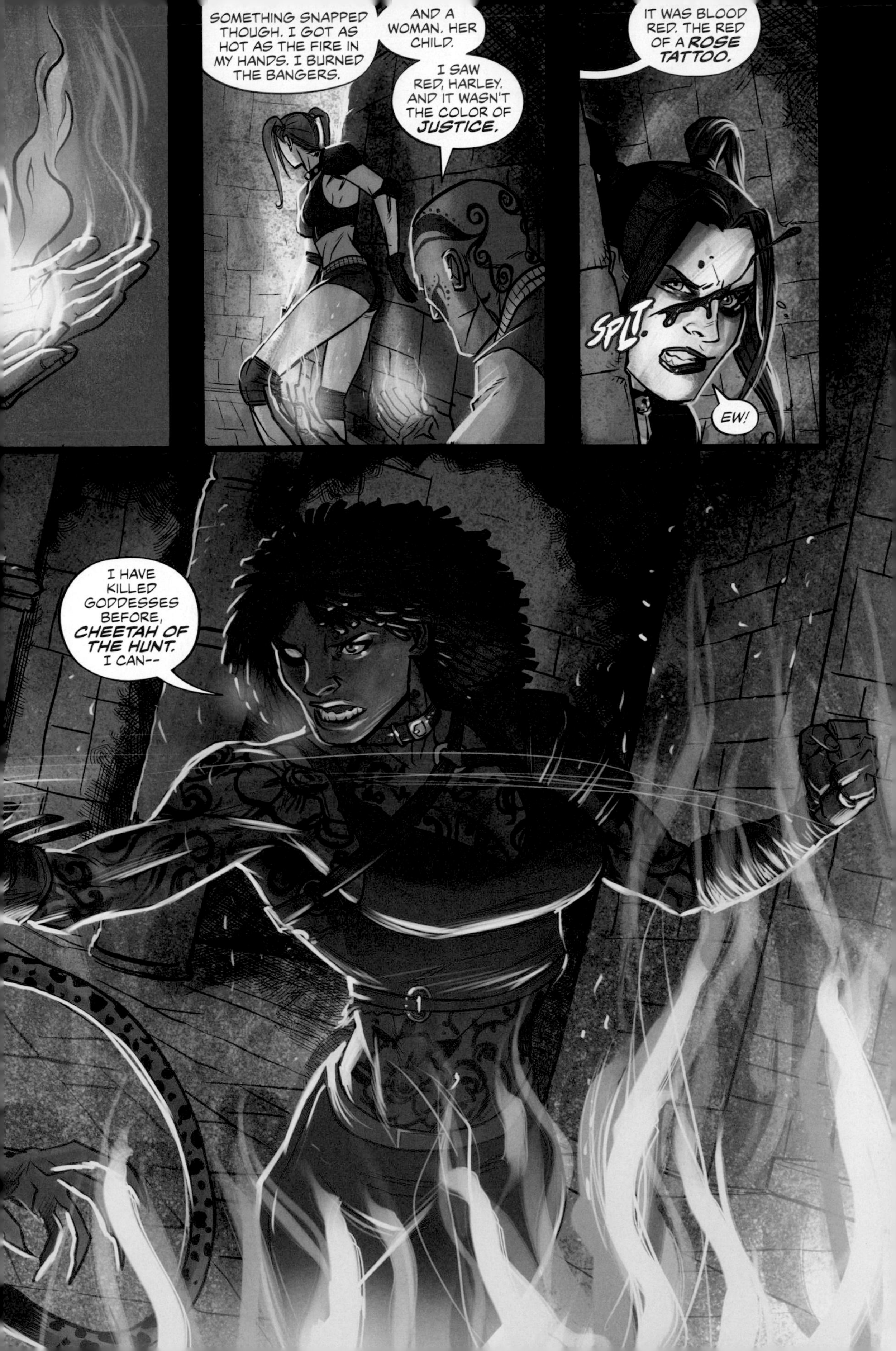
SOMETHING SNAPPED THOUGH. I GOT AS HOT AS THE FIRE IN MY HANDS. I BURNED THE BANGERS.
AND A WOMAN. HER CHILD.
I SAW RED, HARLEY. AND IT WASN'T THE COLOR OF JUSTICE.
IT WAS BLOOD RED. THE RED OF A ROSE TATTOO.
SPLT.
EW!
I HAVE KILLED GODDESSES BEFORE, CHEETAH OF THE HUNT. I CAN--

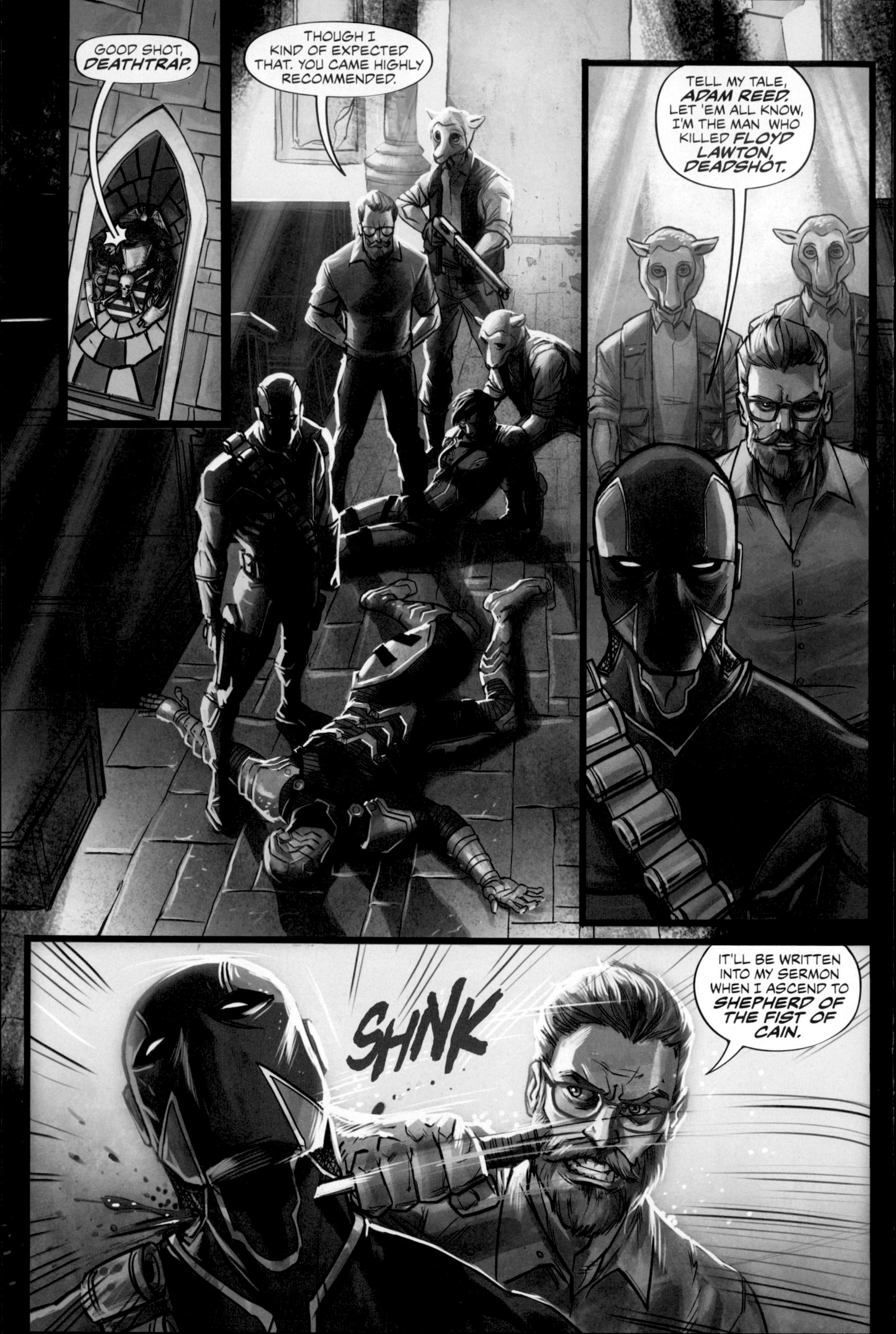

GOOD SHOT, DEATHTRAP.
THOUGH I KIND OF EXPECTED THAT. YOU CAME HIGHLY RECOMMENDED.
TELL MY TALE, ADAM REED. LET 'EM ALL KNOW, I'M THE MAN WHO KILLED FLOYD LAWTON, DEADSHOT.
SHNK
IT'LL BE WRITTEN INTO MY SERMON WHEN I ASCEND TO SHEPHERD OF THE FIST OF CAIN.

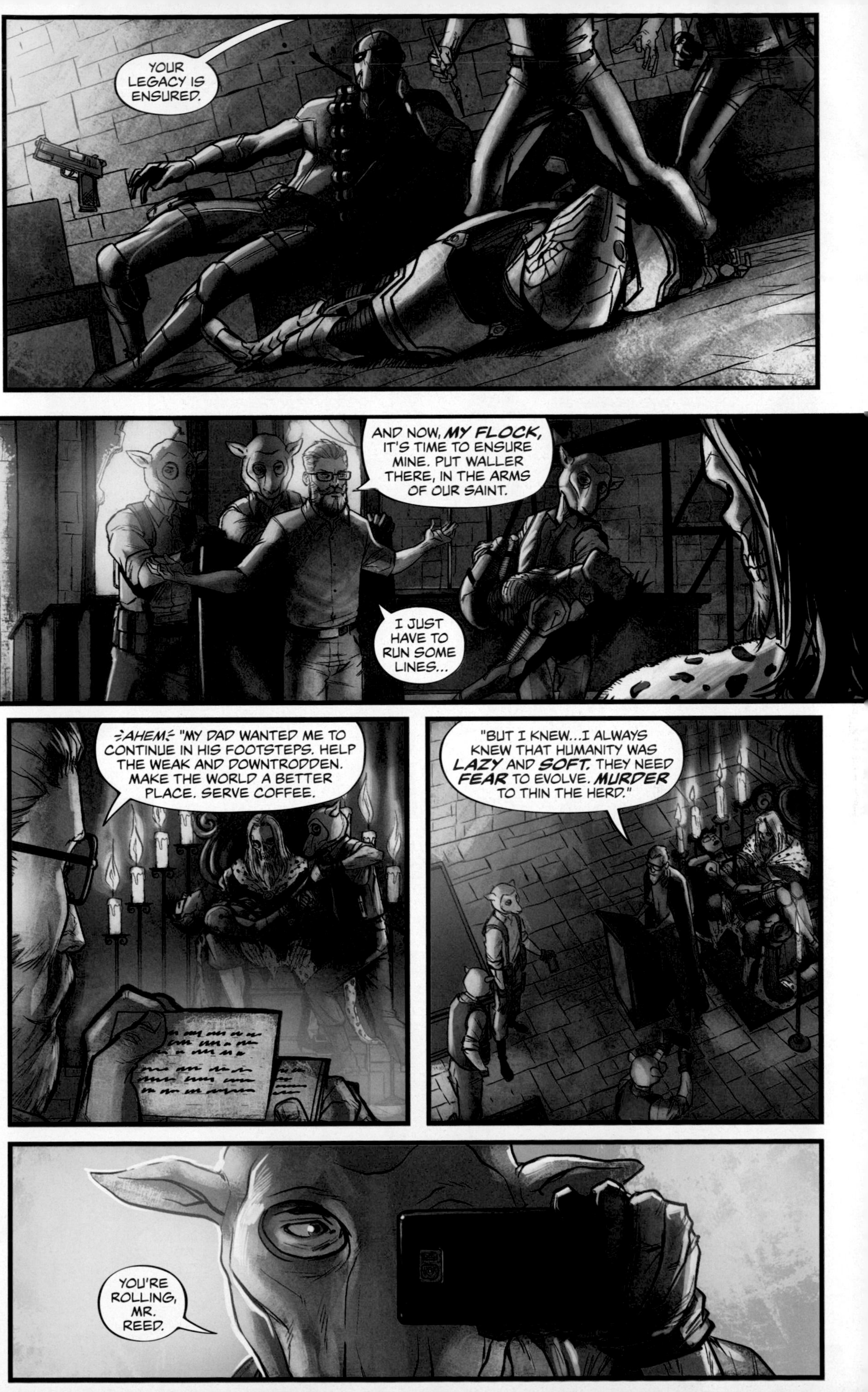
YOUR LEGACY IS ENSURED.
AND NOW, MY FLOCK, IT'S TIME TO ENSURE MINE. PUT WALLER THERE, IN THE ARMS OF OUR SAINT.
I JUST HAVE TO RUN SOME LINES...
-AHEM- "MY DAD WANTED ME TO CONTINUE IN HIS FOOTSTEPS. HELP THE WEAK AND DOWNTRODDEN. MAKE THE WORLD A BETTER PLACE. SERVE COFFEE.
"BUT I KNEW...I ALWAYS KNEW THAT HUMANITY WAS LAZY AND SOFT. THEY NEED FEAR TO EVOLVE. MURDER TO THIN THE HERD."
YOU'RE ROLLING, MR. REED.

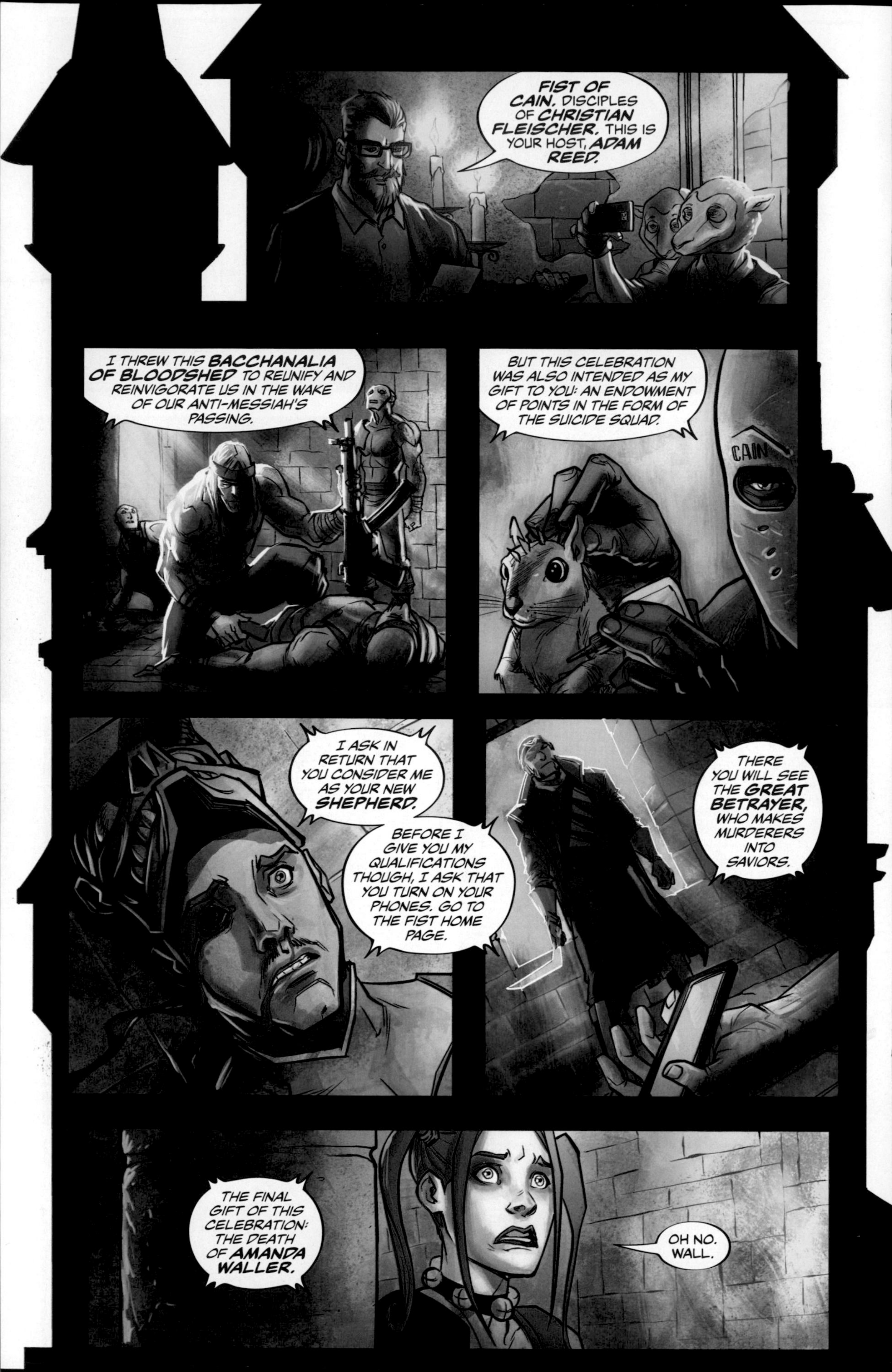
FIST OF CAIN. DISCIPLES OF CHRISTIAN FLEISCHER. THIS IS YOUR HOST, ADAM REED.
I THREW THIS BACCHANALIA OF BLOODSHED TO REUNIFY AND REINVIGORATE US IN THE WAKE OF OUR ANTI-MESSIAH'S PASSING.
BUT THIS CELEBRATION WAS ALSO INTENDED AS MY GIFT TO YOU: AN ENDOWMENT OF POINTS IN THE FORM OF THE SUICIDE SQUAD.
CAIN
I ASK IN RETURN THAT YOU CONSIDER ME AS YOUR NEW SHEPHERD.
BEFORE I GIVE YOU MY QUALIFICATIONS THOUGH, I ASK THAT YOU TURN ON YOUR PHONES. GO TO THE FIST HOME PAGE.
THERE YOU WILL SEE THE GREAT BETRAYER, WHO MAKES MURDERERS INTO SAVIORS.
THE FINAL GIFT OF THIS CELEBRATION: THE DEATH OF AMANDA WALLER.
OH NO. WALL.

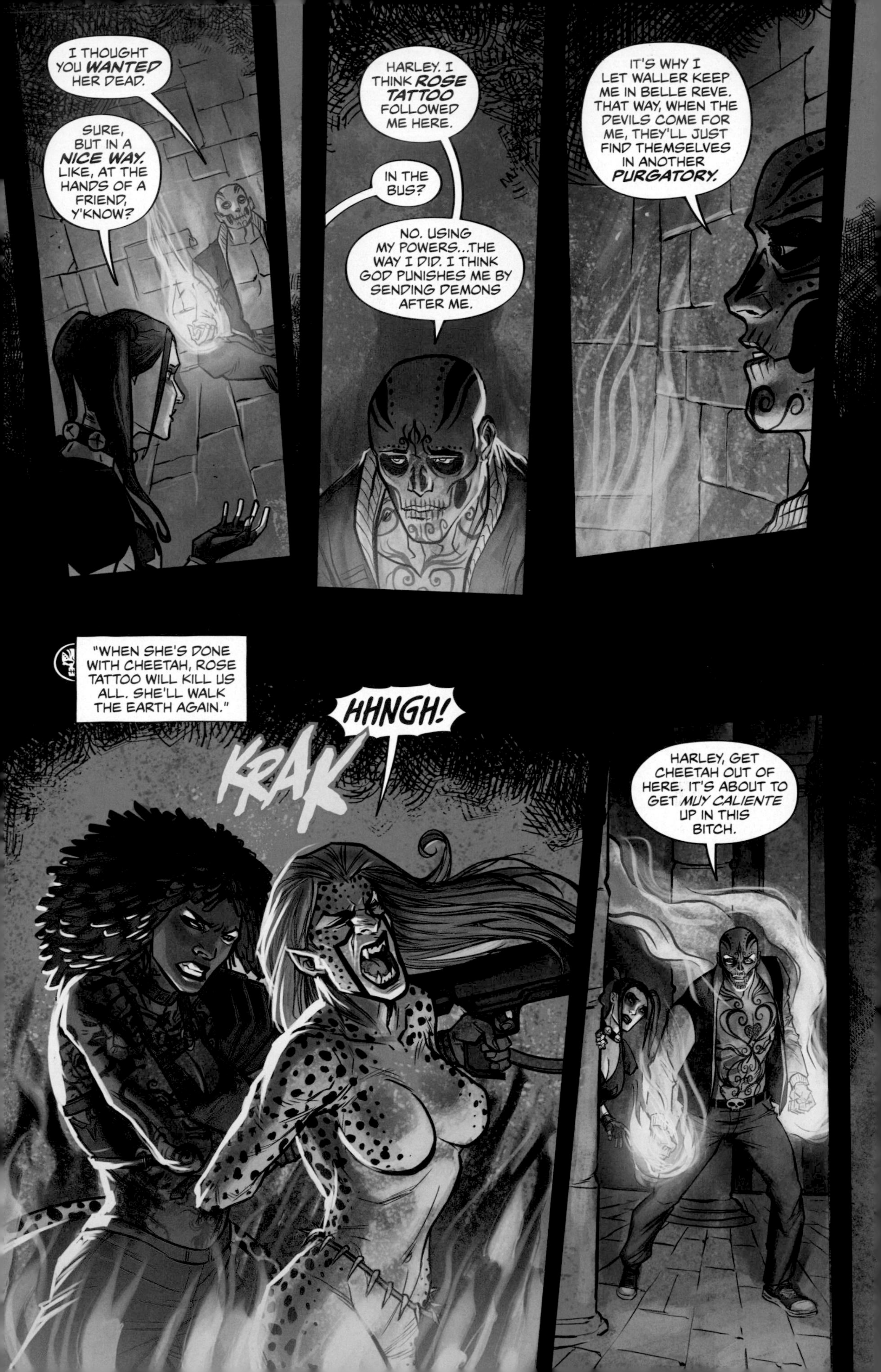

I THOUGHT YOU WANTED HER DEAD.
SURE, BUT IN A NICE WAY. LIKE, AT THE HANDS OF A FRIEND, Y'KNOW?
HARLEY. I THINK ROSE TATTOO FOLLOWED ME HERE.
IN THE BUS?
NO. USING MY POWERS...THE WAY I DID. I THINK GOD PUNISHES ME BY SENDING DEMONS AFTER ME.
IT'S WHY I LET WALLER KEEP ME IN BELLE REVE. THAT WAY, WHEN THE DEVILS COME FOR ME, THEY'LL JUST FIND THEMSELVES IN ANOTHER PURGATORY.
"WHEN SHE'S DONE WITH CHEETAH, ROSE TATTOO WILL KILL US ALL. SHE'LL WALK THE EARTH AGAIN."
HHNGH!
KRAK
HARLEY, GET CHEETAH OUT OF HERE. IT'S ABOUT TO GET MUY CALIENTE UP IN THIS BITCH.

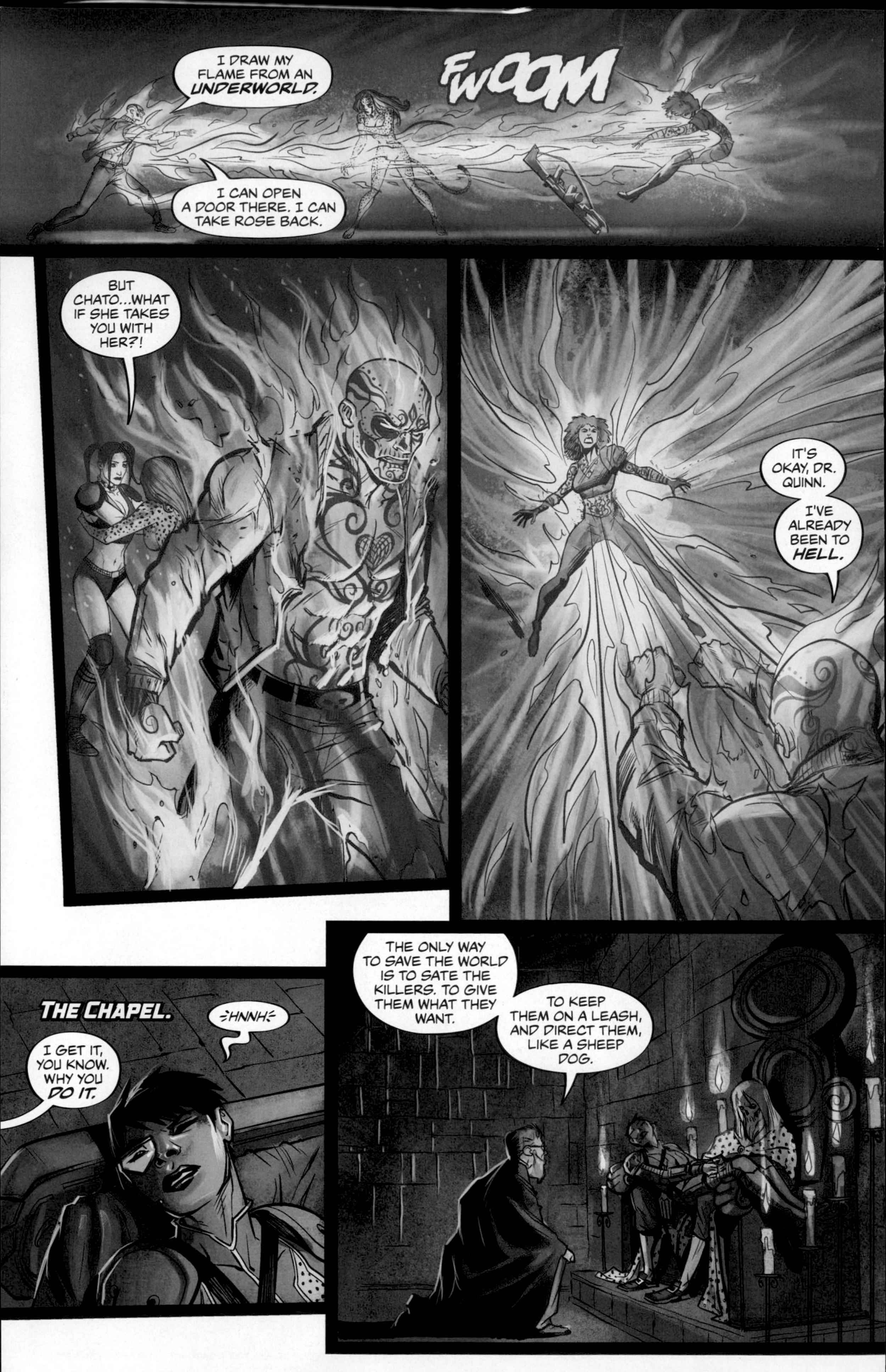
I DRAW MY FLAME FROM AN UNDERWORLD.
FWOOM
I CAN OPEN A DOOR THERE. I CAN TAKE ROSE BACK.
BUT CHATO...WHAT IF SHE TAKES YOU WITH HER?!
IT'S OKAY, DR. QUINN.
I'VE ALREADY BEEN TO HELL.
THE CHAPEL.
I GET IT, YOU KNOW. WHY YOU DO IT.
HNNH
THE ONLY WAY TO SAVE THE WORLD IS TO SATE THE KILLERS. TO GIVE THEM WHAT THEY WANT.
TO KEEP THEM ON A LEASH, AND DIRECT THEM, LIKE A SHEEP DOG.

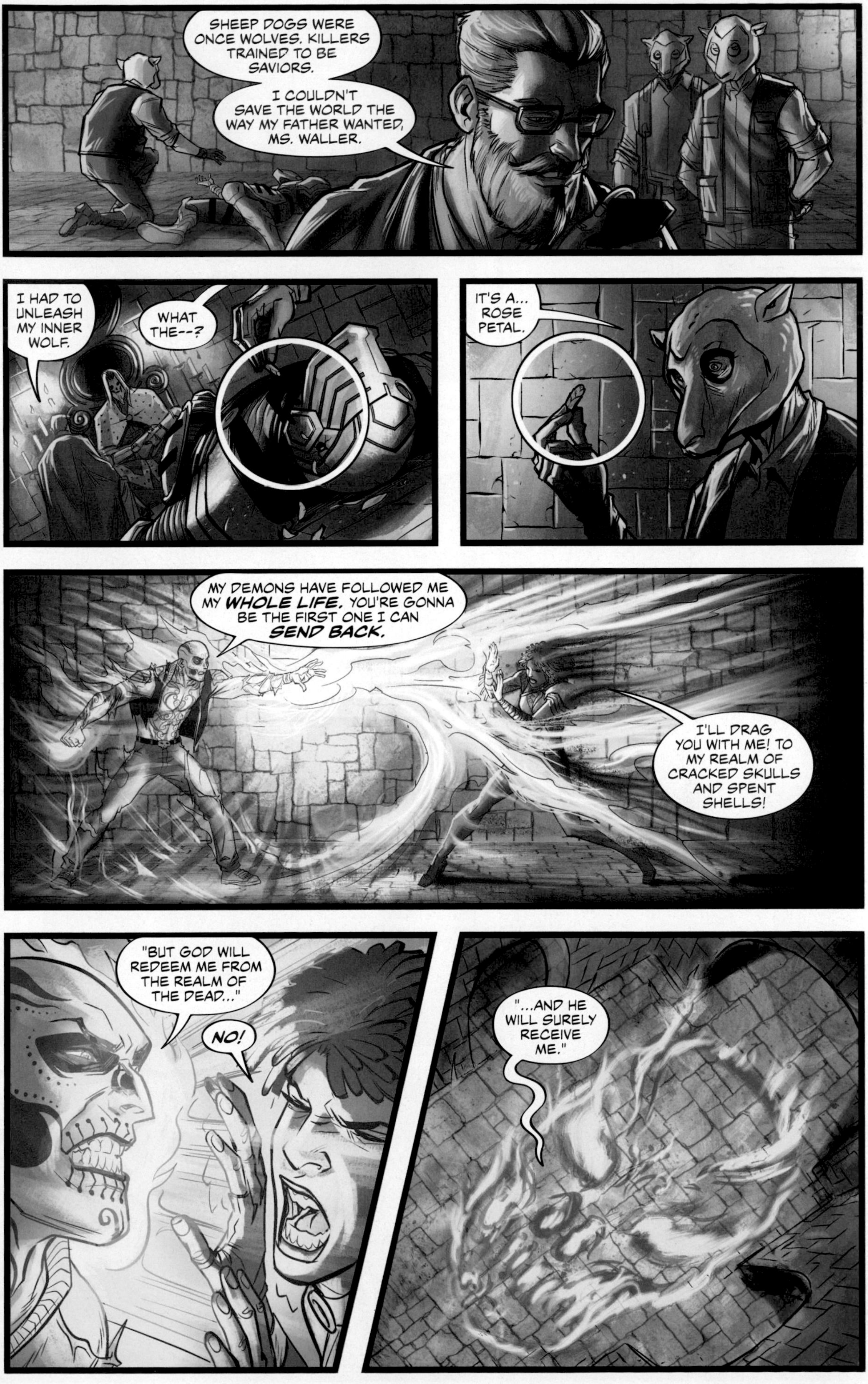
SHEEP DOGS WERE ONCE WOLVES. KILLERS TRAINED TO BE SAVIORS.
I COULDN'T SAVE THE WORLD THE WAY MY FATHER WANTED, MS. WALLER.
I HAD TO UNLEASH MY INNER WOLF.
WHAT THE--?
IT'S A... ROSE PETAL.
MY DEMONS HAVE FOLLOWED ME MY WHOLE LIFE. YOU'RE GONNA BE THE FIRST ONE I CAN SEND BACK.
I'LL DRAG YOU WITH ME! TO MY REALM OF CRACKED SKULLS AND SPENT SHELLS!
"BUT GOD WILL REDEEM ME FROM THE REALM OF THE DEAD..."
NO!
"...AND HE WILL SURELY RECEIVE ME."

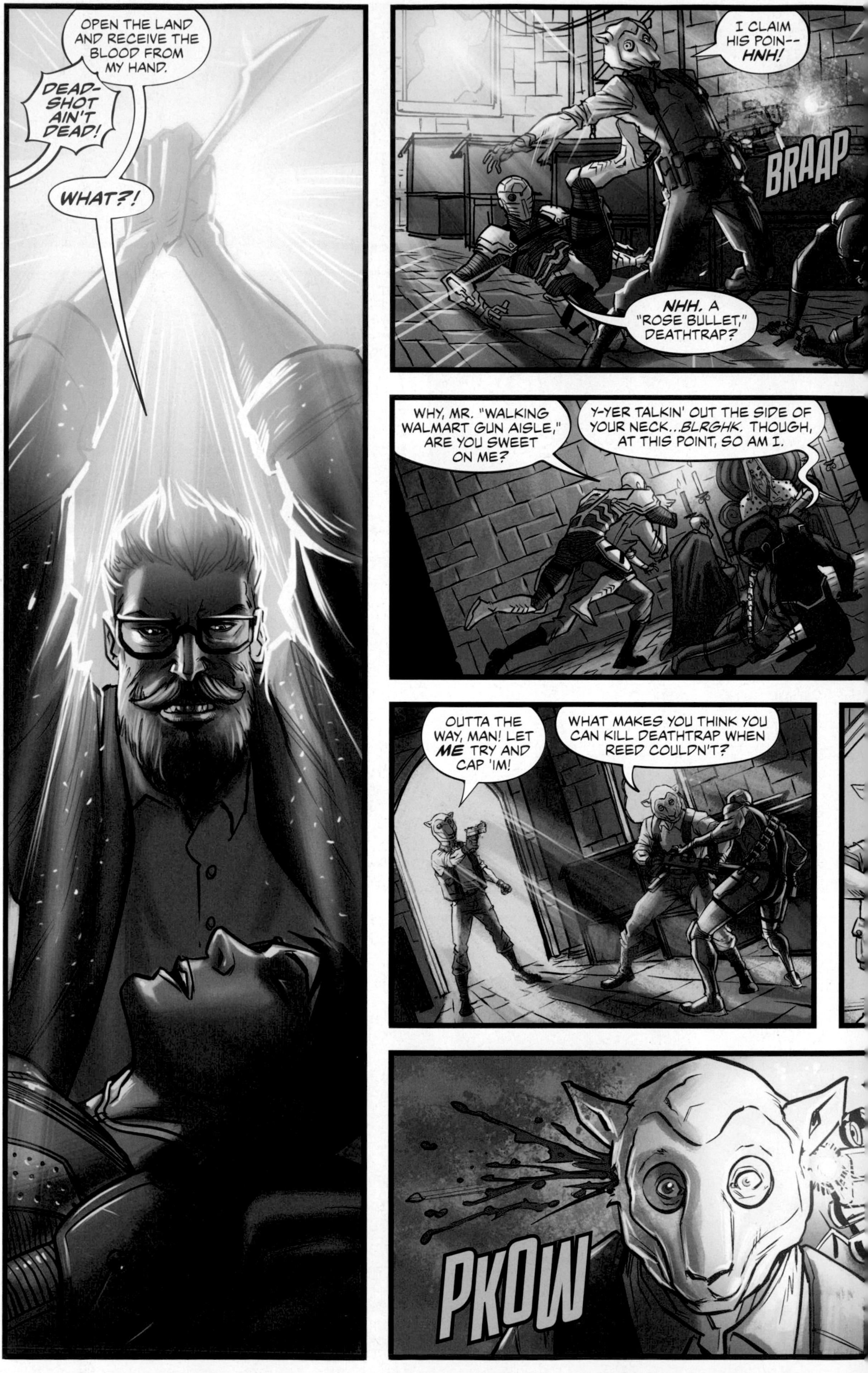
OPEN THE LAND AND RECEIVE THE BLOOD FROM MY HAND.
DEAD-SHOT AIN'T DEAD!
WHAT?!
I CLAIM HIS POIN-- HNH!
BRAAP
NHH. A "ROSE BULLET," DEATHTRAP?
WHY, MR. "WALKING WALMART GUN AISLE," ARE YOU SWEET ON ME?
Y-YER TALKIN' OUT THE SIDE OF YOUR NECK...BLRGHK. THOUGH, AT THIS POINT, SO AM I.
OUTTA THE WAY, MAN! LET ME TRY AND CAP 'IM!
WHAT MAKES YOU THINK YOU CAN KILL DEATHTRAP WHEN REED COULDN'T?
PKOW

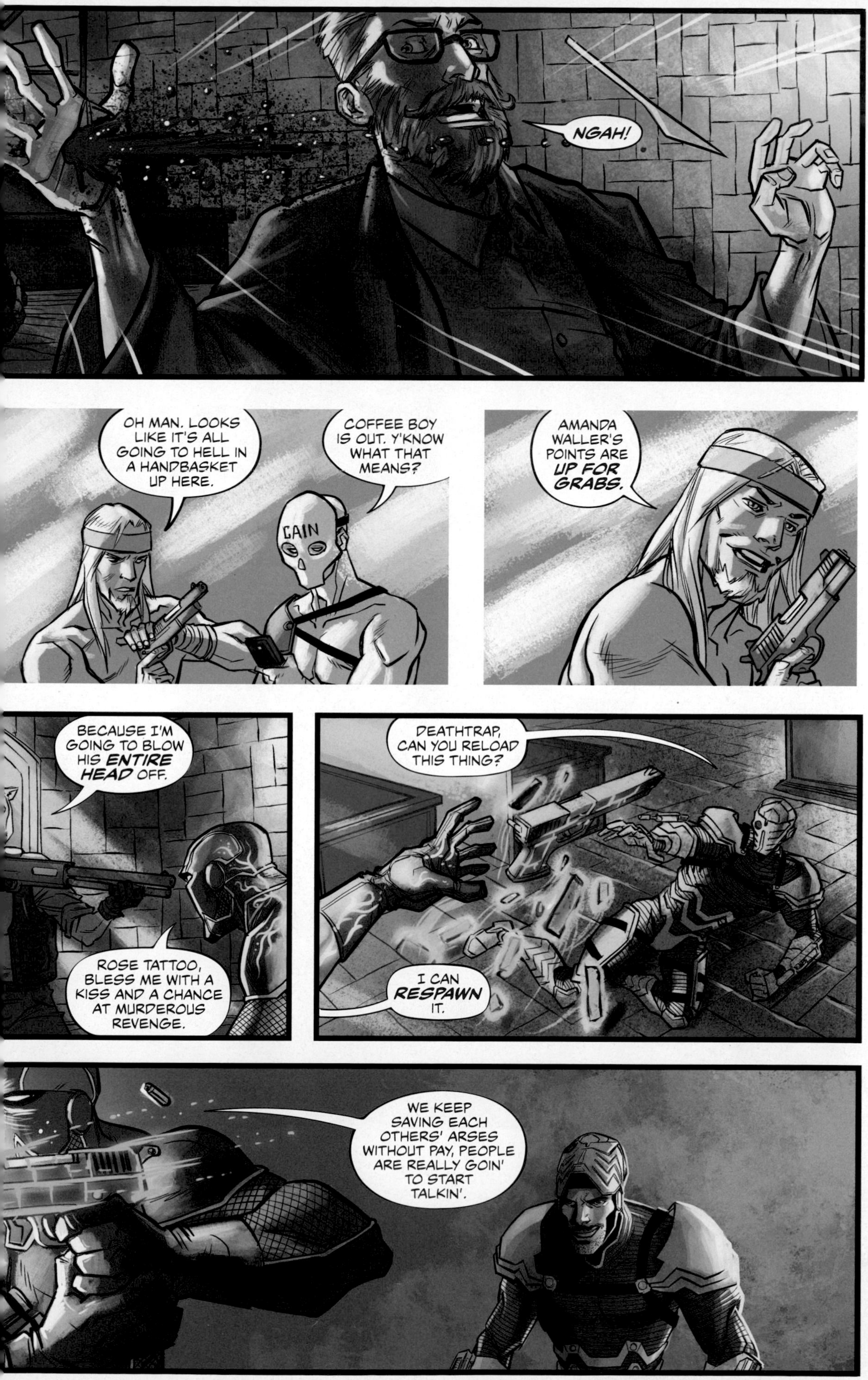
NGAH!
OH MAN. LOOKS LIKE IT'S ALL GOING TO HELL IN A HANDBASKET UP HERE.
CAIN
COFFEE BOY IS OUT. Y'KNOW WHAT THAT MEANS?
AMANDA WALLER'S POINTS ARE UP FOR GRABS.
BECAUSE I'M GOING TO BLOW HIS ENTIRE HEAD OFF.
ROSE TATTOO, BLESS ME WITH A KISS AND A CHANCE AT MURDEROUS REVENGE.
DEATHTRAP, CAN YOU RELOAD THIS THING?
I CAN RESPAWN IT.
WE KEEP SAVING EACH OTHERS' ARSES WITHOUT PAY, PEOPLE ARE REALLY GOIN' TO START TALKIN'.

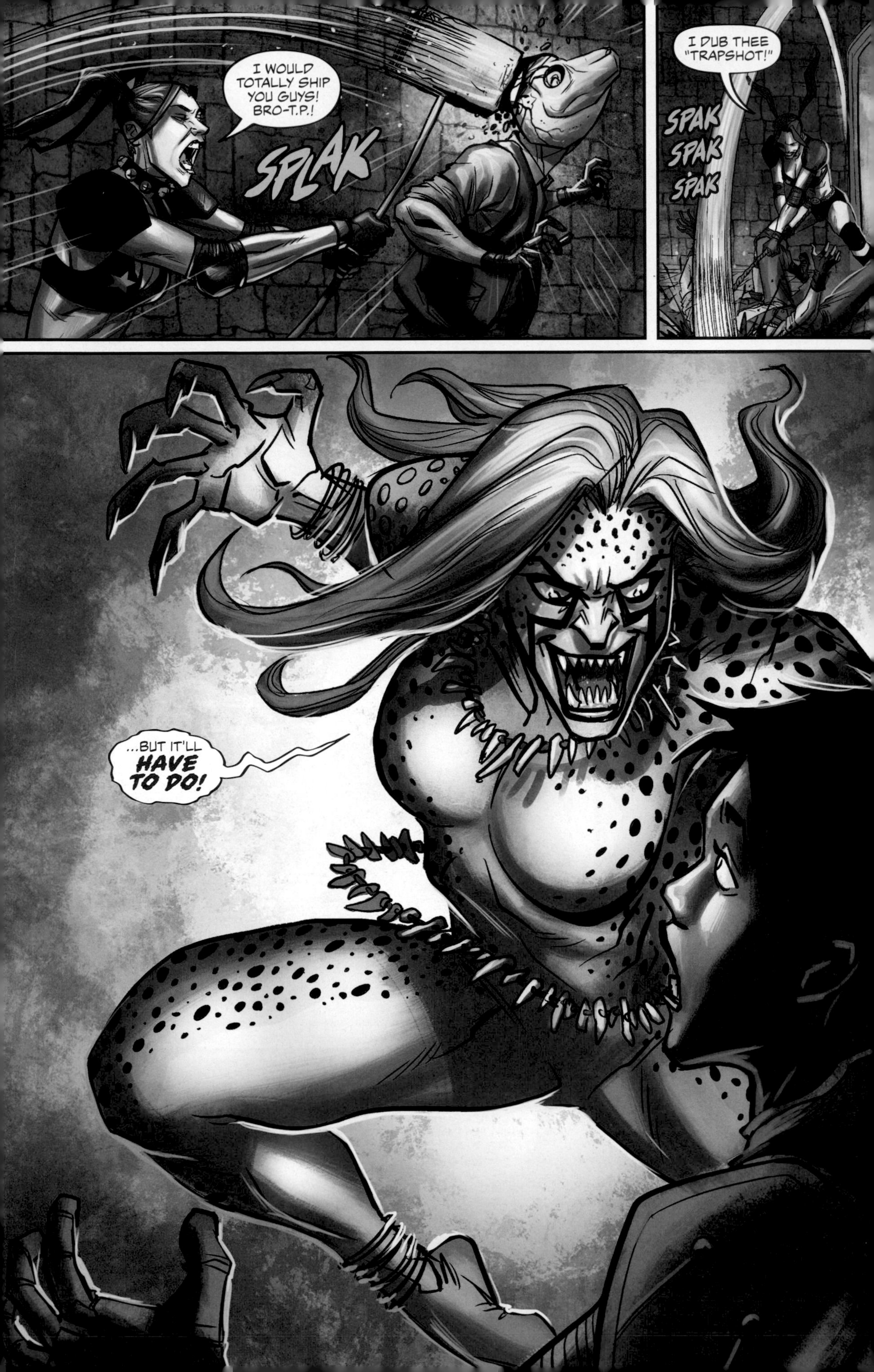
I WOULD TOTALLY SHIP YOU GUYS! BRO-T.P.!
SPLAK
I DUB THEE "TRAPSHOT!"
SPAK
SPAK
SPAK
...BUT IT'LL HAVE TO DO!

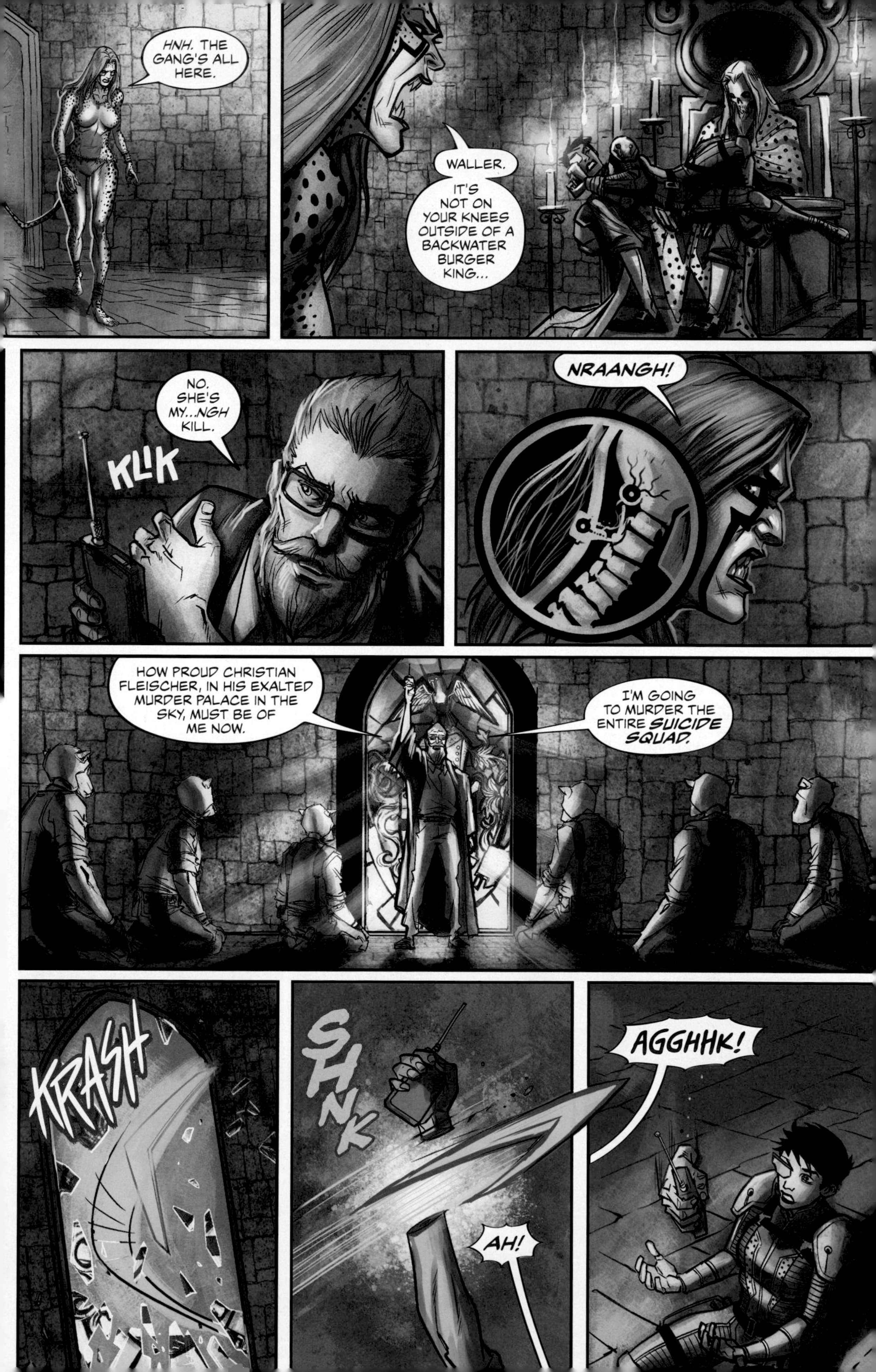
HNH. THE GANG'S ALL HERE.
WALLER.
IT'S NOT ON YOUR KNEES OUTSIDE OF A BACKWATER BURGER KING...
NO. SHE'S MY...NGH KILL.
KLIK
NRAANGH!
HOW PROUD CHRISTIAN FLEISCHER, IN HIS EXALTED MURDER PALACE IN THE SKY, MUST BE OF ME NOW.
I'M GOING TO MURDER THE ENTIRE SUICIDE SQUAD.
KRASH
SHNK
AH!
AGGHHK!

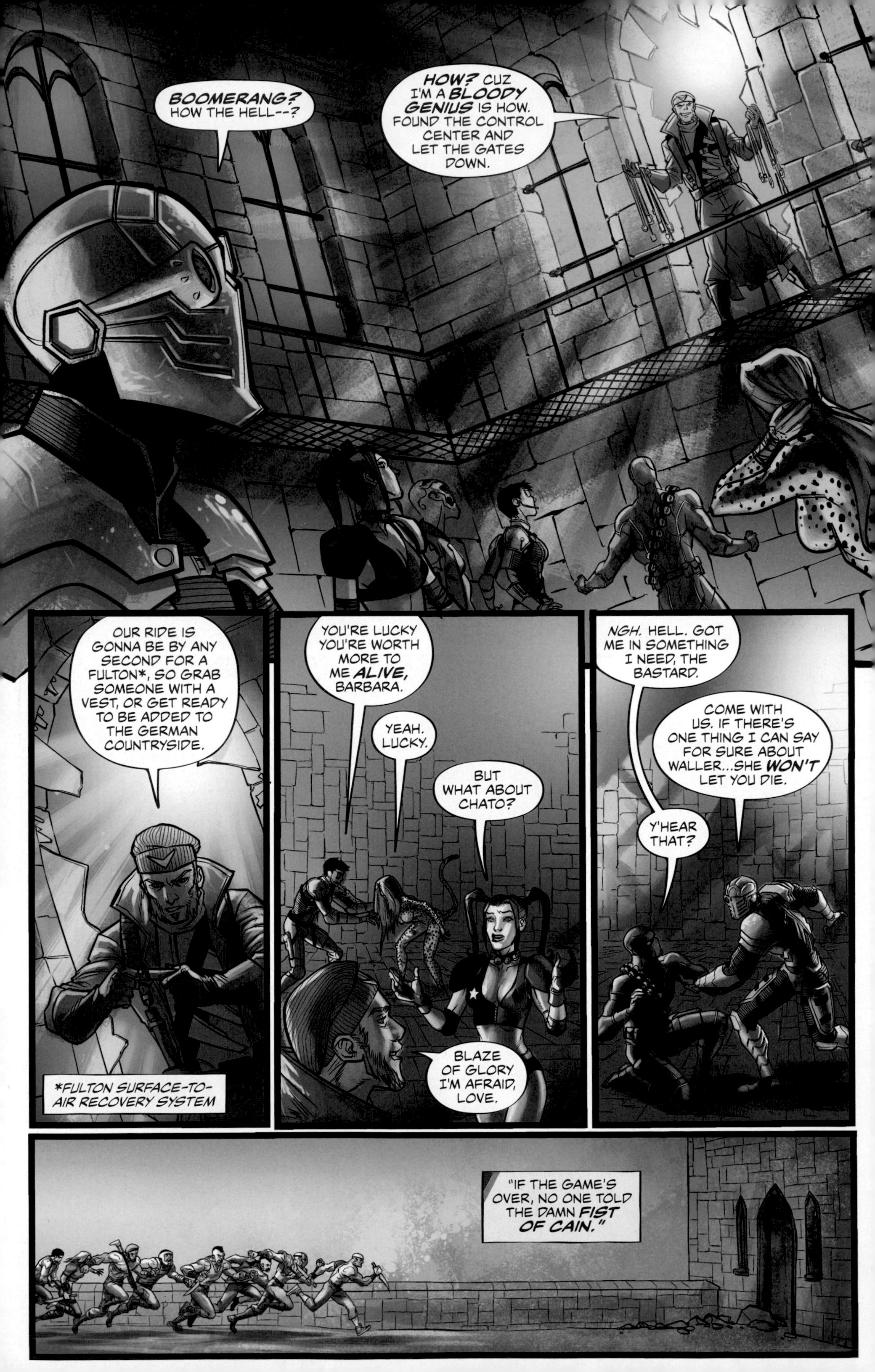
BOOMERANG? HOW THE HELL--?
HOW? CUZ I'M A BLOODY GENIUS IS HOW. FOUND THE CONTROL CENTER AND LET THE GATES DOWN.
OUR RIDE IS GONNA BE BY ANY SECOND FOR A FULTON*, SO GRAB SOMEONE WITH A VEST, OR GET READY TO BE ADDED TO THE GERMAN COUNTRYSIDE.
*FULTON SURFACE-TO-AIR RECOVERY SYSTEM
YOU'RE LUCKY YOU'RE WORTH MORE TO ME ALIVE, BARBARA.
YEAH. LUCKY.
BUT WHAT ABOUT CHATO?
BLAZE OF GLORY I'M AFRAID, LOVE.
NGH. HELL. GOT ME IN SOMETHING I NEED, THE BASTARD.
COME WITH US. IF THERE'S ONE THING I CAN SAY FOR SURE ABOUT WALLER...SHE WON'T LET YOU DIE.
Y'HEAR THAT?
"IF THE GAME'S OVER, NO ONE TOLD THE DAMN FIST OF CAIN."

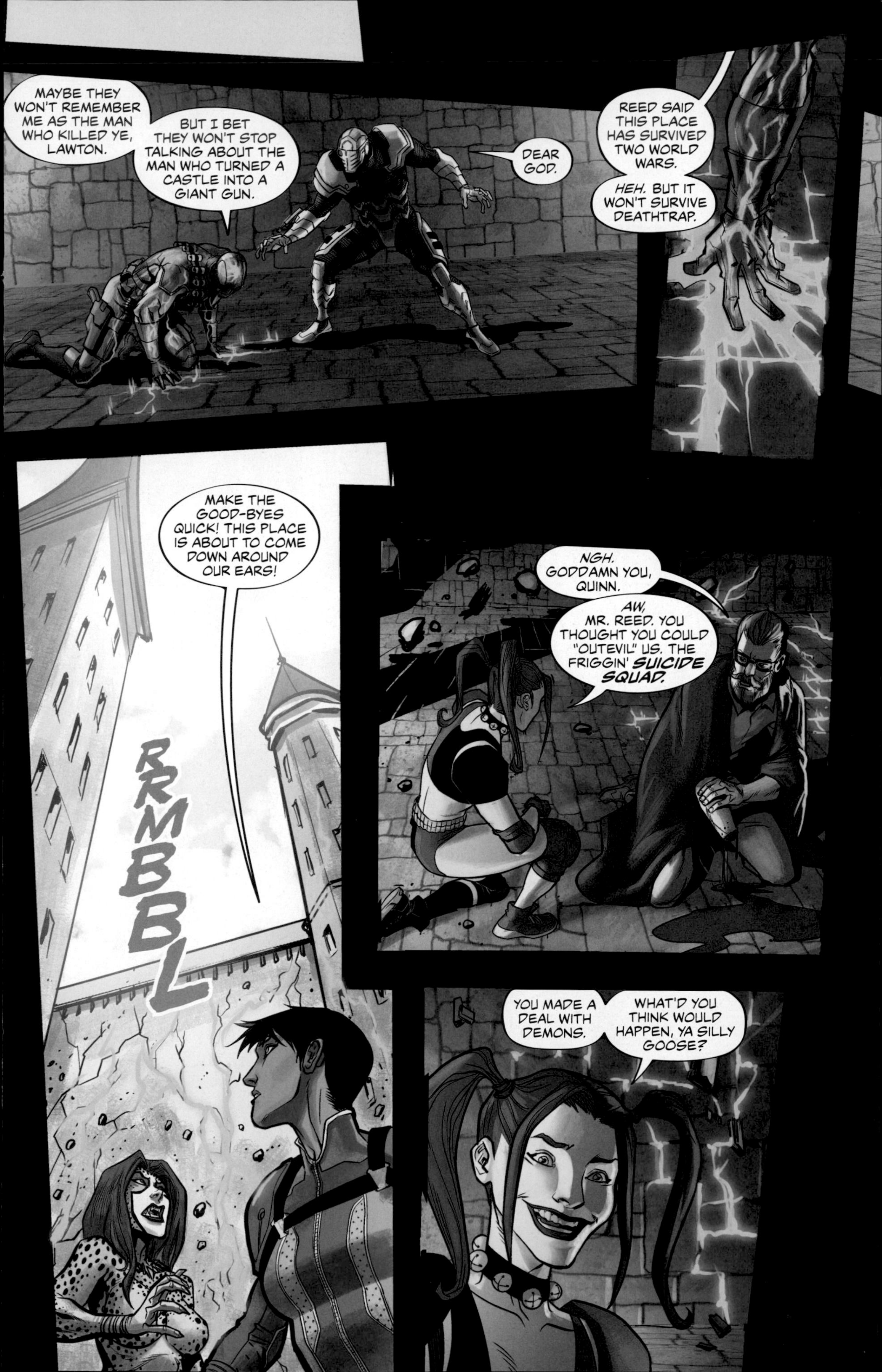
MAYBE THEY WON'T REMEMBER ME AS THE MAN WHO KILLED YE, LAWTON.
BUT I BET THEY WON'T STOP TALKING ABOUT THE MAN WHO TURNED A CASTLE INTO A GIANT GUN.
DEAR GOD.
REED SAID THIS PLACE HAS SURVIVED TWO WORLD WARS.
HEH. BUT IT WON'T SURVIVE DEATHTRAP.
MAKE THE GOOD-BYES QUICK! THIS PLACE IS ABOUT TO COME DOWN AROUND OUR EARS!
RRMBBL
NGH. GODDAMN YOU, QUINN.
AW, MR. REED. YOU THOUGHT YOU COULD "OUTEVIL" US. THE FRIGGIN' SUICIDE SQUAD.
YOU MADE A DEAL WITH DEMONS.
WHAT'D YOU THINK WOULD HAPPEN, YA SILLY GOOSE?

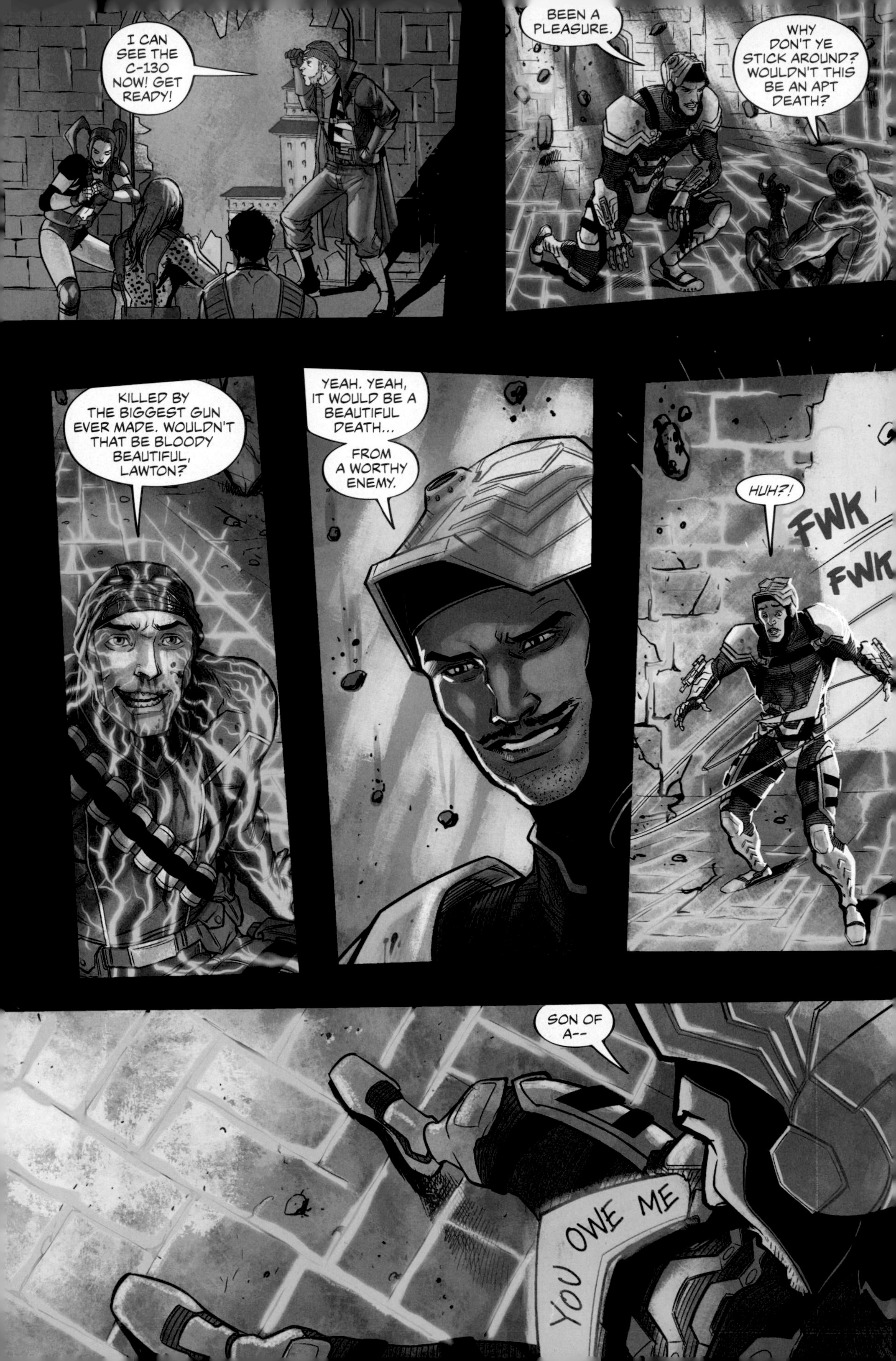
I CAN SEE THE C-130 NOW! GET READY!
BEEN A PLEASURE.
WHY DON'T YE STICK AROUND? WOULDN'T THIS BE AN APT DEATH?
KILLED BY THE BIGGEST GUN EVER MADE. WOULDN'T THAT BE BLOODY BEAUTIFUL, LAWTON?
YEAH. YEAH, IT WOULD BE A BEAUTIFUL DEATH...
FROM A WORTHY ENEMY.
HUH?!
FWK
FWK
SON OF A--
YOU OWE ME

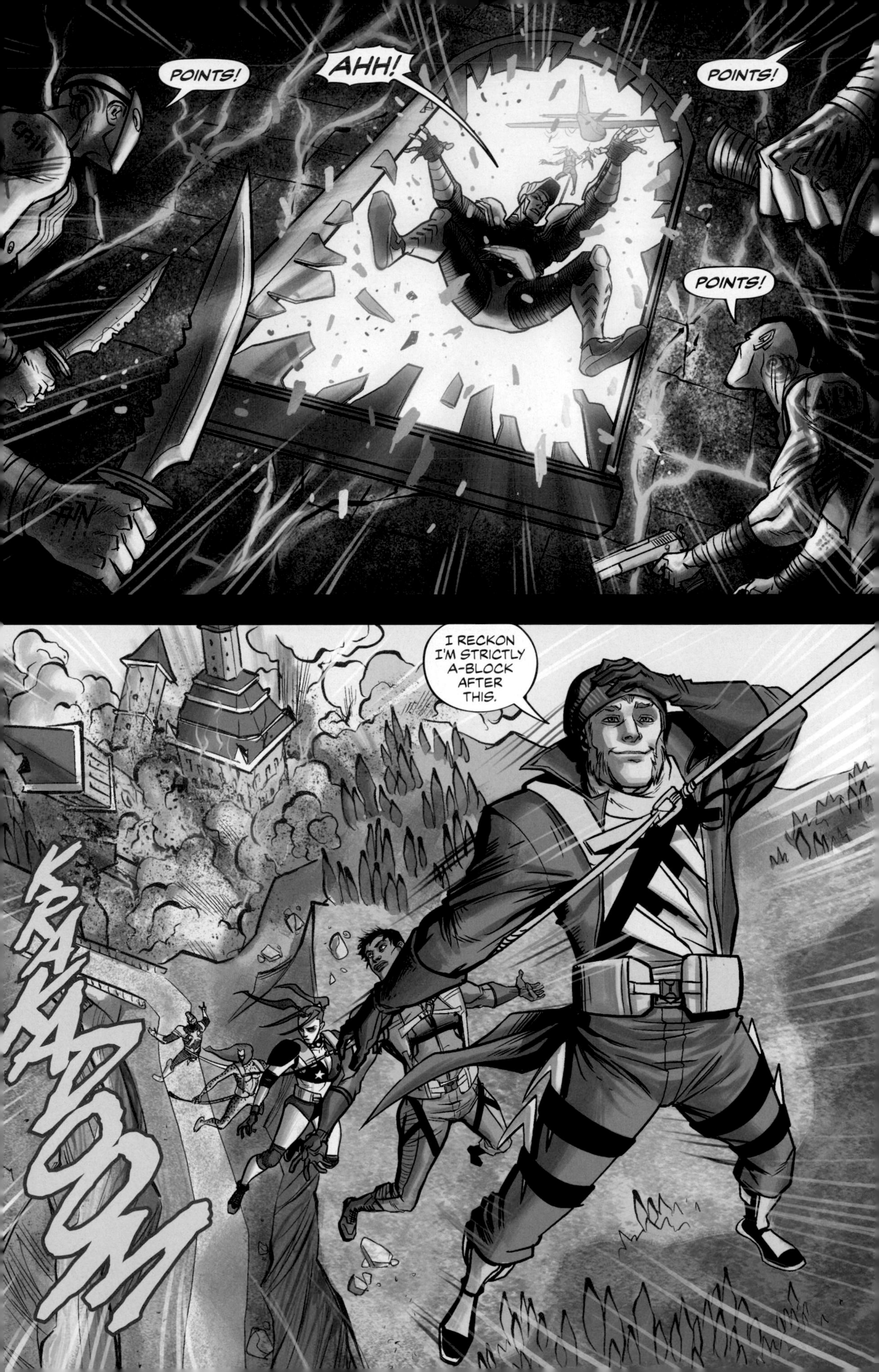
POINTS!
AHH!
POINTS!
POINTS!
I RECKON I'M STRICTLY A-BLOCK AFTER THIS.
KRAKADOOM

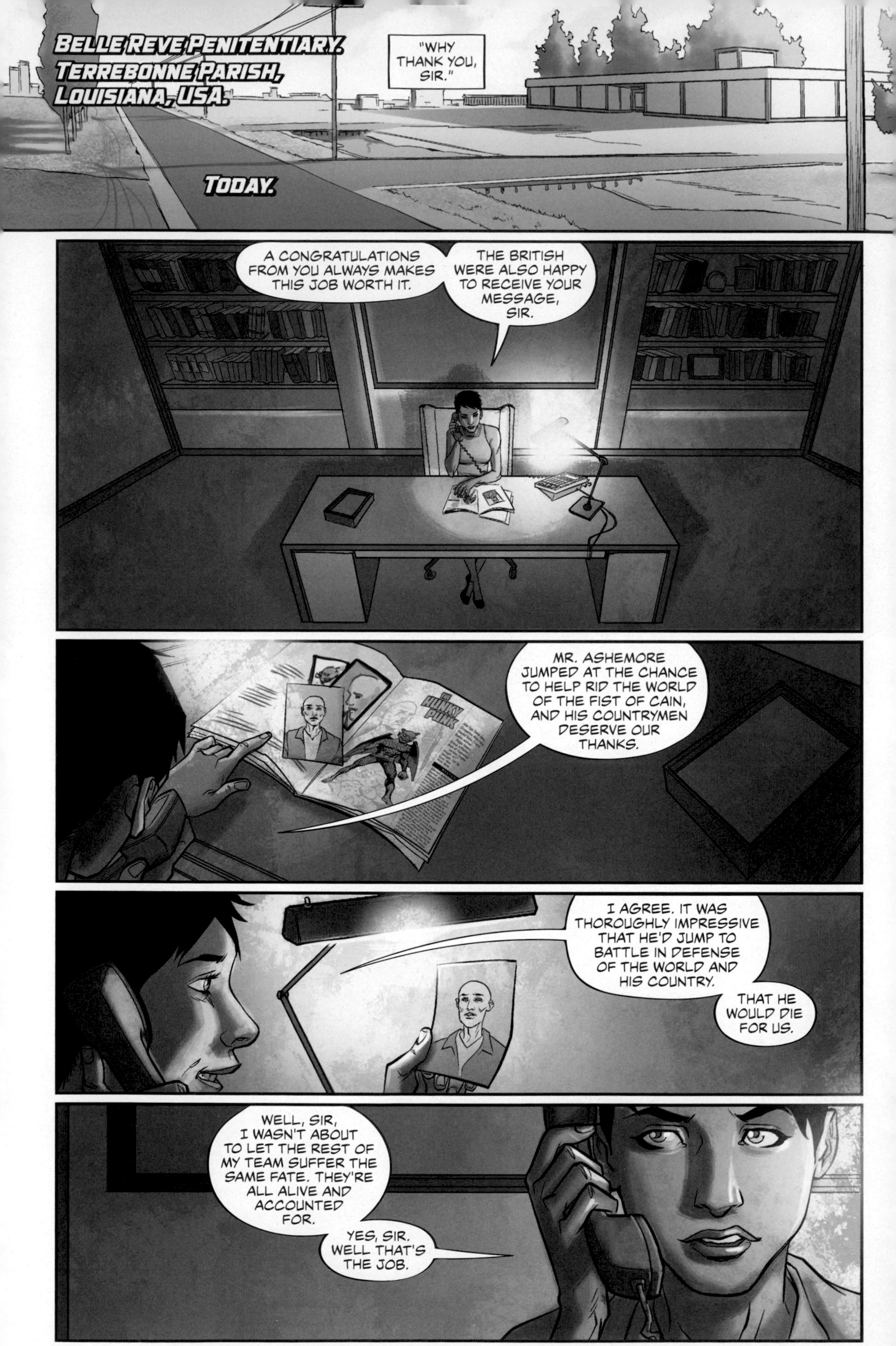
BELLE REVE PENITENTIARY. TERREBONNE PARISH, LOUISIANA, USA.
"WHY THANK YOU, SIR."
TODAY.
A CONGRATULATIONS FROM YOU ALWAYS MAKES THIS JOB WORTH IT.
THE BRITISH WERE ALSO HAPPY TO RECEIVE YOUR MESSAGE, SIR.
MR. ASHEMORE JUMPED AT THE CHANCE TO HELP RID THE WORLD OF THE FIST OF CAIN, AND HIS COUNTRYMEN DESERVE OUR THANKS.
I AGREE. IT WAS THOROUGHLY IMPRESSIVE THAT HE'D JUMP TO BATTLE IN DEFENSE OF THE WORLD AND HIS COUNTRY.
THAT HE WOULD DIE FOR US.
WELL, SIR, I WASN'T ABOUT TO LET THE REST OF MY TEAM SUFFER THE SAME FATE. THEY'RE ALL ALIVE AND ACCOUNTED FOR.
YES, SIR. WELL THAT'S THE JOB.

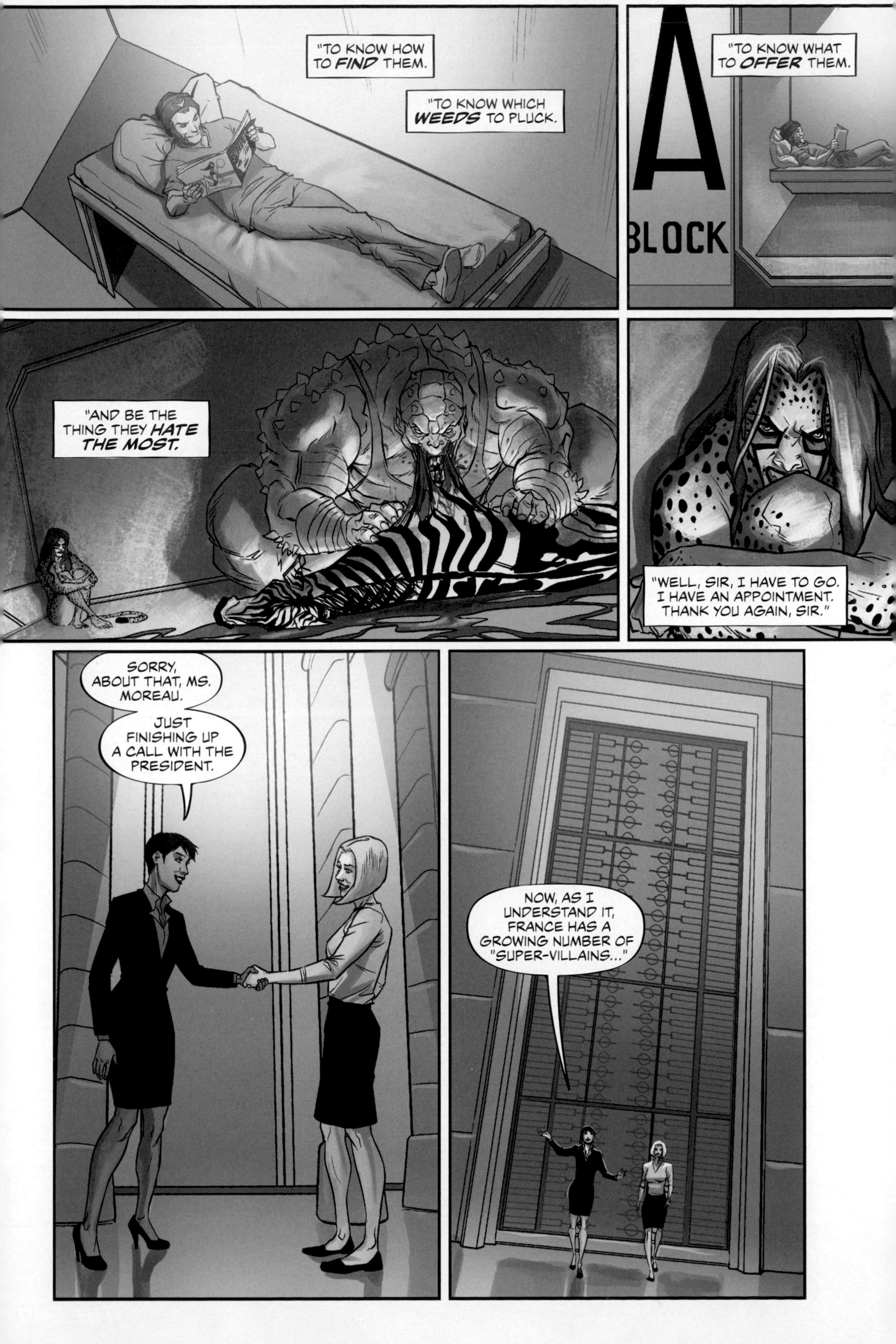
"TO KNOW HOW TO FIND THEM.
"TO KNOW WHICH WEEDS TO PLUCK.
A BLOCK
"TO KNOW WHAT TO OFFER THEM.
"AND BE THE THING THEY HATE THE MOST.
"WELL, SIR, I HAVE TO GO. I HAVE AN APPOINTMENT. THANK YOU AGAIN, SIR."
SORRY, ABOUT THAT, MS. MOREAU.
JUST FINISHING UP A CALL WITH THE PRESIDENT.
NOW, AS I UNDERSTAND IT, FRANCE HAS A GROWING NUMBER OF "SUPER-VILLAINS..."

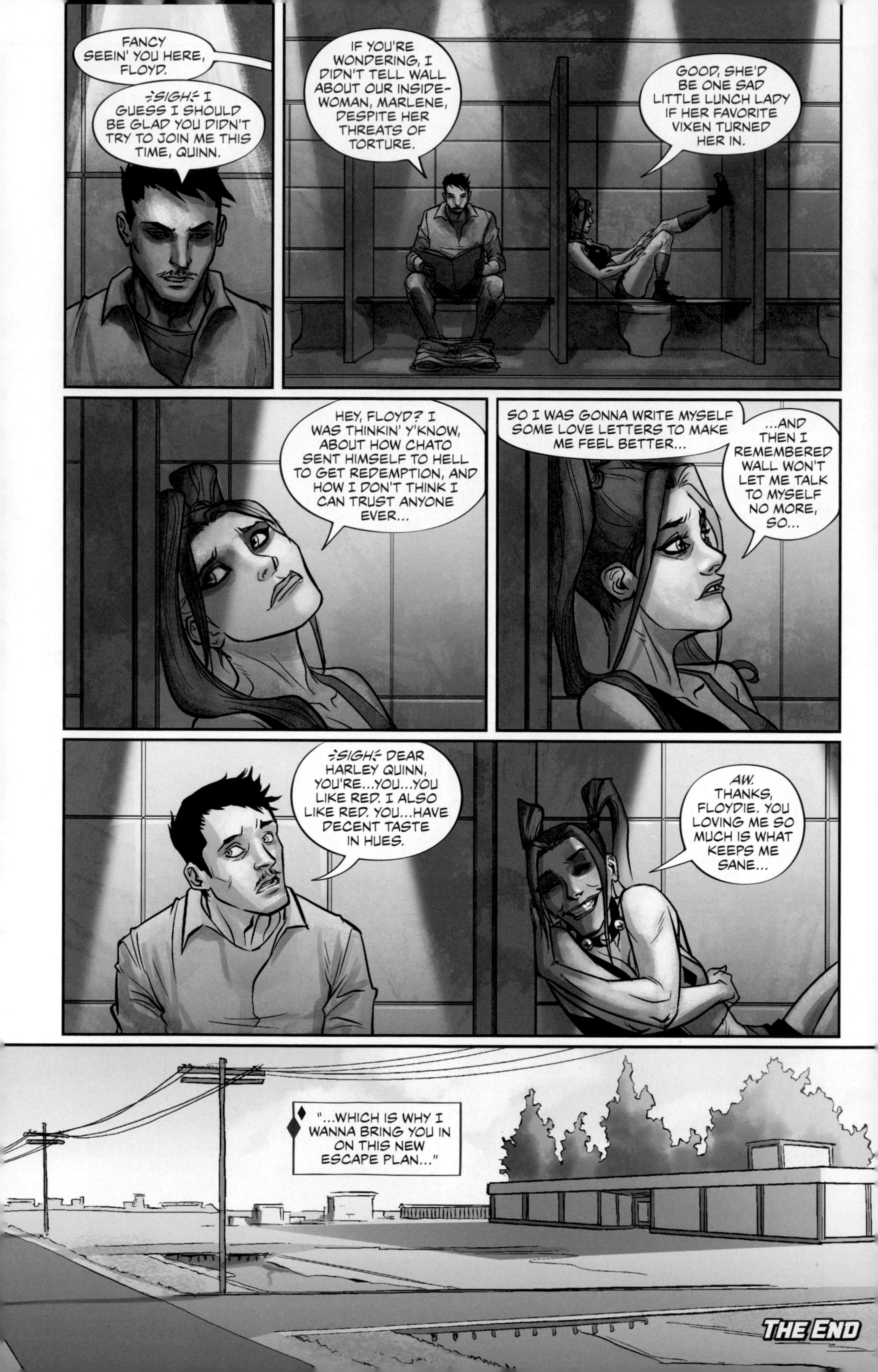
FANCY SEEIN' YOU HERE, FLOYD.
=SIGH= I GUESS I SHOULD BE GLAD YOU DIDN'T TRY TO JOIN ME THIS TIME, QUINN.
IF YOU'RE WONDERING, I DIDN'T TELL WALL ABOUT OUR INSIDE-WOMAN, MARLENE, DESPITE HER THREATS OF TORTURE.
GOOD, SHE'D BE ONE SAD LITTLE LUNCH LADY IF HER FAVORITE VIXEN TURNED HER IN.
HEY, FLOYD? I WAS THINKIN' Y'KNOW, ABOUT HOW CHATO SENT HIMSELF TO HELL TO GET REDEMPTION, AND HOW I DON'T THINK I CAN TRUST ANYONE EVER...
SO I WAS GONNA WRITE MYSELF SOME LOVE LETTERS TO MAKE ME FEEL BETTER...
...AND THEN I REMEMBERED WALL WON'T LET ME TALK TO MYSELF NO MORE, SO...
=SIGH= DEAR HARLEY QUINN, YOU'RE...YOU...YOU LIKE RED. I ALSO LIKE RED. YOU...HAVE DECENT TASTE IN HUES.
AW. THANKS, FLOYDIE. YOU LOVING ME SO MUCH IS WHAT KEEPS ME SANE...
"...WHICH IS WHY I WANNA BRING YOU IN ON THIS NEW ESCAPE PLAN..."
THE END

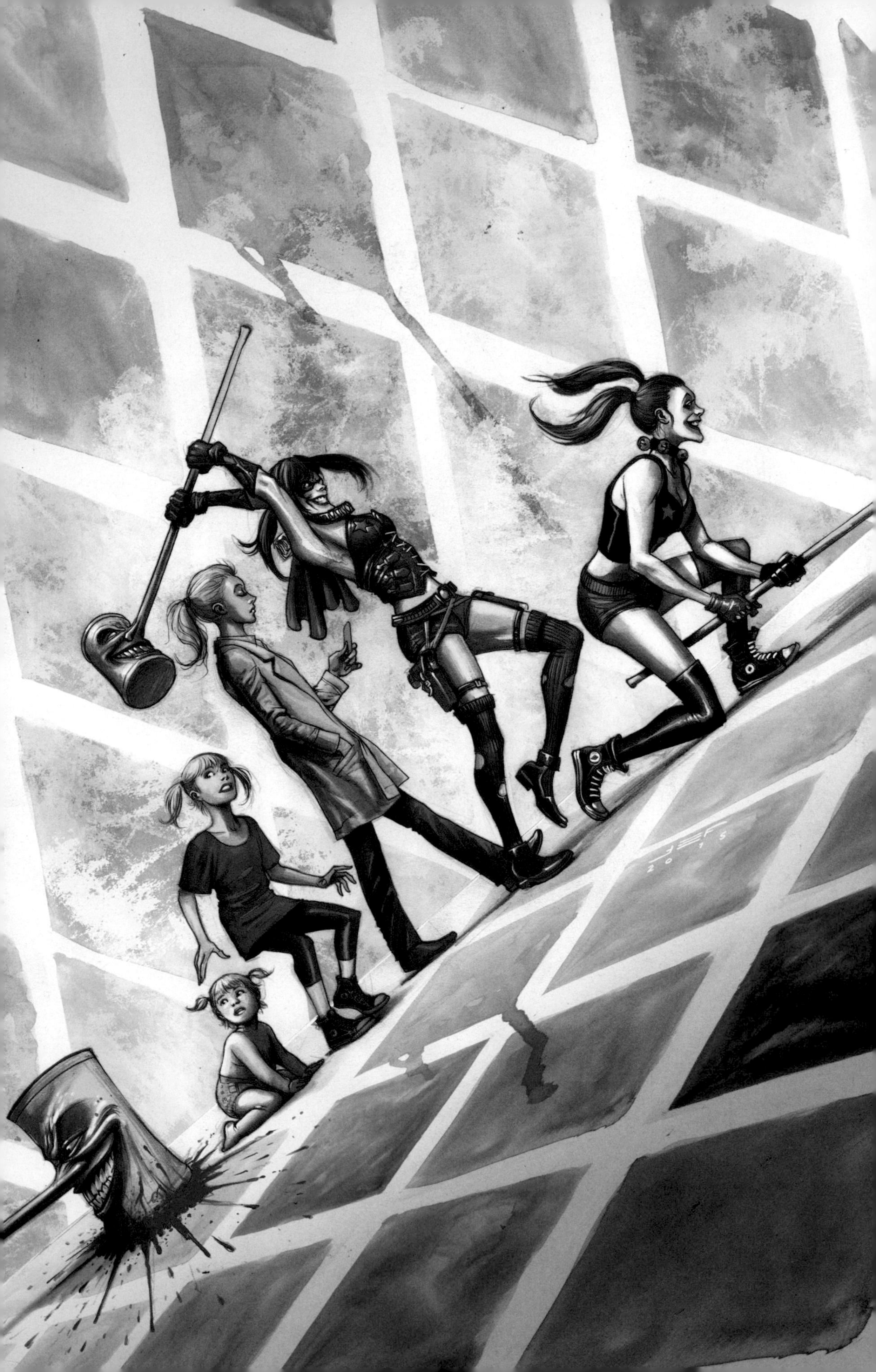

BLANK SPACE

SEAN RYAN writer RONAN CLIQUET artist BLOND colorist DAVE SHARPE letterer

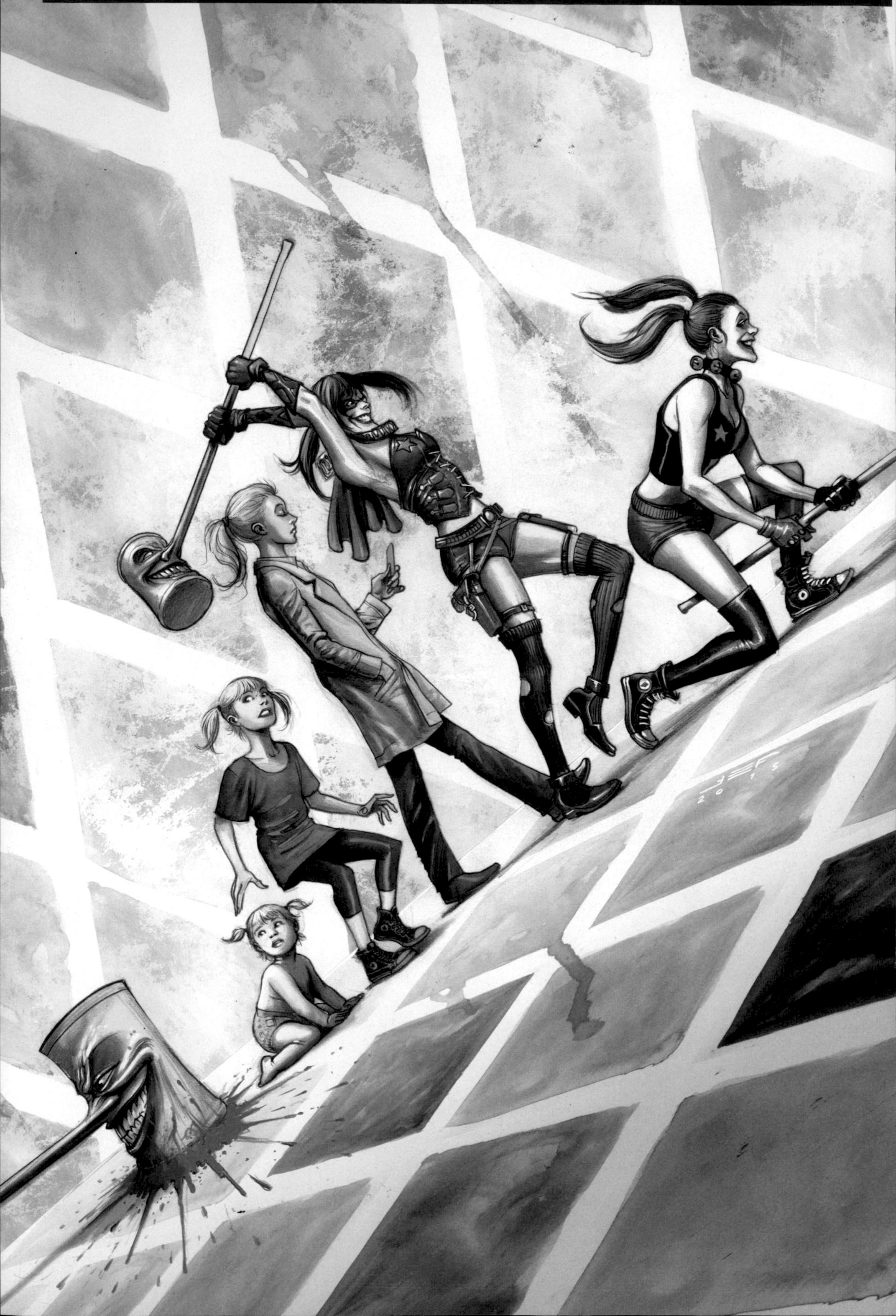

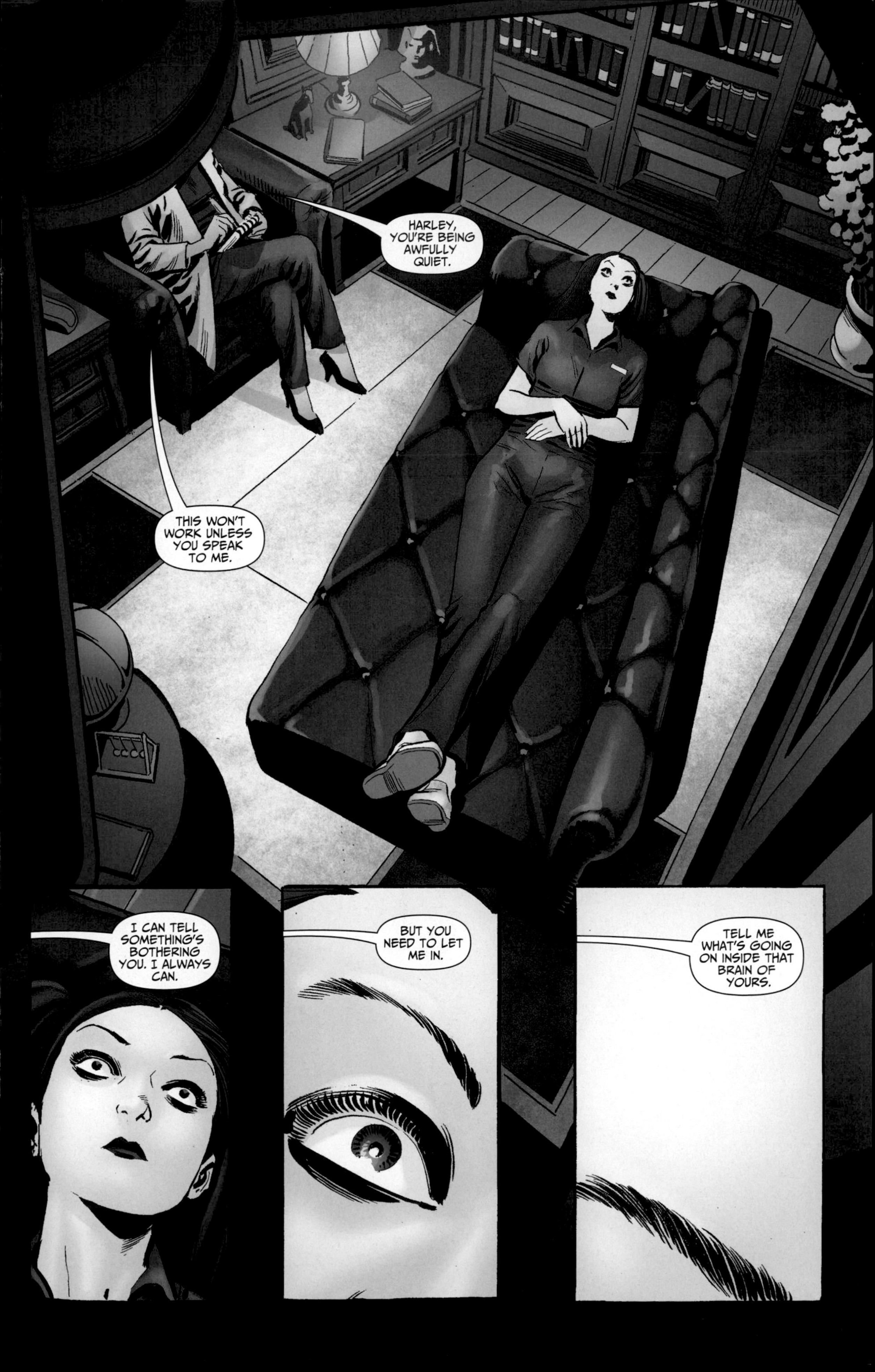
HARLEY, YOU'RE BEING AWFULLY QUIET.
THIS WON'T WORK UNLESS YOU SPEAK TO ME.
I CAN TELL SOMETHING'S BOTHERING YOU. I ALWAYS CAN.
BUT YOU NEED TO LET ME IN.
TELL ME WHAT'S GOING ON INSIDE THAT BRAIN OF YOURS.

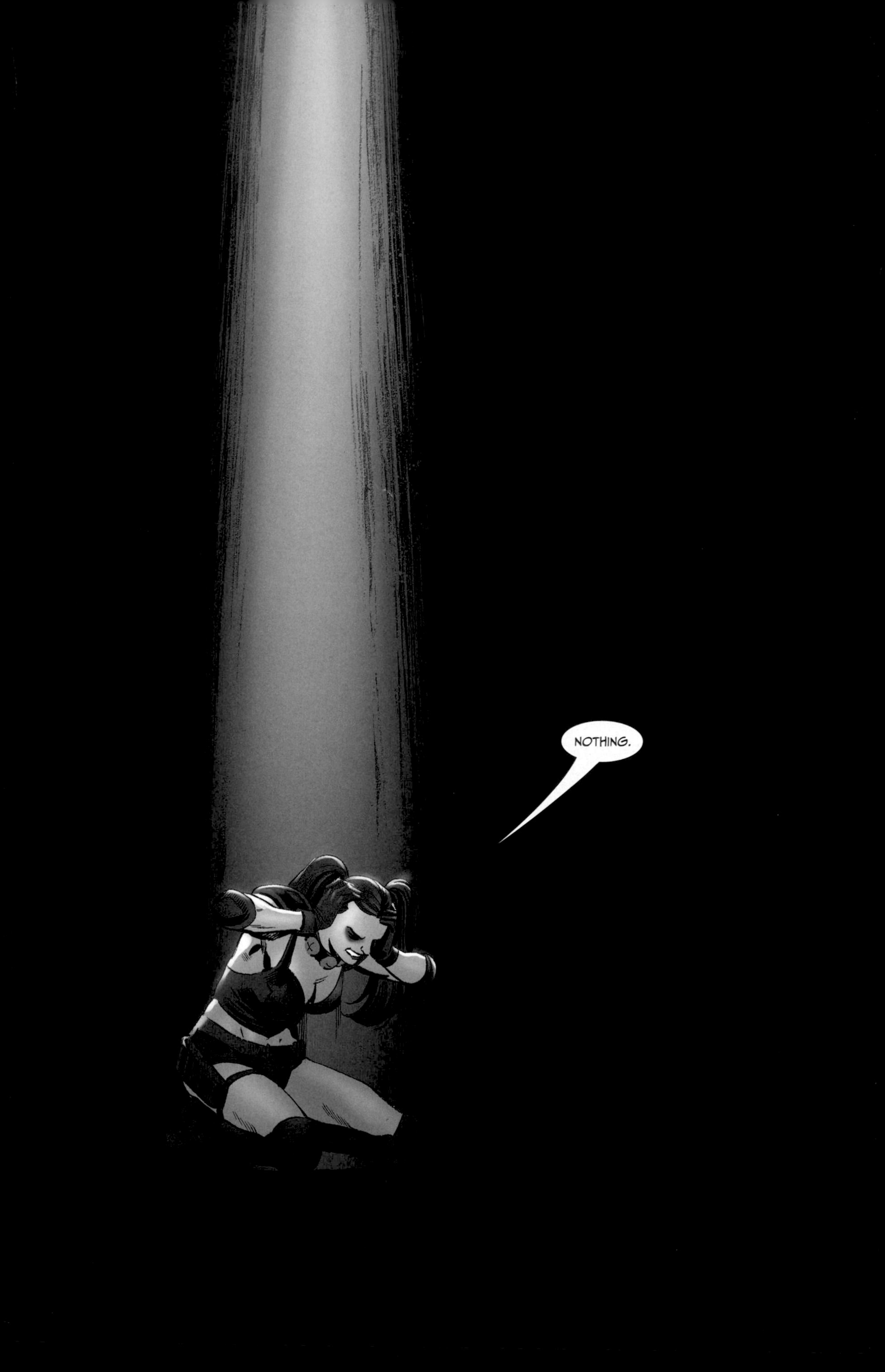
NOTHING.

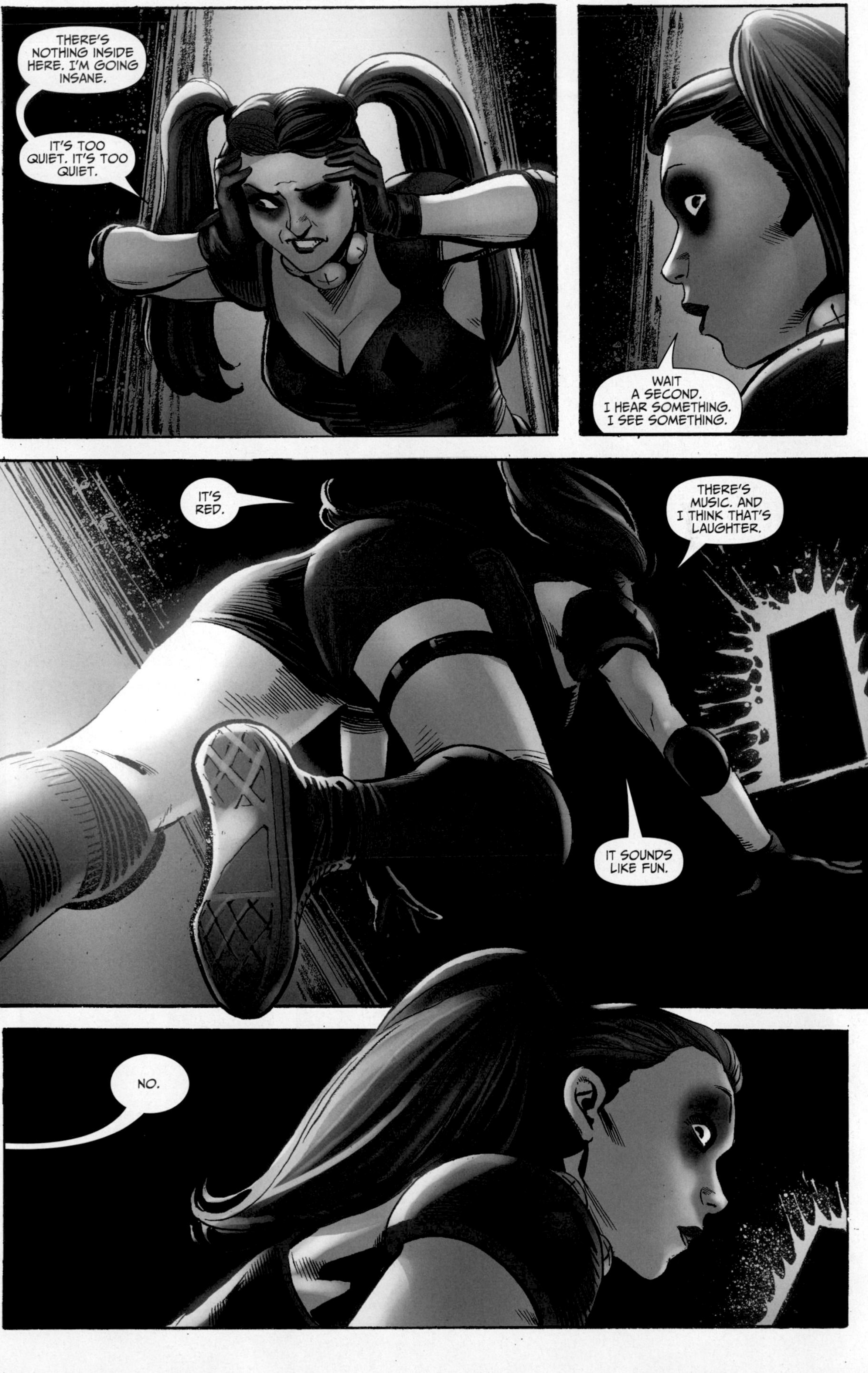
THERE'S NOTHING INSIDE HERE. I'M GOING INSANE.
IT'S TOO QUIET. IT'S TOO QUIET.
WAIT A SECOND. I HEAR SOMETHING. I SEE SOMETHING.
IT'S RED.
THERE'S MUSIC. AND I THINK THAT'S LAUGHTER.
IT SOUNDS LIKE FUN.
NO.

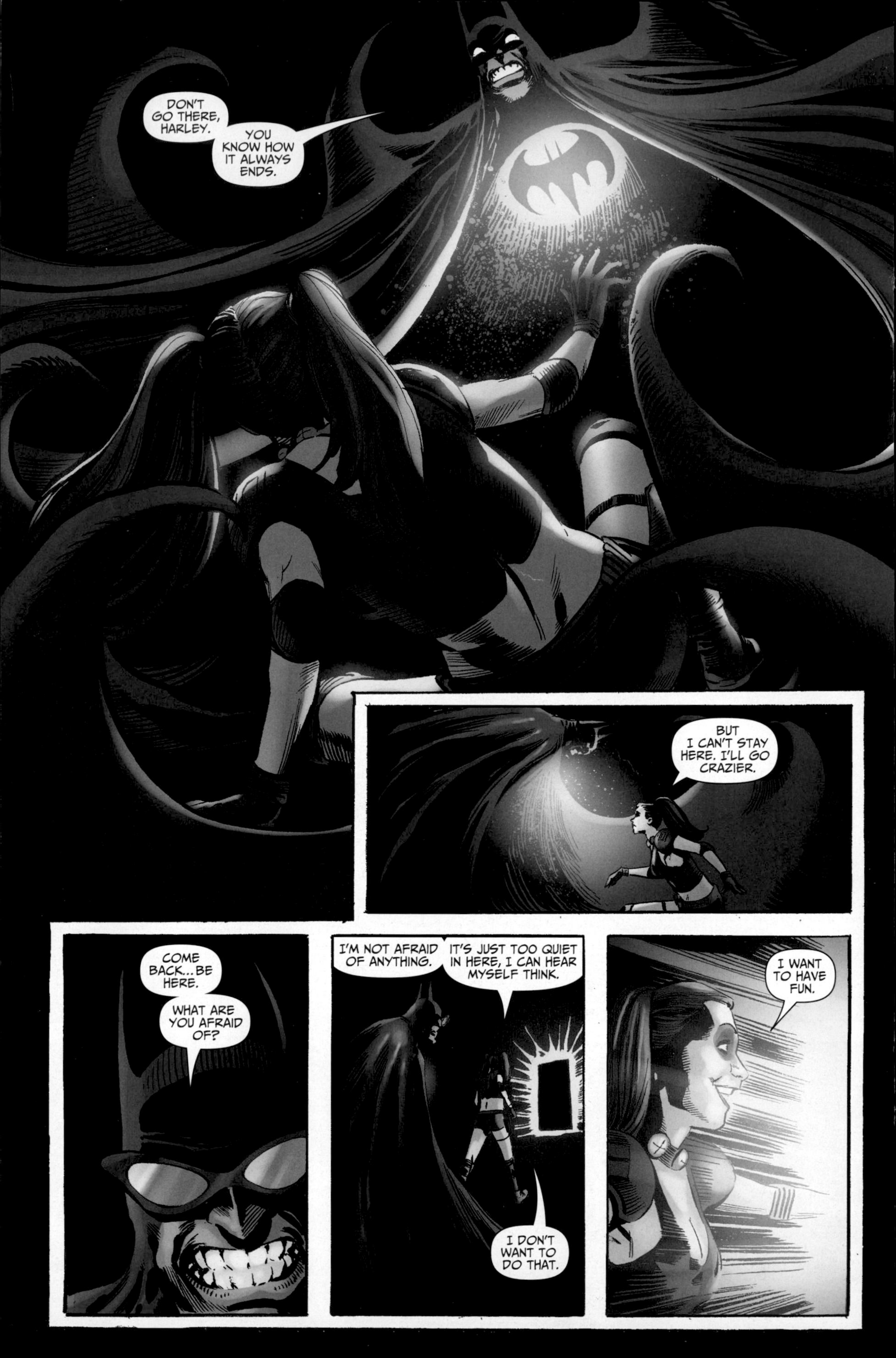
DON'T GO THERE, HARLEY.
YOU KNOW HOW IT ALWAYS ENDS.
BUT I CAN'T STAY HERE. I'LL GO CRAZIER.
COME BACK...BE HERE.
WHAT ARE YOU AFRAID OF?
I'M NOT AFRAID OF ANYTHING.
IT'S JUST TOO QUIET IN HERE, I CAN HEAR MYSELF THINK.
I DON'T WANT TO DO THAT.
I WANT TO HAVE FUN.

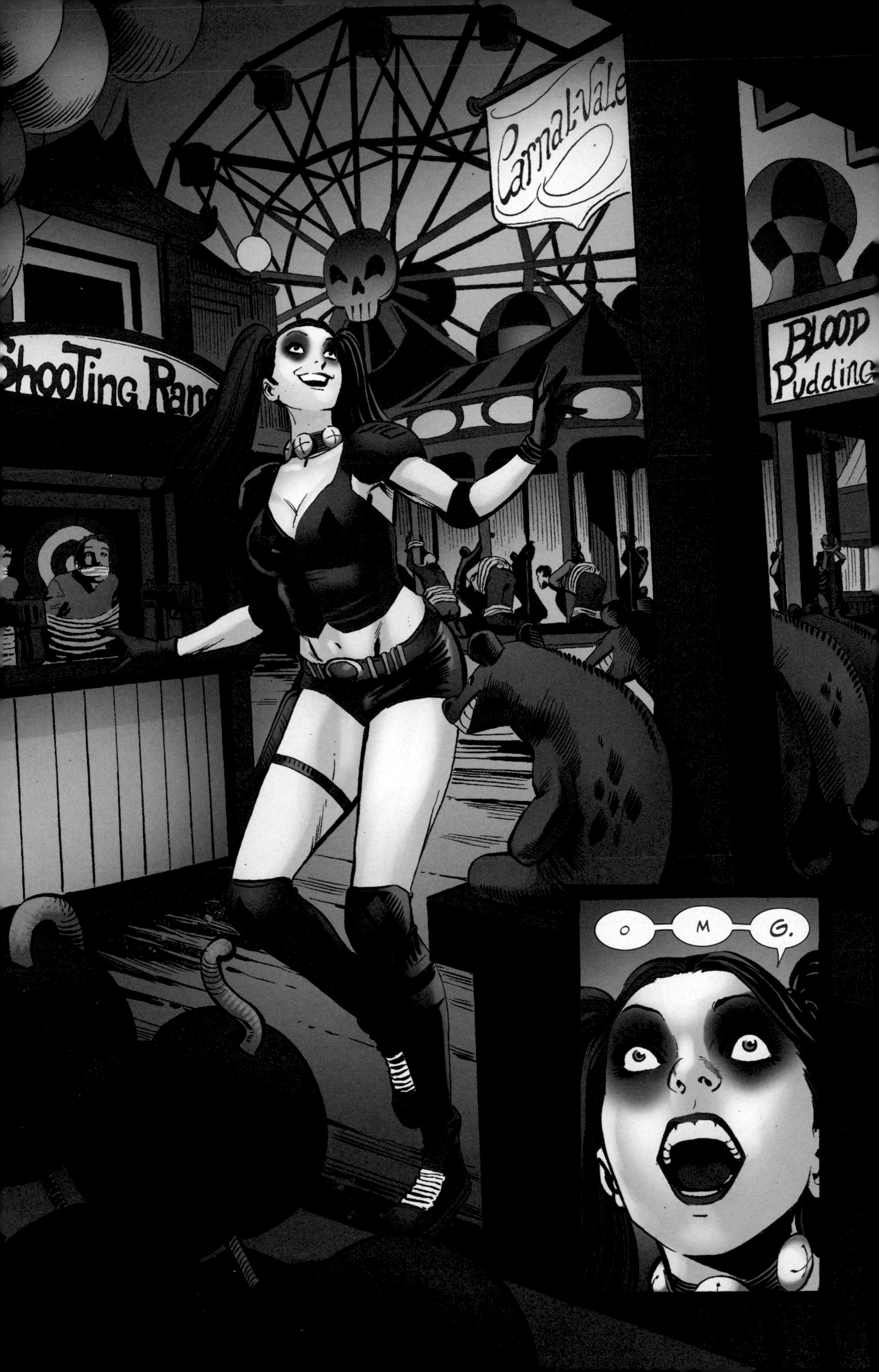
Carnal-Vale
Shooting Rang
Blood Pudding
O M G.

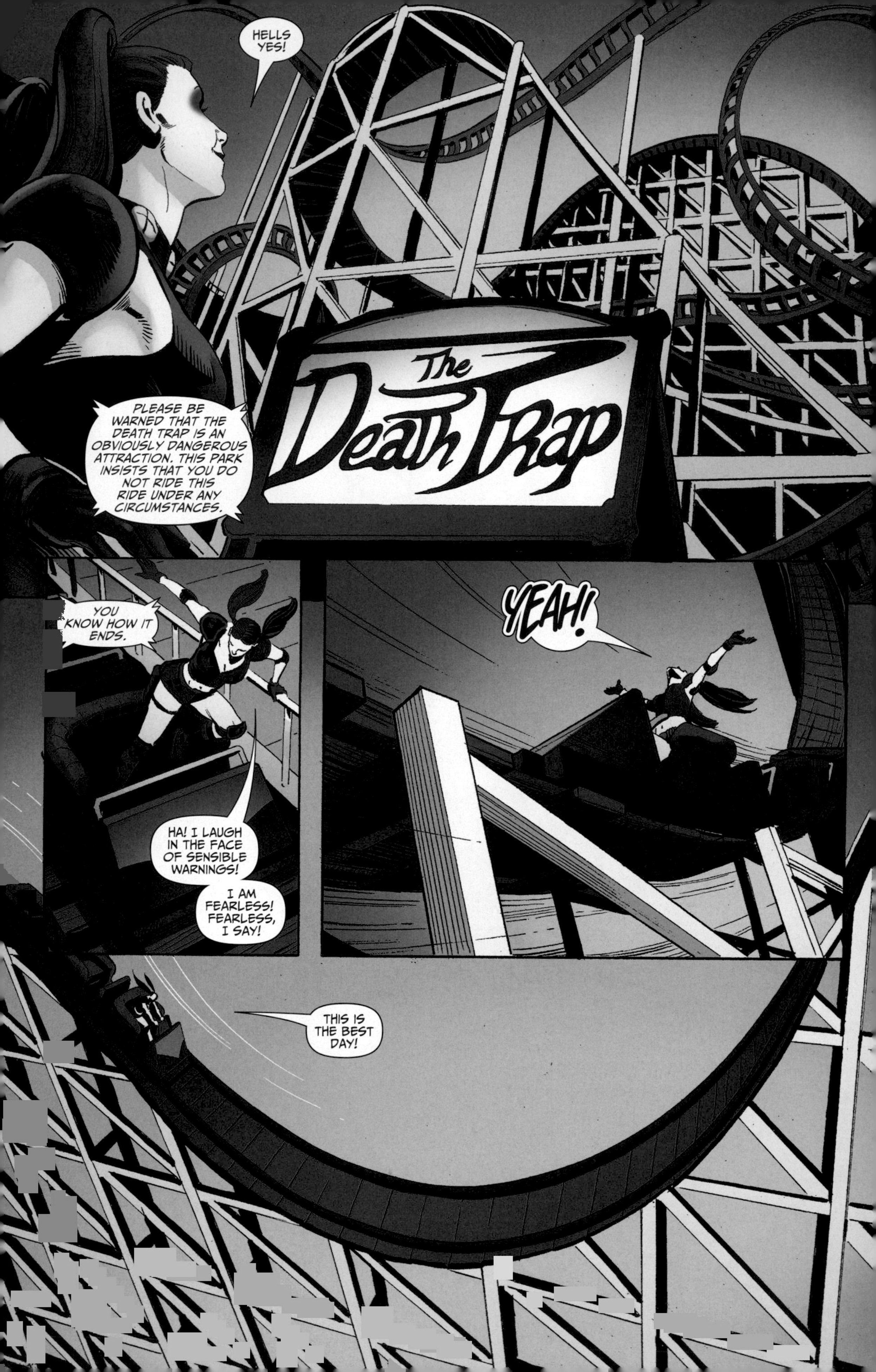

HELLS YES!
The Death Trap
PLEASE BE WARNED THAT THE DEATH TRAP IS AN OBVIOUSLY DANGEROUS ATTRACTION. THIS PARK INSISTS THAT YOU DO NOT RIDE THIS RIDE UNDER ANY CIRCUMSTANCES.
YOU KNOW HOW IT ENDS.
HA! I LAUGH IN THE FACE OF SENSIBLE WARNINGS!
I AM FEARLESS! FEARLESS, I SAY!
YEAH!
THIS IS THE BEST DAY!

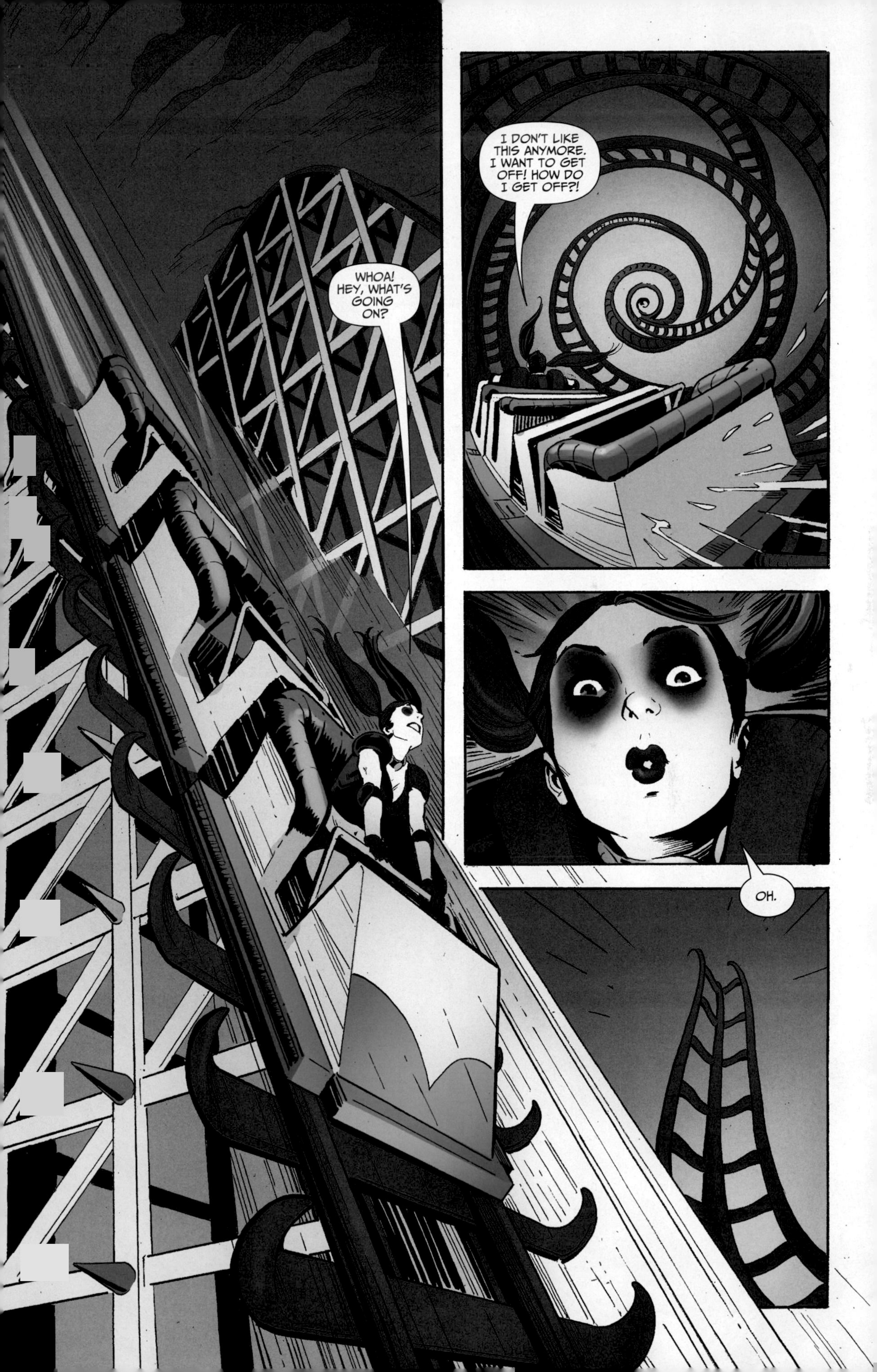
WHOA! HEY, WHAT'S GOING ON?
I DON'T LIKE THIS ANYMORE. I WANT TO GET OFF! HOW DO I GET OFF?!
OH.

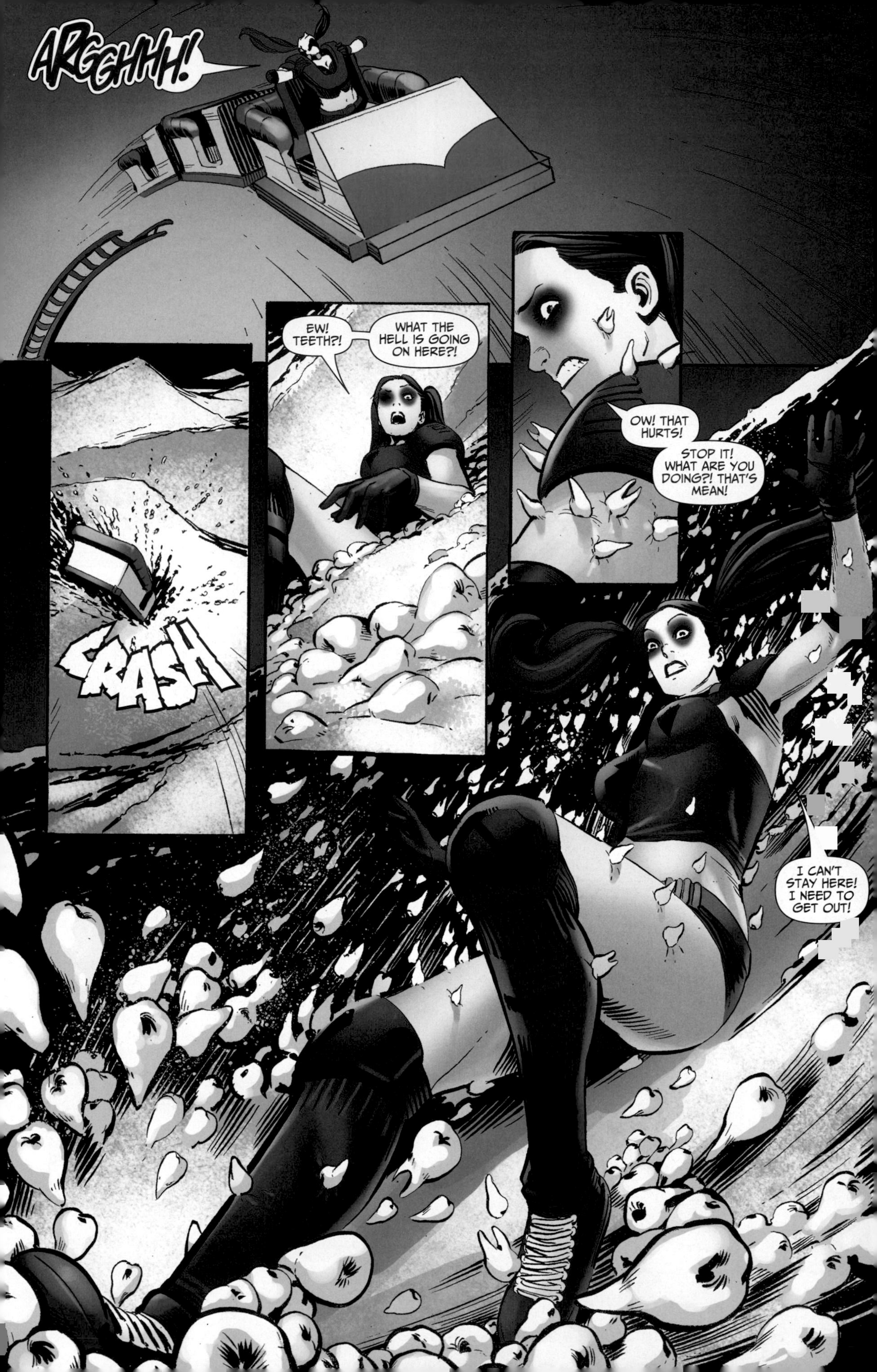
ARGGHHH!
CRASH
EW! TEETH?!
WHAT THE HELL IS GOING ON HERE?!
OW! THAT HURTS!
STOP IT! WHAT ARE YOU DOING?! THAT'S MEAN!
I CAN'T STAY HERE! I NEED TO GET OUT!

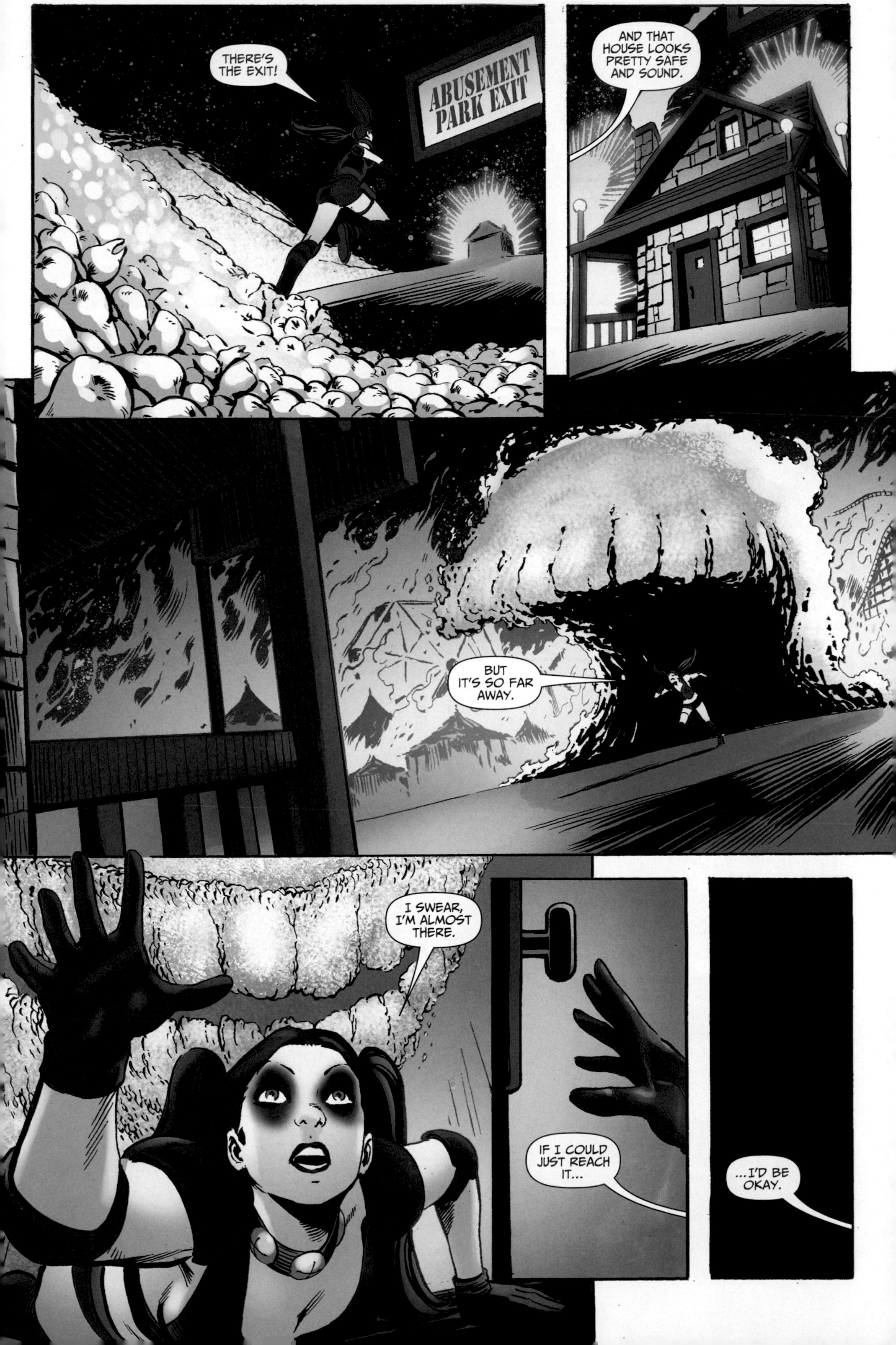
THERE'S THE EXIT!
ABUSEMENT PARK EXIT
AND THAT HOUSE LOOKS PRETTY SAFE AND SOUND.
BUT IT'S SO FAR AWAY.
I SWEAR, I'M ALMOST THERE.
IF I COULD JUST REACH IT...
...I'D BE OKAY.

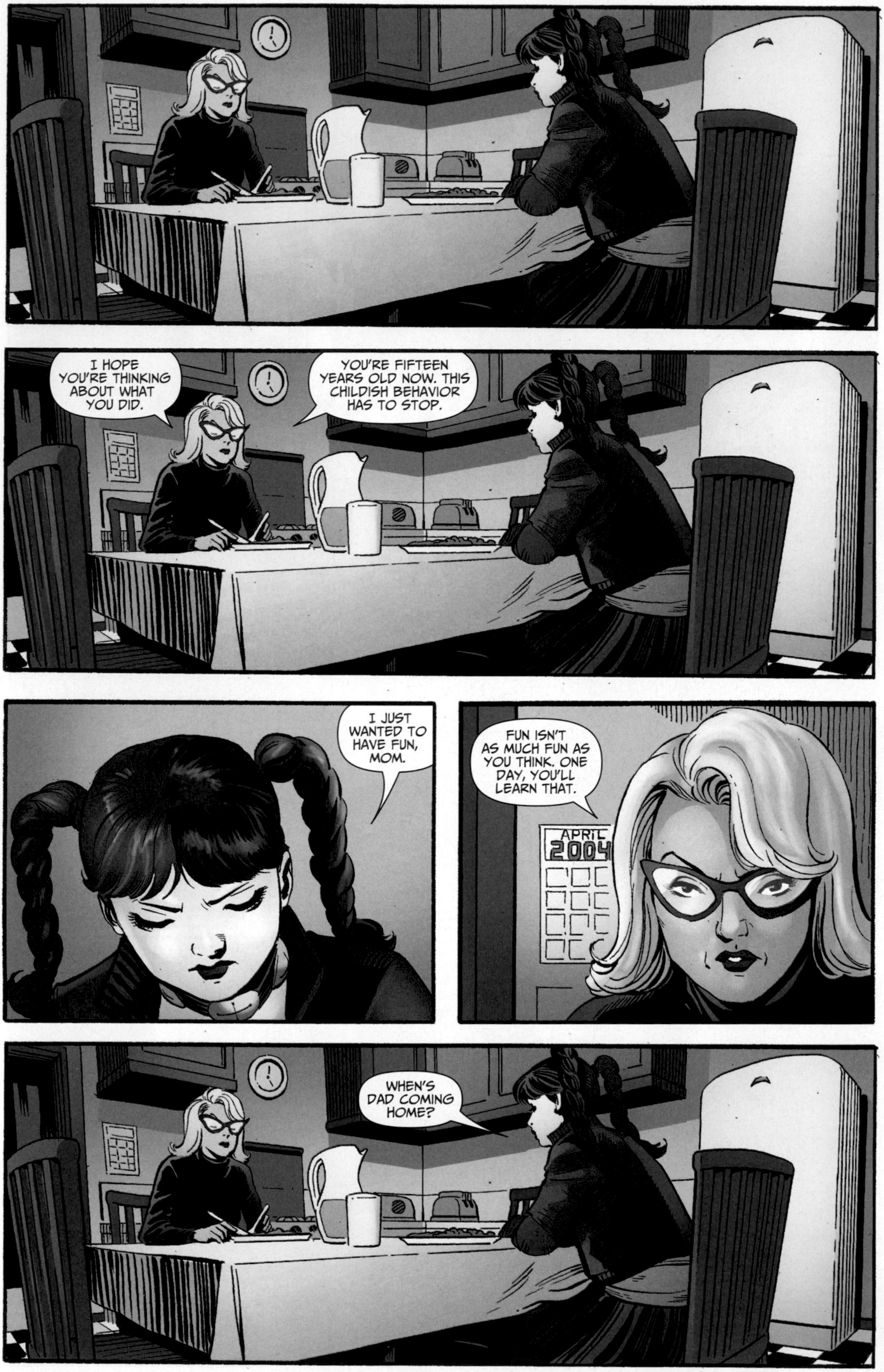
I HOPE YOU'RE THINKING ABOUT WHAT YOU DID.
YOU'RE FIFTEEN YEARS OLD NOW. THIS CHILDISH BEHAVIOR HAS TO STOP.
I JUST WANTED TO HAVE FUN, MOM.
FUN ISN'T AS MUCH FUN AS YOU THINK. ONE DAY, YOU'LL LEARN THAT.
APRIL 2004
WHEN'S DAD COMING HOME?

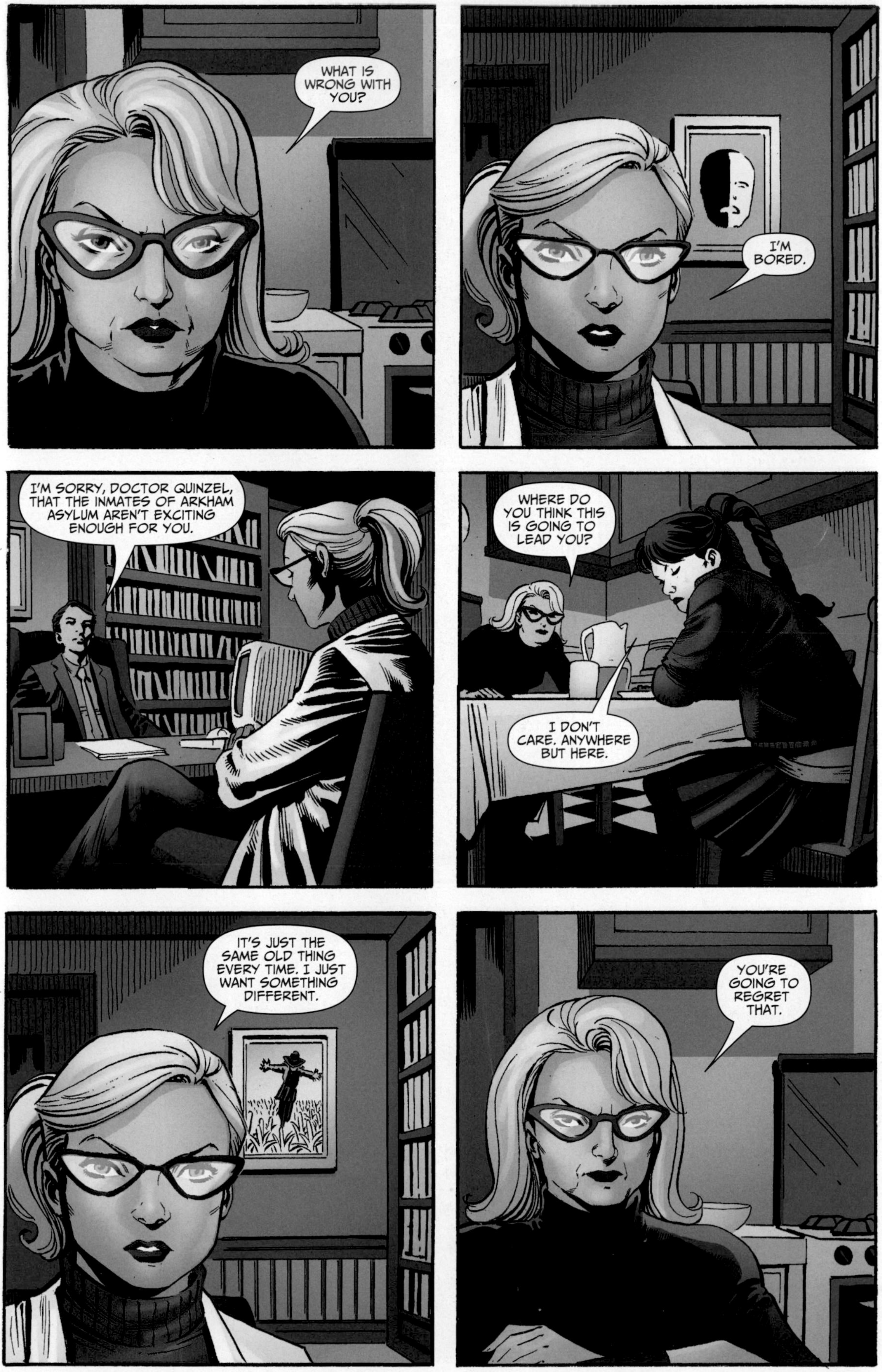
WHAT IS WRONG WITH YOU?
I'M BORED.
I'M SORRY, DOCTOR QUINZEL, THAT THE INMATES OF ARKHAM ASYLUM AREN'T EXCITING ENOUGH FOR YOU.
WHERE DO YOU THINK THIS IS GOING TO LEAD YOU?
I DON'T CARE. ANYWHERE BUT HERE.
IT'S JUST THE SAME OLD THING EVERY TIME. I JUST WANT SOMETHING DIFFERENT.
YOU'RE GOING TO REGRET THAT.

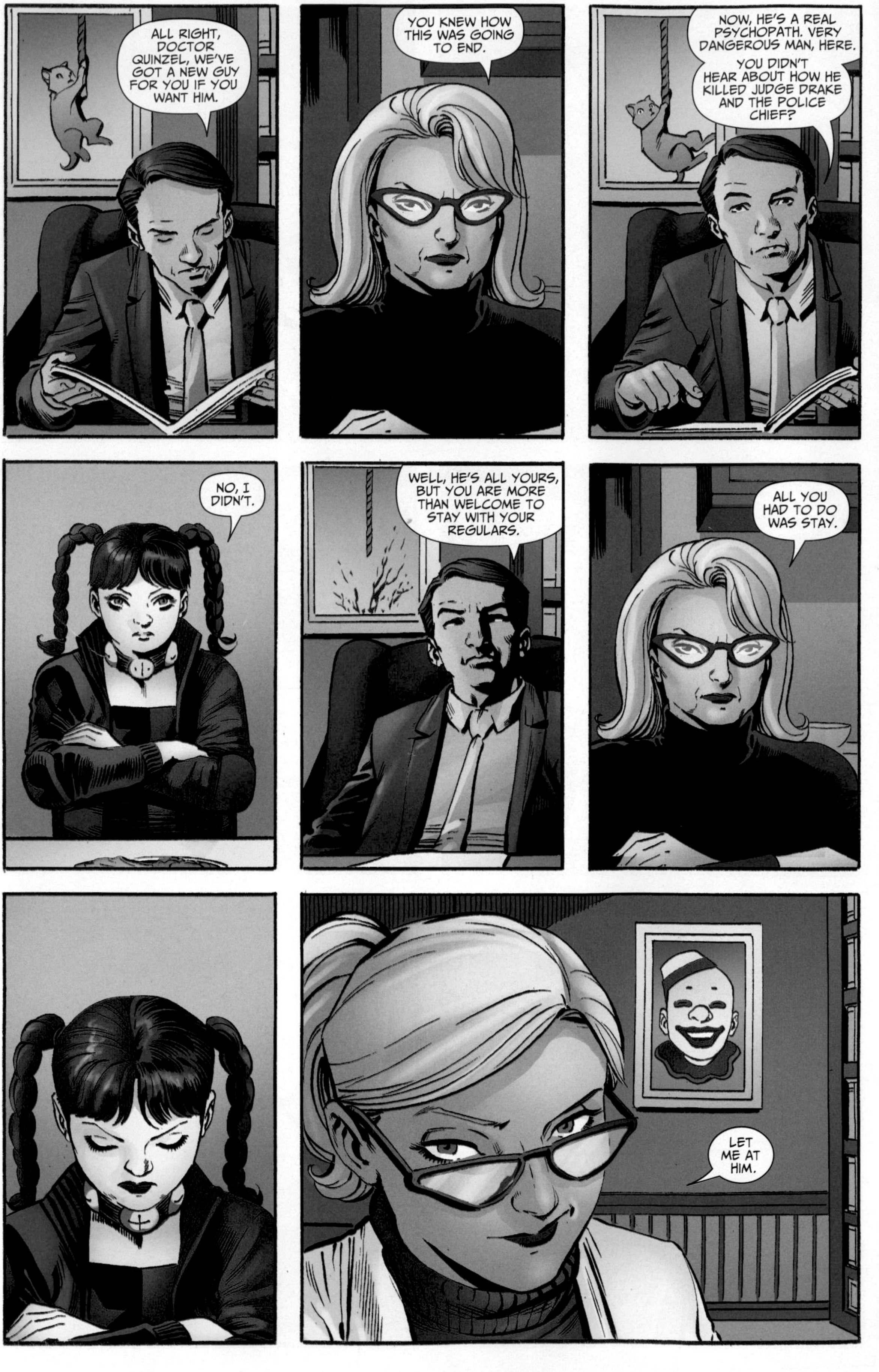
ALL RIGHT, DOCTOR QUINZEL, WE'VE GOT A NEW GUY FOR YOU IF YOU WANT HIM.
YOU KNEW HOW THIS WAS GOING TO END.
NOW, HE'S A REAL PSYCHOPATH. VERY DANGEROUS MAN, HERE.
YOU DIDN'T HEAR ABOUT HOW HE KILLED JUDGE DRAKE AND THE POLICE CHIEF?
NO, I DIDN'T.
WELL, HE'S ALL YOURS, BUT YOU ARE MORE THAN WELCOME TO STAY WITH YOUR REGULARS.
ALL YOU HAD TO DO WAS STAY.
LET ME AT HIM.

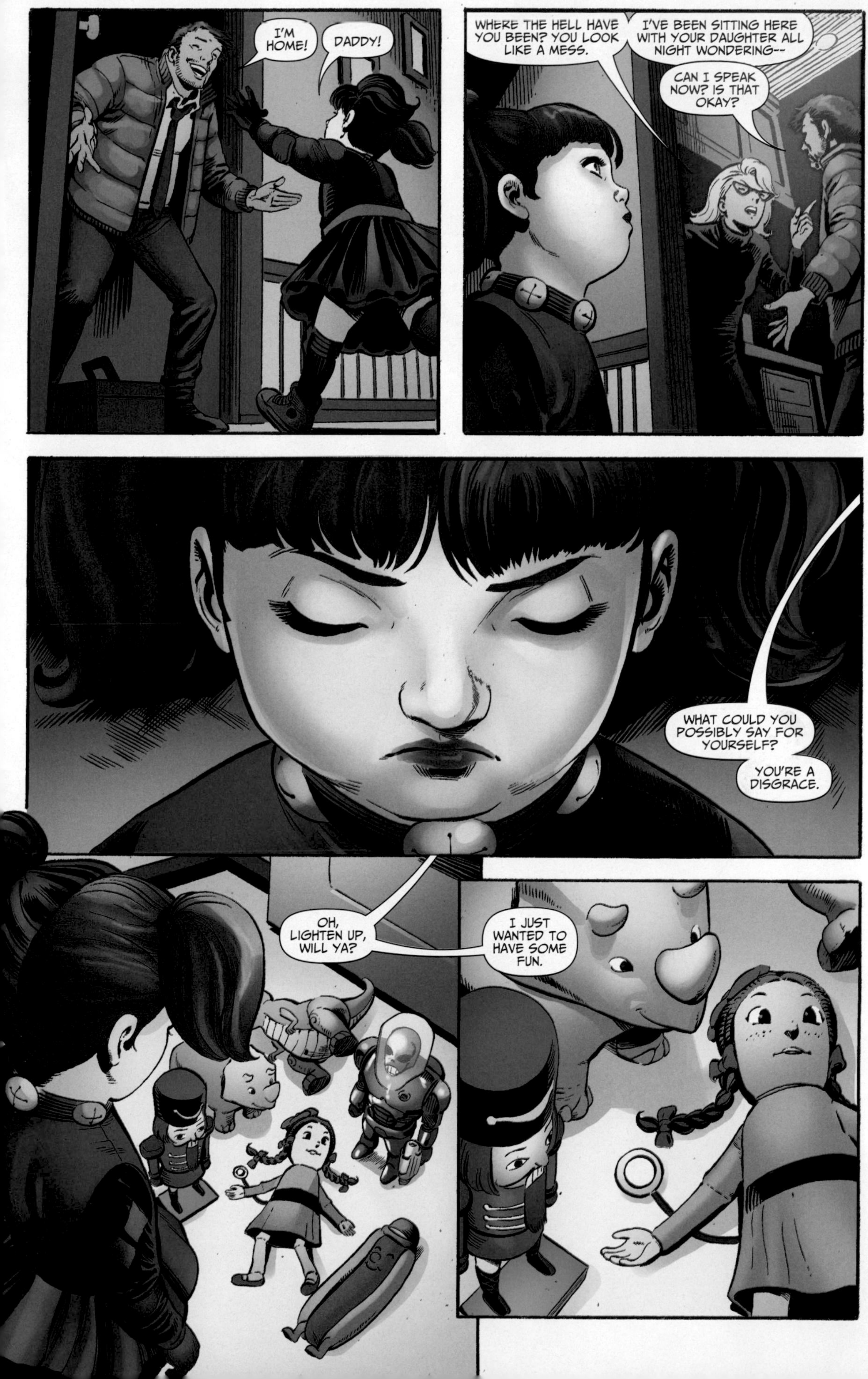
I'M HOME!
DADDY!
WHERE THE HELL HAVE YOU BEEN? YOU LOOK LIKE A MESS.
I'VE BEEN SITTING HERE WITH YOUR DAUGHTER ALL NIGHT WONDERING--
CAN I SPEAK NOW? IS THAT OKAY?
WHAT COULD YOU POSSIBLY SAY FOR YOURSELF?
YOU'RE A DISGRACE.
OH, LIGHTEN UP, WILL YA?
I JUST WANTED TO HAVE SOME FUN.

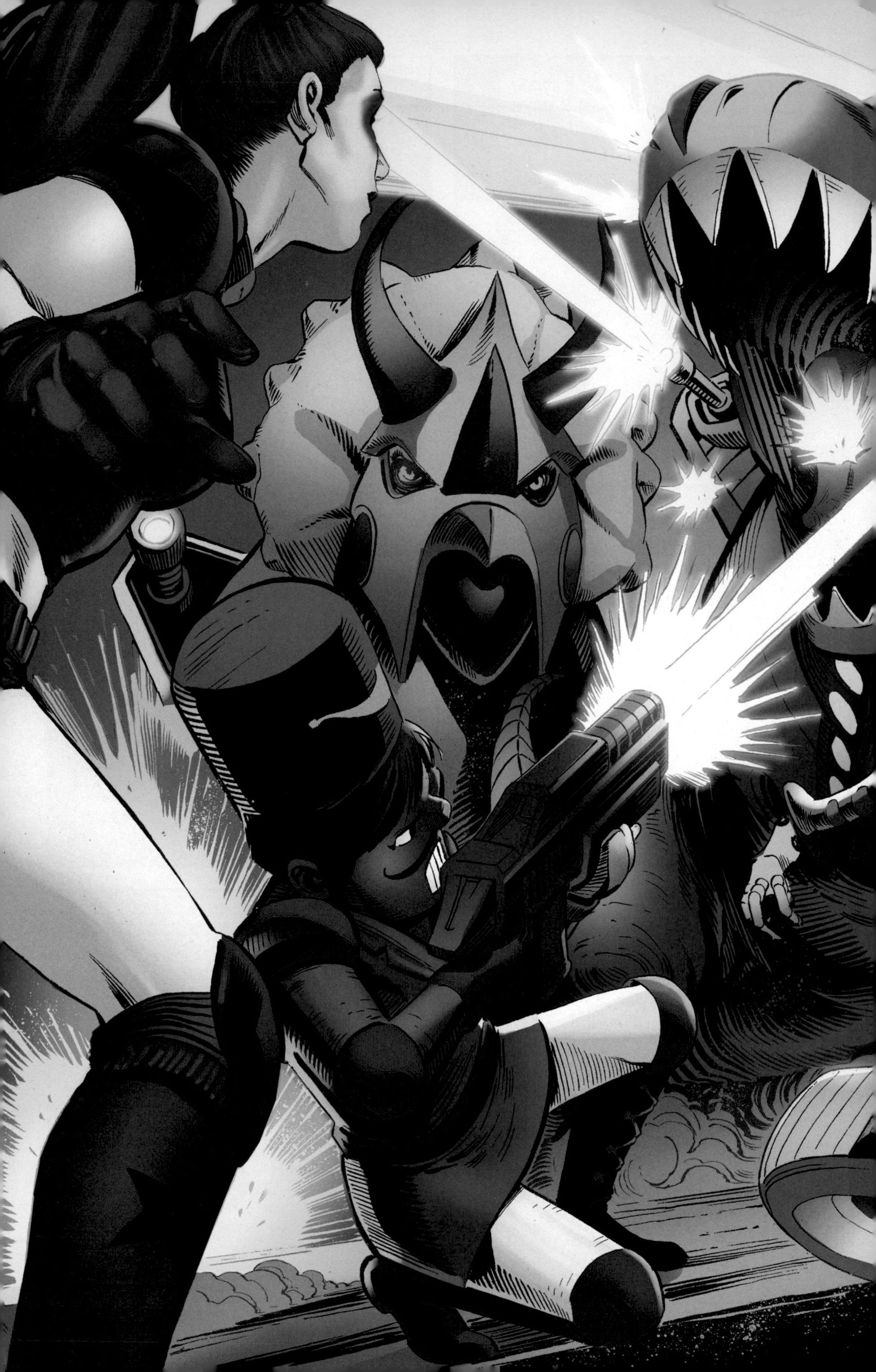

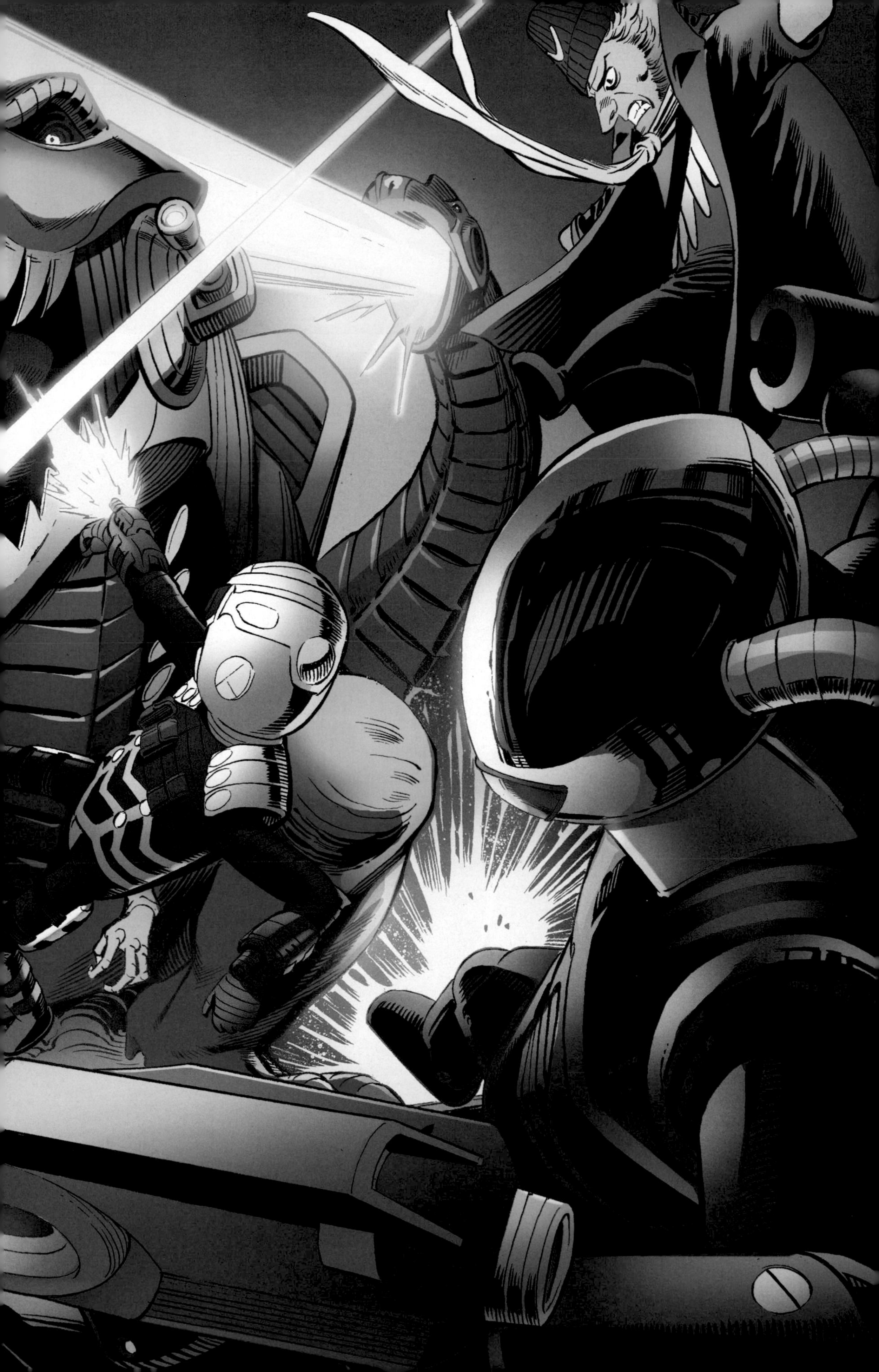

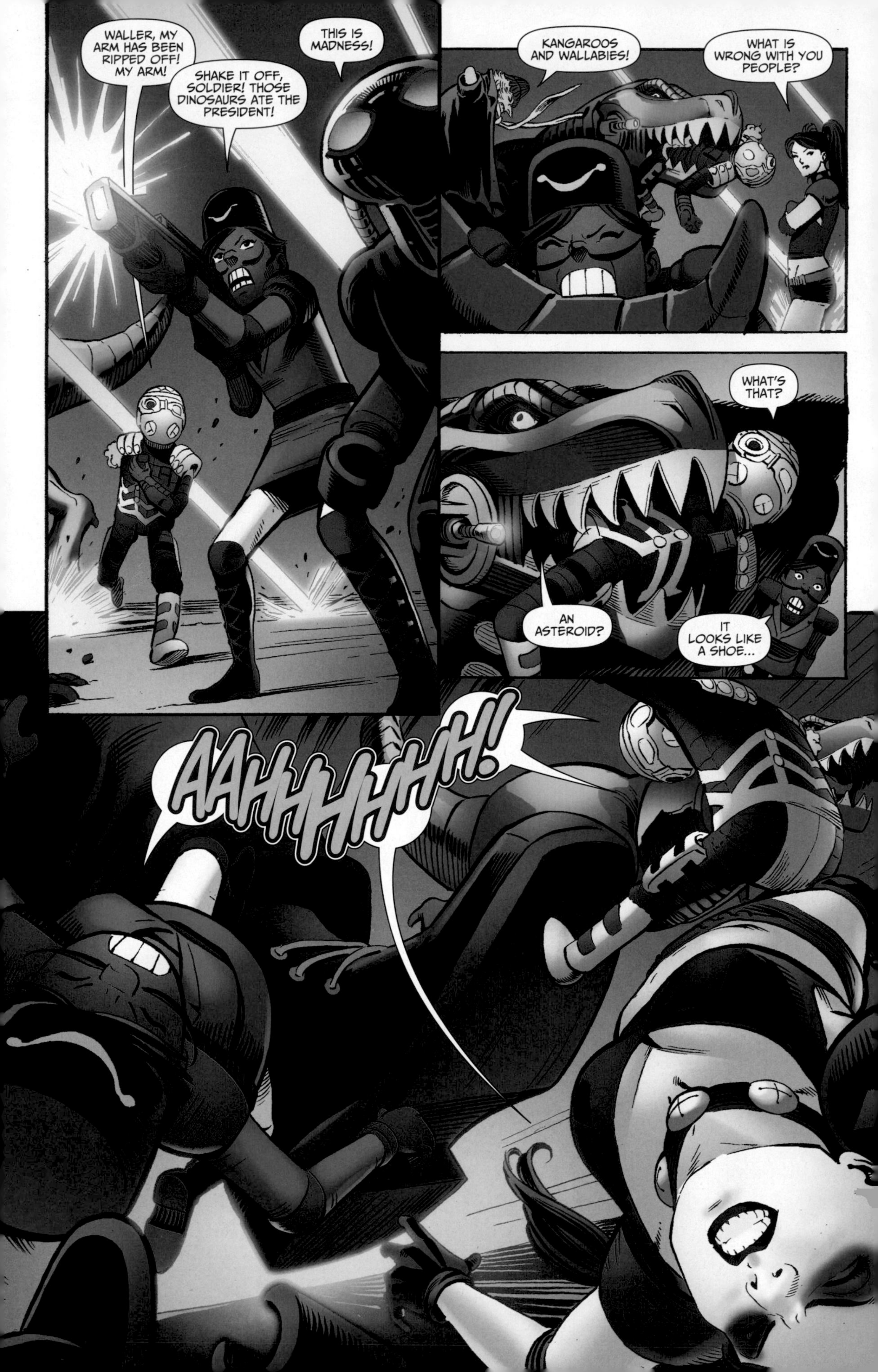
WALLER, MY ARM HAS BEEN RIPPED OFF! MY ARM!
SHAKE IT OFF, SOLDIER! THOSE DINOSAURS ATE THE PRESIDENT!
THIS IS MADNESS!
KANGAROOS AND WALLABIES!
WHAT IS WRONG WITH YOU PEOPLE?
WHAT'S THAT?
AN ASTEROID?
IT LOOKS LIKE A SHOE...
AAHHHHHH!

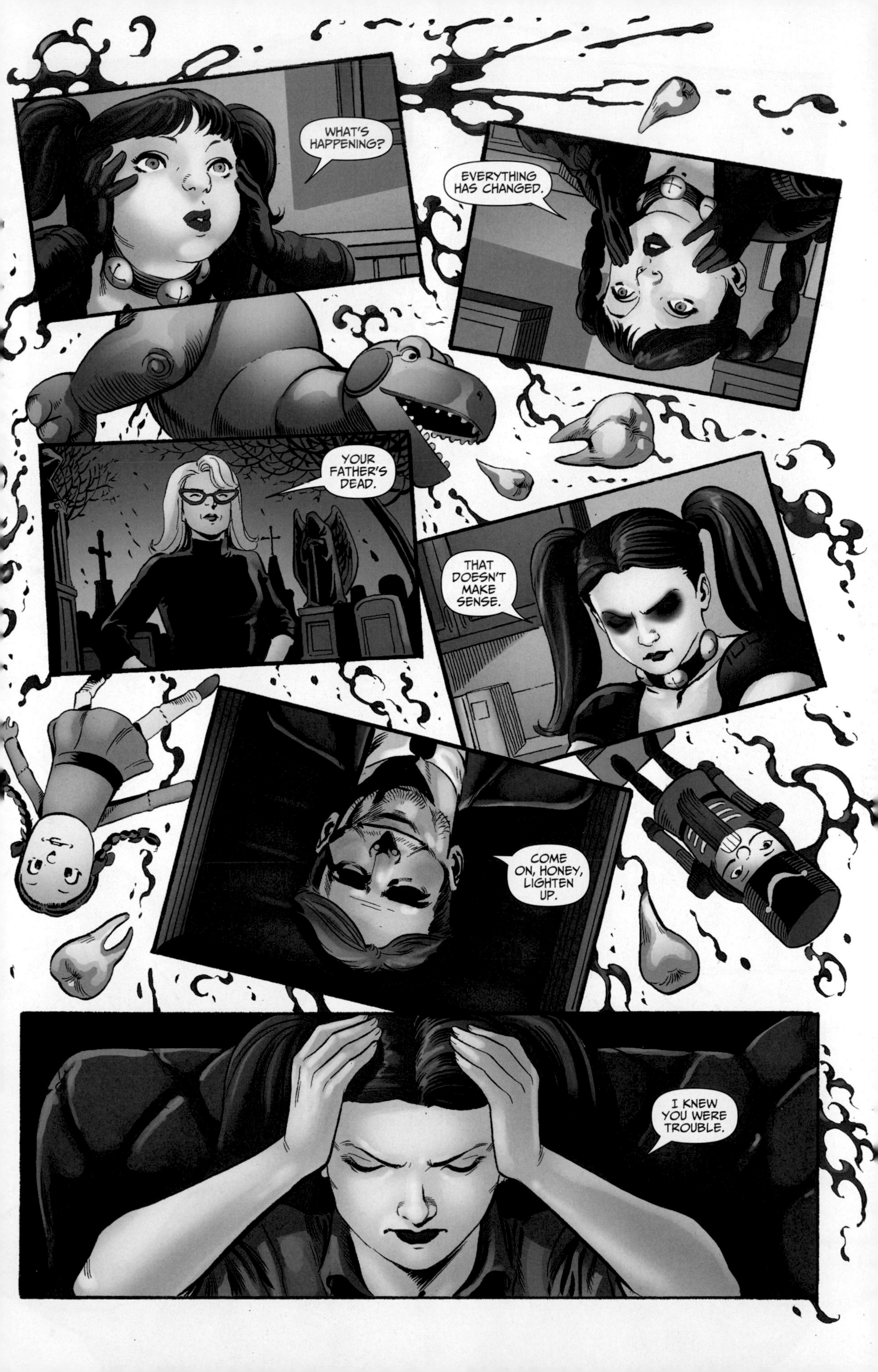
WHAT'S HAPPENING?
EVERYTHING HAS CHANGED.
YOUR FATHER'S DEAD.
THAT DOESN'T MAKE SENSE.
COME ON, HONEY, LIGHTEN UP.
I KNEW YOU WERE TROUBLE.

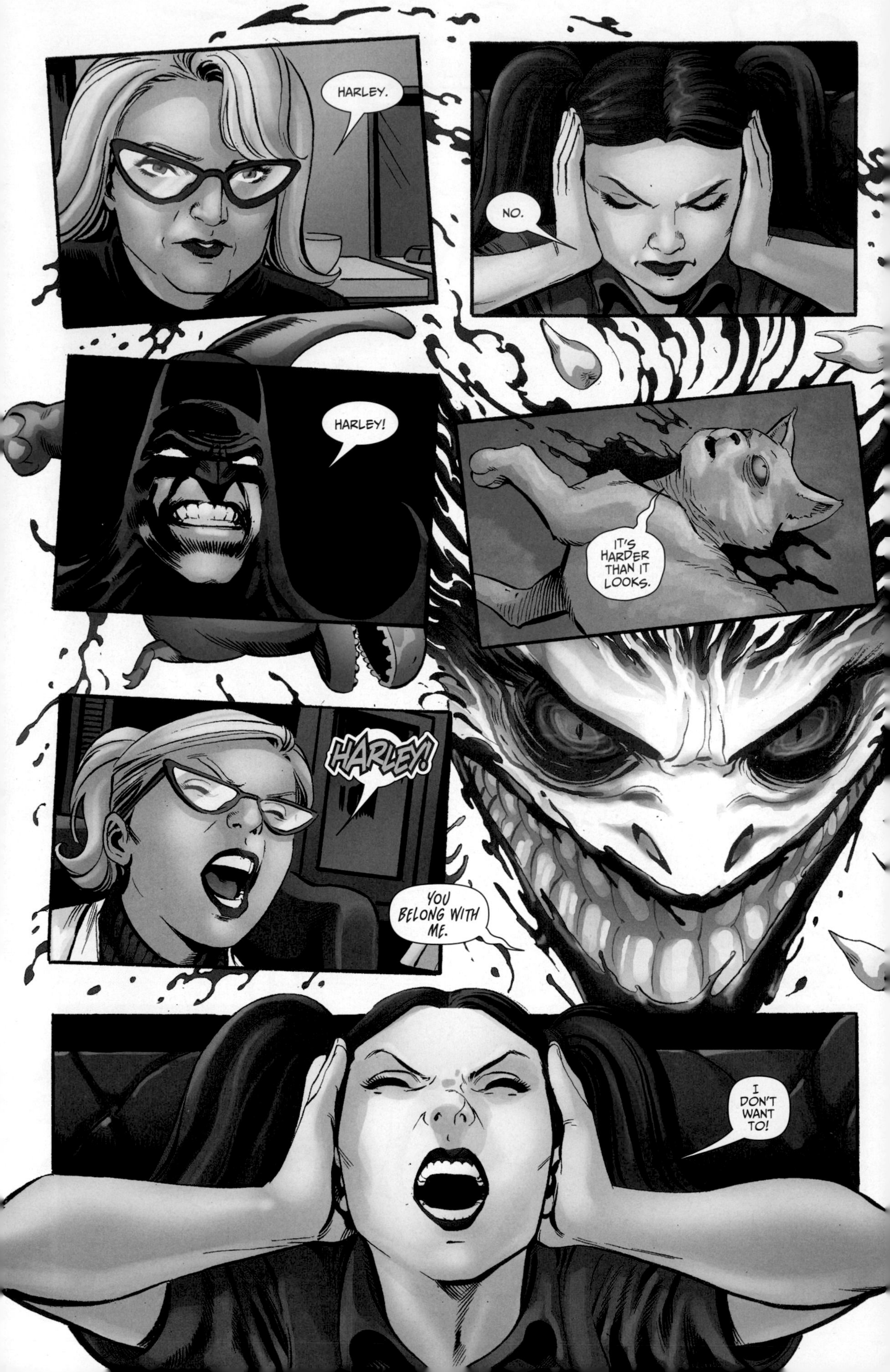
HARLEY.
NO.
HARLEY!
IT'S HARDER THAN IT LOOKS.
HARLEY!
YOU BELONG WITH ME.
I DON'T WANT TO!

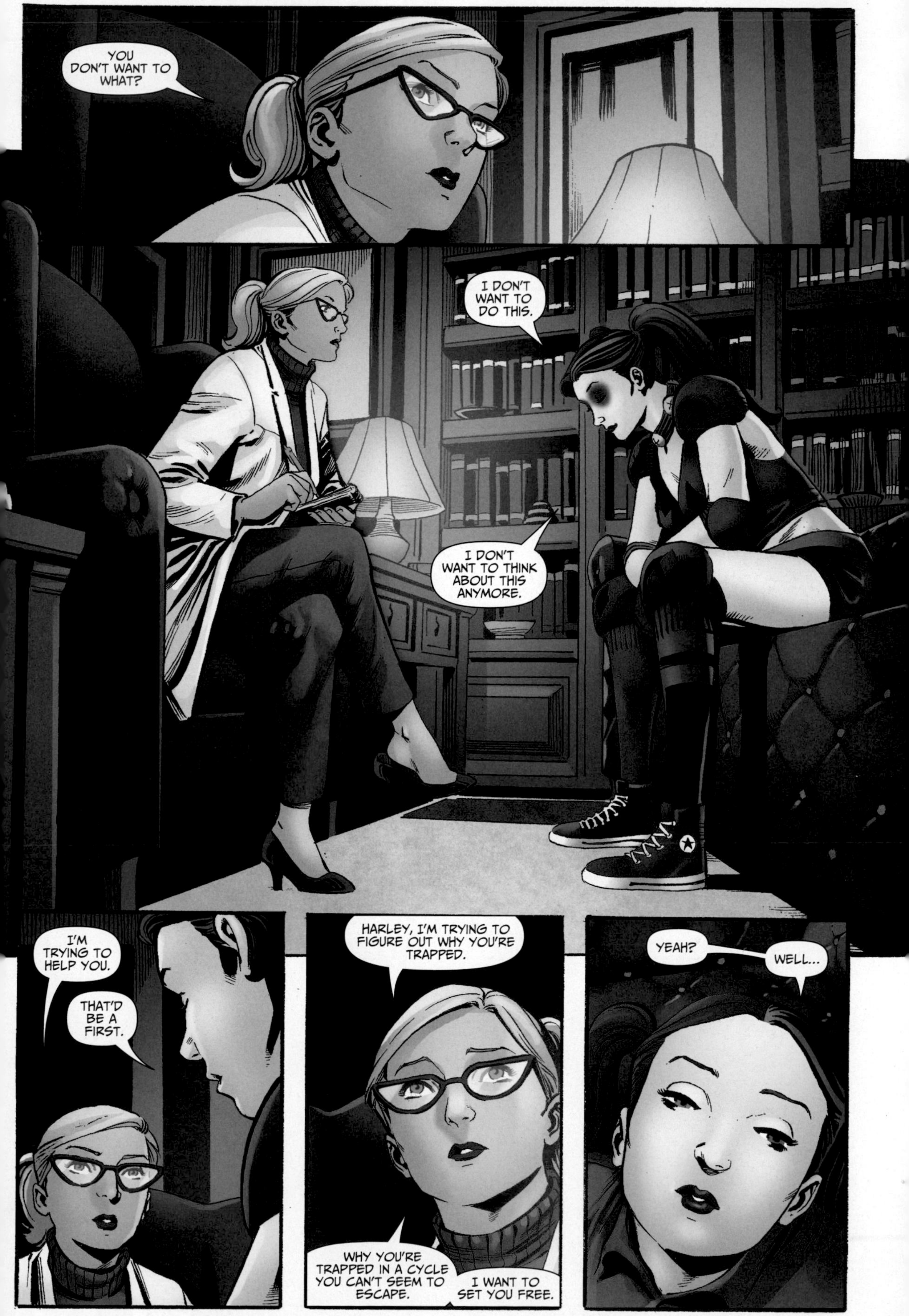
YOU DON'T WANT TO WHAT?
I DON'T WANT TO DO THIS.
I DON'T WANT TO THINK ABOUT THIS ANYMORE.
I'M TRYING TO HELP YOU.
THAT'D BE A FIRST.
HARLEY, I'M TRYING TO FIGURE OUT WHY YOU'RE TRAPPED.
WHY YOU'RE TRAPPED IN A CYCLE YOU CAN'T SEEM TO ESCAPE.
I WANT TO SET YOU FREE.
YEAH?
WELL...

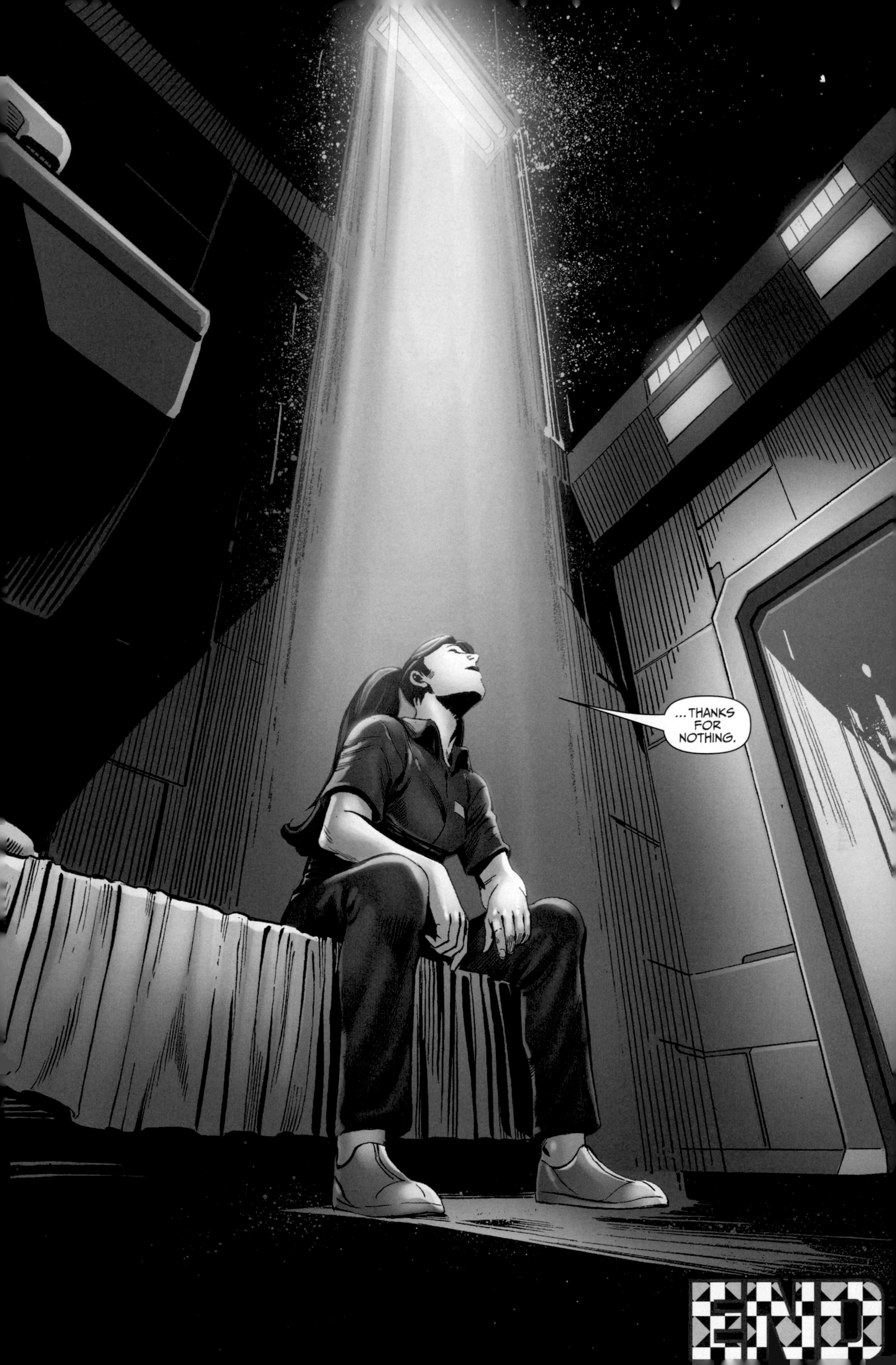
...THANKS FOR NOTHING.
END

NEW SUICIDE SQUAD #18 VARIANT COVER BY
TONY S. DANIEL & TOMEU MOREY

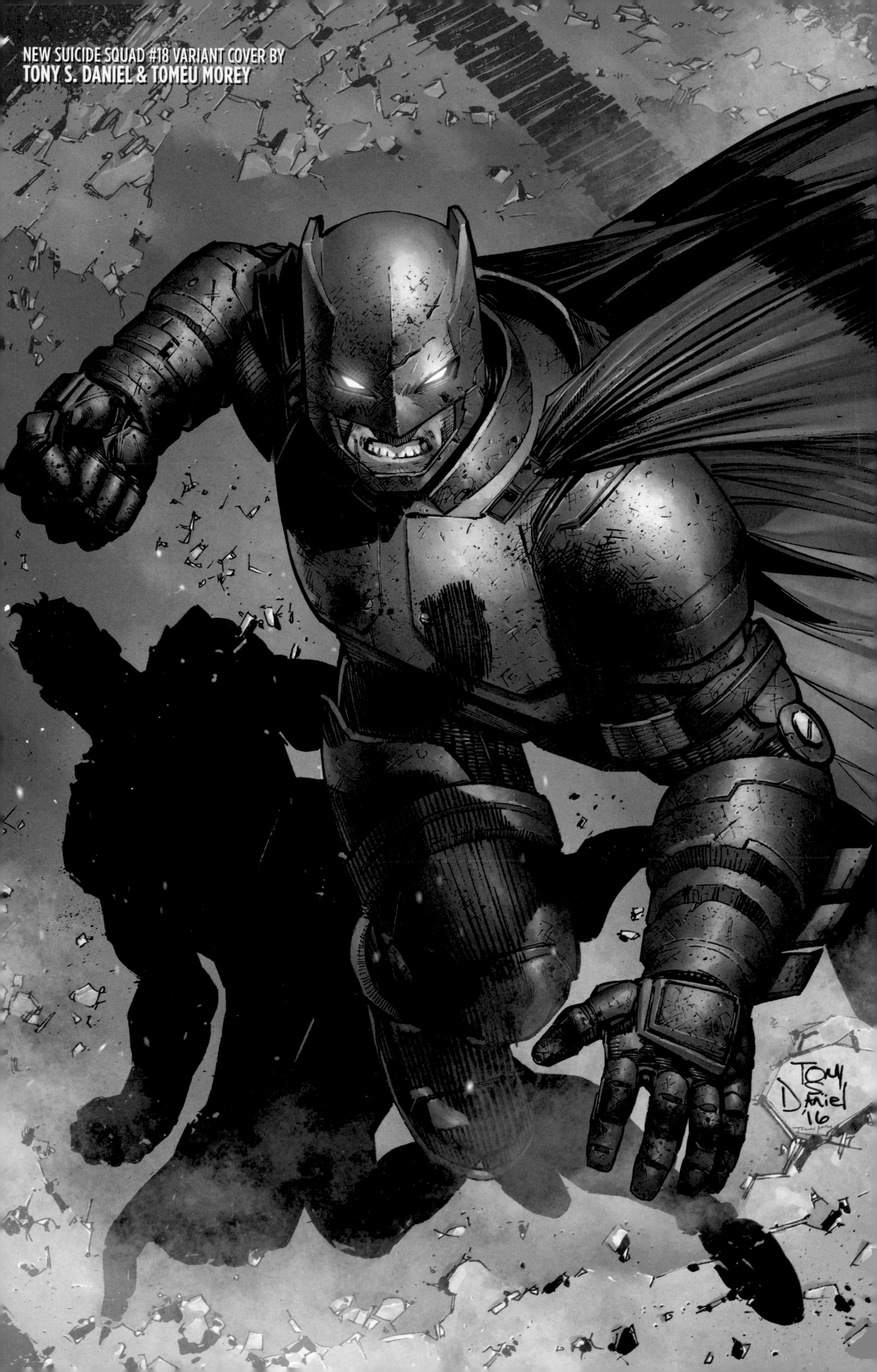

COVER SKETCHES BY JUAN FERREYRA
NEW SUICIDE SQUAD #17

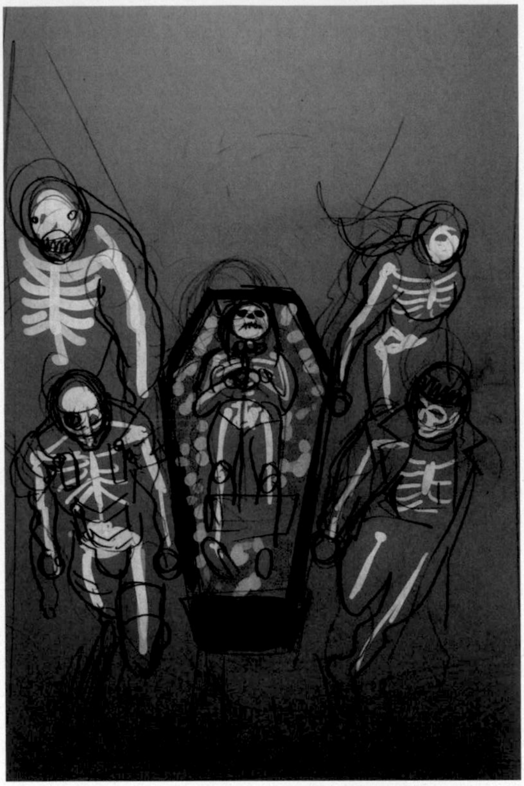

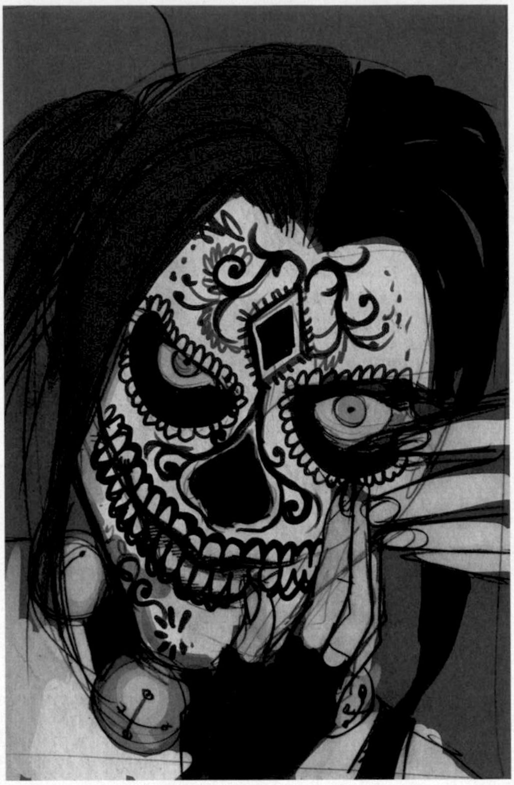

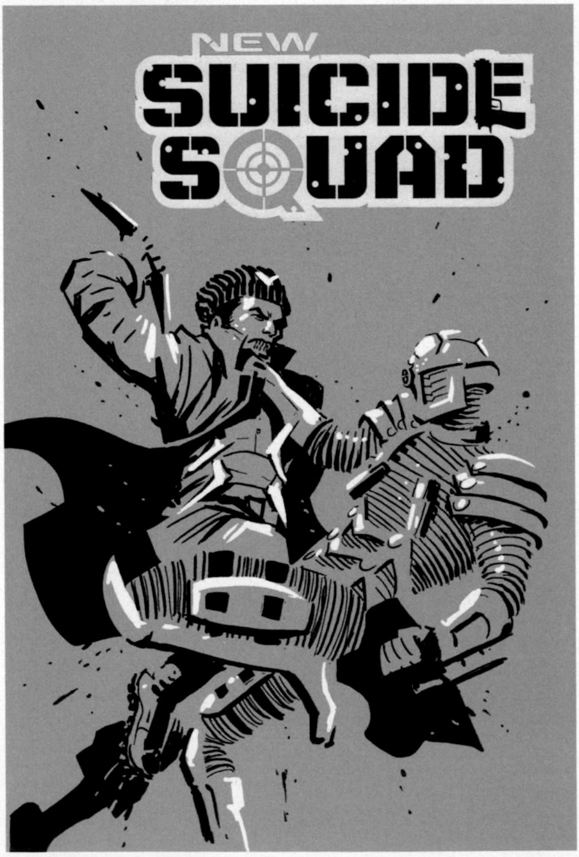
NEW
SUICIDE
SQUAD

NEW
SUICIDE
SQUAD

NEW
SUICIDE
SQUAD

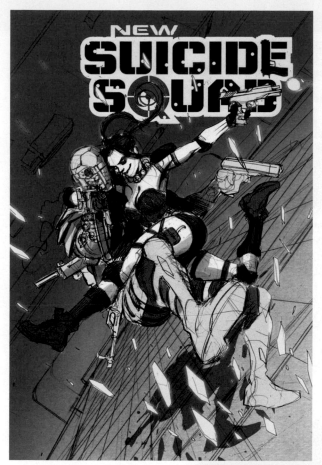

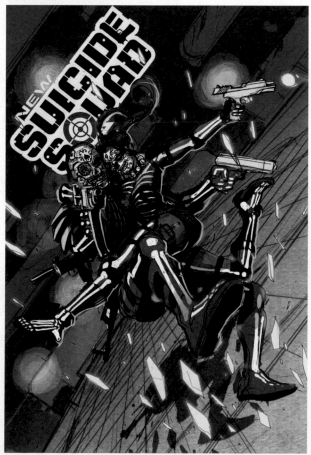

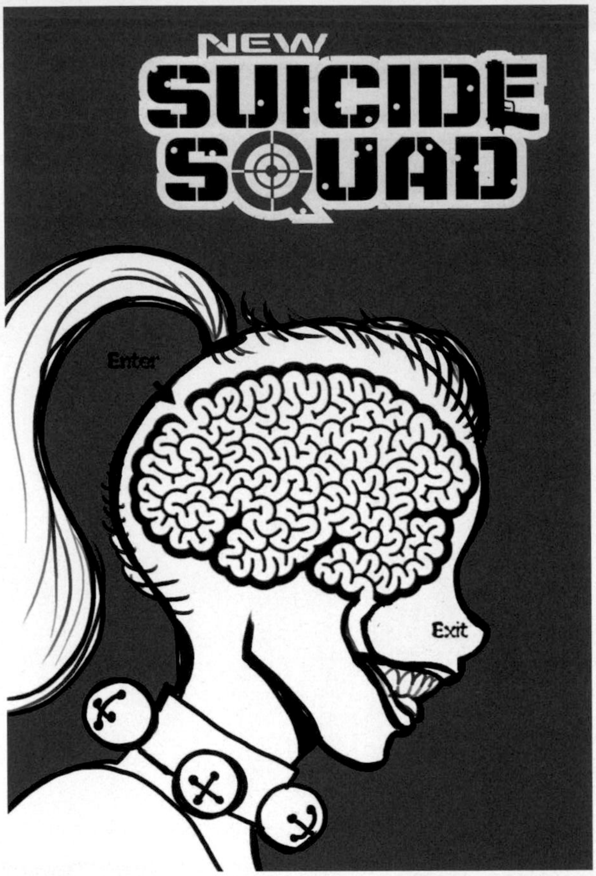
NEW
SUICIDE
SQUAD
Enter
Exit

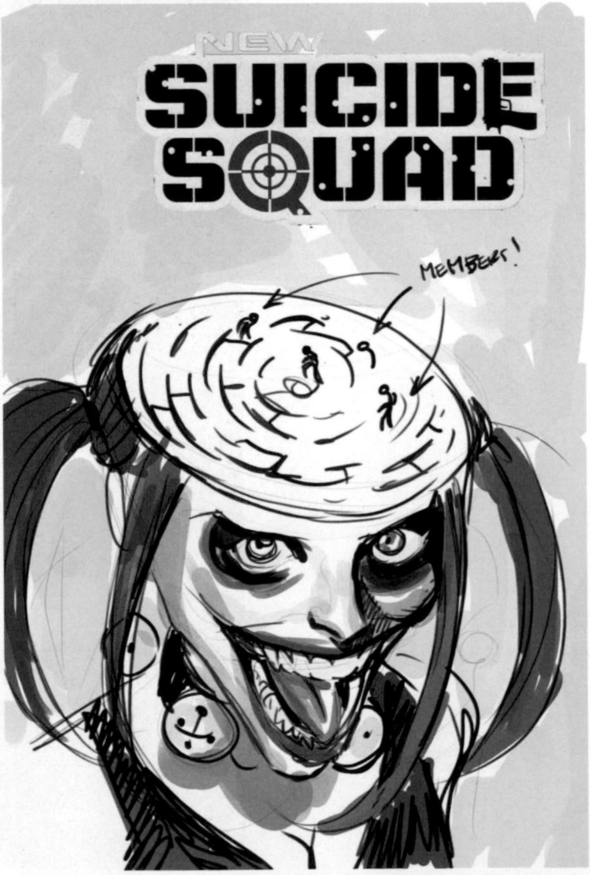
NEW
SUICIDE
SQUAD
MEMBERS!

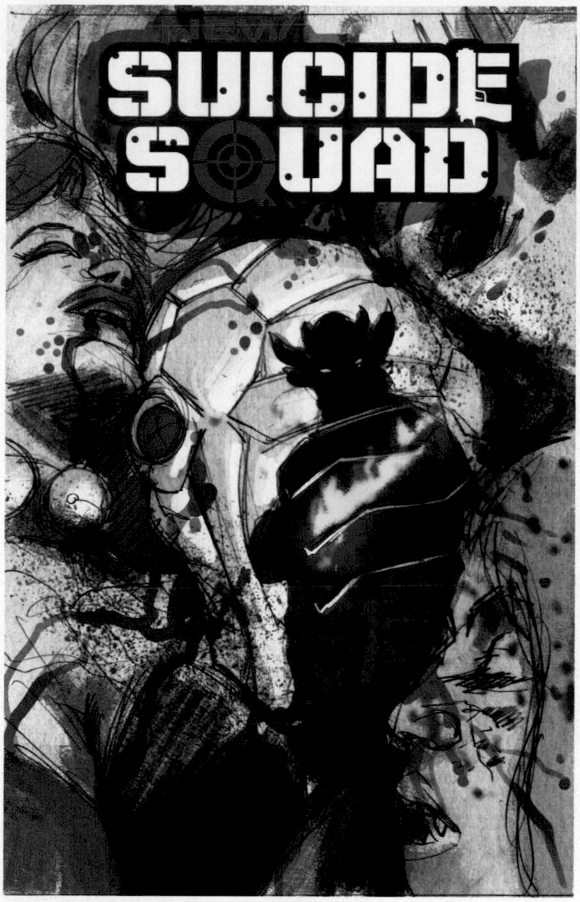
NEW
SUICIDE
SQUAD

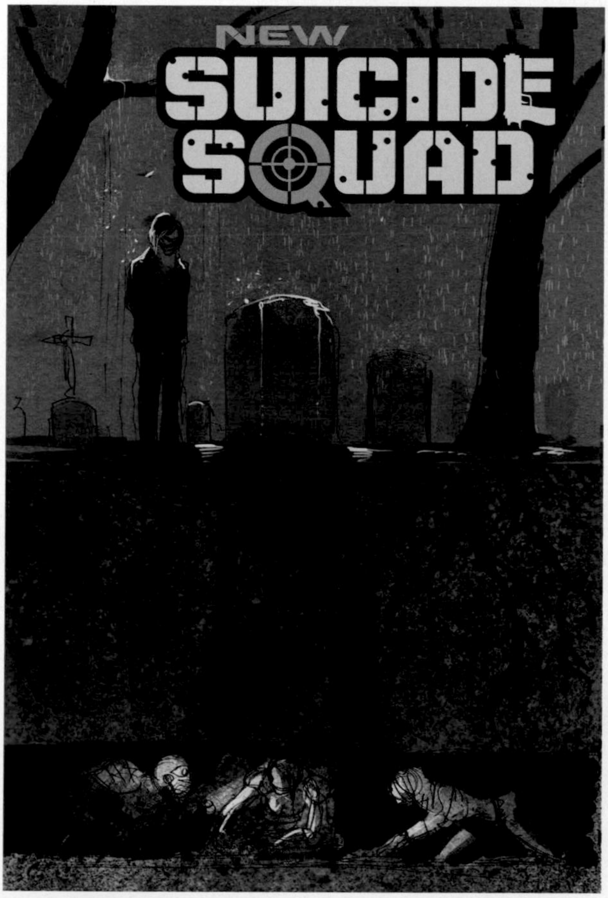
NEW
SUICIDE
SQUAD

NEW
SUICIDE
SQUAD

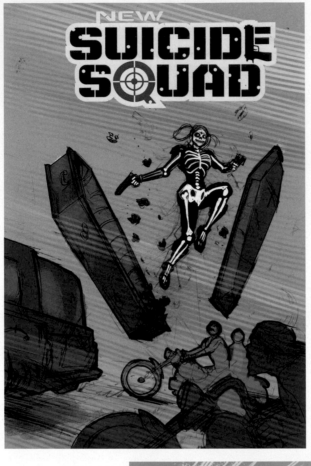

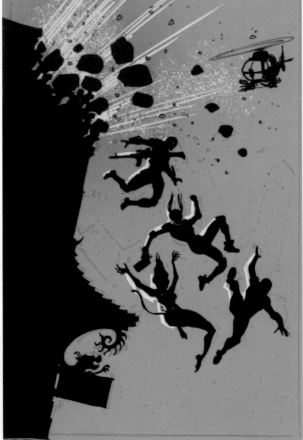

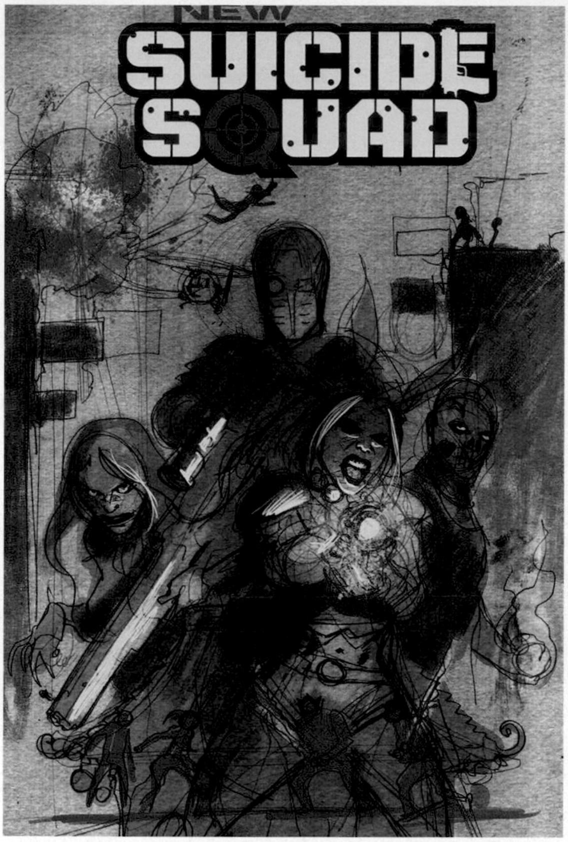
NEW
SUICIDE
SQUAD

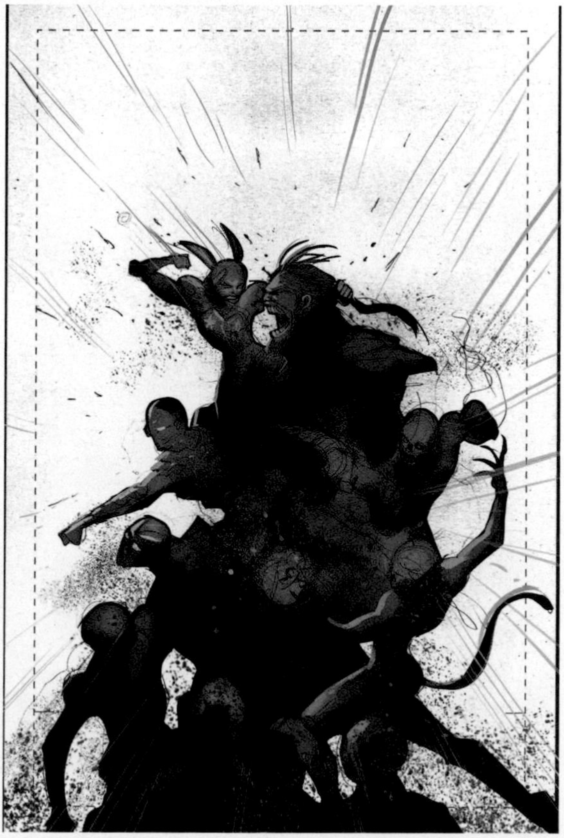

NEW SUICIDE SQUAD #19

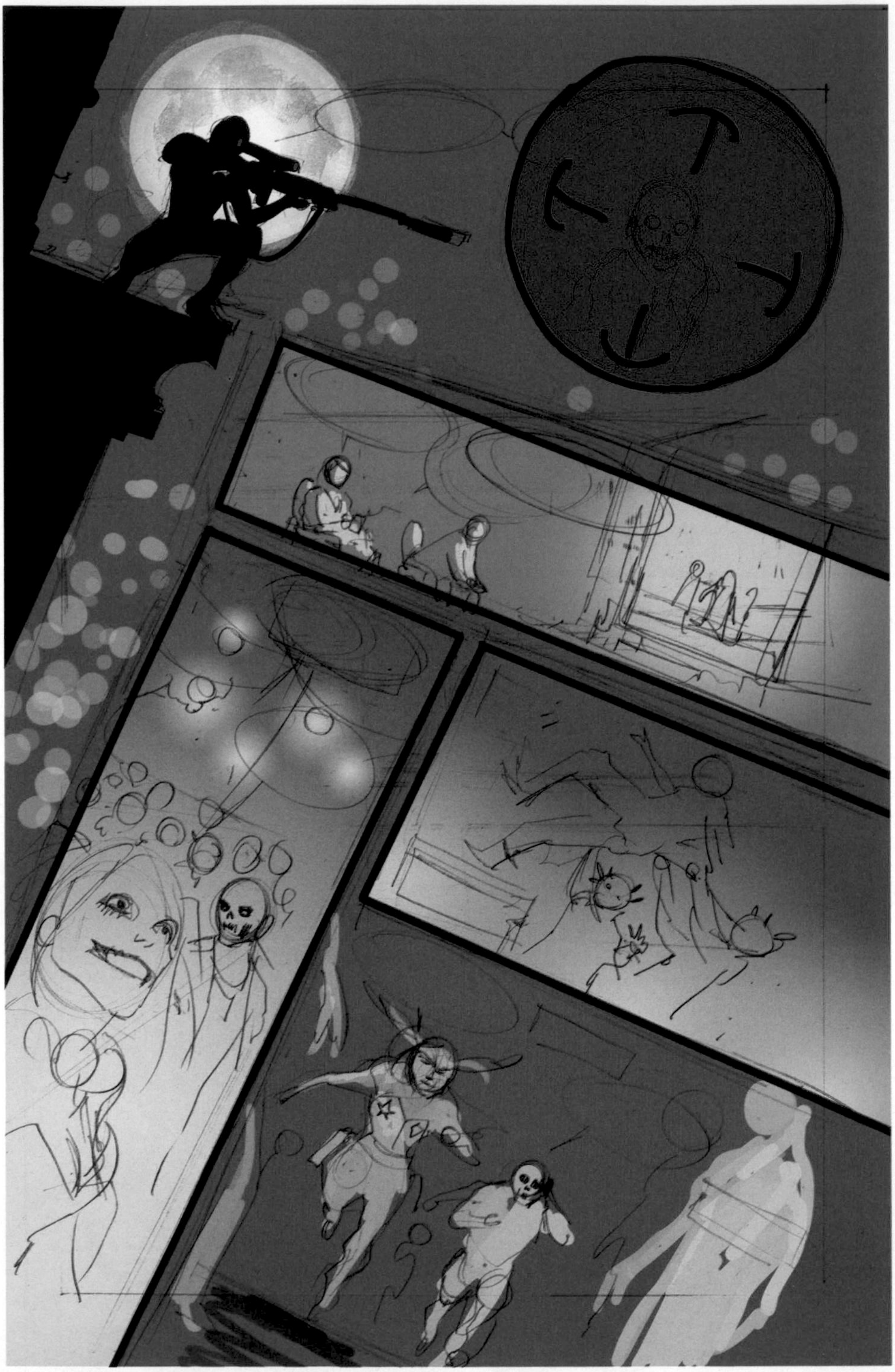

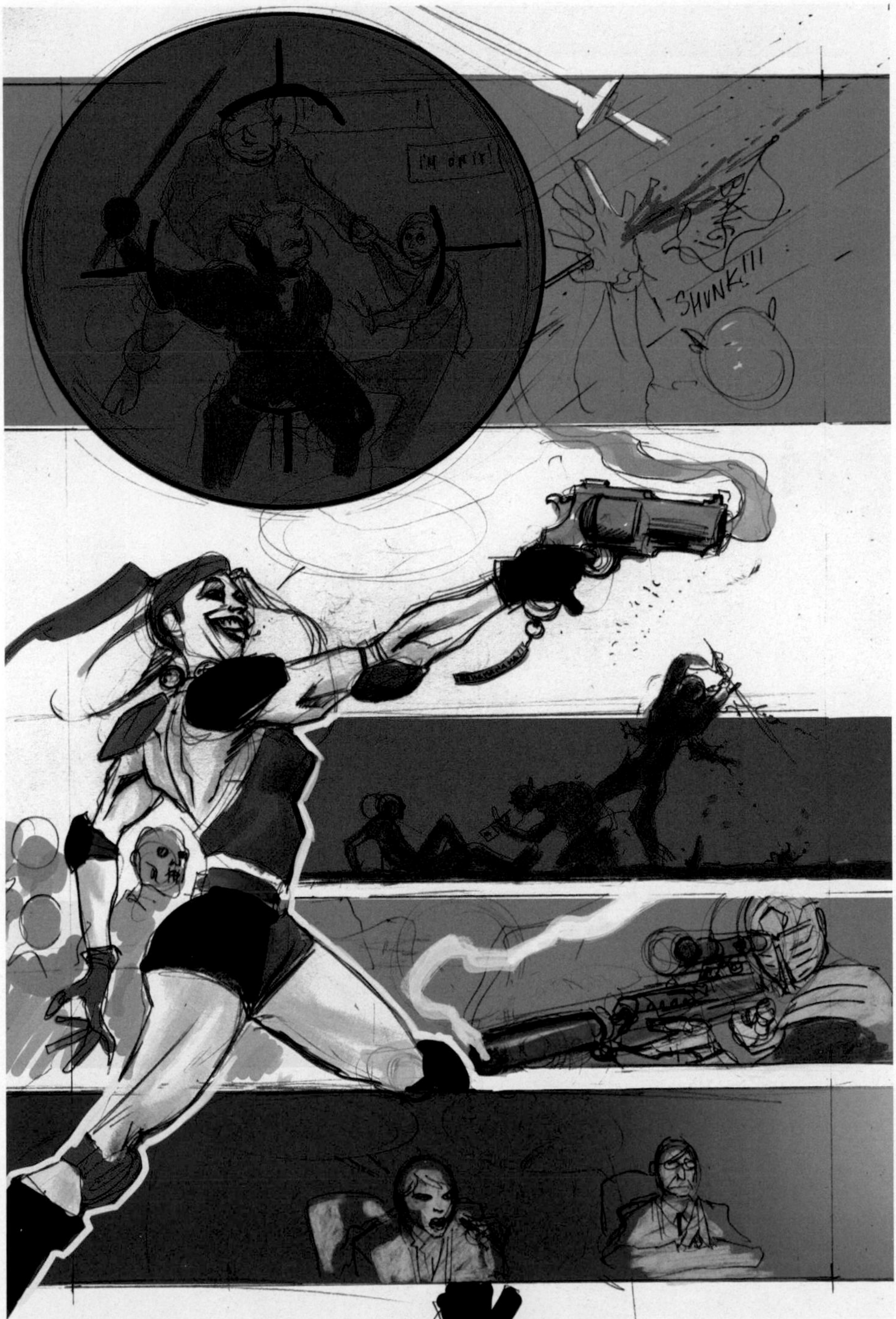
I'M ON IT!
SHUNK!!!

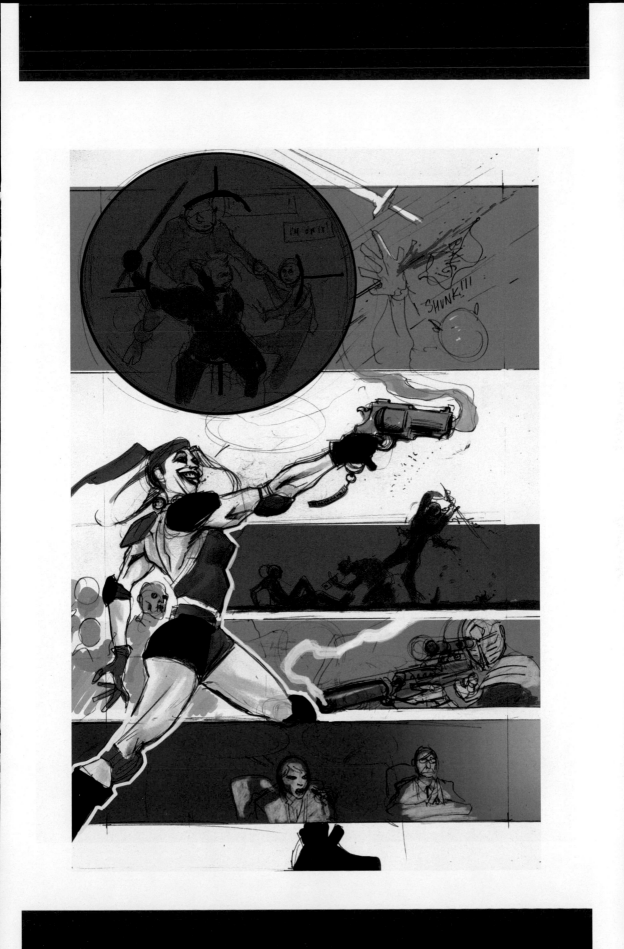

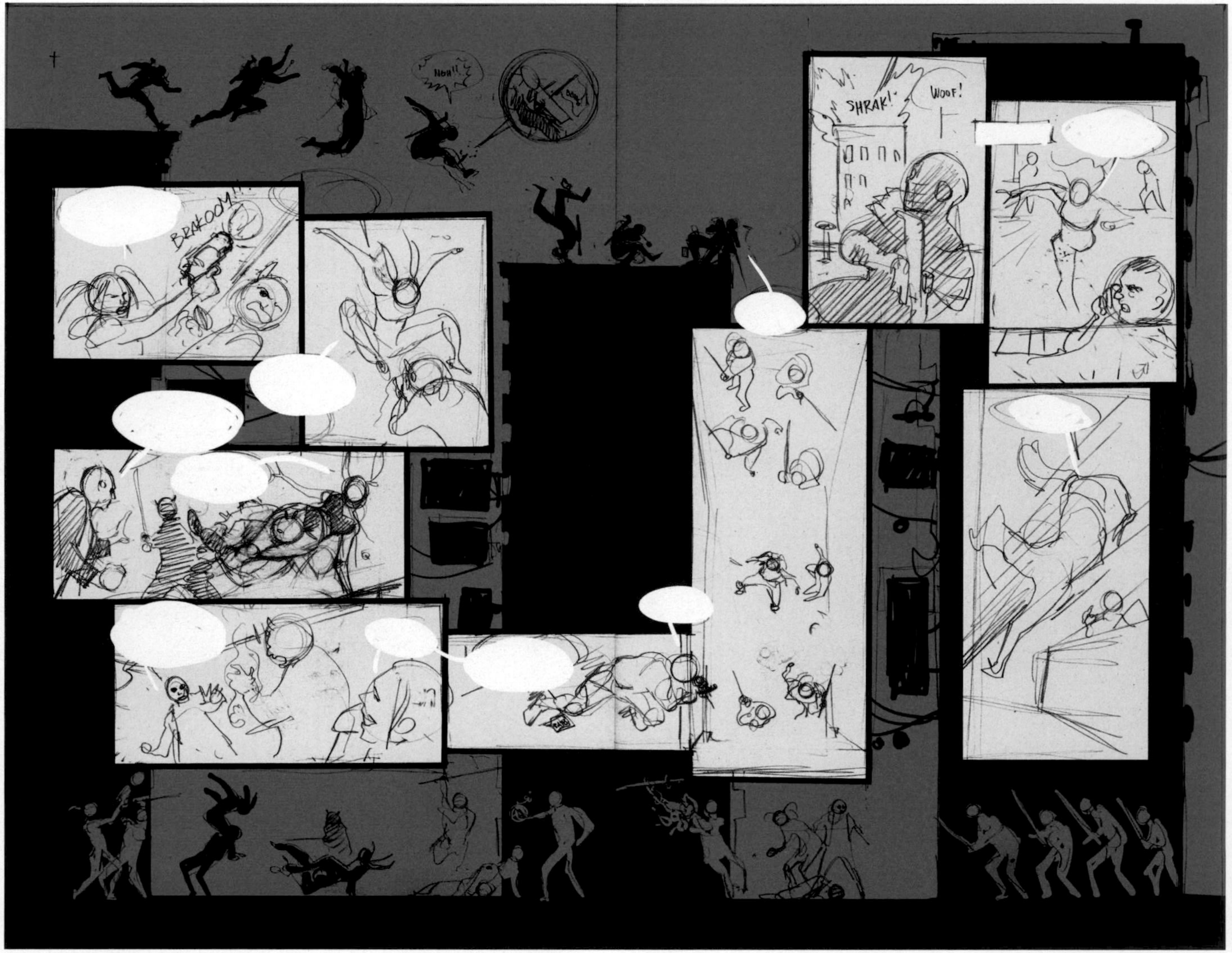
SHRAK!
WOOF!
NGH!!
BRAKOOM!!!

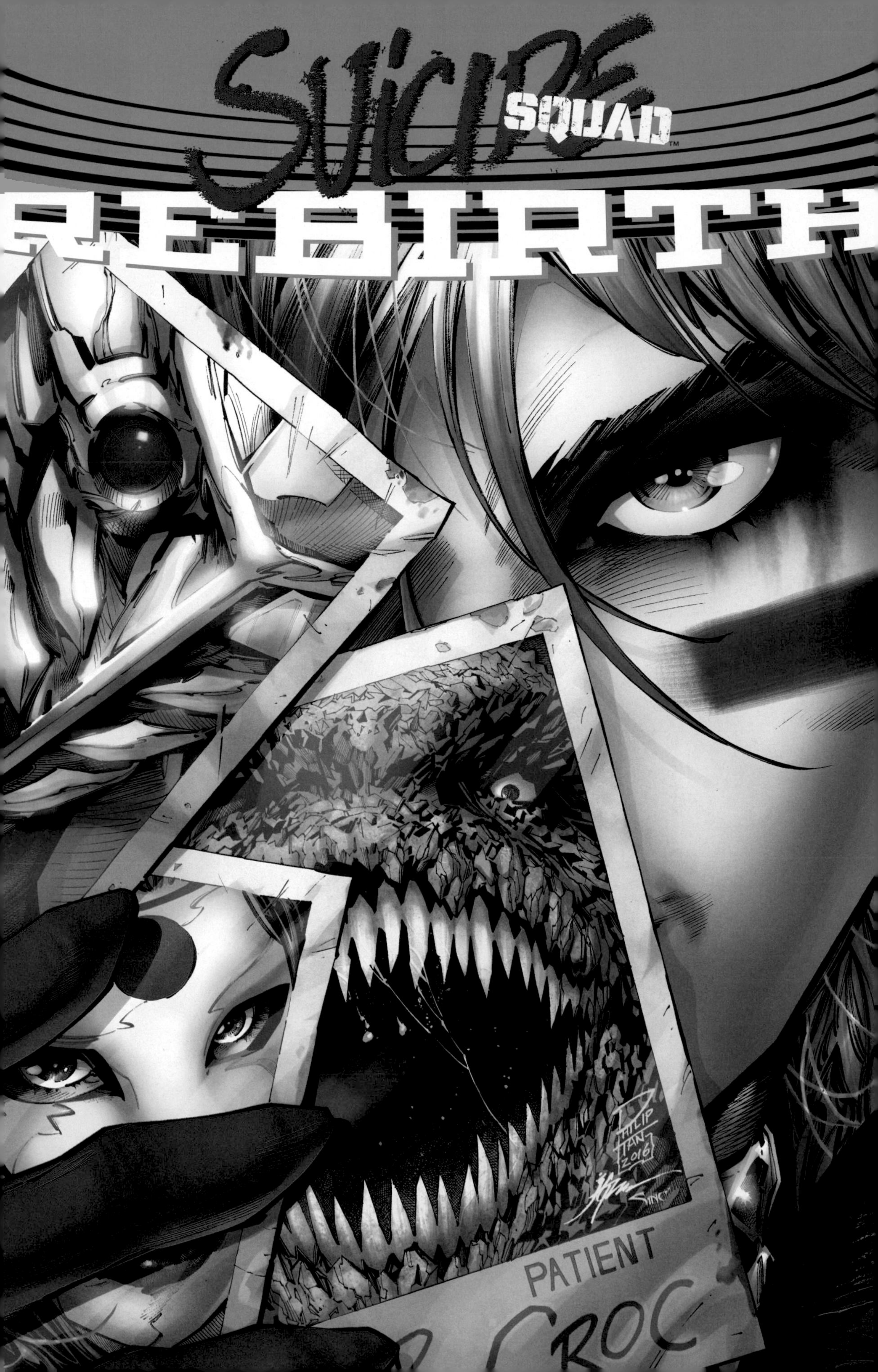
SUICIDE SQUAD
REBIRTH
PHILIP TAN 2016
PATIENT
CROC

The future (and past) of the DC Universe starts with DC UNIVERSE: REBIRTH!

Explore the changing world of Harley Quinn and the rest of Task Force X in this special bonus preview of **SUICIDE SQUAD: REBIRTH #1**.

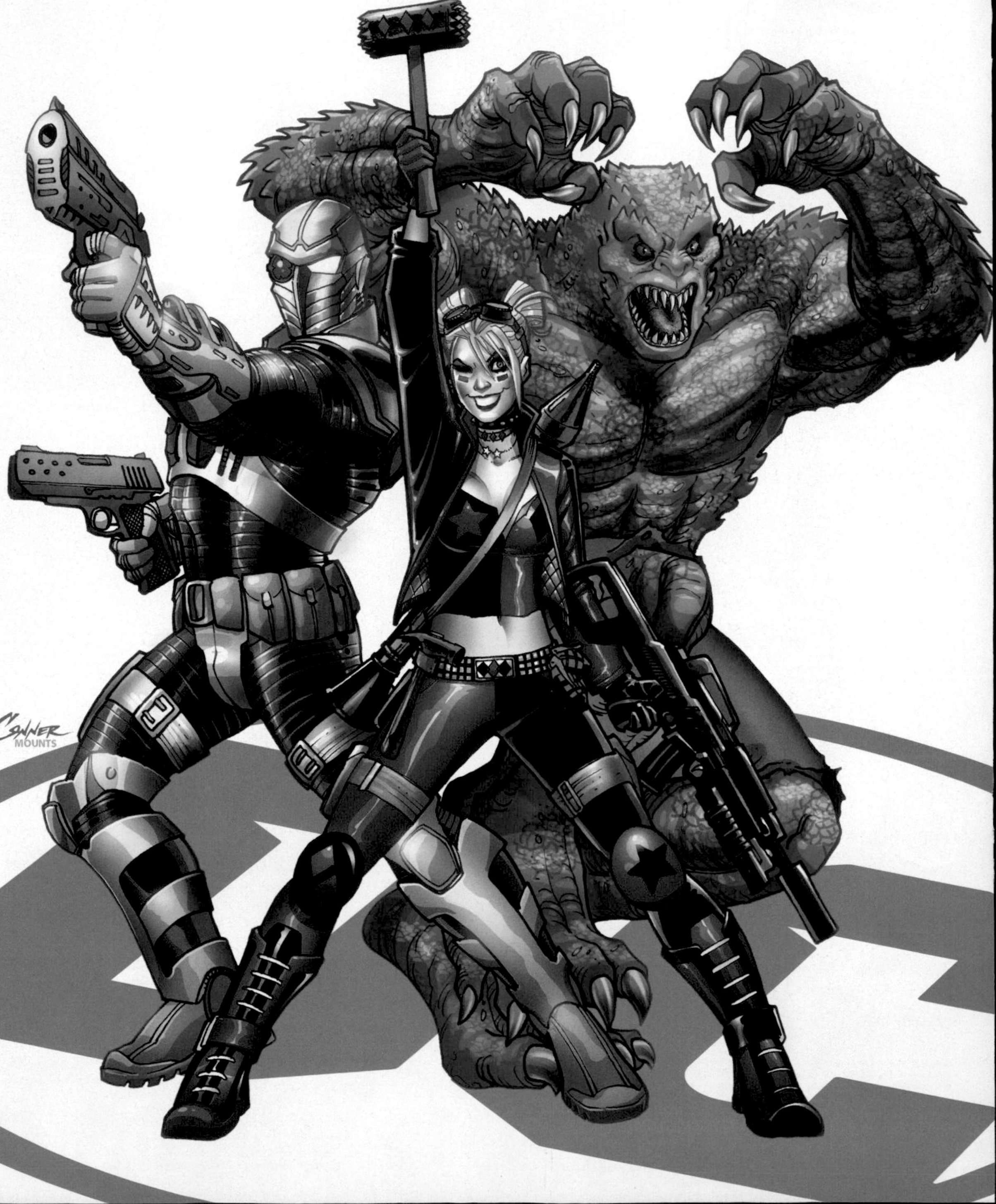
CONNER
MOUNTS

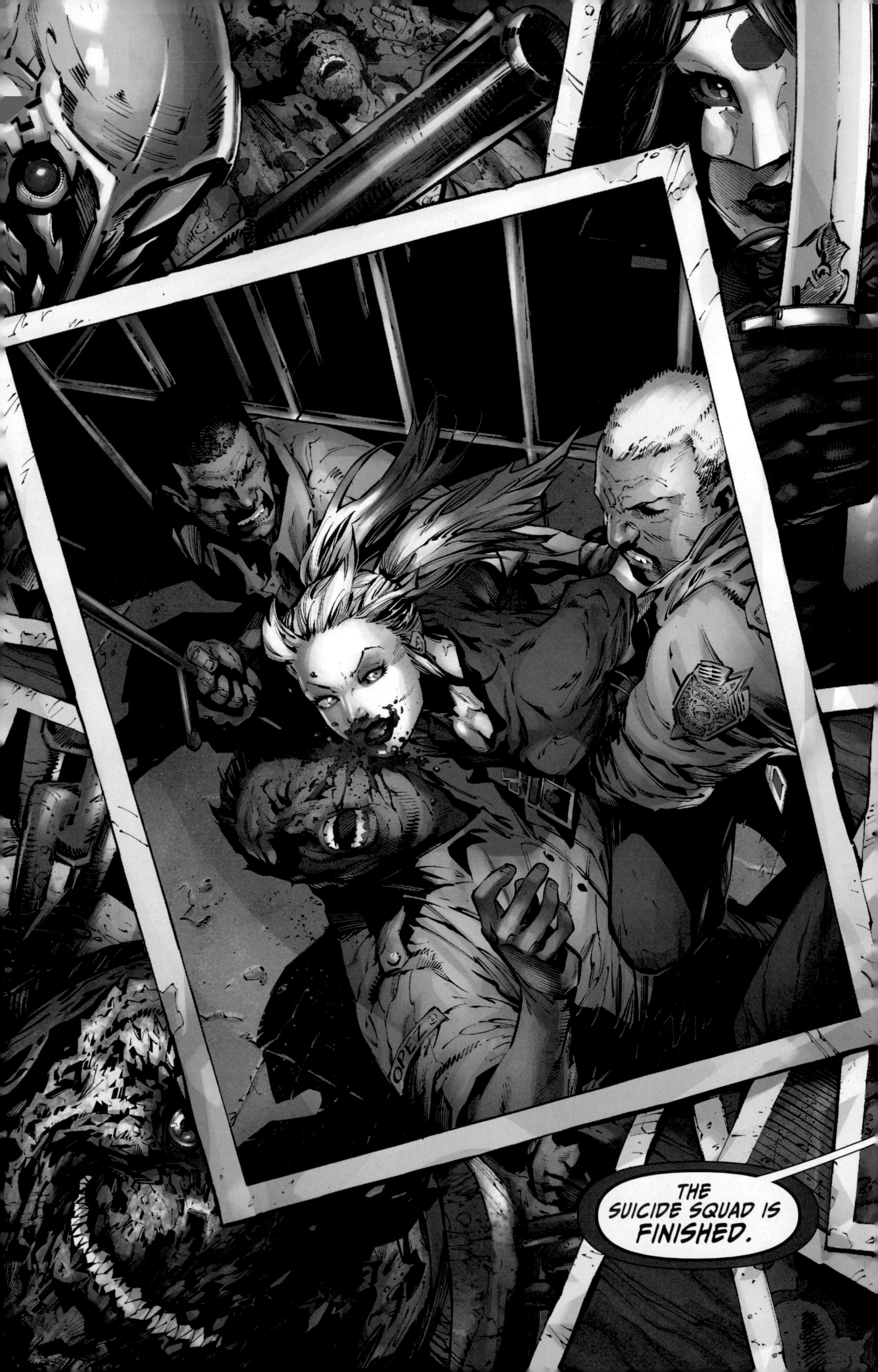
THE SUICIDE SQUAD IS FINISHED.

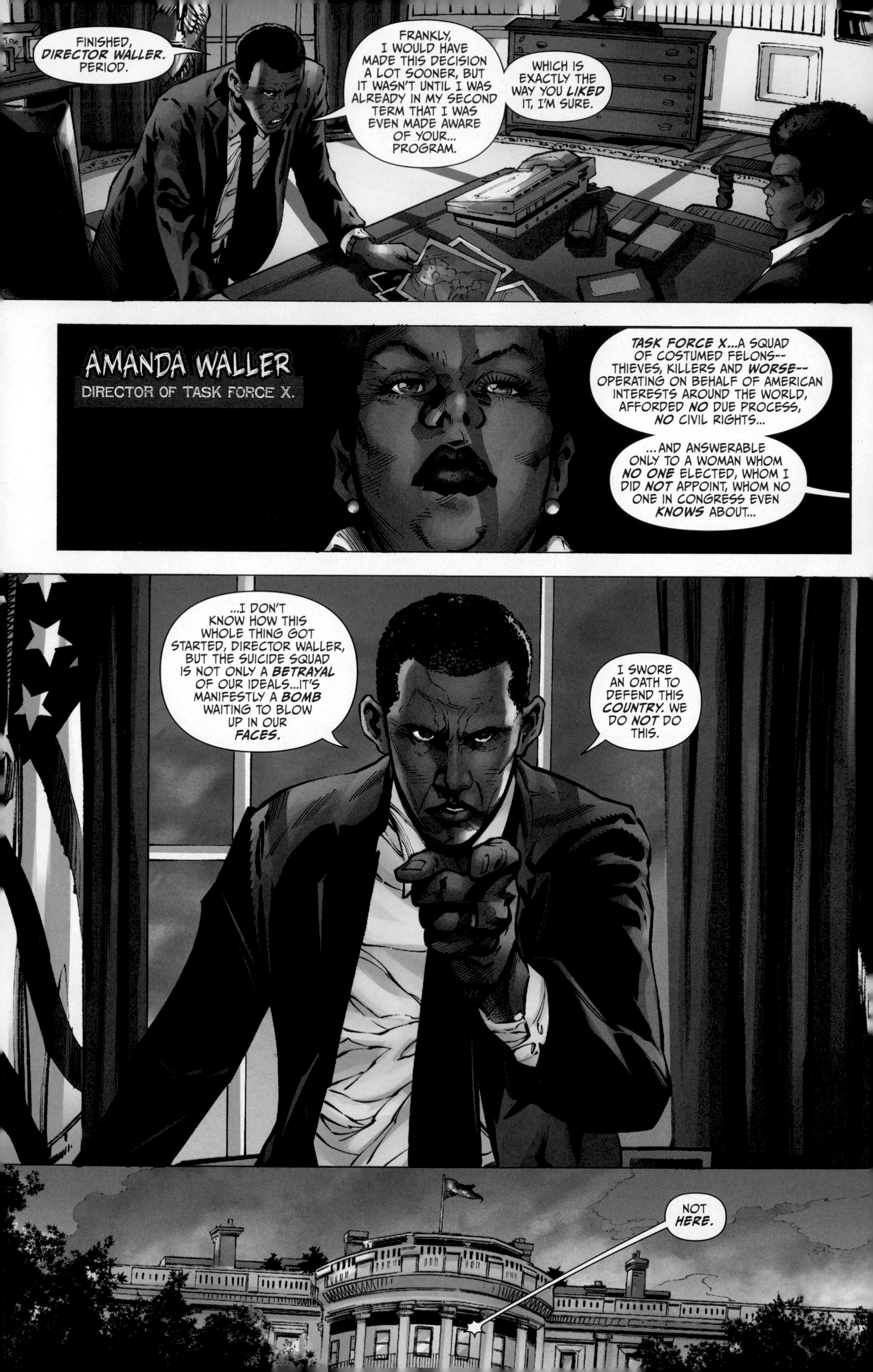
FINISHED, DIRECTOR WALLER. PERIOD.
FRANKLY, I WOULD HAVE MADE THIS DECISION A LOT SOONER, BUT IT WASN'T UNTIL I WAS ALREADY IN MY SECOND TERM THAT I WAS EVEN MADE AWARE OF YOUR... PROGRAM.
WHICH IS EXACTLY THE WAY YOU LIKED IT, I'M SURE.
AMANDA WALLER
DIRECTOR OF TASK FORCE X.
TASK FORCE X...A SQUAD OF COSTUMED FELONS--THIEVES, KILLERS AND WORSE--OPERATING ON BEHALF OF AMERICAN INTERESTS AROUND THE WORLD, AFFORDED NO DUE PROCESS, NO CIVIL RIGHTS...
...AND ANSWERABLE ONLY TO A WOMAN WHOM NO ONE ELECTED, WHOM I DID NOT APPOINT, WHOM NO ONE IN CONGRESS EVEN KNOWS ABOUT...
...I DON'T KNOW HOW THIS WHOLE THING GOT STARTED, DIRECTOR WALLER, BUT THE SUICIDE SQUAD IS NOT ONLY A BETRAYAL OF OUR IDEALS...IT'S MANIFESTLY A BOMB WAITING TO BLOW UP IN OUR FACES.
I SWORE AN OATH TO DEFEND THIS COUNTRY. WE DO NOT DO THIS.
NOT HERE.

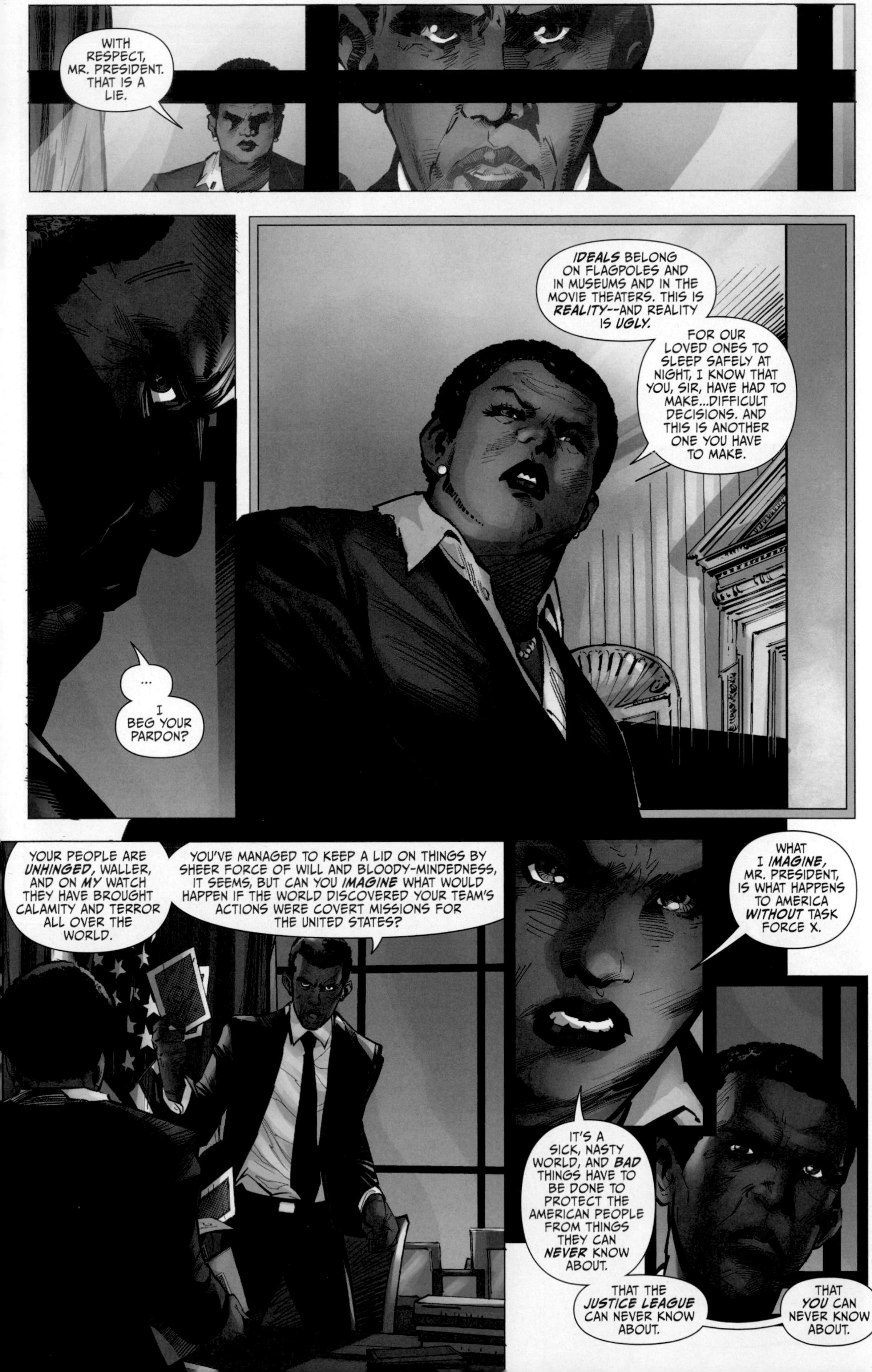
WITH RESPECT, MR. PRESIDENT. THAT IS A LIE.
IDEALS BELONG ON FLAGPOLES AND IN MUSEUMS AND IN THE MOVIE THEATERS. THIS IS REALITY--AND REALITY IS UGLY.
FOR OUR LOVED ONES TO SLEEP SAFELY AT NIGHT, I KNOW THAT YOU, SIR, HAVE HAD TO MAKE...DIFFICULT DECISIONS. AND THIS IS ANOTHER ONE YOU HAVE TO MAKE.
...
I BEG YOUR PARDON?
YOUR PEOPLE ARE UNHINGED, WALLER, AND ON MY WATCH THEY HAVE BROUGHT CALAMITY AND TERROR ALL OVER THE WORLD.
YOU'VE MANAGED TO KEEP A LID ON THINGS BY SHEER FORCE OF WILL AND BLOODY-MINDEDNESS, IT SEEMS, BUT CAN YOU IMAGINE WHAT WOULD HAPPEN IF THE WORLD DISCOVERED YOUR TEAM'S ACTIONS WERE COVERT MISSIONS FOR THE UNITED STATES?
WHAT I IMAGINE, MR. PRESIDENT, IS WHAT HAPPENS TO AMERICA WITHOUT TASK FORCE X.
IT'S A SICK, NASTY WORLD, AND BAD THINGS HAVE TO BE DONE TO PROTECT THE AMERICAN PEOPLE FROM THINGS THEY CAN NEVER KNOW ABOUT.
THAT THE JUSTICE LEAGUE CAN NEVER KNOW ABOUT.
THAT YOU CAN NEVER KNOW ABOUT.

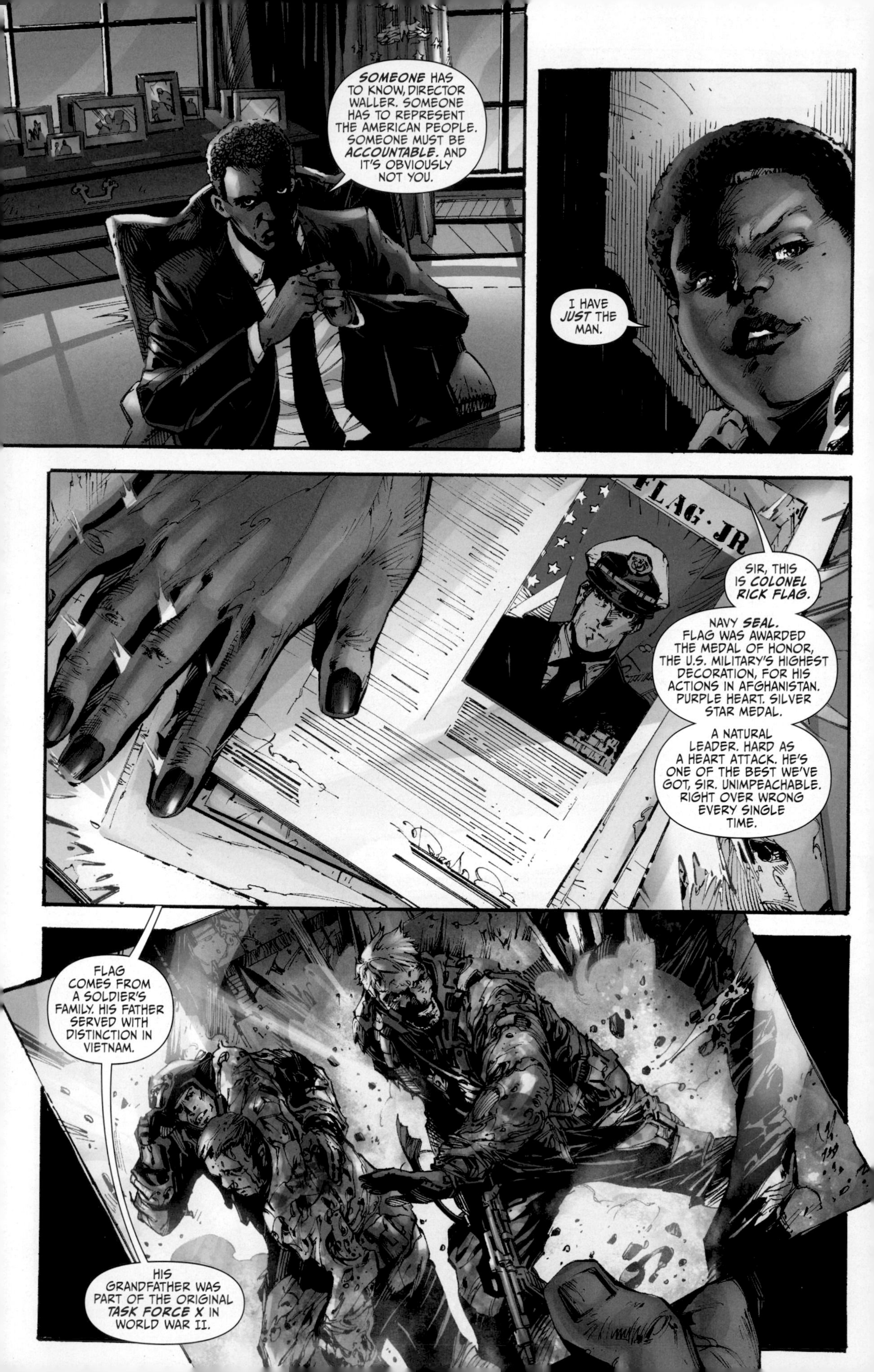
SOMEONE HAS TO KNOW, DIRECTOR WALLER. SOMEONE HAS TO REPRESENT THE AMERICAN PEOPLE. SOMEONE MUST BE ACCOUNTABLE. AND IT'S OBVIOUSLY NOT YOU.
I HAVE JUST THE MAN.
FLAG · JR
SIR, THIS IS COLONEL RICK FLAG.
NAVY SEAL. FLAG WAS AWARDED THE MEDAL OF HONOR, THE U.S. MILITARY'S HIGHEST DECORATION, FOR HIS ACTIONS IN AFGHANISTAN. PURPLE HEART. SILVER STAR MEDAL.
A NATURAL LEADER. HARD AS A HEART ATTACK. HE'S ONE OF THE BEST WE'VE GOT, SIR. UNIMPEACHABLE. RIGHT OVER WRONG EVERY SINGLE TIME.
FLAG COMES FROM A SOLDIER'S FAMILY. HIS FATHER SERVED WITH DISTINCTION IN VIETNAM.
HIS GRANDFATHER WAS PART OF THE ORIGINAL TASK FORCE X IN WORLD WAR II.

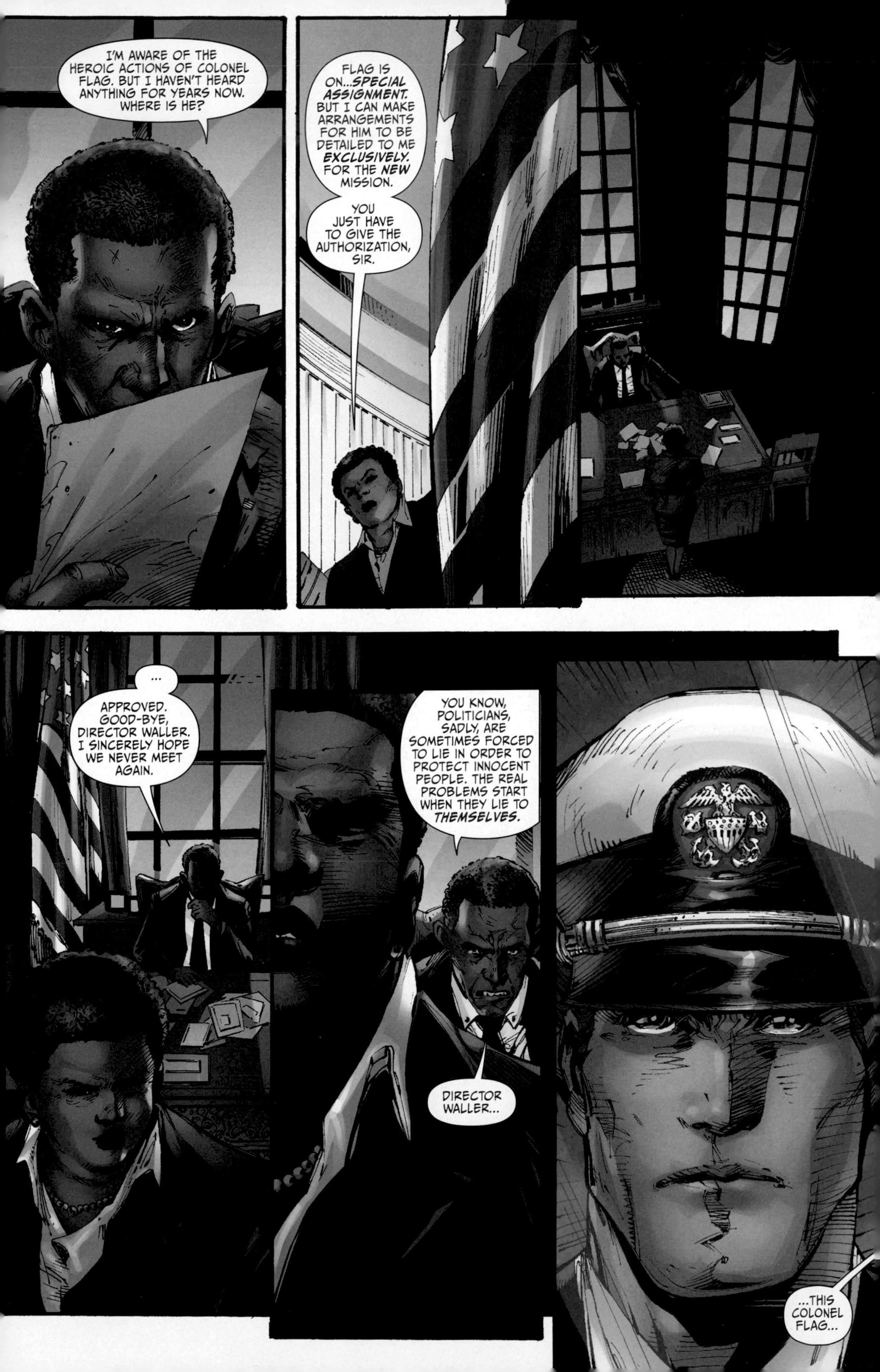
I'M AWARE OF THE HEROIC ACTIONS OF COLONEL FLAG. BUT I HAVEN'T HEARD ANYTHING FOR YEARS NOW. WHERE IS HE?
FLAG IS ON...SPECIAL ASSIGNMENT. BUT I CAN MAKE ARRANGEMENTS FOR HIM TO BE DETAILED TO ME EXCLUSIVELY. FOR THE NEW MISSION.
YOU JUST HAVE TO GIVE THE AUTHORIZATION, SIR.
...
APPROVED. GOOD-BYE, DIRECTOR WALLER. I SINCERELY HOPE WE NEVER MEET AGAIN.
YOU KNOW, POLITICIANS, SADLY, ARE SOMETIMES FORCED TO LIE IN ORDER TO PROTECT INNOCENT PEOPLE. THE REAL PROBLEMS START WHEN THEY LIE TO THEMSELVES.
DIRECTOR WALLER...
...THIS COLONEL FLAG...

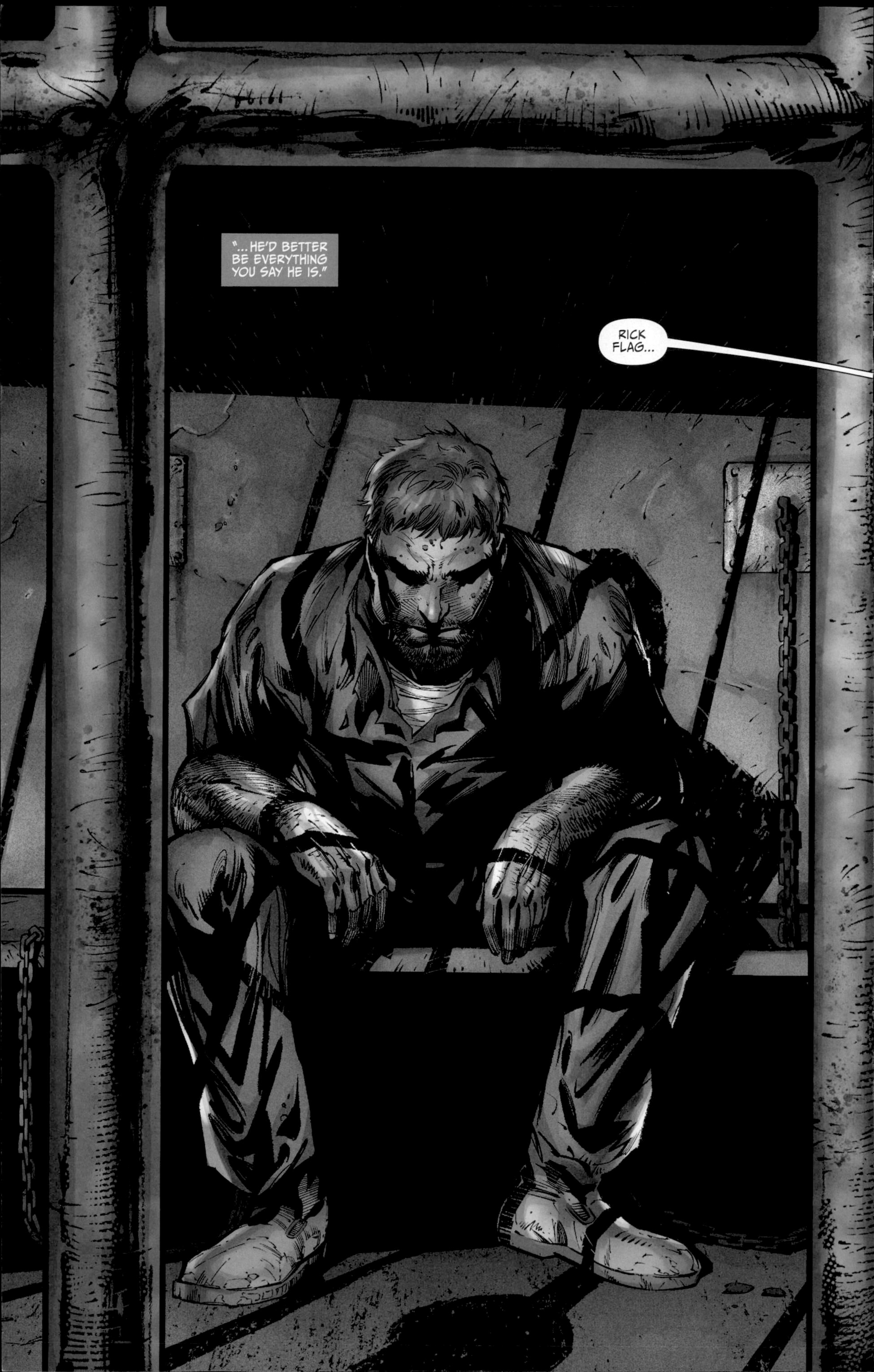
"...HE'D BETTER BE EVERYTHING YOU SAY HE IS."
RICK FLAG...

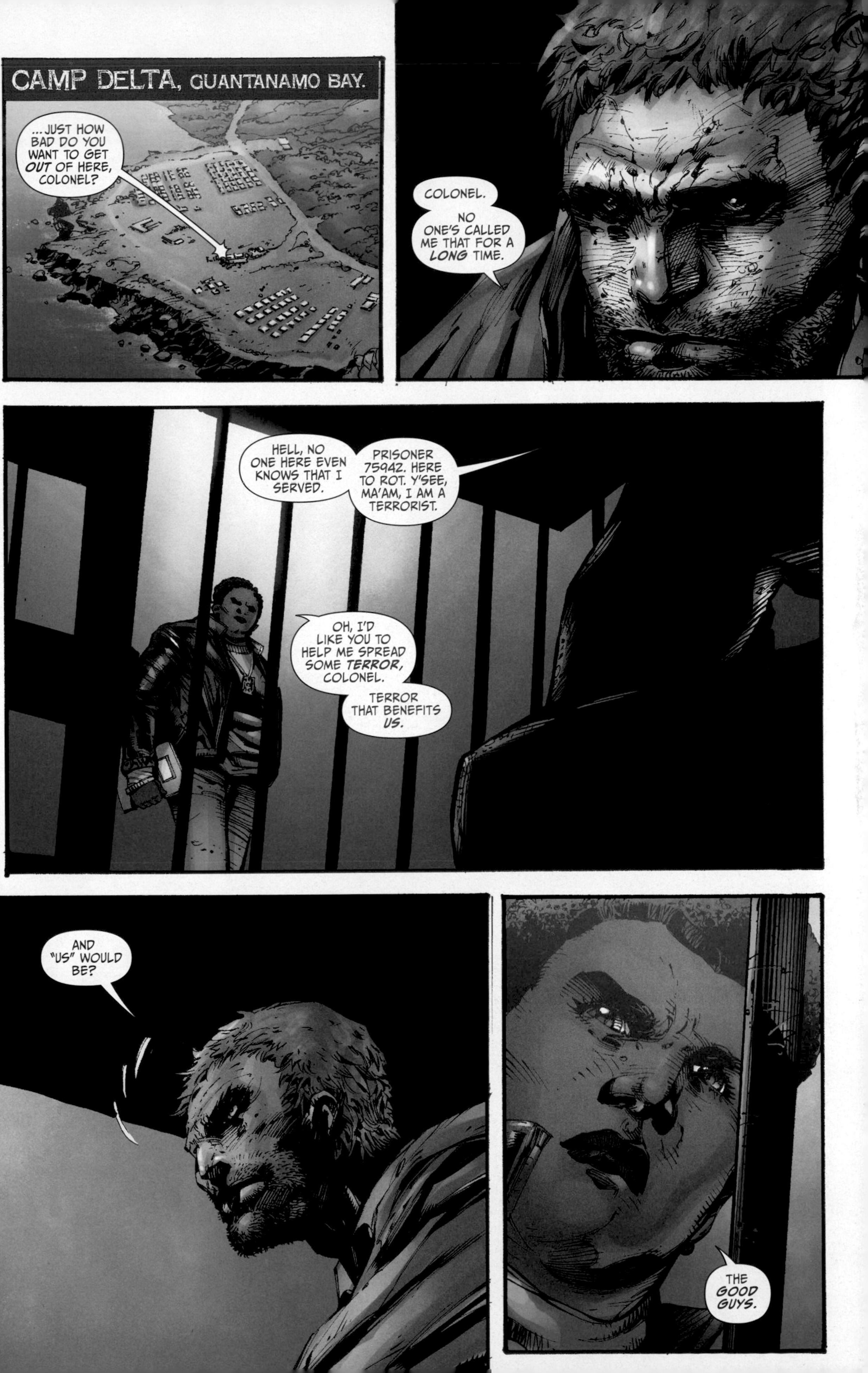
CAMP DELTA, GUANTANAMO BAY.
...JUST HOW BAD DO YOU WANT TO GET OUT OF HERE, COLONEL?
COLONEL.
NO ONE'S CALLED ME THAT FOR A LONG TIME.
HELL, NO ONE HERE EVEN KNOWS THAT I SERVED.
PRISONER 75942. HERE TO ROT. Y'SEE, MA'AM, I AM A TERRORIST.
OH, I'D LIKE YOU TO HELP ME SPREAD SOME TERROR, COLONEL.
TERROR THAT BENEFITS US.
AND "US" WOULD BE?
THE GOOD GUYS.

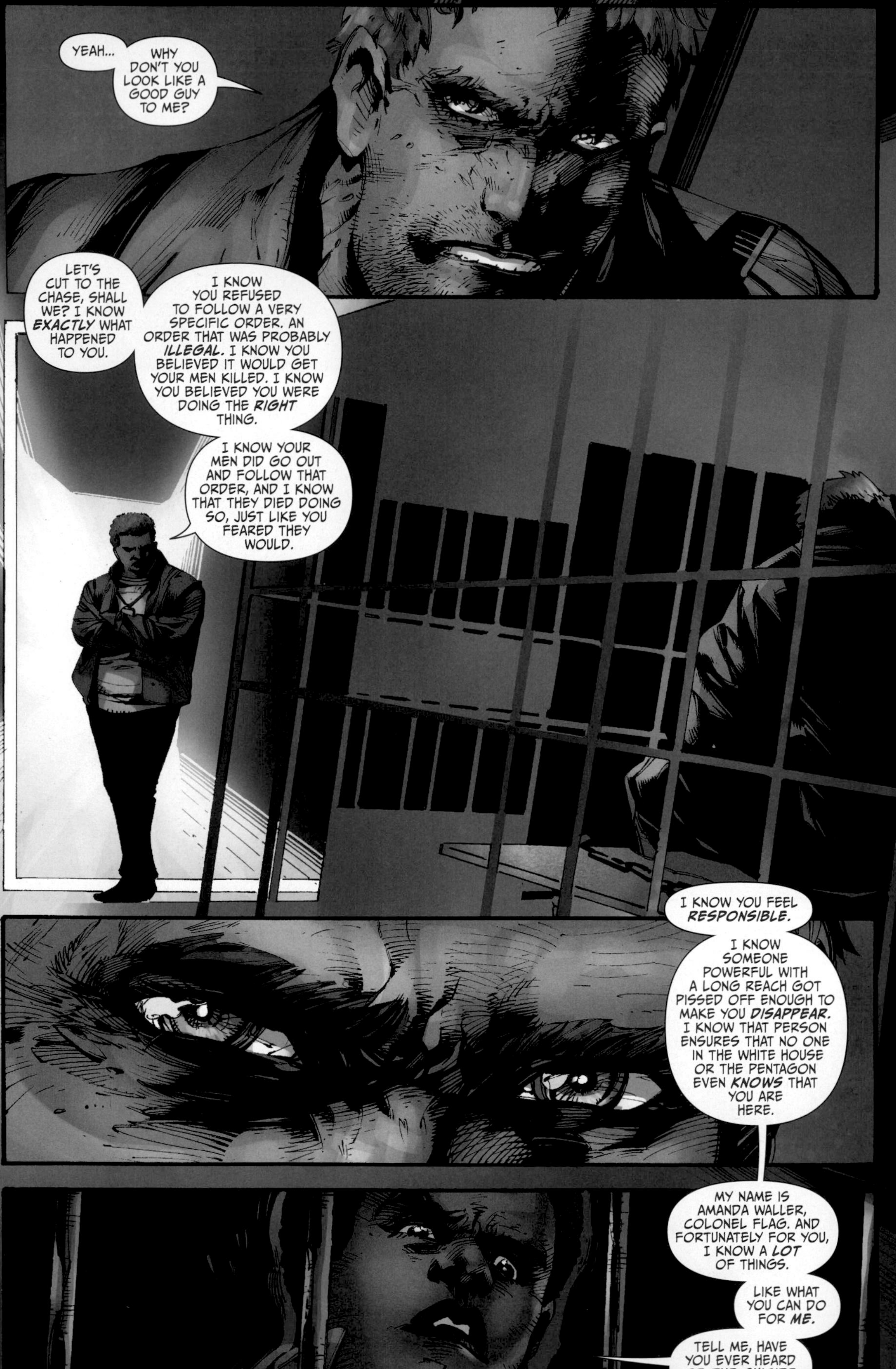
YEAH...
WHY DON'T YOU LOOK LIKE A GOOD GUY TO ME?
LET'S CUT TO THE CHASE, SHALL WE? I KNOW ***EXACTLY*** WHAT HAPPENED TO YOU.
I KNOW YOU REFUSED TO FOLLOW A VERY SPECIFIC ORDER. AN ORDER THAT WAS PROBABLY ***ILLEGAL.*** I KNOW YOU BELIEVED IT WOULD GET YOUR MEN KILLED. I KNOW YOU BELIEVED YOU WERE DOING THE ***RIGHT*** THING.
I KNOW YOUR MEN DID GO OUT AND FOLLOW THAT ORDER, AND I KNOW THAT THEY DIED DOING SO, JUST LIKE YOU FEARED THEY WOULD.
I KNOW YOU FEEL ***RESPONSIBLE.***
I KNOW SOMEONE POWERFUL WITH A LONG REACH GOT PISSED OFF ENOUGH TO MAKE YOU ***DISAPPEAR.*** I KNOW THAT PERSON ENSURES THAT NO ONE IN THE WHITE HOUSE OR THE PENTAGON EVEN ***KNOWS*** THAT YOU ARE HERE.
MY NAME IS AMANDA WALLER, COLONEL FLAG. AND FORTUNATELY FOR YOU, I KNOW A ***LOT*** OF THINGS.
LIKE WHAT YOU CAN DO FOR ***ME.***
TELL ME, HAVE YOU EVER HEARD OF ***THE SUICIDE SQUAD?***

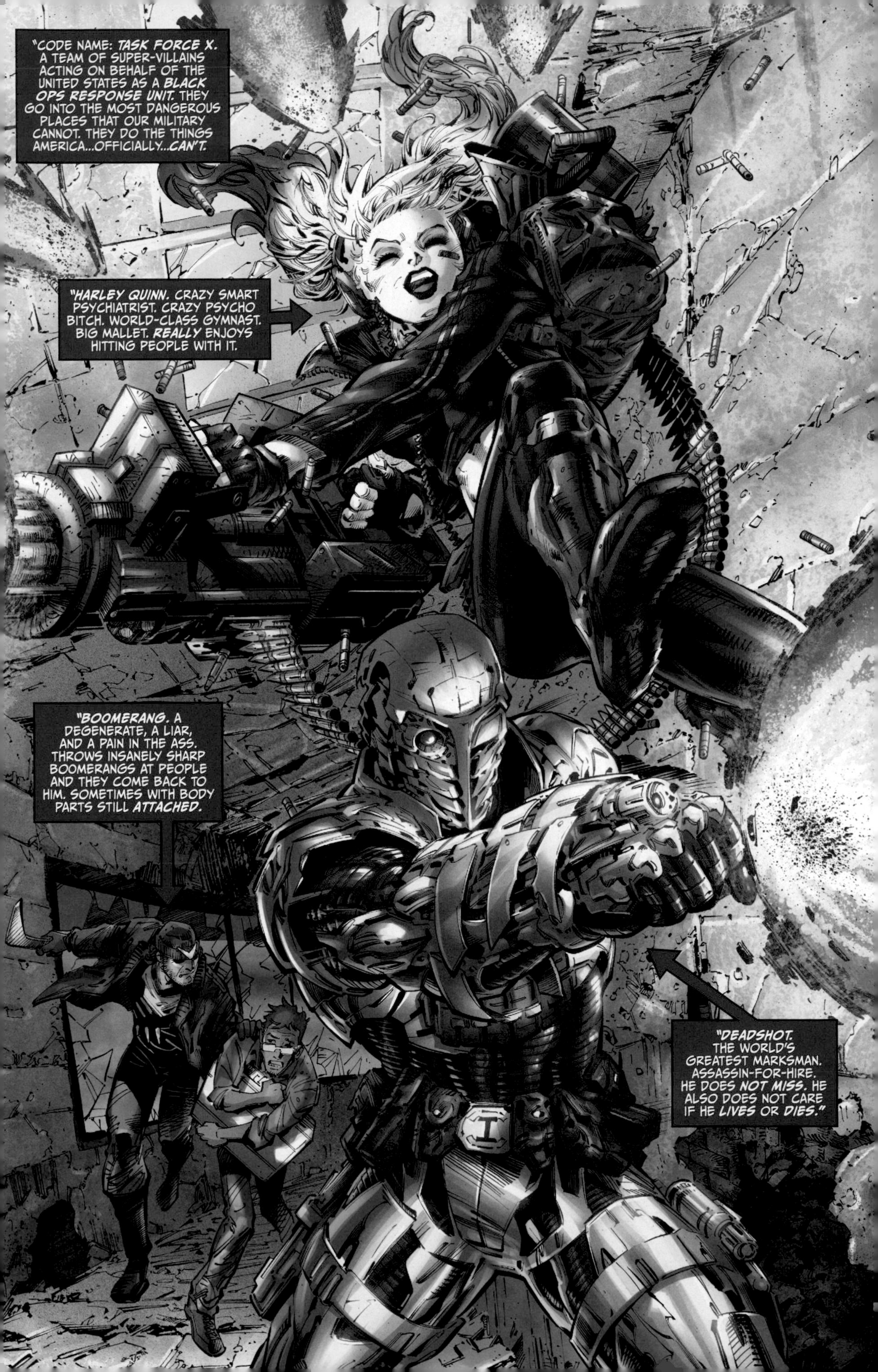
"CODE NAME: TASK FORCE X. A TEAM OF SUPER-VILLAINS ACTING ON BEHALF OF THE UNITED STATES AS A BLACK OPS RESPONSE UNIT. THEY GO INTO THE MOST DANGEROUS PLACES THAT OUR MILITARY CANNOT. THEY DO THE THINGS AMERICA...OFFICIALLY...CAN'T.
"HARLEY QUINN. CRAZY SMART PSYCHIATRIST. CRAZY PSYCHO BITCH. WORLD-CLASS GYMNAST. BIG MALLET. REALLY ENJOYS HITTING PEOPLE WITH IT.
"BOOMERANG. A DEGENERATE, A LIAR, AND A PAIN IN THE ASS. THROWS INSANELY SHARP BOOMERANGS AT PEOPLE AND THEY COME BACK TO HIM. SOMETIMES WITH BODY PARTS STILL ATTACHED.
"DEADSHOT. THE WORLD'S GREATEST MARKSMAN. ASSASSIN-FOR-HIRE. HE DOES NOT MISS. HE ALSO DOES NOT CARE IF HE LIVES OR DIES."

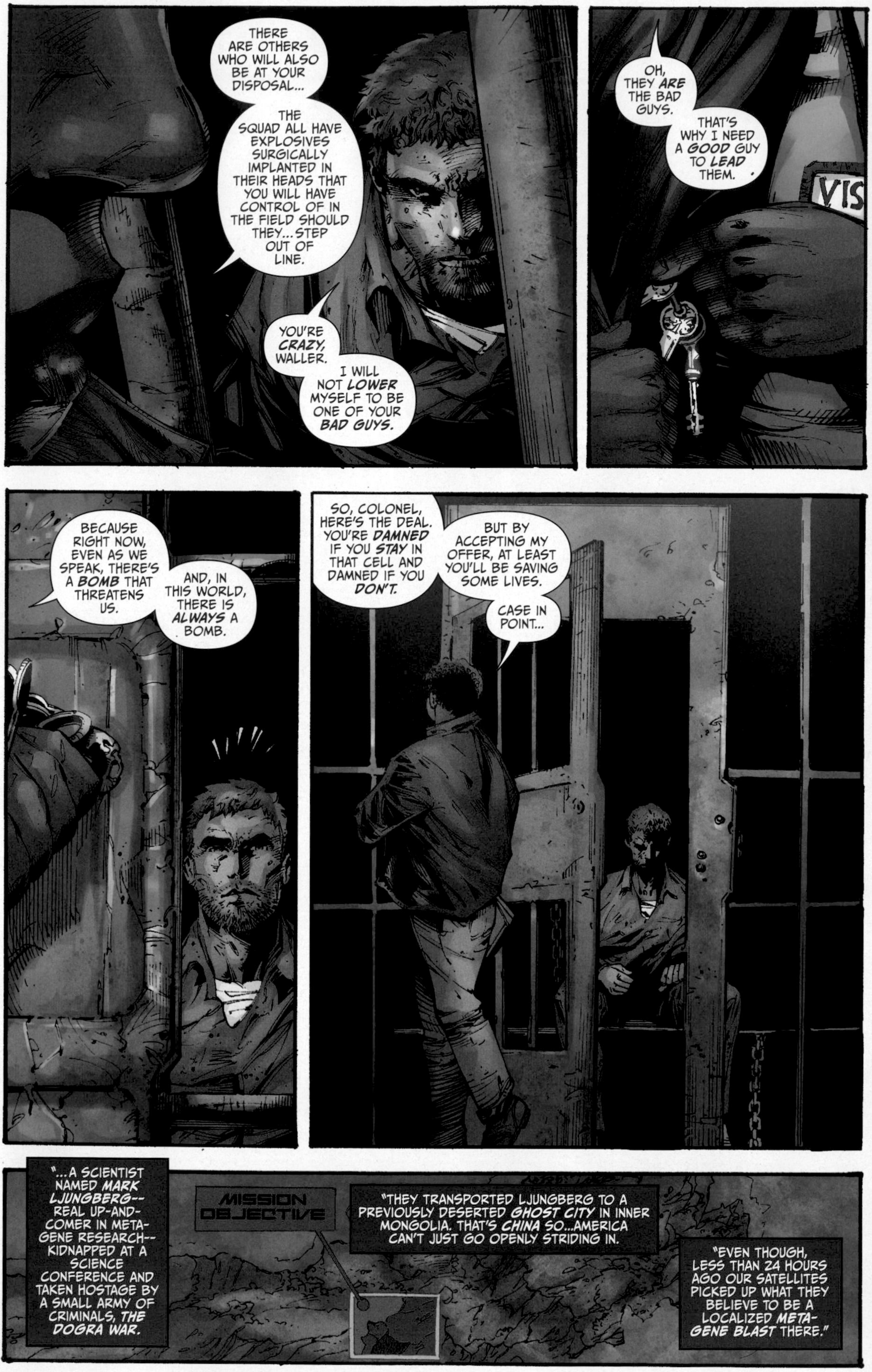
THERE ARE OTHERS WHO WILL ALSO BE AT YOUR DISPOSAL...
THE SQUAD ALL HAVE EXPLOSIVES SURGICALLY IMPLANTED IN THEIR HEADS THAT YOU WILL HAVE CONTROL OF IN THE FIELD SHOULD THEY... STEP OUT OF LINE.
YOU'RE CRAZY, WALLER.
I WILL NOT LOWER MYSELF TO BE ONE OF YOUR BAD GUYS.
OH, THEY ARE THE BAD GUYS.
THAT'S WHY I NEED A GOOD GUY TO LEAD THEM.
VIS
BECAUSE RIGHT NOW, EVEN AS WE SPEAK, THERE'S A BOMB THAT THREATENS US.
AND, IN THIS WORLD, THERE IS ALWAYS A BOMB.
SO, COLONEL, HERE'S THE DEAL. YOU'RE DAMNED IF YOU STAY IN THAT CELL AND DAMNED IF YOU DON'T.
BUT BY ACCEPTING MY OFFER, AT LEAST YOU'LL BE SAVING SOME LIVES.
CASE IN POINT...
"...A SCIENTIST NAMED MARK LJUNGBERG--REAL UP-AND-COMER IN META-GENE RESEARCH--KIDNAPPED AT A SCIENCE CONFERENCE AND TAKEN HOSTAGE BY A SMALL ARMY OF CRIMINALS, THE DOGRA WAR.
MISSION OBJECTIVE
"THEY TRANSPORTED LJUNGBERG TO A PREVIOUSLY DESERTED GHOST CITY IN INNER MONGOLIA. THAT'S CHINA SO...AMERICA CAN'T JUST GO OPENLY STRIDING IN.
"EVEN THOUGH, LESS THAN 24 HOURS AGO OUR SATELLITES PICKED UP WHAT THEY BELIEVE TO BE A LOCALIZED META-GENE BLAST THERE."

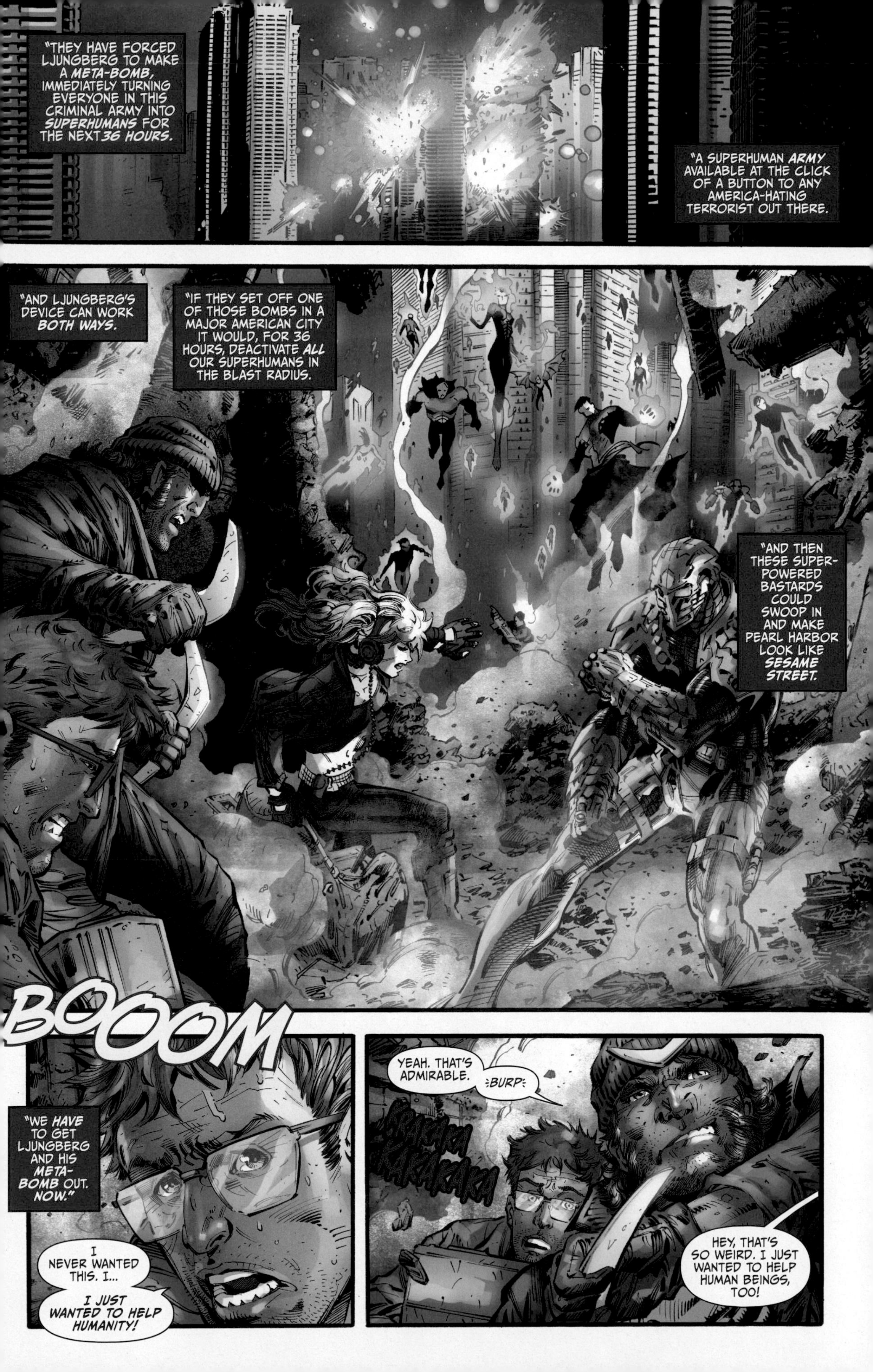
"THEY HAVE FORCED LJUNGBERG TO MAKE A META-BOMB, IMMEDIATELY TURNING EVERYONE IN THIS CRIMINAL ARMY INTO SUPERHUMANS FOR THE NEXT 36 HOURS.
"A SUPERHUMAN ARMY AVAILABLE AT THE CLICK OF A BUTTON TO ANY AMERICA-HATING TERRORIST OUT THERE.
"AND LJUNGBERG'S DEVICE CAN WORK BOTH WAYS.
"IF THEY SET OFF ONE OF THOSE BOMBS IN A MAJOR AMERICAN CITY IT WOULD, FOR 36 HOURS, DEACTIVATE ALL OUR SUPERHUMANS IN THE BLAST RADIUS.
"AND THEN THESE SUPER-POWERED BASTARDS COULD SWOOP IN AND MAKE PEARL HARBOR LOOK LIKE SESAME STREET.
BOOOM
"WE HAVE TO GET LJUNGBERG AND HIS META-BOMB OUT. NOW."
I NEVER WANTED THIS. I...
I JUST WANTED TO HELP HUMANITY!
YEAH. THAT'S ADMIRABLE.
BURP
KRAKAKA KAKAKAKA
HEY, THAT'S SO WEIRD. I JUST WANTED TO HELP HUMAN BEINGS, TOO!

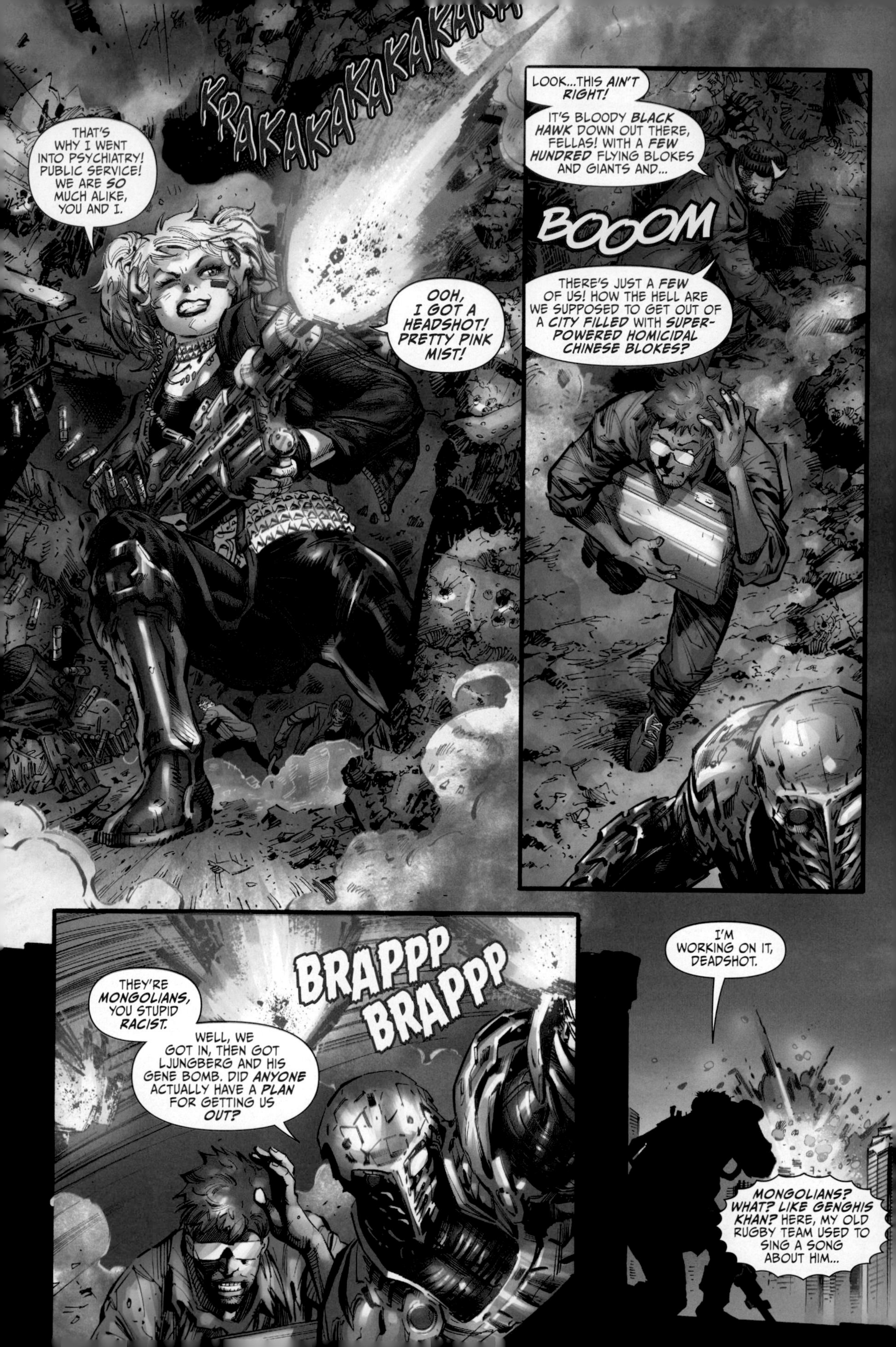
KRAKAKAKAKAKAKANN
THAT'S WHY I WENT INTO PSYCHIATRY! PUBLIC SERVICE! WE ARE SO MUCH ALIKE, YOU AND I.
OOH, I GOT A HEADSHOT! PRETTY PINK MIST!
LOOK...THIS AIN'T RIGHT!
IT'S BLOODY BLACK HAWK DOWN OUT THERE, FELLAS! WITH A FEW HUNDRED FLYING BLOKES AND GIANTS AND...
BOOOM
THERE'S JUST A FEW OF US! HOW THE HELL ARE WE SUPPOSED TO GET OUT OF A CITY FILLED WITH SUPER-POWERED HOMICIDAL CHINESE BLOKES?
BRAPPP BRAPPP
THEY'RE MONGOLIANS, YOU STUPID RACIST.
WELL, WE GOT IN, THEN GOT LJUNGBERG AND HIS GENE BOMB. DID ANYONE ACTUALLY HAVE A PLAN FOR GETTING US OUT?
I'M WORKING ON IT, DEADSHOT.
MONGOLIANS? WHAT? LIKE GENGHIS KHAN? HERE, MY OLD RUGBY TEAM USED TO SING A SONG ABOUT HIM...

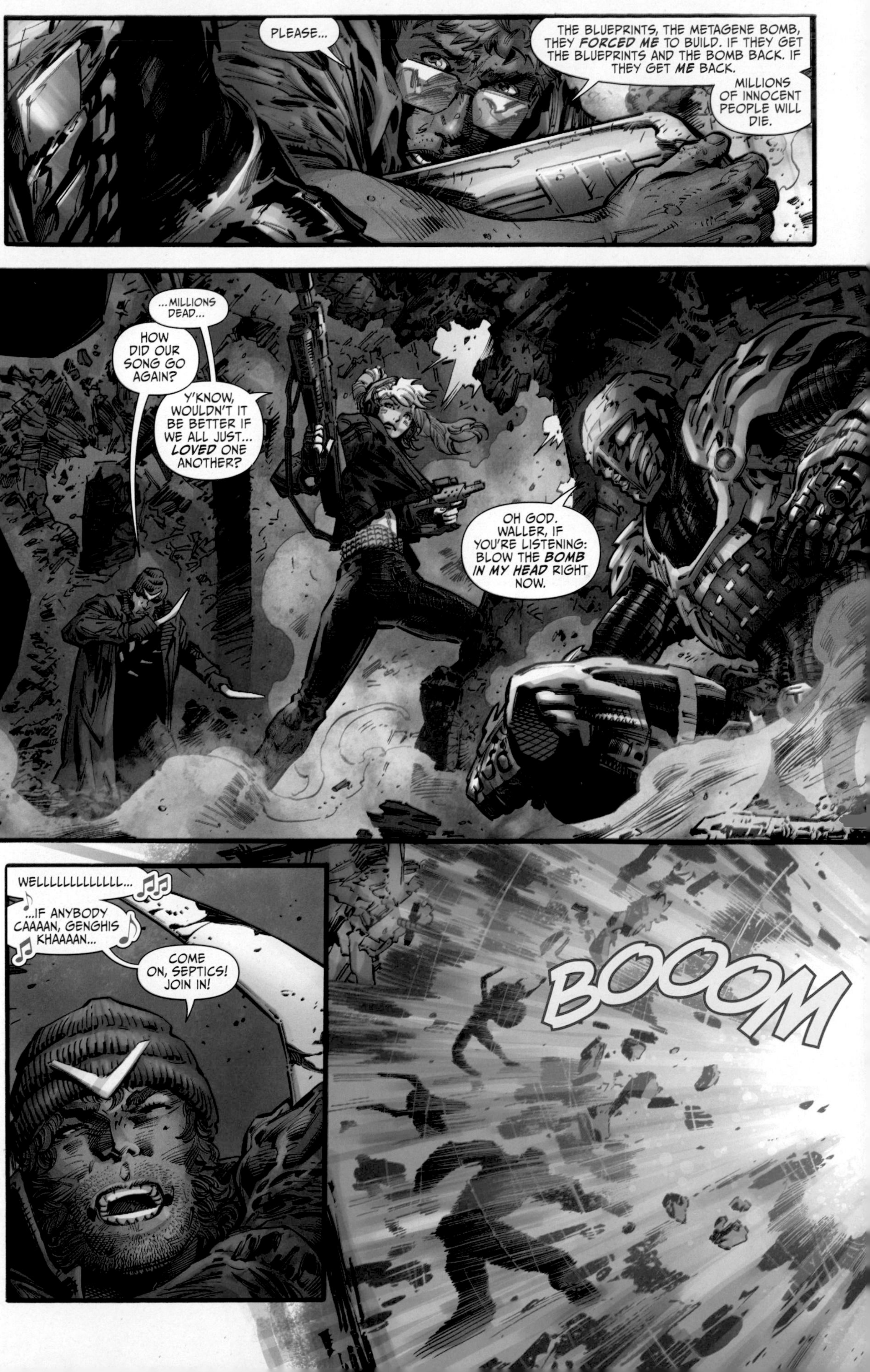
PLEASE...
THE BLUEPRINTS, THE METAGENE BOMB, THEY FORCED ME TO BUILD. IF THEY GET THE BLUEPRINTS AND THE BOMB BACK. IF THEY GET ME BACK.
MILLIONS OF INNOCENT PEOPLE WILL DIE.
...MILLIONS DEAD...
HOW DID OUR SONG GO AGAIN?
Y'KNOW, WOULDN'T IT BE BETTER IF WE ALL JUST... LOVED ONE ANOTHER?
OH GOD. WALLER, IF YOU'RE LISTENING: BLOW THE BOMB IN MY HEAD RIGHT NOW.
WELLLLLLLLLLLLLL...
...IF ANYBODY CAAAAN, GENGHIS KHAAAAN...
COME ON, SEPTICS! JOIN IN!
BOOOM

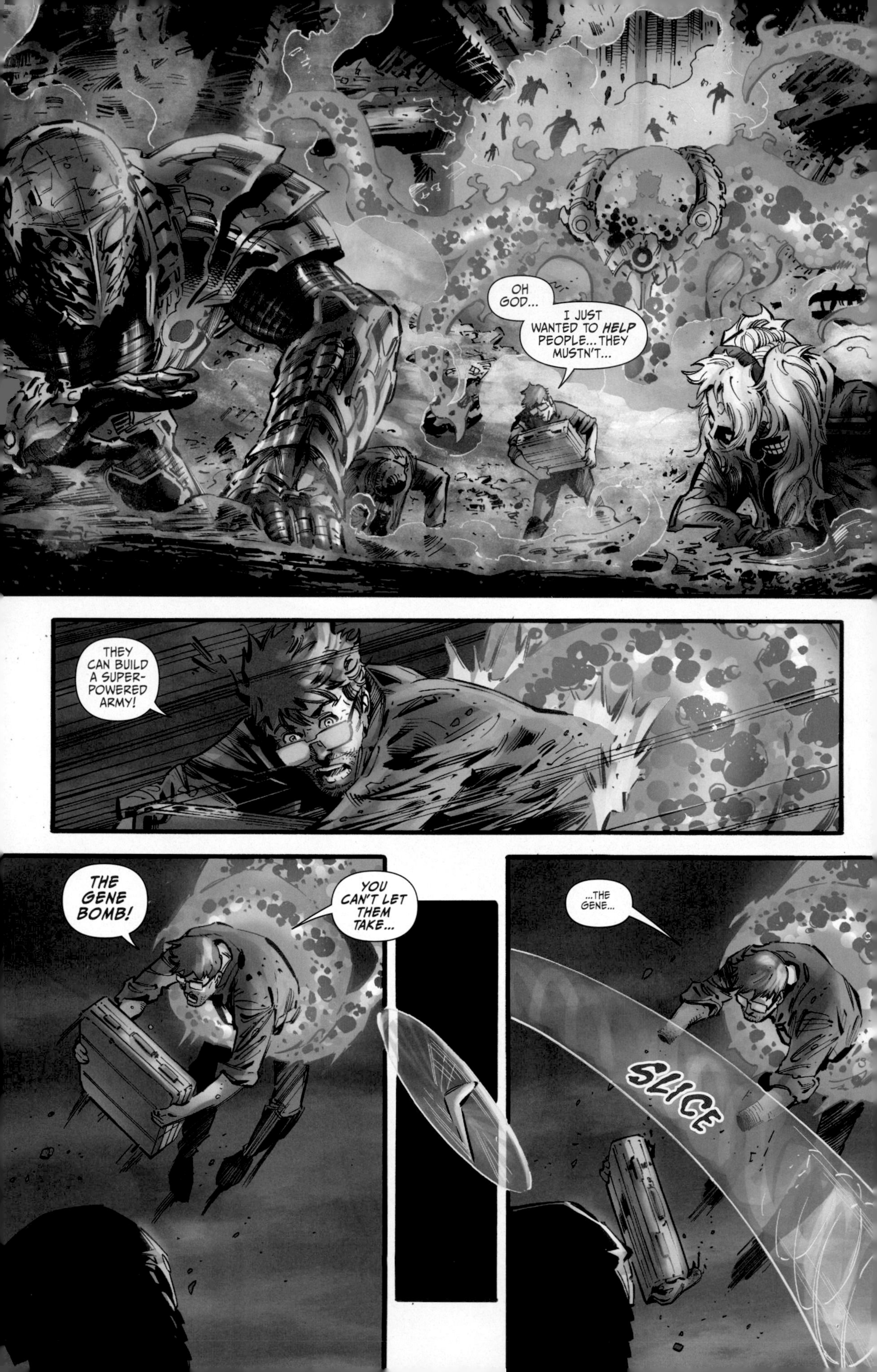
OH GOD...
I JUST WANTED TO HELP PEOPLE...THEY MUSTN'T...
THEY CAN BUILD A SUPER-POWERED ARMY!
THE GENE BOMB!
YOU CAN'T LET THEM TAKE...
...THE GENE...
SLICE

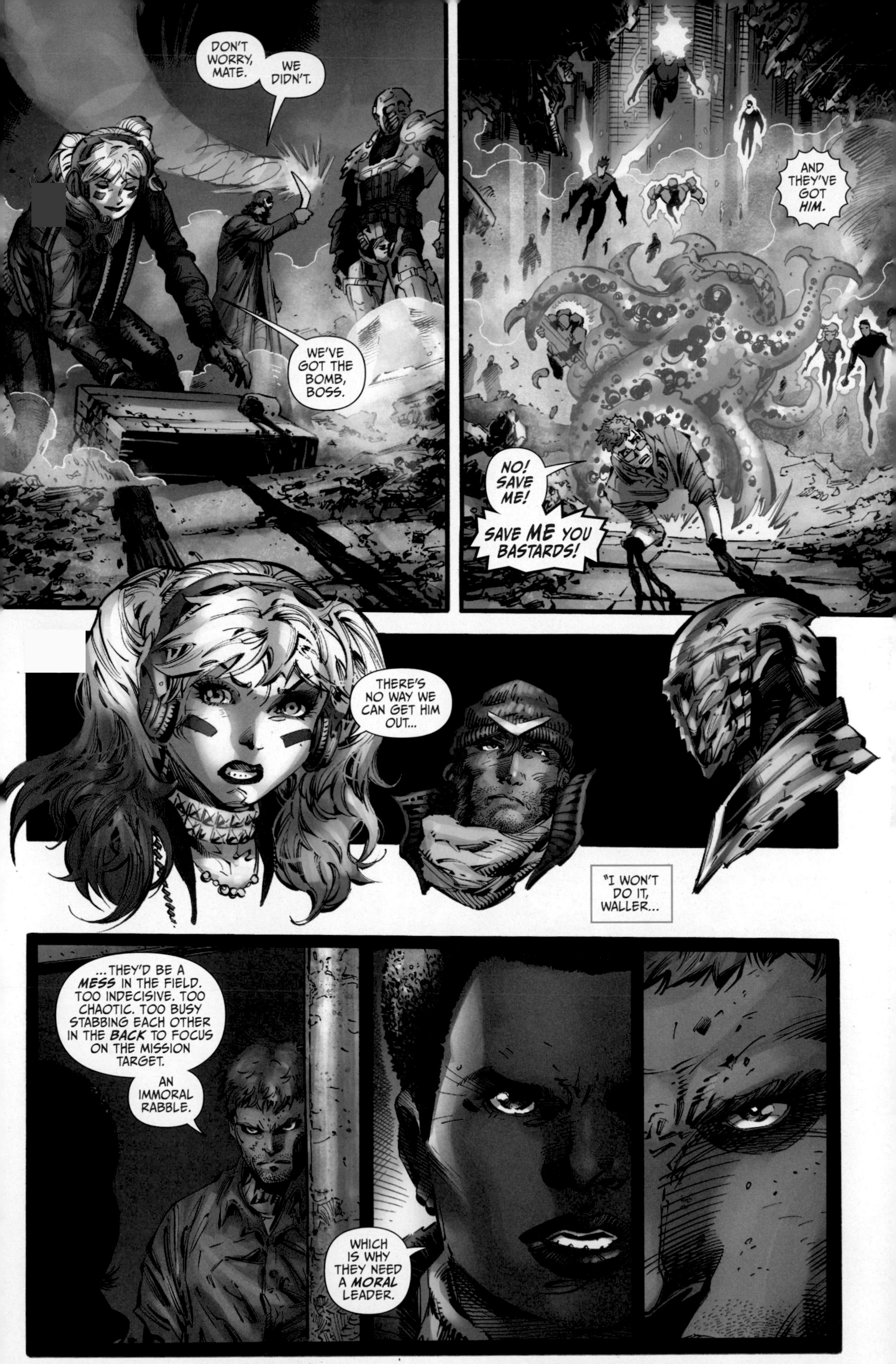
DON'T WORRY, MATE.
WE DIDN'T.
WE'VE GOT THE BOMB, BOSS.
AND THEY'VE GOT HIM.
NO! SAVE ME!
SAVE ME YOU BASTARDS!
THERE'S NO WAY WE CAN GET HIM OUT...
"I WON'T DO IT, WALLER...
...THEY'D BE A MESS IN THE FIELD. TOO INDECISIVE. TOO CHAOTIC. TOO BUSY STABBING EACH OTHER IN THE BACK TO FOCUS ON THE MISSION TARGET.
AN IMMORAL RABBLE.
WHICH IS WHY THEY NEED A MORAL LEADER.

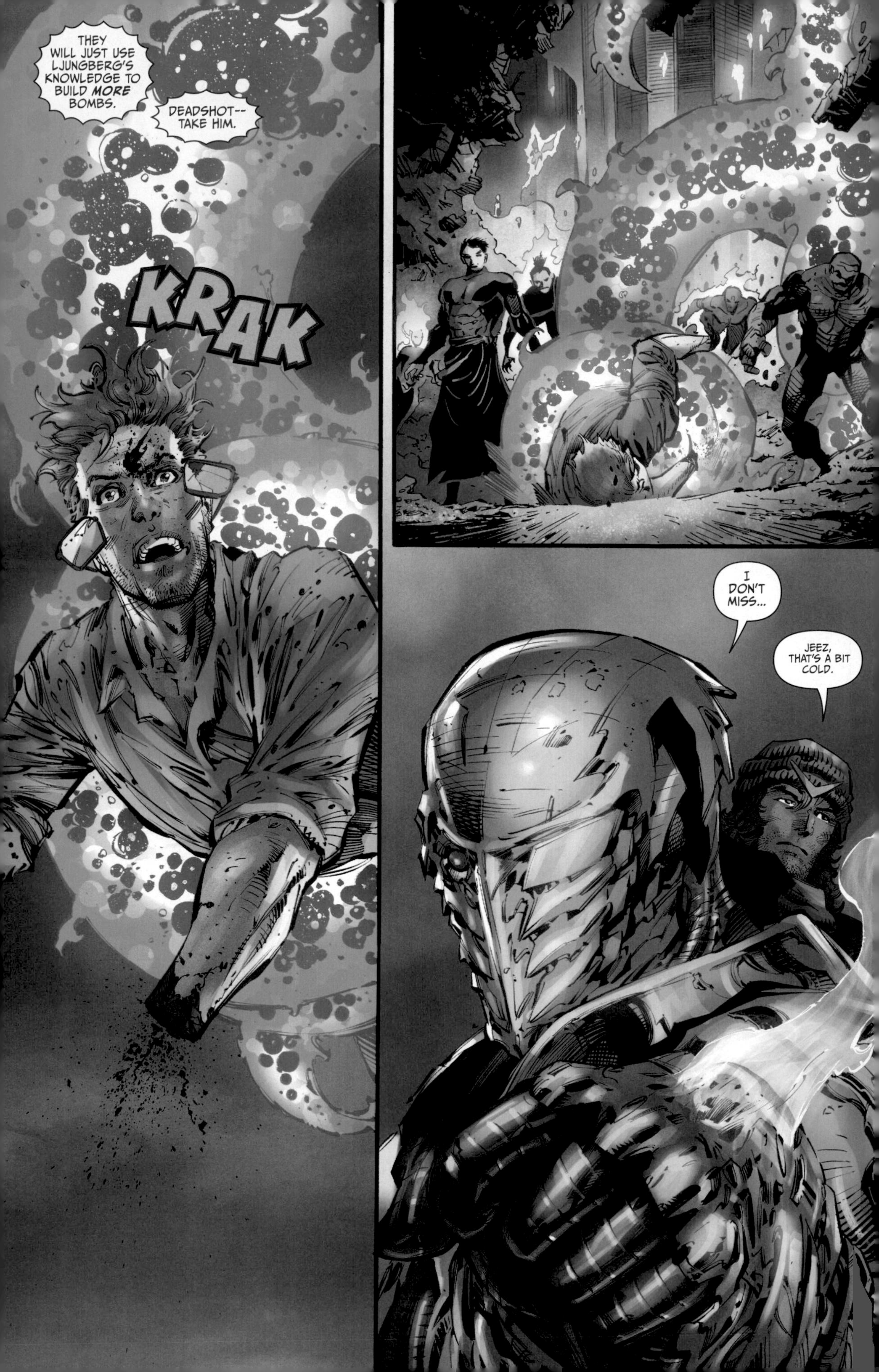
THEY WILL JUST USE LJUNGBERG'S KNOWLEDGE TO BUILD *MORE* BOMBS.
DEADSHOT-- TAKE HIM.
KRAK
I DON'T MISS...
JEEZ, THAT'S A BIT COLD.

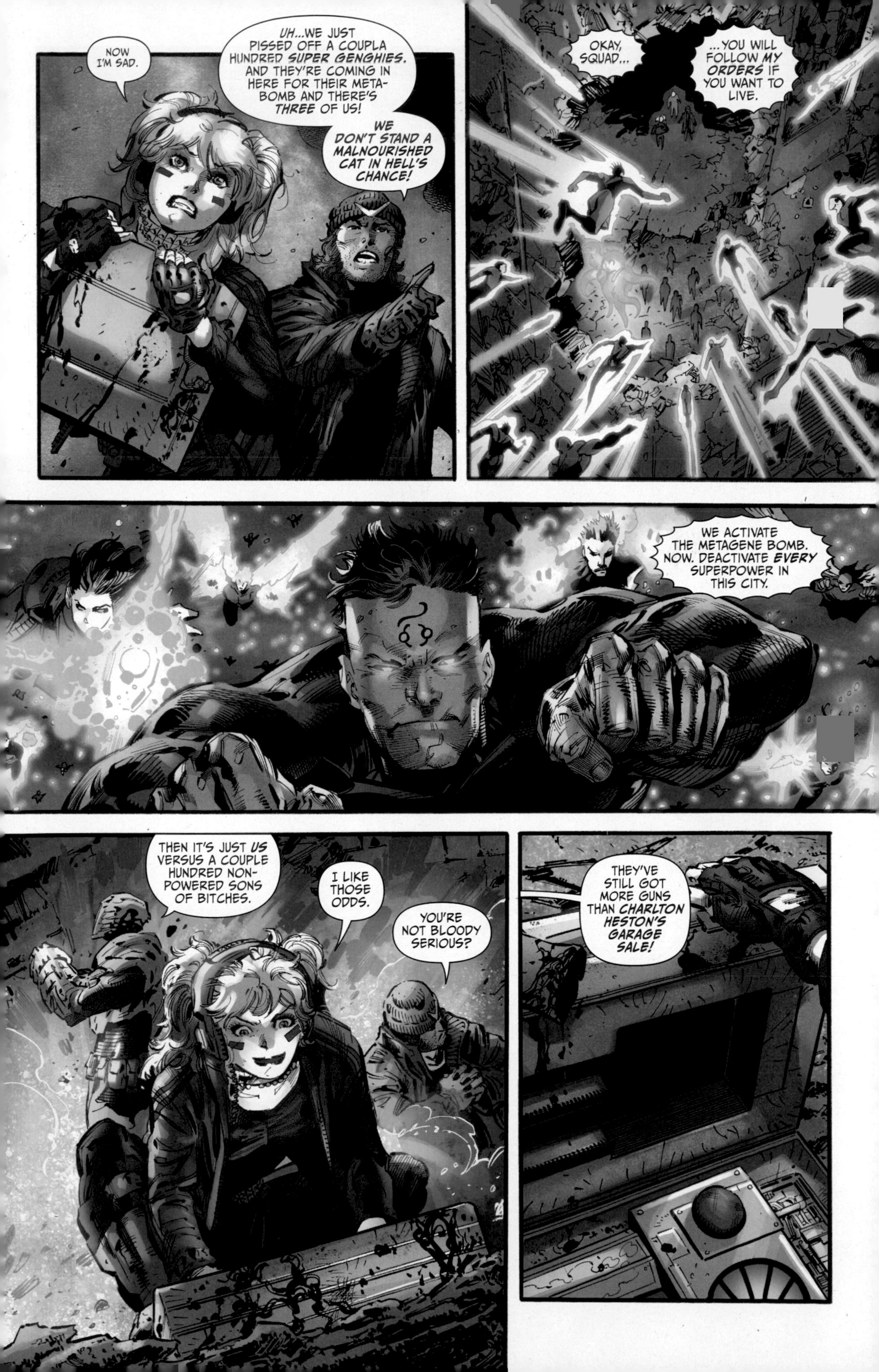
NOW I'M SAD.
UH...WE JUST PISSED OFF A COUPLA HUNDRED SUPER GENGHIES. AND THEY'RE COMING IN HERE FOR THEIR META-BOMB AND THERE'S THREE OF US!
WE DON'T STAND A MALNOURISHED CAT IN HELL'S CHANCE!
OKAY, SQUAD...
...YOU WILL FOLLOW MY ORDERS IF YOU WANT TO LIVE.
WE ACTIVATE THE METAGENE BOMB. NOW. DEACTIVATE EVERY SUPERPOWER IN THIS CITY.
THEN IT'S JUST US VERSUS A COUPLE HUNDRED NON-POWERED SONS OF BITCHES.
I LIKE THOSE ODDS.
YOU'RE NOT BLOODY SERIOUS?
THEY'VE STILL GOT MORE GUNS THAN CHARLTON HESTON'S GARAGE SALE!

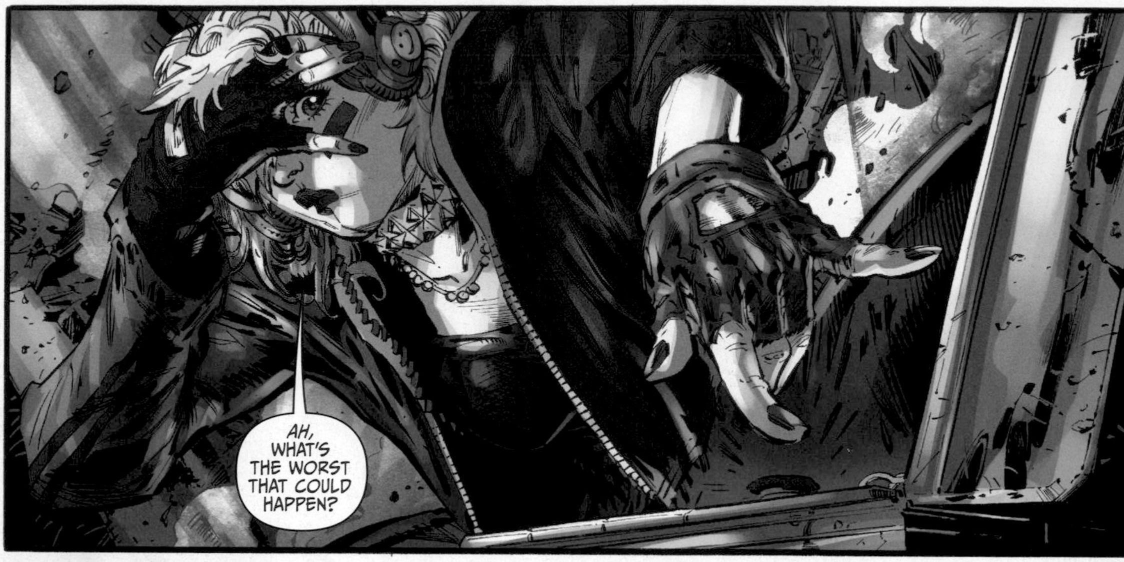
AH, WHAT'S THE WORST THAT COULD HAPPEN?

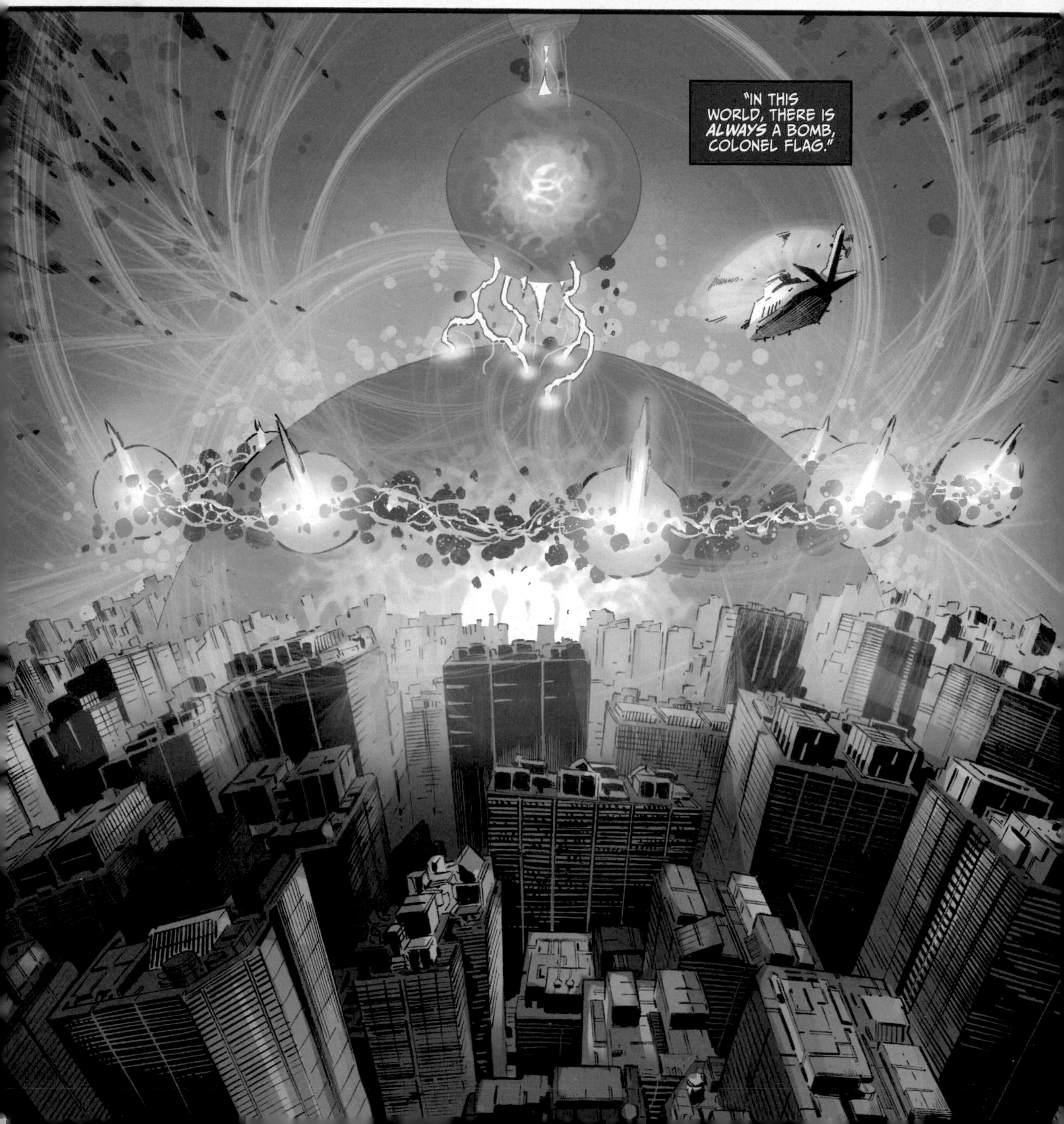
"IN THIS WORLD, THERE IS ALWAYS A BOMB, COLONEL FLAG."

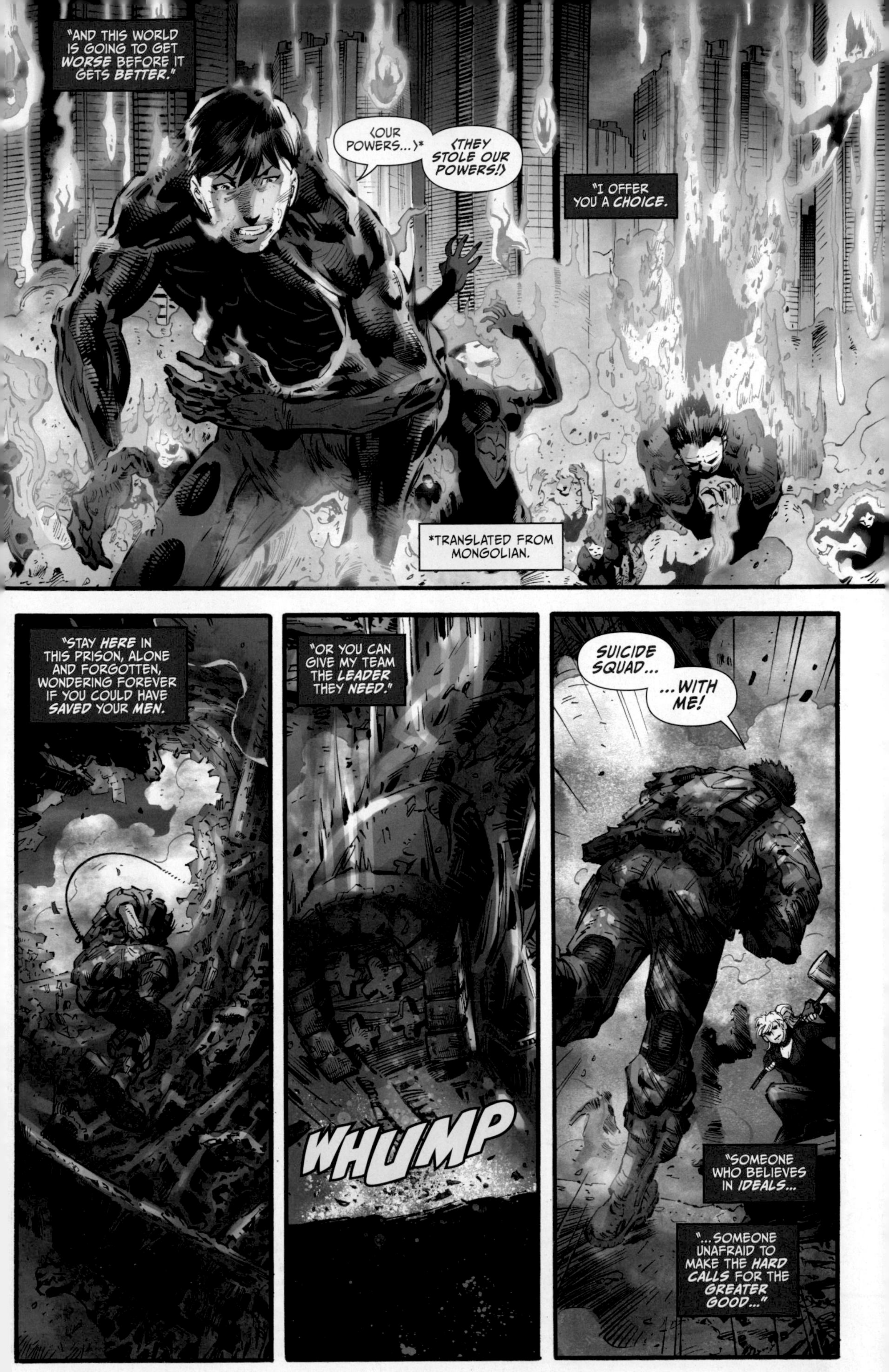

"AND THIS WORLD IS GOING TO GET *WORSE* BEFORE IT GETS *BETTER*."
‹OUR POWERS...›*
‹THEY STOLE OUR POWERS!›
"I OFFER YOU A *CHOICE*.
*TRANSLATED FROM MONGOLIAN.
"STAY *HERE* IN THIS PRISON, ALONE AND FORGOTTEN, WONDERING FOREVER IF YOU COULD HAVE *SAVED* YOUR *MEN*.
"OR YOU CAN GIVE MY TEAM THE *LEADER* THEY *NEED*."
WHUMP
SUICIDE SQUAD...
...WITH ME!
"SOMEONE WHO BELIEVES IN *IDEALS*...
"...SOMEONE UNAFRAID TO MAKE THE *HARD CALLS* FOR THE *GREATER GOOD*..."

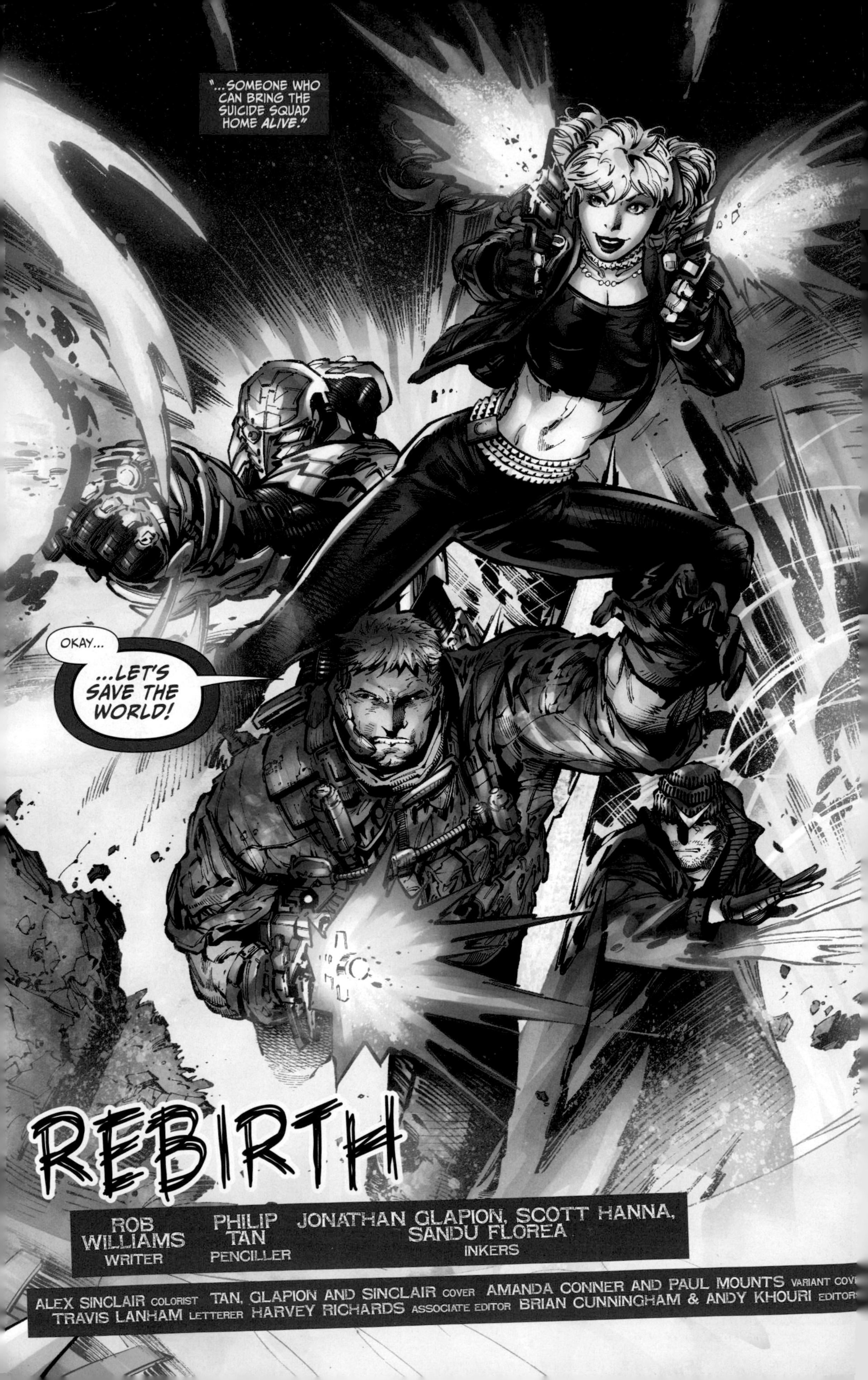
"...SOMEONE WHO CAN BRING THE SUICIDE SQUAD HOME ALIVE."
OKAY...
...LET'S SAVE THE WORLD!
REBIRTH
ROB WILLIAMS WRITER
PHILIP TAN PENCILLER
JONATHAN GLAPION, SCOTT HANNA, SANDU FLOREA INKERS
ALEX SINCLAIR COLORIST TAN, GLAPION AND SINCLAIR COVER AMANDA CONNER AND PAUL MOUNTS VARIANT COV
TRAVIS LANHAM LETTERER HARVEY RICHARDS ASSOCIATE EDITOR BRIAN CUNNINGHAM & ANDY KHOURI EDITORS